THE ALL★STAR ★★★Companion

VOLUME TWO

An Overview of the JUSTICE SOCIETY OF AMERICA and Related Comics Series, 1935-1989

Compiled, Edited, and (Partly) Written by
ROY THOMAS

With the Special Contributions of:

FRANK BRUNNER

CREIG FLESSEL

DENNIS MALLONEE

JERRY G. BAILS

CRAIG DELICH

MIKE W. BARR

DAVID STUDHAM

PEDRO ANGOSTO

KURT MITCHELL

Design
CHRISTOPHER DAY

Cover
CARLOS PACHECO
(WITH THE ASSISTANCE OF JESUS MERINO)
COLORED BY TOM ZIUKO

> "Follow your bliss."
> —Joseph Campbell.
> [still *words to live by, six years later*]

Acknowledgments

Dusty Abell, Christian Voltan Alcala, Jim Amash, Pedro Angosto, Manuel Auad, Rodrigo Baeza, Brian H. Bailie, Jerry G. Bails, Mike Baron, Mike W. Barr, Michael Baulderstone, Howard Bender, Jack Bender, Al Bigley, Dave Billman, Bill Black, Dominic Bongo, Ray Bottorff, Jr., Mike Bromberg, Frank Brunner, Tim Burgard, Mike Burkey, Jack Burnley, Carmen Q. Bryant, Glen Cadigan, Brian S. Carney, R. Dewey Cassell, Mike Catron, Bob Cherry, Gerry Conway, J. Randolph Cox, Dale Crain, Larry Crook, Christopher Day, John Day, Fred De Boom, Kim DeMulder, Craig Delich, David Delich, Al Dellinges, Michaël Dewally, Tony DeZuniga, Tony DiPreta, Shel Dorf, Michael Dunne, Ric Estrada, Michael Eury, Jennie-Lynn Falk, Chris Fama, Michael Feldman, Linda Fields, Greg Fischer, Stephen Fishler, Creig Flessel, Shane Foley, Ramona Fradon, Todd Franklin, Keif A. Fromm, Carl Gafford, Frank Giella, Joe Giella, Keith Giffen, Michael T. Gilbert, Louis Glanzman, Glenn David Gold, "Gone and Forgotten" website, Luz Gonzales, Ron Goulart, Grand Comic Book Database, Robert Greenberger, Doug Greene, George Hagenauer, Jim Harmon, Joey Harris, Merrily Mayer Harris, Ron & Jan Harris, Irwin Hasen, Fred Hembeck, Dave Hennen, Freeman Henry, Heritage Comics, Rick Hoberg, Tom Horvitz, Richard Howell, Bob Hughes, Carmine Infantino, Chris Irving, Arvell Jones, Bill Jourdin, Rafael Kayanan, Michael Kelly, Robert Klein, Glenn Koenig, Robert Knist, Alan Kupperberg, Paul Kupperberg, Stan Lee, Paul Levitz, Mark Lewis, Jim Ludwig, Mike & Eve Machlan, Mad Mona, Russ Maheras, Dan Makara, Dennis Mallonee, Joe & Nadia Mannerino, Scott Maple, Pablo Marcos, Don Maris, Bruce Mason, Lanny Mayer, Todd McFarlane, Jesus Merino, Al Milgrom, Kurt Mitchell, Sheldon Moldoff, Fred Mommsen, Tom Morehouse, John Morrow, Frank Motler, Mark Muller, Will Murray, Jim Murtagh, Mart Nodell, Michelle Nolan, Eric Nolen-Weathington, Scott Nybakken, Martin O'Hearn, Jerry Ordway, Carlos Pacheco, Fred Patten, Barry Pearl, George Pérez, Kenny Picklesimer, Jr., Michael Posner, Ethan Roberts, Don Rosa, Paul Ryan, Bill Schelly, Carole Seuling, Rick Shurgin, David Siegel, Keif Simon, J.E. Smith, Robert M. Socha, Joe Staton, Rob Stolzer, Cory Stroke, David Studham, Dann Thomas, Leona Thomas, Eric Toth, Mark Trost, Chris Wallace, Hames Ware, Len Wein, Gregg Whitmore, Jeff Wiegel, John Wilcox, Kevin Wilkens, Jim Woeltje, Marv Wolfman, Bill Wormstedt, Alex Wright, "Mr. Z," Ed Zeno, Michael Zeno, Tom Ziuko

FOR YOUR READING EXCITEMENT

SUPERMAN

COMIC MAGAZINES

SUPERMAN • BATMAN • FLASH ACTION • FUN • ALL-STAR and other popular titles

NEW ISSUES EVERY WEEK

WHELAN DRUG STORES

An early-1940s notice from DC to retailers; thanks to Don Maris. Art by Joe Shuster & his art shop. [© DC Comics.]

Dedicated to the memory of Mark Hanerfeld, comics fan—and friend—who guarded the legacy of "The Will of William Wilson" for all those years

Published by TwoMorrows Publishing, 10407 [...] 919-449-0344 • www.t[...]

© 2006 Roy Thomas & Tw[...] ISBN 1-8939[...] First printing, November 20[...]

Title page art from Green Arrow story in *Adventure Comics* #269 (Feb. 1960), as reprinted in [...]; art by Lee Elias, script by Robert Bernstein. [© DC Com[...]

All-Star Comics, All-Star Squadron, America vs. the Justice Society, Last Days o[...] The Young All-Stars, the Justice Society of America, and all associated characters a[...] All associated artwork reproduced in this volume is © DC [...]

Table of Contents

Covers culled from house ads, mid-1940s. [© DC Comics.]

HITCHING MY WAGON TO *ALL-STAR*
Another Personal Introduction
by Roy Thomas

Ralph Waldo Emerson's line "Hitch your wagon to a star" is one those phrases so often quoted that it's become so much verbal wallpaper—making it hard to imagine it was *ever* a new combination of words and image. Like "My kingdom for a horse" or "It was Greek to me," or, God help us, "Tomorrow is another day." (You think that, if the latter hadn't been coined by Margaret Mitchell in her novel *Gone with the Wind*, producer Darryl Zanuck would've let his nearly-four-hour *movie version* end with it?)

But I digress, as someone once said… and the book's barely begun.

It's hard to believe it's really been six years since TwoMorrows and I brought out *The All-Star Companion*—the first volume of what was, at that time, definitely intended to be a one-volume series. Maybe that's partly because we issued a second edition of same in 2004, with dozens of corrections and additional information and even a couple of new photos.

All along, though, I kept getting these messages from folks augmenting—even *arguing* over—certain points made in the book. Heroic Publishing headman Dennis Mallonee had a controversial new theory about the original identity of one hero who was re-drawn in several mid-'40s *All-Star Comics* solo segments—and retired college prof Jerry G. Bails, who's spent decades ruminating on similar subjects, agreed with some of

TO WARREN — THANKS FOR REMEMBERING US—
Winky Blinky Noddy
Jay Garrick (THE FLASH)
and E.E. Hibbard   8/10/'77

A Flashy Pair Of Illos

A number of illustrators who'd contributed to that very first JSA story in 1940's All-Star Comics #3 did new drawings of its classic heroes in later years.

(Left:) Everett E. Hibbard became artist of The Flash feature with the third issue of Flash Comics in 1940, and probably drew the cover of All-Star #3. In 1977 he executed this drawing (in color!) of the Fastest Man Alive and his sidekicks, The Three Dimwits—Winky, Blinky, and Noddy—his and writer Gardner Fox's answer to the movies' Three Stooges. To the best of our knowledge, this artwork has never before been published. With thanks to Michael Zeno.

(Above:) Mart Nodell was the original artist and major co-creator of the Golden Age Green Lantern, and continues to this day to do occasional (oft-color) sketches of him—in this instance, chumming around with The Flash, his pal from all those Comic Cavalcade covers. Maybe they're going to see if Wonder Woman can come out and play? Art courtesy of Marty.

[Green Lantern, Flash & 3 Dimwits TM & © DC Comics.]

Dennis' conclusions and respectfully begged to disagree with others. Craig Delich explored the Batman chapter in *All-Star* #36, whose artist has never been satisfactorily identified. From Australia David Studham wrote about variants of the Junior Justice Society membership kits—which only reminded me that we'd shortchanged the JSA "Laboratory Notes" that were featured in later issues. And, astonishingly, out of the blue, my old friend and occasional artistic collaborator Frank Brunner—just about the last person I'd have figured would *have* any thoughts about *All-Star*—sent me a tongue-in-cheek (?) rant about the famous cover of its famous third issue.

What's more, after we printed material prepped for but not used in the *Companion* about the 1963-85 JLA-JSA team-ups and the 1970s JSA revival in our monthly magazine *Alter Ego* (available from TwoMorrows at **www.tomorrows.com**), I started getting letters from people encouraging me to do a second volume gathering all that material together. Some folks also asked for coverage of "my" 1980s *All-Star Squadron* and related series (*America vs. the Justice Society*, *The Young All-Stars*, *Secret Origins*, *Infinity, Inc.*, and the *Last Days of the Justice Society Special*). I'll confess, such suggestions appealed to me—as long as any second volume also dealt with the 1940-51 *All-Star Comics* which will always be, in my eyes, the one and only totally 100% legitimate source of stories about the JSA.

In addition, I myself was eager to assemble in one place all the existing artwork from the unpublished mid-1940s Justice Society story "The Will of William Wilson" that hadn't made it into the 2000 *Companion*. Only after that book's publication had photocopies of several additional panels—and even of the entire 5-page JSA introductory chapter—found their way into my hands, and been printed spread out over five issues of *Alter Ego*.

So, what the hell—publisher John Morrow and I talked it over, and we decided we'd do it. A second volume of *The All-Star Companion*.

Only thing is, to get everything in, we soon realized we'd have to do *two* additional books, not one—so that's what we've planned. This one deals primarily with new information and added speculation about the 1940-51 JSA/*All-Star Comics* and with the 1980s *All-Star Squadron*, though with a nod to other series published between 1963 and our cut-off year of 1989—and benefiting from the substantial contributions of Pedro Angosto, Kurt Mitchell, Jerry Ordway, and a passel of very generous collectors.

The third volume, set for autmun of 2007, will collect—and greatly expand—the pieces published in *A/E* #7 & #14 about the original JLA-JSA team-ups and the 1970s JSA revival, in those halcyon days before the *Crisis on Infinite Earths* wiped out several generations of continuity in one tsunamic sweep. But yes, there'll be more in *Volume Three* about both the Golden Age *All-Star* and the 1980s features I developed, as well, including *The Young All-Stars* and *Secret Origins*.

That said, there really isn't that much left to write about *The All-Star Companion, Volume Two*, before you plunge into it for yourself.

Except to admit in advance that I shamelessly enjoyed myself putting together the part of this book that deals primarily with *All-Star Squadron* and my other 1980s work—and I make no apologies for devoting 100+ pages to a series which was never, save for a short time at the very outset, a best-selling or trend-setting comic book.

But then, of course, it was never really *meant* to be a "hot title."

Oh, sure, I'd have *loved* it if *All-Star Squadron* had been the smash hit that my buddies Marv Wolfman and George Pérez's *New Teen Titans* was becoming at that time. In fact, somewhere deep in my heart of hearts, I always felt it *deserved* to be at least nearly as popular. After all, it dealt with many of the greatest super-heroes in the history of comic books… it was blessed from the outset with excellent art by Rich Buckler and Jerry Ordway… and I myself hadn't had too shabby a sales record at Marvel between 1965-80, or else the powers-that-be at DC would never have allowed me to set the series in the World War II period.

Still, *The Invaders* comic I'd launched at Marvel in the mid-1970s

Johnny Rings The Belle

Recent artists have found inspiration in the work done by Rich Buckler and Jerry Ordway in early issues of All-Star Squadron. This fine commission drawing of Johnny Quick and Liberty Belle (the latter during her caped period) is by penciler Paul Ryan, who did well-remembered stints on Fantastic Four *and* Avengers West Coast *and now draws the syndicated* Phantom *strip—and by inker Kim Mulder, who has inked such comics as* Superboy, Swamp Thing, *and* Nick Fury, Agent of SHIELD. *Thanks to Michael Zeno—and to Paul and Kim. [Characters TM & © DC Comics.]*

to spin war-era yarns of Captain America, Sub-Mariner, and Human Torch had never really set the world on fire, though it had garnered respectable sales for some time. At DC, though, I had a far more stellar lineup to choose from—at least a dozen heroes I considered among the best ever created, while at Marvel there'd been only three such (albeit they were a trio of *great* characters, and they had reasonably good backup).

I was willing to risk such creative capital as I'd accrued under Stan Lee on a comic set in 1942 instead of the 1980s—because, frankly, I'd have been bored out of my skull just adding to the already-large legacy of Superman or Batman or even Wonder Woman or, heaven forfend, the Legion of Super-Heroes. Fine concepts all, certainly… but of all the characters DC controlled at that time, only an assignment to scribe new adventures of (the real) Captain Marvel and his Family could've pushed my buttons with anything resembling the force that writing the JSA did. And DC wasn't in a mood, just then, to launch a full-scale *Shazam!* revival. I know. I asked.

All-Stars All?

(Above:) Roy in 1944 at age three—sneaking a peek at a stranger's Sunday comics section near the zoo in Forest Park, in St. Louis. RT started in early as a comics fan! Photo courtesy of boyhood chum Jim Woeltje & Roy's mother, Mrs. Leona Thomas.

(Right:) The breathtaking cover of All-Star Squadron #1. It's reproduced from a scan of the original (autographed) art sent by proud owner Keif A. Fromm. Roy considers this cover among his all-time favorites—and recalls it as being the concept of the series' first editor, Len Wein. The art has been signed by RT and artists Rich Buckler (pencils) and Dick Giordano (inks). [Art © DC Comics.]

Okay, so, since you're perusing this book, you probably understand about my love for the original JSA—but, you may be asking, why didn't I inaugurate a *Justice Society of America* title set in 1981, rather than this *All-Star Squadron* thing—a name derived half-unconsciously from the 1970s "All-Star Super Squad"?

Well, you need to remember that the '70s *All-Star* revival had ended only a year or so before—so the bloom was definitely off that particular rose for the immediate future. DC appreciated the fact that I wanted to "do something" with the JSA heroes; but, under the circumstances, it wasn't hard for me to talk them into letting that "something" be to create a group that contained, absorbed, and even *dwarfed* the total lifetime membership of the older combo, and even into letting me set the story in the period during which, let's face it, all those heroes had enjoyed their first and in some ways greatest flush of success.

So I took the ball and ran with it.

Maybe I stumbled, eventually. Certainly I feel in retrospect that I should've written somewhat fewer dialogue balloons. I got carried away, I suppose, because I was enjoying myself so immensely, and the readers seemed to like the end result.

One thing I *don't* regret, though—not one whit—is my tossing in all those footnotes about old comics, a feature that a few folks disparaged. My feeling was and is that, after all, no one had to actually *read* those back issues in order to enjoy the new ones. I told readers all they needed to know in the body of the new story. Even so, it's nice, this time around, for example, to be able to show an image of The Flash time-traveling in *All-Flash* #4 as well as the 1982-83 recasting of that image by Jerry Ordway. This book would have needed to include dozens more panels from 1940s comics to illustrate those flashbacks and footnotes, if not for DC's excellent *Archives* volumes of the past decade and a half.

Another thing I definitely don't regret is my decision to include *so many* heroes in the mix. Oh, I argued back and forth with myself briefly about what to do concerning the Quality characters, because of the earlier "Earth-X" thing—*and* because, in my mind, Busy

Arnold's heroes, great as they are, will never be fully a part of 1940s DC continuity. (The same is true of the Fawcett-generated Marvel Family, though I'd have been glad to see them in the Squadron had DC allowed it.) In the end, it was my love for Plastic Man and my intention of making Phantom Lady one of the series' rare super-heroines that tipped the scales on including the Quality bunch. And then I wound up not doing much with either character, after all.

But, as for the others—all those vintage DC heroes (including a few, like Liberty Belle, that I backdated slightly to squeeze them into late 1941/early 1942) and even new creations Amazing-Man and the femme Firebrand—I considered them, each and every one, part of the verbal and visual tapestry I wanted to weave out of the Golden Age of Comics. If Hawkman knew Green Lantern, why shouldn't they both know Belle and Johnny Quick and Robotman and Shining Knight and…?

But, enough about that…for now. You've got roughly a hundred pages to peruse before you reach the 1980s "retro" material. First come more revelations and speculations about the original JSA of 1940-51—and the excitement of the revivals of the 1960s and '70s.

I've also tossed in photos of as many creators who weren't seen in *Vol. 1* as I could get hold of. If there's no photo of your favorite artisan herein, it's because I couldn't reach him/her to ask for one. At one time or another, all of them—like me—hitched their wagons to *All-Star*… and I hope *you* will, too.

WHY I HATE ALL-STAR COMICS #3

(Or, How Boring Can A Cover Get!)

by Frank Brunner

It seems that if you look at almost any fanzine, price guide, or auction catalog, there it is!... that darn cover to *All-Star Comics* #3.

Frankly (no pun), I'm really tired of seeing that "classic" underachievement of the Golden Age... so, just for fun, I started thinking about how this "oh, so famous" cover might have come about... with a little imagination and the assistance of a Mr. Rip Hunter (Time Master). Let's return to that hallowed time and fateful day in 1940!

(Note: Real names have been omitted to protect the innocent, mainly *me!*)

DC Comics offices, and in particular *All-Star* editor Shmoe's desk. A cloud of cigar smoke circles his furrowed brow. He is deep in thought... and through the magic of bad writing, let's eavesdrop on his mental machinations.

Editor Shmoe's thinking... thinking. Suddenly, a light bulb appears over his balding cranium.

Shmoe: "Gee, we've got all these great super-hero characters. Hmmm, why not combine them into... a... a... team!! YEAH, THAT'S IT! A TEAM!"

Editor Shmoe clicks on his intercom and shouts to his secretary: "Miss White! Are there any artists in the offices right now?"

"Well, there's Sneezy, Sleepy, and I think Dopey is here somewhere."

"This is too important for Dopey. Send in Sleepy."

A few moments later and Sleepy appears before editor Shmoe's desk.

"Hiya, Chief. What's up?"

Editor Shmoe irritatedly barks, "How many times have I told you, don't call me Chief!!"

"OK, OK!... Your Majesty!"

"That's better. Now sit down and listen up! I've got a great idea for the next issue of *All-Star Comics*. We're gonna take a bunch of these super-heroes and make a team out of them. And you're gonna draw me a cover!"

Sleepy tries to seem excited. "Wow! That sounds great... er... What is the name of this team?"

Frank-ly Spectral

The Spectre, in a moody, previously-unpublished pencil illustration by Frank Brunner, conjures up E.E. Hibbard's cover for All-Star Comics #3 (Winter 1940). [Spectre TM & © DC Comics; cover © DC Comics.]

Editor Shmoe thinks a minute. "Why, they are called... the... the All-Star Team!!... of course!"

Sleepy raises an eyelid and sarcastically mumbles, "Yeah, that's really gonna sit well with the baseball people!"

Editor Shmoe weakly retorts, "Gee, I guess that could be a problem. Let's think again... hmm... They fight for... justice... and they... protect society, right? So... let's call them the Justice Society??!!"

Sleepy sinks back into his chair, almost sliding off it, and replies, "Society? Sounds a little too high-falutin'. What about the rest of America?"

Editor Shmoe angrily shoots back, "Of *course* they are all Americans. Every man jack of 'em! Er... wait, is one of the guys Polish?"

Sleepy, in a rare display of knowledge replies, "You're thinking of that Blackhawk guy over at Quality Comics."

Editor Shmoe, looking relieved, sez, "Then it's settled! They are the Justice Society of America. Boy, what a genius I am!"

Sleepy ignores Shmoe's golden glow of self-indulgence and inquires further: "OK, so who's on the team?"

Editor Shmoe recites his list: "Our main strip characters, of course. Flash, Hawkman, Spectre, Dr. Fate, Green Lantern, Hour-Man, Sandman, and The Atom!"

It's Déjà Vu All Over Again!

Along with a couple of early comics covers depicting Superman or Batman, that of All-Star #3 is one of the Golden Age covers most often paid homage to. Above left, the cover of Fighting Fun Comics #3 (2002) by Robert M. Socha and Kenny Picklesimer, Jr.—above right, a recent drawing by Carl Barks' latter-day successor on the Ducks, Don Rosa, done as a commission. [Fighting Fun art © Robert M. Socha & Kenny Picklesimer, Jr.; duck art © Disney Enterprises, Inc.; All-Star Comics logo TM & © DC Comics.]

Sleepy's eyes suddenly pop open. "What? No Superman or Batman? They're the top sellers this company has!"

Editor Shmoe looks wistfully up at the ceiling fan rotating amidst the cigar smoke and says, in a low whisper-like voice, "Now why would we want to do that? A team book *with* Superman *and* Batman might sell in the millions! The publisher might even *notice* what I've done... and that's... not good. No, that's not good at all."

Sleepy protests, "But... but... *selling comics*, isn't that what it's all..."

Editor Shmoe cuts Sleepy off. "You're just trying to use logic. Forget about it. No bats or buts about it!"

Sleepy, exasperated, slumps back into his chair again. "OK. Whatever. Let's talk about the cover. What are they doing? What evil menace are they confronting?"

A Place At The Table

Cartoonist Fred Hembeck's inimitable take on the cover of All-Star #3 (Winter 1940). Frank Brunner specifically asked that Fred's version accompany his article—and Fred happily obliged. We just didn't want it to be lonely! [Hembeck art © Fred Hembeck; JSA & logo TM & © DC Comics.]

Look Out, All-Stars—Here We Come!

(Right:) Longtime Marvel artist & editor Al Milgrom drew the Timely take on All-Star #3 (at right) as a cover for *Alter Ego #20* (2003), with *The Whizzer* impatiently drumming on the tabletop.
[Heroes TM & © Marvel Characters, Inc.]

Editor Shmoe, with another wistful smile, replies, "No evil, no menace. In fact, they are doing *nothing!*"

Sleepy, inspired by this statement: "Well, I think I can handle this job. But what exactly do you mean by 'doing nothing'?"

Editor Shmoe continues, "They are all just sitting around... around... a *Round Table!* Do I have to think of *everything?*"

Sleepy, now satirically, pushes further: "Are they smoking cigars and swapping tall tales, maybe?"

Editor Shmoe: "Don't be ridiculous. Half of them don't have *faces!* And we all know that Good Guys don't smoke cigars!'

Sleepy continues his questions with complete innocence. "But, Chief... you smoke cigars!"

Editor Shmoe suddenly explodes at the observation. "*Blast it! I'm not a comic book character...* and don't call me *Chief!*" He continues in a lower, softer, again wistful voice: "Yes, this is gonna be a classic cover! Eight action heroes just sitting around. Oh, listen, Sleepy, can you put a kind of Mona Lisa smile on Hour-Man's face? That'd be just great!"

Sleepy, no longer listening, now dozing quietly: "ZZZZZZZZZZZZZZZZ"

And thus was created the cover of *All-Star Comics* #3.

Just'a Shazam Association

Big Bang Comics artist Mark Lewis drew a fine original illo that'll appear in Vol. 3 of this series—but meanwhile, have a sneak peak at his pencils for that Fawcett-filled nod to a certain classic cover that dare not speak its name (at least not in Frank Brunner's presence).
[Heroes TM & © DC Comics.]

There've been numerous other All-Star #3 homages, of course, including Al Dellinges' version in *Alter Ego* V3#9 of that scene featuring the 1940 DC heroes who weren't at that first JSA meeting. And you'll find yet another artful homage to the cover of All-Star #3 on p. 102 of this very volume.

Okay, fellas—can we all quit now? We're upsetting poor Frank!

FRANK BRUNNER has been a professional comics artist only since the late 1960s, and thus can be forgiven for not knowing that Blackhawk originated *after* the Justice Society. He has also worked in the field of animation. He is known especially for his work on *Howard the Duck* and *Dr. Strange* for Marvel Comics. Frank currently draws re-creations and original commissions. Visit his website at www.frankbrunner.net, or write him at 312 Kildare Court, Myrtle Beach, SC 29588.

Frank Brunner.

Chapter II

PLAYING WITH SAND(MAN)

by Roy Thomas

Artist (and ofttimes writer) Creig Flessel, as per his interview in *Alter Ego* #45 (2005), was one of the earliest artists to go to work for Major Malcolm Wheeler-Nicholson's National Allied Publications in 1935—and he stuck around for a few years after Harry Donenfeld and associates took over the company and turned it into what is now DC Comics. While Creig also drew The Shining Knight and other features there before leaving for other commercial art endeavors by 1942 or so, he is especially noted for drawing the very first Sandman covers for *Adventure Comics*, and for taking over the Sandman writing and art chores when original artist Bert Christman left for China in 1941 to become a fighter pilot with Claire Chennault's Flying Tigers.

Creig believes that reports crediting him as artist of the Sandman tales in *All-Star Comics* #1 & 3 are in error. But he opines as how he *might* have penciled the pre-JSA Sandman story in issue #2, and art-ID expert Craig Delich believes that he *did*, with Chad Grothkopf inking. (All this material is on view in DC's *All Star* and *Golden Age Sandman Archives* volumes—and see p. 56 for more of Flessel's work.)

In his mid-90s and still drawing, in August 2005 the artist sent Ye Editor photocopies of some of his work (part of it quite recent) which simply cried out for inclusion in this second volume of *The All-Star Companion*. In the accompanying letter, he wrote: "My part of the Golden Age is so small that people now say, 'Creig Who?' However, the Major, Whit [Ellsworth], Vin [Sullivan], and I were there in 1935, starting the industry known as 'the comics.' And your efforts to give credit to the Henry Fords of the comic book are admirable."

The honor is all ours, Creig.

So here it is—a special art bonus, courtesy of one of the finest gentlemen (and talents) to work in comic books.

Mr. Sandman, Send Me a Dream...

Creig Flessel in his California studio in 2005—as seen in both sketch (top of page) and photo. The original of this superb piece of artwork belongs to Rob Stolzer. [Art © Creig Flessel; Sandman TM & © DC Comics.]

It's A Gas!

We're constantly astounded by the variations that Creig Flessel manages to work on Sandman drawings, when he's really just this masked guy with a gas-gun! [Sandman TM & © DC Comics.]

Maybe They Should've Called It "DC Cola"!

Besides his having probably penciled the Sandman story in All-Star Comics #2, Creig Flessel's art was often on display in that and other DC mags, especially in the "'R.C.' and Quickie" comics-style commercial pages he drew for what was then called Royal Crown Cola. (The soft drink's name wasn't officially changed to "RC Cola" till years later.) Western movie stars like Johnny Mack Brown, Sunset Carson, and even John Wayne—despite the Duke's having been an "A"-lister ever since 1939's *Stagecoach*—plugged the product, as well. Flessel writes: "Royal Crown Cola was one of my early accounts at Johnstone & Cushing. I did 'em, grabbed the money, and ran. Had I known I would have to face all my sinful scratchings 60+ years later, I would have done a better job." Oh, we dunno, Creig—they look pretty good to us!

(Above left:) This "R.C. and Quickie" page from *All-Star* #41 (June-July 1948) is Ye Editor's personal favorite. It made him go ape at age 7!

(Above right:) The back cover ad from *All-Star* #42 (Aug.-Sept. 1948) was a quasi-parody of the long-running Charles Atlas sand-in-the-face, 90-pound-weakling ads—which also occasionally appeared in *All-Star*. A bit of art and copy have been lost at right because the page was photocopied from Ye Editor's bound volumes.

(Left:) From the back cover of *All-Star* #48 (Aug.-Sept. 1949).

[All three ads © the respective copyright holders.]

CHAPTER III

MORE MYSTERIES OF *ALL-STAR COMICS*

An Alternate View

by Dennis Mallonee

Until recently, those of us who loved the Justice Society of America, but who weren't sentient when it was still possible to acquire a complete set of *All-Star Comics* without taking out a second mortgage, had access only to the few JSA stories that were reprinted from time to time.

Since the publication of DC's *All Star Comics Archives*, the adventures we'd only heard about are now available at reasonable prices. And, as often happens when a fresh look is taken by new eyes, certain inconsistencies in the conventional wisdom have been perceived.

Understand that, in regard to the remaining mysteries of *All-Star Comics*, the conventional wisdom isn't necessarily *wrong*. There are, however, certain facts that have previously been overlooked. And there remain several mysteries of that comics title, all stemming from one unassailable fact. Specifically:

All-Star Comics *was neither conceived of, nor in its early years regarded as, a vehicle for the Justice Society of America.*

All-Star Genesis

It's well known to aficionados that the JSA was originally devised as nothing more than a clever framing device for an anthology comic book. Yet, the conventional wisdom that *All-Star* was the JSA's comic is so ingrained that even DC chose to begin its *All Star Archives* with the group's first appearance in #3, skipping #1-2. Still, it's in those first two issues—which have since seen print in their own *Archives* volume—that we can clearly see what *All-Star Comics* was intended to be. It was conceived in the aftermath of the extraordinary success of DC's solo *Superman* comic, which had proven that a comic book featuring a single strong character was capable of outperforming an anthology title. Clearly, there was money to be made.

For DC's second solo title, the choice was obvious. But after *Batman*, who? Was there any character from *Detective Comics*, *Action Comics*, *Adventure Comics*, or *More Fun Comics* who could sell comics all on his own? And over at M.C. Gaines' related All-American house, were there any characters from *Flash Comics* or *All-American Comics* who might be strong enough?

One way to find out would be to put them to the test. You'd start by preparing a comic book featuring a lineup of the two most promising characters from each of four of the above monthly anthologies—but (though the reasoning gets a bit shaky here) minus any heroes from *Action* or *Detective*, whose lead characters Superman and Batman had already reached stellar heights. The 1939 and 1940 *New York World's Fair* anthology issues had shown a market for a comic featuring a roster of characters taken from other

comics. And then you could *ask* your readers which of these showcased heroes they liked best.

The house ads for *All-Star* follow this model precisely. Readers are told that Superman and Batman have their own titles, and now there's also a comic featuring favorite characters from each of four other "DC" anthologies. Moreover, in *All-Star* #1 itself, a poll asks readers to name their favorite heroes who *didn't* appear therein. A follow-up poll in #2 invites readers to vote for the hero they'd most like to see follow Superman and Batman into a third solo title.

Simply put:

All-Star *was conceived of, and in its early years was regarded as, a profitable promotional vehicle for the rest of the DC/All-American line.*

The Gang's All Here!

(Above:) Here's a rarity you won't find in a volume of The All Star Comics Archives: namely, a full-page house ad for All-Star Comics #3! With thanks to Jim Ludwig. [© DC Comics.]

(Top left:) Chances are the All-Star Comics logo was designed and executed by All-American editor (and cartoonist) Sheldon Mayer, who oversaw the line until 1948, around the time this photo was taken. This studio portrait appeared in Comic Book Artist [Vol. 1] #11, courtesy of daughter Merrily Mayer Harris & son Lanny Mayer.

The Early Honorary Members— And The Wonder Woman Anomaly

There's Never A Wayback Machine Around When You Really Need One

(Left:) This full-page house ad for Flash Comics #1 appeared in All-American Comics #9 (Dec. 1939). Interesting that The Whip is depicted, rather than Hawkman—but we wonder whether it was original Flash artist Harry Lampert or (far more likely) editor Shelly Mayer who drew the cartoony figure of the Fastest Man Alive. With thanks to Bob Hughes.

(Below:) A house ad for the forthcoming Sensation Comics #1 (Jan. 1942) faced the last page of Wonder Woman's 8-page origin in All-Star #8, but wasn't reprinted in All Star Comics Archives, Vol. 2. Note that famed boxer Gene Tunney's congratulatory note addresses AA publisher M.C. Gaines as "Charley." It was apparently as "Charley/Charlie," never as "Max," that Gaines was known to his friends; his middle name became the front half of the "Charles Moulton" byline which appeared on all Wonder Woman stories for years, added to the middle name of major WW creator Dr. William Moulton Marston. Apparently, artist H.G. Peter (WW's co-creator, who even designed her costume) was supposed to consider himself lucky he was allowed to sign his work! [Both pages © DC Comics.]

It's for that reason that DC's most popular heroes, Superman and Batman, were relegated from the beginning to the status of "honorary" membership, and why, as soon as The Flash and Green Lantern received their own quarterly titles, *they* were required to leave the team. Given *All-Star*'s creation as a promotional vehicle, no purpose was to be served by continuing to use it to promote a hero who already had his own comic book.

As an important corollary to this: it was doubtless the promotional structure of *All-Star* that dictated who the *replacements* for departing members would be. When The Flash and Green Lantern gained honorary status, their replacements were Johnny Thunder and Dr. Mid-Nite, heroes likewise from *Flash Comics* and *All-American*, respectively. And when Starman, a promising new lead feature in *Adventure*, joined the JSA, the hero dropped was *Adventure*'s Hour-Man. In this way, the mandated symmetry of *All-Star* was maintained.

Even after all this time, however, there remain several mysteries concerning the Golden Age *All-Star Comics* and the Justice Society of America.

The *first* of these concerns issue #8, in which, even as Starman replaces Hour-Man, Wonder Woman was introduced, with no fanfare whatever, in a bonus 9-page feature which added 8 pages to the thickness of the comic, at no increase in cover price. While it may be true, as some believe, that there were "trademark reasons" for wanting to get a Wonder Woman story into print as quickly as possible (and *Alter Ego* V3#2 demonstrated that the WW story originally earmarked for *Sensation Comics* #2 became the cover feature of #1 instead), early publication of her adventures could've been accomplished in any number of less expensive ways.

Wonder Woman made her debut in *All-Star* #8 because, as a promotional tool, *All-Star* had worked. Flash and Green Lantern had already graduated from it into their own titles, and surely the expec-

tation was that more characters would follow. DC had high hopes for the new Starman, for instance, and, after the AA branch's good fortune with Flash and GL, putting him into *All-Star* must have seemed the pathway to success. But where DC used *All-Star* #8 to promote a new character (Starman), its sister company All-American used it to promote a whole new *magazine*. What better way to boost sales on the first issue of *Sensation* than by giving *All-Star*'s readers a sneak peak at its lead feature a few weeks early?

Again the DC/AA strategy worked. Wonder Woman not only supposedly won a poll asking which of *Sensation*'s six features characters should be inducted into the JSA—she also won her own magazine in record time. This created a peculiar problem, and with it the *second* great mystery of *All-Star*.

The original idea had surely been to add the Amazon as a 9th active JSAer, even though there were only pages enough for 8 heroes to have

Ancient Jewish Curse: "May You Always Have Partners!"

If, as Dennis theorizes, there was ever a tug-of-war over which heroes should belong to the JSA, it would've been between these three co-publishers of the All-American Comics line, seen toasting each other in 1940. (L. to r.:) M.C. Gaines, Harry Donenfeld, and Jack Liebowitz. Gaines, who was involved only in the AA company, would've been on one end of the rope—with Donenfeld (co-publisher of both AA & DC/National) and Liebowitz (whom Donenfeld promoted from being his accountant to co-publisher of DC, and eventually also of AA) pulling on the other. Gaines' son Bill—later the publisher of Mad, Tales from the Crypt, Weird Science, and other EC comics—maintained that, by the mid-'40s, his father and his two partners squabbled constantly. This photo appeared in The Mad World of William M. Gaines by Frank Jacobs; thanks to Michael Feldman for reminding us of that fact. [© the respective copyright holders.]

solo adventures in any given issue. (Thus, in *All-Star* #11-13, first The Spectre, then Wonder Woman, then Dr. Fate played little part in the story; indeed, Fate missed the entire meeting!) But, by the time of #13, *Wonder Woman* #1 was on sale, and by the editorial rules then in place, she *had* to become the JSA's 5th honorary member. Yet, were she to disappear entirely from *All-Star*, there would be nothing therein that would cross-promote *Sensation*!

Becoming the JSA's secretary allowed Wonder Woman to remain visible in *All-Star* without interfering with that magazine's principal purpose of promoting characters who didn't yet have their own magazines. It was an elegant solution to the dilemma.

The Consequences of War

We can only guess what might have happened at DC/AA had America not entered World War II. Perhaps DC's third chairman would have won his own magazine; artist Shelly Moldoff has said that co-publisher M.C. Gaines once talked to him about drawing a projected *Hawkman* title. But with wartime paper rationing plus reduced page counts across the entire DC/AA line, there was no chance between mid-1942 and war's end in 1945 to launch any new titles. Indeed, the gradual drop in interior page count, from 64 to 56 to 48, meant that *heroes*, too, had to be dropped. The last Dr. Fate story in *More Fun* appeared in the July-Aug. 1944 issue; The Spectre lasted there till the Jan.-Feb. 1945 issue. In *Adventure*, Sandman and Starman both continued through Feb.-March 1946.

The looming disappearances of these characters from DC's monthly anthologies had a profound impact on *All-Star*. Although chapters featuring Sandman and Dr. Fate had been planned for #20, the reduction in page count from 56 to 48 led to the scrapping of already-scripted chapters for that pair, just as Jerry Bails once theorized and JSA writer/co-creator Gardner Fox later confirmed from his own records (see *The All-Star Companion, Vol. 1*). From

#20 on, there were to have been only *six* active JSA members, instead of eight. Yet that wasn't how it worked out—at least not for two more issues.

And this constitutes the *third* great mystery of *All-Star*.

In #21, although they don't appear on the cover, Dr. Fate and Sandman both have solo chapters in the story, instead of the cover-featured Spectre and Atom. It's been theorized that the former pair were retained for an issue or two longer because there were still Junior Justice Society membership kits to sell, with likenesses of Fate and Sandman on the certificates. But I argue there was a much more basic reason for keeping those characters in *All-Star*:

I believe it happened because DC *insisted* they remain!

Note that every hero being dropped from the JSA roster was a *DC* (as opposed to AA) character. The only DC stalwart who'd have remained in what had always been a cooperative venture between DC and AA was Starman. DC was about to stop publishing stories about Fate and Spectre, though a few stories with that pair may well have been in the can; and a decision had been made to continue the Sandman feature for a time in *Adventure* (without Simon and Kirby, who were in the armed services), as well as Starman. I believe that, for as long as DC continued to publish those four heroes, they wanted them featured in *All-Star*—even if it meant that some pages of existing artwork had to be redrawn.

More Terrific Than You Ever Knew

Jerry Bails has theorized that the Sandman and Dr. Fate chapters in *All-Star* #21 ("The Man Who Relived His Life!") were originally written to feature The Atom and The Spectre. While I think the Atom-into-Sandman part of that theory is right, I'm convinced the part about Spectre-into-Fate is wrong.

There are good reasons to believe that the last actual intended appearance of Spectre in *All-Star* was the one in #20—and that, while there was indeed one more chapter of a JSA adventure written originally with The Spectre in mind, it *wasn't* either that Dr. Fate chapter from #21, or either of the Spectre chapters that would appear in #22 or #23 (which one it *was* is revealed on p. 20—but don't be impatient.)

It has often been said that, toward the end of their runs in *All-Star*, The Spectre didn't act very ghostlike, and Dr. Fate wasn't much of a sorcerer. But, in fact, The Spectre acts *very much* like himself up through #20, and it's only in #21 that Dr. Fate doesn't act much like Dr. Fate.

The perspicacious among you may see where I'm going with this. We know that Dr. Fate and Sandman were to be dropped, and The Spectre vanished soon afterward. So the question regarding the latter is: why in the world would plans have been made to continue to feature an abandoned DC hero once promoting him would serve no purpose?

The obvious answer is—there would have been *no* such plans. Not only wasn't that really Dr. Fate in *All-Star* #21—it wasn't even The Spectre! And the reason The Spectre didn't act much like himself in #22-23 is that those chapters weren't originally written for him. I believe that, before DC insisted its heroes continue to be featured in the JSA, *someone else* was on tap to serve as The Spectre's replacement.

Who?

Is There A Doctor In the House?

By the time of 1944's All-Star #21, Dr. Fate had long since ceased to be the all-powerful mage he was in his 1940 More Fun debut. His original incarnation is captured wonderfully at right by Frank Brunner, who in the '70s became a major artist of Marvel's own "Sorcerer Supreme," Dr. Strange (below). Both illos were done by Frank as commission drawings. [Dr. Fate TM & © DC Comics; Dr. Strange TM & © Marvel Characters, Inc.]

One corrective: Dennis says Dr. Fate "may call himself a doctor, [but] diagnostic ability isn't a talent we'd ever seen [him] display." Actually, in More Fun #85 (Nov. 1942), Fate's alter ego, Kent Nelson, did get a medical degree—in the space of a page or two. After that, as Don Thompson wrote in Xero #7 in 1961, Fate "used modern medicine... completely dropping the wizard bit." So far as we know, in 1942 Dr. Fate co-creator Gardner Fox—shown here applauding that hero (though he also scripted Dr. Strange briefly in the '70s)—was still writing Fate's solo exploits, as well as his All-Star chapters. Thanks to Bill Schelly for researching this point... and to Fred Mommsen for finding Fox's photo in an early Phil Seuling comicon program book.

There are some clues in *All-Star* #21:

Take a close look at the 3rd page of the Dr. Fate chapter. (For this and following comparisons, you'll need to consult a copy of various volumes of *The All Star Archives*.) In panel 5 of that 3rd page, Joe Fitch's aiming of his handgun is disrupted by a thrown object—something neither Fate nor Spectre would've had to do. In panel 6, in the only quasi-supernatural event in the chapter, Fate "steps from a glowing halo of light." But a close examination of even the *Archives* reprinting of *All-*

Star #21 reveals that this caption has been completely *re-lettered*, in a style different from the rest of the lettering in the chapter; thus, we may infer there was originally no mention of a "glowing halo of light" at all. [**EDITOR'S NOTE:** *See p. 22.*]

Next, on page 4, panel 1, Dr. Fate easily identifies a dead man's condition as symptomatic of hydrocyanic poisonic. Though Fate may call himself a doctor, that level of diagnostic ability isn't a talent we'd ever seen him, let alone The Spectre, display.

In the first panel on page 5, there are two different weights of lettering. The first half of the caption, ending with the word "man," is in a lighter weight and of a slightly different style than the rest of it, beginning with "of mystery." From this, we may infer that the caption originally referred to a "man of"—something else.

Finally, in the last panel on page 5, there's extra white space after the world "good-bye." It's just enough space to fit a two-letter abbreviation.

In *All-Star* #22, The Spectre's chapter deals with 19th-century Luddites trying to destroy an electrical motor. Not once does "The Spectre" do anything supernatural. The only mention that he's a spirit occurs in panel 2 of the 2nd page—in a caption lettered in a different style from the rest of the story.

Beginning in the last panel of the 3rd page, and continuing into the first panel of the next, "The Spectre" rattles off an historical narrative describing the troubles other inventors had faced when they developed something new.

Finally, in the 3rd panel of the 5th page, an outraged "Spectre" declares that beating up innocent men is going to get downright unpopular—while he himself thwacks the Luddites with his fists. Obviously, the hero of this chapter—whoever he was supposed to be—doesn't consider the beating up of innocent men to be fair play.

In *All-Star* #23, there's only one panel in which "The Spectre" does anything even remotely ghostlike. Instead, he receives a telegram, climbs through windows, hides behind a curtain, uses mops and buckets as weapons, tosses an object through a window in order to get fresh air, and punches out one of The Psycho-Pirate's henchmen. None of these are things The Spectre would normally do.

Figured it out yet?

On the basis of the contextual evidence, in all likelihood the character who was intended to have been The Spectre's JSA replacement was a true believer in fair play, the definitely non-supernatural Man of a Thousand Talents—the one and only *Mr. Terrific!*

Taking Inventory

When the full split between DC and AA finally came in late 1944, not only was there no longer any need to continue featuring any of DC's heroes in *All-Star*—it was no longer even *possible* to do so. As of the hastily-prepared #24 (with its theme of "What do we do with a defeated Germany?"), Mr. Terrific finally made his long-delayed debut as a replacement for The Spectre—and Wildcat was tapped to step in for Starman.

All-Star #24 was, in a strange way, a precursor to the reality-altering *Crisis on Infinite Earths* four decades in the future. Reality had changed. As reflected in the 1945 JJSA certificate, Superman and Batman were completely out of the picture, no longer listed even as honorary members; the JSA's only remaining honoraries were Flash and Green Lantern. Wonder Woman stayed as secretary, and the active membership was to have consisted of Hawkman and Johnny Thunder from *Flash*, Dr. Mid-Nite and The Atom from *All-American*, and Wildcat and Mr. Terrific from *Sensation*. It was a new symmetry composed entirely of heroes of the All-American group. And one wonders if, given the chance, it might have worked.

But there was a problem.

We now know that, because of the wartime paper-quota-induced cutback of *All-Star* from bimonthly to quarterly, there were several *unpublished issues* in various stages of production, each of which had probably been written with a "Starman" chapter. Given the financial outlay already made, there had to be a certain pressure to publish those stories. But what to do about Starman himself?

The All-Star Companion, Vol. 1, related what happened: Starman was changed into Green Lantern. Not a difficult trick. But if you were using GL, then you were abandoning the editorial stricture against using in the JSA heroes who had their own magazines. And if you were doing *that*, then why weren't you also using the equally popular Flash?

In *All-Star* #25, and thereafter in those issues in which Starman chapters were redone to star Green Lantern, there were also chapters in which *someone* was converted into The Flash. And I believe the answer to the question of how Spectre

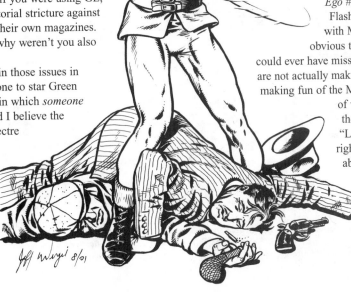

chapters were converted into chapters featuring the Scarlet Speedster is actually quite simple:

In the stories that appeared in All-Star *#25 and beyond, there never were any chapters that had originally featured The Spectre!*

A Flash Of Green

Examine the Flash episode in #25. Take away the speed lines, and Flash isn't doing any super-speed tricks at all. Look at the spacing of the lettering in the first word balloon in the 4th panel of page 2. There's a terrific amount of white space. Give you two guesses what was originally there. The same thing can be seen in the 4th panel of page 3. And on page 5, where "The Flash" makes a point of saying he doesn't gamble, one also has to wonder why the lone thug left standing would be surprised that the Fastest Man Alive would be capable of taking on three opponents at once.

The same sort of thing holds in *All-Star* #26. Even in the *Archives* edition, we can observe that, wherever the words "The Flash" or in one instance "the speedster" are lettered, there's an inordinately large amount of white space. And even though in this story Flash actually performs a few super-speed tricks, we note that there's no detail to the panels in which he does, but that the lettering in the captions describing those tricks is of a style significantly different from that in the rest of the story. [**NOTE:** *Re this paragraph, see p. 23.*]

In *All-Star* #28 (be patient—there's a *reason* we're skipping #27), which was much more extensively reworked than the stories in #25 or #26, there are two distinct styles of lettering. One style always appears where The Flash *doesn't*; the other appears only in panels where Flash is doing something speedy. And, to support the surmise that this chapter wasn't originally written with him in mind, "The Flash" refers on page 5, panel 1, to a trick he once saw "worked in Asia." That's not a reference Flash would normally make; it is, however, something the well-traveled Mr. Terrific might have said.

It's *All-Star* #29 (not the previously-theorized #28, which contains panels in which Green Lantern's left hand could have once held an invisible Gravity Rod) that, I believe, is the first issue in which chapters were written specifically with Flash and GL in mind. In #29's Flash chapter, the Scarlet Speedster comes across like Mercury unleashed, doing well-delineated speed trick after speed trick.

The next of the published Starman-into-GL and Mr.-Terrific-into-Flash *All-Stars* was #30, which the internal evidence of Joe Kubert's evolving art style has long since shown to have been published well over a year after it was prepared (as detailed in both *All-Star Companion, Vol. 1*, and in *Alter Ego* #44, 2005). Once you realize the Flash chapter was originally written with Mr. Terrific in mind, the joke is so obvious that you wonder how anyone could ever have missed it. The funny animals in #30 are not actually making fun of The Spectre. They're making fun of the Man of a Thousand Talents, none of which has done him any good. So the beasties fit him with a "Laughing Stock" placard that slips right down over his trademark abdominal "Fair Play" logo, and fits him to a... wait for it... "T."

There's one more published issue of *All-Star* that might conceivably have been a Starman-into-GL and Mr.-Terrific-into-Flash one. The

Wildcattin'

Virtually the only Wildcat story ever drawn by Joe Kubert appeared in Sensation Comics #66 (June 1947). The villain is The Yellow Wasp. Repro'd from an Australian black-&-white reprint, with thanks to Shane Foley.
[© DC Comics.]

evidence for #31 is much less persuasive than we have for any of the others, but there are panels in which GL seems once again to be holding an invisible Gravity Rod. And in the Flash chapter, although research chemist Jay Garrick might well be capable of tracking the criminals by examining the soil thrown up their digging machine, that's much more a Mr. Terrific thing. And, once again, if you take away the speed lines, you'll find that The Flash isn't really doing much in the way of super-speed stunts.

The Other "Wildcat" Story

The *fourth* remaining mystery of *All-Star* involves why Wildcat made one more appearance in that magazine, displacing The Atom in #27. One theory put forward is that, because the Mighty Mite's last appearance in *All-American Comics* was in its April 1946 issue, as of the Winter 1945-46 edition of *All-Star* he was on the verge of being dropped totally by AA. I believe that *All-Star* #27, as originally written, *did* in fact have an Atom chapter. In this issue, it was The Atom who was redone as The Flash, and (amazingly enough) Mr. Terrific who was redone as Green Lantern!

If you doubt it, take a look at Flash using props to take down a bunch of thugs. Take a look at GL walking around instead of flying.

Sure, Flash does some speed tricks; there are also a couple of panels in which GL uses his ring, plus one in which he bangs his head against a tree. But it's always the case, whenever a character substitution was made, that there are clearly redrawn panels. And even in the panel on page 5 in which "GL" is using his ring, his young ally rather pointedly remarks: "G-Golly! That's.. That's terrific!"

Need a clincher? Look at the word balloon on page 5, panel 6. The words "Green Lantern" don't even come close to lining up with the rest of the text. "Green Lantern" isn't what was originally lettered there!

The explanation for Wildcat's anomalous appearance in *All-Star #27 isn't* that he'd been tapped as a replacement for The Atom. The explanation is that #27 is the only issue besides #24 that was initiated with a roll call that included Mr. Terrific and Wildcat. The Mr. Terrific chapter got redrawn. For some reason, the Wildcat chapter didn't. It's as simple as that.

"The Will of William Wilson"

Finally, there's the mystery of those four "unpublished" Gardner Fox JSA stories, as named by Fox himself in 1965. Jerry Bails has hypothesized that one of those stories ("The Men of Magnifica") may have become the "5 Drowned Men" tale in *All-Star #36*, with Superman and Batman substituted for Johnny Thunder and The Atom. And that's most likely true. Jerry also theorized that another of those "unpublished" tales ("Peril of the Paper Death") was rewritten for *All-Star #28* as "The Paintings That Walked the Earth!" That may be true, as well. For the third story ("The Emperors of Japan"), no existing artwork has yet been discovered, and it's quite possible none was ever done, because of the war's abrupt end after the dropping of two atomic bombs on Japan.

But artwork for the fourth story, "The Will of William Wilson," *does* exist, as seen in *The All-Star Companion, Vol. 1*, and in *Alter Ego #7, 14, 21, 44, & 50*—as well as in the book you hold in your hands. And the *fifth* JSA/*All-Star* mystery—that of why "Will" was never published—was solved, as recounted in *A/E #21* (2003) and in Chapter VI of this volume.

On the first page of the introductory JSA chapter of "Will," a note reveals that at some stage it had been scheduled to appear in *All-Star #31*. But there's also something resembling proof positive that "Will" had been written and even drawn as a 48-page story—ten pages too long to fit into a 1945 issue of *All-Star*. So it got yanked and put on the shelf.

Signs Of The Times

Perhaps the strongest argument in favor of Dennis' Mr. Terrific theory is the placard that the talking animals hang around The Flash's neck in a Brain Wave-induced dream in All-Star #30. The sign makes little sense if written for either speedster or Spectre—but, put there to cover up the "Fair Play" logo on Mr. T's abdomen, it would've made a perfect last panel for that chapter, as shown by the slight modifications done by amiable Al Dellinges, first depicting the possible Spectre version, then the same panel featuring Mr. Terrific! Either way, chances are the art was done only after Flash was "written in." Basic art by Martin Naydel. [© DC Comics.]

Under The Green Star?

Dennis suggests that, in the never-published 1940s JSA story "The Will of William Wilson," Paul Reinman (seen in photo) may have originally drawn a Starman solo chapter rather than a Green Lantern outing. Ye Editor finds that debatable, since GL is emphasizing his left (Power Ring) hand in most of the panels of it we've seen, while Starman often wielded his Gravity Rod with his right. Still, in this panel from "Will," GL is extending his right hand, and it's not impossible the Gravity Rod was whited out therein. At right, Al Dellinges shows us what that panel would've looked like with the Astral Avenger instead of the Emerald Gladiator. Photo thanks to Frank Motler. [© DC Comics.]

Beastly Behavior

This art, as re-created by Al Dellinges, is what the Flash chapter's splash page might've looked like if drawn by Martin Naydel, but featuring Mr. Terrific instead. [© DC Comics.]

This, of course, begs the question of *why* "Will" was 48 pages long. It's been postulated that either DC was planning to make *All-Star* into an oversized 15¢ comic like *World's Finest* and *Comic Cavalcade*, or that "Will" was originally intended as the lead feature in a second 128-page *Big All-American Comic Book*, such as had been published in 1944. But there's a simpler explanation that doesn't require postulating something for which no evidence exists.

"The Will of William Wilson" is probably a lot *older* than the existing artwork makes it look.

The fact is that, during the brief 1944 period when DC and AA titles were at 56 pages, around the time of *All-Star* #20-21, 48 pages was the standard page count for a JSA story. If we surmise that the decision to drop Dr. Fate and Sandman from the JSA roster came just before the decision was made to cut another eight pages out of all the company's titles, then we have a situation in which there might well have been a 48-page JSA adventure featuring a six-man active roster, which was originally slated for *All-Star* #20 or so.

And that, I maintain, is precisely what "The Will of William Wilson" is.

This would explain why, in a few panels of the existing Paul Reinman artwork, Green Lantern appears to be holding that invisible Gravity Rod which slipped by in *All-Star* #26. It would also explain why it was necessary to come up with a trick that would allow Flash to travel backwards in time.

But if "Will" does in fact date from around the time of *All-Star* #20, then why do the records of Gardner Fox indicate it was intended for a much later issue—and why does The Psycho-Pirate put in an appearance, when he doesn't make his debut until issue #23?

The answer to the last question is that "The Will of William Wilson" isn't really a Psycho-Pirate story at all! It has nothing to do with the psychology of the JSA, as do the villain's other two Golden Age appearances. Rather, it's a straightforward quest adventure in which each hero is assigned an "impossible" task, then proceeds to accomplish it. When this inventory story was being prepared for publication, I believe William Wilson was transformed into The Psycho-Pirate in precisely the same way Starman was so often transformed into Green Lantern. In this case, not only were heroes being redrawn to be other characters—the *villain* was recast, too.

So, given all of this, what was the likely sequence of events that led to "The Will of William Wilson" never being published? I believe things went like this:

First, the story was written at a specific moment in time, just after the decision had been made to drop Dr. Fate and Sandman, and just prior to the decision to drop another eight pages from *All-Star*. Because the JSA tale was now too long, whatever artwork was finished was put on the shelf. Some months later, after M.C. Gaines had sold AA to DC lock, stock, and barrel, all existing "JSA" adventures, whether finished or incomplete, were scheduled for various issues, and were handed off to the artists to make whatever changes were necessary to get them ready for publication. For "Will," this involved substituting GL for Starman—reworking the Spectre chapter into a Flash one (See? I *told* you back on p. 15 that there was one more JSA chapter written for The Spectre that got altered)—and (for reasons unknown) dropping in a gratuitous appearance of The Psycho-Pirate. Perhaps, carelessly, it wasn't until much of the artwork for "Will" was assembled that the editors realized it was 48 pages long—at which point it went back on the shelf and was sadly never pulled down again.

Conclusion

Understand that I don't claim with any certainty that these alternate explanations of the mysteries of *All-Star* are the *right* explanations. They are, however, explanations that seem to fit the facts. They do connect the dots, and they do form a consistent pattern.

And that, after all, is what storytelling is all about.

ADDENDUM (EDITED FROM A LATER LETTER TO ROY THOMAS):

Odd that it hadn't registered before, but *Alter Ego* #14 (April 2002) actually printed one of Gardner Fox's plots for a Mr. Terrific story. In the context of this ongoing discussion, that's a useful thing, because it demonstrates how Gardner wrote for that character. Whenever he did a Mr. Terrific tale, he always—*always*—tossed in tidbits of scientific or historical information. He liked to do that anyway, and the fact that the Man of a Thousand Talents was a super-genius who knew a lot about everything gave him the perfect excuse.

It was this pattern of Gardner tossing those little factoids into his Mr. Terrific stories that finally clued me in on why, in their final *All-Star* appearances, Dr. Fate and The Spectre weren't acting like Dr. Fate and The Spectre. Doesn't it make perfect sense that, if a replacement for the vanishing Spectre were needed, it would be a character from *Sensation Comics* whom Gardner was already writing?

The point here is that Mr. Terrific was a hero largely unfamiliar to old-time fans of the JSA. He appeared in just one issue of *All-Star*, and was never seen again (except in a JJSA ad or two). So it's not surprising that it had never previously occurred to JSA historians to look for him in those peculiar Fate and Spectre chapters. But, the instant you start looking for him, he jumps out at you.

As soon as I figured out I might be looking at Mr. Terrific in disguise, I also realized this same pattern carried through into the Flash chapters in those issues of *All-Star* in which Starman was redrawn as Green Lantern, and that the Green Lantern chapter in *All-Star* #27 also displays evidence of Terrific's presence.

That's why I was so keen on seeing the artwork for the "William Wilson" story. Because I do think the story—if not necessarily the artwork—dates from that specific moment in time, just after Sandman and Dr. Fate were dropped from the roster, and just before the page count was trimmed from 56 to 48.

Having looked again at the five pages of the JSA introduction printed in *A/E* #14 (and on pp. 27-31 of this book), I also observe a peculiarity that gives us a clue as to what the actual ending of the story was originally intended to be. Take a look at the man depicted on the splash page. Yes, that's Abel Northrup, the elderly recluse from the Dr. Mid-Nite chapter. Now ask yourself why in the world a minor character from a single chapter would be given such a prominent position on the splash? The obvious answer is—this fellow is *William Wilson!* If you substitute him for The Psycho-Pirate, and The Spectre and Starman for The Flash and GL, then you have substantially the story that Gardner originally wrote. At the end of the story, the guy Mid-Nite met turns out also to be both Fiddle and Wilson. It's Mister X (from *All-Star* #5) redux.

This also relates indirectly to *All-Star* #36. Jerry thinks this was originally the missing "Men of Magnifica" tale, and I'm pretty sure he's right. He's further observed that the Batman chapter was likely originally written for The Atom, and the Superman chapter for Johnny Thunder. What Jerry didn't point out was some pretty obvious evidence that the latter wasn't a Superman story at all. Take a look at what Superman *does*. When a skyscraper is blown up, he effortlessly puts it back together! Even for the Superman of 1965, that would have been a difficult trick. For the Superman of 1947, it would have been impossible. What we see in *All-Star* #36 is Superman doing what must have been conceived of originally as a bit of magic that Johnny's Thunderbolt could've done.

The contextual evidence is overwhelming that, during that strange period in the history of *All-Star Comics*, characters were being substituted, not just once or twice but systematically, as a matter of editorial policy. Read some of those peculiar chapters again, and I promise that you will see Mr. Terrific under there. It may even, come to think of it, be the reason Gardner's Flash chapter in *All-Star* #36 had to be completely redone.

DENNIS MALLONEE is the president of Heroic Publishing, Inc., and a principal writer/creator of *Flare*, *The League of Champions*, *Chrissie Claus*, and many other Heroic Publishing characters. He graduated from Caltech with a degree in economics. From 1981 through 1987 he was editor of the fantasy/sf magazine *Fantasy Book*.

Will The Real William Wilson Please Stand Up?

Instead of The Psycho-Pirate, could the reclusive Abel Northrup—shown at far left from Dr. Mid-Nite chapter of "Will"—have secretly been the story's main villain (or at least prime mover)? Maybe... though Ye Editor feels an equally plausible reason for Northrup's appearing on the splash of the "lost" story (see p. 27) is that obtaining his signature was one of the six "impossible feats" the JSA had to accomplish, and therefore something related to Northrup had to be there along with the other five quest objects. The only alternatives would've been the signature itself or the pen with which he wrote it. Michael T. Gilbert went the latter route when concocting his own version of a cover for "Will" (see p. 25). All the same, Dennis' general theories concerning those mid-1940s All-Stars may well have merit. Thus, in this composite panel, we've juxtaposed Abel Northrup with The Psycho-Pirate (right)—the two William Wilson wannabes. Thanks to Ethan Roberts. [Dr. Mid-Nite TM & © DC Comics.]

THE SPECTRE DOES ANOTHER FADE-OUT AFTER AN UNGHOSTLY BREATH

by Jerry G. Bails

"The Mr. Terrific Hypothesis"

Dennis Mallonee has done a truly amazing job in pinpointing the anomalies in the handling of the heroes in the troublesome issues of *All-Star Comics* running from #20 through #36. Without question, most of these troublesome events were prompted by the rapid changes in the ownership of the characters, the fateful demise of some of the latter in their monthly anthology series, and the loss of story pages in *All-Star* beginning with #20.

A number of JSA stories were already drawn and in inventory when a number of disrupting orders came down from the publisher. The poor editors were required to make a number of last-minute changes in work that was either in progress or already completed. Evidence of changes in art gave us the first clue that this had happened, the most glaring of which is Green Lantern's wielding Starman's Gravity Rod in two panels in #26, as shown in *The All-Star Companion, Vol. 1*. There are other such examples, first pointed out by Phil Castora in his groundbreaking 1965 essay which revealed that numerous JSA stories had appeared out of the order in which they had been drawn.

Phil (as quoted in *ASC V1*) based his analysis on Joe Kubert's evolving renderings of Hawkman, and his argument stands unscathed after decades of scrutiny. In fact, Gardner Fox himself confirmed that his stories appeared out of the order in which he had written them, and he gave us his best determination of what the exact order was. However, Gardner never cleared up the question of precisely which characters he had written in each of his scripts. That's the puzzle that still haunts us, and which Dennis has addressed so eloquently.

Dennis operates on the reasonable assumption that some of Gardner's scripts were changed in significant ways before or after they reached the artists, and that some characters wound up playing parts that Gardner had intended for a quite different hero. Dennis has combed through the JSA stories to look for inconsistent handling of the characters, or other out-of-whack features in the art or story. He has succeeded admirably in pushing back the inquiry to 1943-44 and the very beginning of the page reduction prompted by wartime paper rationing. He has *added* significantly to the list of problems that plague those of us trying to tease out every last drop of intelligence from the published works of those early DCs.

There's no denying that Dennis has identified the most bothersome episodes in which a hero acts out of character, or in which the context selected by the writer doesn't jibe with the nature of the hero. Gardner Fox was too systematic and conscientious to have mishandled these characters, with which he was so familiar. The quirks Dennis identifies show other signs of hurried editorial manipulations, such as an unexpected artist handling the chapter in question. I think therefore that Dennis has identified genuine editorial changes that resulted in story blips. For that he is to be commended.

Dennis also spots a few apparent lettering changes. These, however, are more "iffy." In some of these instances, it appears he is stretching to find supporting evidence rather than putting his hypothesis to the most severe test. Nevertheless, he demonstrates admirably

Making A Terrific Entrance

The splash panel of the very first Mr. Terrific story, from Sensation Comics #1 (Jan. 1942), with script by Charles Reizenstein and art by Hal Sharp. Before long, he lost the gloves. [© DC Comics.]

that his theory of what *may* have occurred, which I'll refer to as "The Mr. Terrific Hypothesis," would explain the anomalies he has found. The question is: are there *other* possible explanations for those oddities? If we discover other possibilities, we are obliged to use Occam's Razor to select the simplest explanation—i.e., the one that requires the fewest *ad hoc* assumptions. I can think of a couple of possibilities. I'll leave it to you readers to decide whether I apply the Razor in the right place.

Those "Lost" JSA Stories Again

I wanted to test Dennis' theory by checking its consistency with information derived from the artists' assignments. The editors tended to assign the same artist to a particular character in consecutive stories. Because the stories were published out of order, the art assignments appear to flip-flop more than they did in real life. Most of these flip-flops are eliminated by first putting the issues in the order in which they were written, which is also most likely the order in which they were originally *drawn*. The order I've used below is based entirely on data supplied by Gardner Fox himself. After this re-arrangement, we can see more clearly any genuine blips in the art.

A classic example of this is the complete Flash episode drawn by Martin Naydel in *All-Star* #30 ("Dreams of Madness"), which was part of a JSA story completed several issues before Naydel began as a regular in the magazine. As we established in *ASC V1* and elsewhere, Naydel touched up some stories, substituting The Flash and Green Lantern for other characters in numerous places. The question is: exactly who were those original characters?

Letter Rip!

Since Dennis suggests that the lettering of the caption of page 3, panel 6, of the Dr. Fate chapter in All-Star Comics #21 had been "completely re-lettered" at some point, we're printing panels 5 & 6 from the original comic, not the Archives volume.

Why did we include panel 5? Because all captions in the chapter are lettered in italics (possibly by teenage artist Joe Kubert), so one needs to compare two captions, not a caption with a non-italicized dialogue balloon. The spacing of the lettering in panel 6's caption seems to us, at most, marginally different from the tighter spacing in panel 5—but not enough so as to be proof positive either that it was re-lettered... or that it wasn't. What do you think? [© DC Comics.]

Rather than reproduce the whole database I constructed to examine the issue, let me just pull out the relevant sections. Here again, for reference, is the actual order in which a number of the stories seem to have been written, using the issue number to designate the story, with one-word listings for the four "unpublished" stories:

All-Star #20, 21, 23, 22, 30, 25, 26, 24, 28, 29, 27,
[Japan, Magnifica, Will], 31, 32, Peril, 33, 34, 35, 36.

Gardner's first three unpublished tales are listed in brackets because he did not know exactly what their order was. His "Emperors of Japan" tale may well have been the earliest, but that provides no relevant information to my inquiry here.

Since we now know most of the artists on "The Will of William Wilson," I used data on "Will" to fill this gap in the published record, and it appears to confirm Gardner's placement of this story after issue #27, not earlier as Dennis suggests. The art assignments are just as one would expect them to be, given what we know of issues #27 and #31. The only outstanding question is whether Chester Kozlak or Joe Kubert handled the missing Hawkman chapter in "Will." My money is on Kubert, precisely because the art is still unaccounted for.

Gardner seemed confident that his fourth supposedly-unpublished story, "Peril of the Paper Death," was written just after #32 ("The Return of the Psycho-Pirate"). We have no further data on this story, so I'll drop it from my discussion of artist assignments.

Issue #35 is traditionally assigned to writer John Broome, with the scripter of #36 "undetermined"—though with a rewrite by Robert Kanigher (according to editor Julius Schwartz) on at least the Flash episode in the latter issue. This story, which features Superman and Batman, is clearly one of the most doctored stories in the entire run. Craig Delich discusses some of the problems with this issue in the following chapter. I myself still see the distinct possibility that this is an altered version of Gardner's "The Men of Magnifica," but there's no need to repeat my reasoning from *ASC VI* here. What I see

as Fox may simply be the plotting influence of editor Sheldon Mayer.

Master Of My Fate (Not To Mention Of Sandman And Spectre)

To test Dennis' hypothesis, let me examine the art assignments on those episodes he believes were originally written for Mr. Terrific. Dennis argues that they were altered along the way to feature different heroes, for reasons he explores.

The significant fact about issue #20 is that Sandman and Dr. Fate do not have individual chapters, although Gardner acknowledged writing them. An altered word balloon in the introduction accounts for two solo-hero chapters that were scrapped because of the page reduction DC's comics were undergoing at the time. It is of some significance that these two members are the first to be permanently dropped from the JSA roll two issues later. Dropping Fate was understandable, since he was to lose his spot in *More Fun Comics* about that same time. But the decision to drop Sandman is a puzzle. He outlived the split-off of the All-American line, continuing in *Adventure Comics* for another year and a half. The Spectre would lose his monthly spot in *More Fun* a full year before Sandman. Furthermore, Sandman would remain the cover feature of *Adventure*, while The Spectre had long since relinquished his cover spot to Green Arrow. This is my first clue that Shelly Mayer showed a preference for The Spectre over Sandman.

For some reason, Sandman is given one more outing in the JSA. In #21, it appears that an Atom episode drawn by Joe Gallagher was converted into a Sandman segment—an 11th-hour reprieve for Sandman. Dr. Fate is also given one last shot in #21. Newcomer Joe Kubert handles the gold-and-blue wizard. This switcheroo was the beginning of all kinds of havoc.

As Dennis points out, this Dr. Fate episode could very well have been written for a non-powered hero. Fate's hurling an ashtray at a protagonist is not only out of character for Fate, but out of character for Fox, who had created Fate as a sorcerer. Dennis thinks Gardner wrote this part originally for Mr. Terrific and offers some interesting arguments. Nevertheless, The Spectre and Wildcat are also possibilities we must consider.

Kubert, who drew this curious episode, was emulating Mort Meskin, whose pencils on Vigilante tales in *Action Comics* Joe frequently inked at that time. This is Kubert's first penciling job at DC, six months before Mayer made him the regular penciler on Hawkman, replacing the departing Shelly Moldoff. We may conclude that this first Kubert outing is probably a last-minute fill-in assignment.

This lends credence to the proposition that the original chapter (drawn much earlier) was scrapped. *Why* was it scrapped? It is reasonable to conclude that it featured a character who was to be dropped from the story. Since the introduction and conclusion still feature the same eight members that had been around since before the war, the prime candidate for the lost episode is The Spectre. The simplest explanation is that this chapter was originally written (and drawn?) for the first Dark Knight. It requires too many additional assumptions to put Mr. Terrific in the lineup that early. Maybe he'll fit in later on, but it stretches things to suggest he makes it into the JSA this soon.

So, you ask, how does that explain the hero hurling an ashtray? Further, Dennis points out, Dr. Fate offers an instant forensic analysis of the dying man. The latter is easy to explain: The Spectre was a homicide detective in his civilian identity. The first question requires a closer look at the Ghostly Guardian. The Spectre was characteristically written to display varied visual solutions to handle a situation.

Telekinetically transporting an ashtray across the room to deflect a gun's aim was not out of character for The Spectre. My conclusion: Gardner wrote this chapter originally for The Spectre, but it appears to have been completely redrawn as the last shot of Dr. Fate.

In #23 and #22 (which were published in reverse order), both Dr. Fate and Sandman are gone. The unusual chapter in both issues is the Spectre tale—drawn by Cliff Young in #23 and by Joe Gallagher in #22. While Gallagher is a regular on *All-Star*, Young's appearance is strange. He did an early Sandman chapter in *All-Star*; however, by the date of #23, he was doing most of his work on Green Arrow for the DC line proper. Why was Mayer calling on Young, who rarely drew *anything* at that time for the All-American line?

A Wildcat Strike?

Dennis suggests that these two Spectre tales were originally written for Mr. Terrific. That's possible, but it is equally likely, given the artist assignments, that they were intended for Wildcat. Gallagher is assigned chapters in #25 and 26 that are modified to become Flash episodes, and in #24, the next in the sequence, Gallagher draws the first published appearance of Wildcat in the JSA.

The Flash chapter in #30 (published *after* five other issues that postdated it) has a completely redrawn story by Martin Naydel. It seems likely that the original chapter had been Gallagher's regular assignment; otherwise, he lost work on that issue. Which character did he draw? Well, he regularly handled Wildcat in *Sensation Comics*, not Mr. Terrific. The latter was Stan Aschmeier's assignment (as "Stan Josephs"), but Aschmeier had his hands full in *All-Star* with Dr. Mid-Nite and Johnny Thunder, and sometimes even Starman. (I'll get to the latter in a moment.)

In terms that make sense of the use of his artists, Mayer would have been more likely to use Wildcat to fill the JSA slot than Mr. Terrific. The fact that Wildcat appeared in *two* published JSA stories tells me that we should be looking for more evidences of *Wildcat* in the run. Could those tales altered by Naydel to show The Flash against a Gallagher background have been Wildcat tales? I see nothing in these segments to rule against this.

While an earlier use of Wildcat is possible, I want to raise one other possibility. It's a little further out, but it *also* fits the facts and may explain another anomaly. All these episodes that Dennis wants to ascribe to Mr. Terrific, and which I suggest could be Wildcat tales, could also be *Sandman* chapters. This would have Sandman running through all the issues that also originally featured Starman (viz., #30, 25, and 26). Both these characters continued in *Adventure* well past #24 when the AA line split off. In fact, Sandman's picture strangely shows up on the JJSA certificate pictured in #24—at a time when Sandman has been out of the JSA for two published issues. Let's consider that Gardner continued to use both Starman and Sandman, who were outlasting both Dr. Fate and The Spectre in their own monthly series, and that only some last-minute change, which didn't get reflected in the JJSA ad, knocked Sandman out of the JSA a bit before his time.

The use of Spectre to replace Sandman (or anyone else) would entail a decision at Mayer's level to alter Gardner's scripts for issues #23 and 22. Perhaps the same editorial judgment applied to the scripts for #30, 25, and 26 before those chapters got altered into Flash tales. The thing we have to remember is that Gardner was working well ahead of the deadline for publication. Any last-minute change affecting the JSA roll call would not reach him for many issues. Lots of changes were made in this period that came after the scripts were turned in. I suspect even *double* switches were necessary in some cases. The appearance of The Spectre rather than Sandman in #23 and 22 cries out for an explanation, and suggests

Flash In The Pan(els)

Dennis Mallonee is on firm ground on p. 17 when he says, re such panels of *All-Star #26* as the splash at left (repro'd from the original comic), that there's often "an inordinately large amount of white space" after the words "The Flash" in that hero's chapter. Of course, it's long been recognized by art-spotters that this chapter is the work of Joe Gallagher, except for the Flash figures, which are all by Martin Naydel—which means Naydel almost certainly redrew some hero to turn him into Flash. So it's just a matter of what name (probably one with more than eight letters in it) The Flash's replaced. [© DC Comics.]

that it may have been Sandman who was replaced—first by The Spectre, and then by The Flash.

I argue that Fox was too sharp to have written a story in which The Spectre is overcome by gas, as he is in the published #23. (This is a test, not a boner on my part; see below.) This chapter could have been written for Dr. Fate, since his lungs were his Achilles heel. The Spectre had no need of air. Dennis may be right to look for a non-powered hero to fill this slot and the chapters handled by Gallagher in #22, 25, and 26 (and probably the chapter that is completely replaced in #30). I personally think it is more likely to be Wildcat or Sandman. Remember that the artist Mayer is initially assigning to these episodes is Gallagher, not Aschmeier. Had the story called for Mr. Terrific, he would, following precedent, have called on Aschmeier, who regularly handled Mr. Terrific in *Sensation*.

In *All-Star #24* Wildcat and Mr. Terrific both show up for the first time. The latter is Starman's replacement, and Aschmeier handles the assignment. To my way of thinking, #24 was Mr. Terrific's only shot at the JSA. The next issue Gardner wrote was #28. By then he had gotten the message. He wrote episodes typical of Green Lantern and Flash.

Wildcat, on the other hand, shows up again three issues later, in #27. Could he have been in the two intervening issues, #28 and 29? If so, he would have replaced The Atom, who had lost his berth in *All-American Comics*. It is not something I can confirm from either the story or art. The Atom and Wildcat are too similar, and Gallagher drew the Atom chapter in #28 and Kozlak in #29. Each of these artists handled both characters, at one time or another.

At present, the two compelling reasons prompting me to insert Wildcat for The Atom in additional stories are: (1) the two *All-Star* appearances of Wildcat; and (2) The Atom's unhappy circumstances in *All-American*. Still, the decision was soon made to find a new home base for the Mighty Mite over in *Flash Comics*, so maybe he was never written out of the JSA longer than one issue (#27). He's back for "The Will of William Wilson," which followed #27. While the Atom chapter in #31 (the next to be drawn) contains a strange mix of Irwin Hasen and Chester Kozlak art, I can't determine that this was a Wildcat story that was altered to revive The Atom, though I suppose it's possible.

Up An Atom

The Atom chapters are real puzzlers. He's drawn in a one-time art job by Harry Lampert in #34, and another by Paul Reinman in #35, and still another by Alex Toth in #37 (after skipping #36), which suggests that the Tiny Titan's presence was more than just a little precarious until he got his makeover. By then, other artists had tried their hand with him. The art assignments on The Atom do not show the pattern that exists in almost every other JSAer. He was on stand-by, probably close to being dropped at any moment in this entire sequence of issues.

Without further evidence, it seems prudent to let The Atom hang on to his precarious membership, and focus on those earlier anomalies in Spectre chapters. If Sandman was allowed to hang around long enough for Gardner to write him into several stories, then why is he replaced by The Spectre? If these were really Wildcat or Mr. Terrific tales, then we are still stuck with: why did Mayer go with The Spectre, who is on the way out well before Sandman? If there was some kind of contractual agreement that *All-Star* must feature a prominent character from the DC line, it would doubtless be Sandman in late 1944 and early 1945. If those six issues (#21, 23, 22, 30, 25, and 26) were written for Sandman (which makes sense because Starman was written into all those issues originally), then why is he drawn out? I have to wonder if Simon and Kirby had some say in the way Sandman was handled, but they weren't available, so it was just easier to go with the dying Spectre.

"A Stroke Of His Red Pencil"

All this is all the more curious because Gardner didn't bother to alter the powers of Dr. Fate or The Spectre as they were being portrayed in *More Fun Comics* at this time, although he was entirely familiar with these characters. Apparently, the editors at 480 Lexington didn't insist on consistent treatment. Were they even paying attention? It appears that Shelly Mayer was pretty much free to do what he wanted, even before the AA split-off occurred. We may never know what prompted his decisions. I doubt that any of this mattered to Gardner. I'm inclined to believe Mayer simply liked using The Spectre more than Sandman, and was not constrained, possibly because the word was out that both characters were biting the dust. None of this is a satisfactory resolution at this time, but Mr. Terrific seems to me to be the least likely of the possibilities. All the other characters, even Wildcat, were clearly more popular with the readers.

I just have the feeling that Gardner Fox wouldn't have made the same mistake twice and have portrayed The Spectre as vulnerable to gas. As JSA fans know, The Spectre was felled by gas in the introductory chapter of *All-Star* #13 and was shipped off by rocket to

Shelly Vs. Shelly

In the above photo, which was first published in Alter Ego, Vol. 3, #4, 1940-44 Hawkman artist Sheldon "Shelly" Moldoff squares off with AA editor Sheldon "Shelly" Mayer (seen on left) for a mock slugfest in the early 1940s. Jerry believes Mayer had a "soft spot" for The Spectre, and kept him in the JSA as long as possible. Photo courtesy of S. Moldoff.

The 1998 "Comics for Boys and Girls" Moldoff illo depicts seven JSAers—including two (Batman and Hawkman) whose exploits he drew for a combined total of 16 years from 1940 through the late '60s. With thanks to Shel Dorf. [Heroes TM & © DC Comics.]

Pluto. I have to believe it was Gardner's intention to send the vulnerable-lunged *Dr. Fate* to Pluto in that issue, but that Mayer decided it was more of a Spectre thing. (I do think Mayer had a soft spot for The Spectre, as shown in the earlier contest for who would win the next solo quarterly.) I can just see Mayer pausing for a moment, then dismissing the very idea that any reader would ever spend even one second worrying over how gas could overcome The Spectre. He did it with a stroke of his red pencil.

Since then, we JSAficionados have spent decades pondering this profundity.

Dr. Jerry G. Bails, in a photo taken by Dann Thomas in Detroit, 2002.

DR. JERRY G. BAILS, though originally a native of Kansas City, Missouri, spent his career as a professor of natural science at Wayne State University, Detroit, Michigan, from 1960 through 1997. He is now retired. In the early 1960s he launched the first super-hero comics fanzine (*Alter-Ego*), the first comics adzine (*The Comicollector*), and the first comics newszine (*On the Drawing Board*, later *The Comic Reader*); he also wrote and published *The Authoritative Index to All-Star Comics*, the first publication ever dedicated wholly to the Justice Society of America. Since the 1970s he has produced various editions of his landmark *Who's Who in 20th-Century American Comic Books*. To access the new online edition, go to: www.bailsprojects.com. No password required.

CHAPTER V

WHERE THERE'S A "WILL"— THERE'S "WILLIAM WILSON"!

Still More *Of That Long-Lost Issue Of* All-Star Comics

by Roy Thomas

[Adapted in part from material appearing in Alter Ego, *Vol. 3, #7, 14, 21, 44, & 50.]*

As every real fan of the Justice Society knows, in 1965 the concept's co-creator Gardner F. Fox informed Jerry G. Bails by mail that his personal records indicated he had actually scripted four JSA tales in the mid-'40s in addition to issues #3-34. That quartet, he said, "apparently were scrapped, or came out under different titles." But that's *all* Fox's records contained concerning them—just their tantalizing *titles*, and nothing more:

"The Men of Magnifica"
"The Emperors of Japan"
"The Will of William Wilson"
"Peril of the Paper Death"

The first of these is discussed in Chapter VI of this volume by Craig Delich; and all four were speculated upon at length in *Vol. 1* of this series, and to a lesser extent in Dennis Mallonee's article in Chapter III of this one. In the late 1960s it was learned that a considerable amount of original art-and-story from the third-named "lost" tale had actually *survived*, although most of it had been sliced into "tiers"—i.e., rows of panels—so that often only *parts* of pages were known to exist. That JSA tale, and a lot of other unpublished Golden Age material from canceled features, had been "written off" by DC for tax purposes on Sept. 30, 1949. Approximately two decades later, much of this art had been reluctantly sliced into horizontal thirds by future pro writer and editor Marv Wolfman, who was then working at DC as an editorial "intern," as the only way he could *keep* any of the artwork as opposed to consigning it to the company incinerator. (The situation is described more fully in our previous volume and in *The Alter Ego Collection, Vol. 1*.)

The first *All-Star Companion* printed 42 of the 44 tiers of art (that's 14 ⅔ pages worth!) from "The Will of William Wilson" that were then acknowledged to exist—including a problematical Dr. Mid-Nite page that, we now know, definitely *was* from that adventure. The other two rows of panels saw print in *A/E* V3#7 (Winter 2001). Shown between those two places were most of the story's Flash solo segment and the JSA conclusion, and several tiers each from the Green Lantern, Atom, and Dr. Mid-Nite chapters. Most of this art from Wolfman's late-'60s cache had come into the hands of the late Mark Hanerfeld, an inveterate comics fan and sometime editorial assistant at DC; he eventually sold it to the present writer in the early 1980s. A handful of other art tiers from that book-lengther turned out to be in the collections of Wolfman himself, his friend (and fellow pro writer/editor) Len Wein, Jerry Bails (via a trade with Hanerfeld), and collector Ethan Roberts. Each of these gents kindly provided copies of the art he owned.

Even after all the above material was printed in 2000, several key mysteries remained:

Why did *no* art seem to have survived from the JSA introduction or from the Hawkman and Johnny Thunder chapters?

Since the extant pages revealed that the tale dealt with half a dozen "impossible feats" that the JSAers accomplished on solo missions at the behest of attorney Harvey Davis, to fulfill the terms

of the will of a Mr. William Wilson (who in the end was revealed to be their old enemy, The Psycho-Pirate, and very much alive!), what the heck was that roundish object Hawkman was shown carrying in the group finale? And what was the pie-slice-shaped thing in Johnny's hands? The present writer speculated that Hawkman's prize might be either Nostradamus' (poorly-drawn) crystal ball or, more likely, "the egg of some mythical animal such as a roc—or of an extinct dinosaur or dodo." And that JT might be toting "a piece of the green cheese out of which the moon is sometimes said to be

There Will *Be A Cover For "Will"!*

Chances are that no cover was ever done for the never-published Justice Society of America story "The Will of William Wilson" back in the mid-1940s when it was written and drawn—so Michael T. Gilbert decided to draw one, in his own tongue-in-cheek style, as the cover of Alter Ego #14 (April 2002). It's numbered as "No. 31" because "Will" was, at one time, scheduled to be printed in that issue of All-Star Comics.
[JSA & characters TM & © DC Comics.]

Naydel Revamped

If "Will" had been published circa 1945-46 like other stories drawn by the same artists around the same time, it would undoubtedly have sported a cover by JSA/Flash artist Martin Naydel. Covers at this time sometimes duplicated, in whole or in part, the splash pages inside...so collector/artist Al Dellinges combined the will itself and the six "impossible" items with adapted JSA figures from the cover of the actual All-Star #32, and came up with this intriguing approximation of what a cover for "The Will of William Wilson" might have looked like. It was first printed in Alter Ego #21 (2003). [Art © DC Comics.]

made." Just a handful of half-wild guesses.

For that matter, while the surviving art revealed that GL's task had been to locate a goblet carved by 16th-century metalsmith Benvenuto Cellini, that Doc had apparently brought back the signature of a recluse named Abel Northrup (but *who he?*), and that Flash had retrieved Genghis Khan's sword—what precisely was that huge gem in The Atom's hands?

Moreover: since the Flash chapter was 6 pages long, and since in all *published All-Stars* of that era all solo segments in a given issue were of exactly the same length (except for the Hawkman chapters, which sometimes contained an extra page), that meant it was a dead certainty that the six solo chapters of "Will" had taken up at least 36 pages. That, plus the 6-page group finale, meant the entire adventure was at least 42 pages long—even before we add in the AWOL *group intro*, which would've surely been at least three pages long, bringing the total to an absolute minimum of 45! And this in a period (circa 1944-46) when each and every printed JSA tale was either 38 or 39 pages long—never more, never less! *What was going on?*

What's more, beginning in #18 *All-Star* solo segments were usually 5 pages long, not 6—and concluding group chapters usually

contained just two or three pages (not a half dozen!)—in that era after the interior page count of issues had been gradually dropped from 64 to 56 to 48. A 45-page story would have left virtually no room in an issue for paid or house ads. *Where in blazes did DC intend to print that story??*

Alas, it seemed we might never know the answers to *any* of the above questions.

But then, in late 2001, the present writer learned from *A/E* associate editor Jim Amash that Stephen Fishler, owner of Metropolitan Comics in New York City, had recently purchased five *intact, unsliced* pages of a Justice Society story from persons unknown. These pages were marked as being from "*All-Star Comics #31*," but Fishler quickly realized that, in fact, they had never been published. Supplied with photocopies, the present writer determined that they constituted a JSAficionado's "holy grail" of sorts: the introductory JSA chapter of "The Will of William Wilson," drawn by Martin Naydel, which had somehow (like one Dr. Mid-Nite page) escaped being chopped into thirds! Through Fishler's generosity, we printed those pages in *A/E #14*. More about them in a minute.

As it turned out, however, there was *even more* artwork out there from that MIA saga, which had clearly been drawn circa 1945, and certainly no later than 1946.

In *Alter Ego #21*, courtesy of Jack Bender, current artist of the *Alley Oop* comic strip, we printed another surprising find: the only known surviving *splash panel* from any of the half dozen solo chapters—that of the Atom segment, drawn by Chester Kozlak.

But wait, there's *more!*

In late 2004, pro artist and regular *A/E* contributor Michael T. Gilbert was one of a couple of folks who e-mailed Ye Editor that two Naydel-drawn panels from "Will" had surfaced on eBay. They were being sold by comics historian (and science-fiction and mystery novelist, as well as sometime comic book/strip writer) Ron Goulart. Ron and his friend John Wilcox provided a photocopy—and so did Dominic Bongo, the collector who had just purchased it. That tier appeared in *A/E #44*, a Justice Society/All-Star Squadron/Infinity, Inc. special.

And that's still not quite *all!*

The previously-mentioned Ethan Roberts soon sent us a photocopy of yet another Dr. Mid-Nite tier to go with the full, uncut page from that chapter he already owned. That row of panels was printed in *A/E #50*.

That made it a total of 20⅔ pages, or something like 45%, of "The Will of William Wilson" that was now known to exist, virtually all of it seeing the light of day for the first time in the 21st century, more than five decades after it was written and drawn!

Beginning on the next page, with added commentary, are the panels from that missing Justice Society tale which weren't printed in *All-Star Companion, Vol. 1*. All art on the following 9 pages is, of course, © DC Comics. First, the story's splash page:

Notations at the top indicate this story was once scheduled for *All-Star Comics #31*—that it had an illegible code number that started with the letters "OH" ("On Hand"?) that may have had something to do with its inventory status—that it was "KILLED" at some point (possibly well before the 9-30-49 date when it was officially "written off")—and, as per note to left of "A.S.#31," that it was 48 pages long! A 5-page intro, a 6-page conclusion, and 6 solo chapters of 6-page length, equal 47 pages—making it all but certain that the missing Hawkman segment was 7 pages long, to account for that 48th page.

Unusually, the JSAers were to appear on the splash only in circles (but why are the latter *blacked in?*), off to one side, perhaps with name labels. To the left of the splash here, we've placed the (mostly reversed) cameo heads that were printed in *All-Star* #24, the only published issue with a similar layout. (But why the blank shield at bottom right for the "Roll Call," if the members were to be named elsewhere on the same page?)

A notation says that the words "Last Will and Testament" on the parchment were to be rendered in the style of "Old English

Lettering," and there is a note to "Sol"—doubtless production manager Sol Harrison—that the body of the will was to be re-lettered "like type," in "upper & lower" case with "seriphs" (a misspelling of "serifs"), the style used in the text you're now reading. For some reason, the note-writer (probably 1940-48 *All-Star* editor Sheldon Mayer rather than his 1944-48 story editor Julius Schwartz) didn't like the idea of the will being handwritten.

The splash art, which shows the six objects sought by the JSAers, made it clear that Ethan Roberts' earlier page of Dr. Mid-Nite art was indeed from "Will," rather than from a Doc tale once slated for the monthly *All-American Comics*. A comparison of head and clothing confirms the seated figure is the reclusive Abel Northrup, merely drawn by Martin Naydel rather than Stanley Aschmeier (a.k.a. Stan Josephs), who did the Mid-Nite caper. (See *Vol. 1* of this series.)

What's more, along with Northrup, a gem, a chalice (not *quite* the

same thing as a goblet, but close enough), a sword, and a big egg-shaped thingie, a *sixth* object is shown overhead. Is it the moon, as this writer had speculated? With its bright aura, it looks more like the sun… but read on.

Incidentally, the name "The Will of William Wilson" is handwritten at the end of the caption—but why only in *pencil*, when the rest of the page had been lettered in ink? It seems unlikely that a change in story title was ever contemplated.

Page "B" clears up a couple of mysteries.

Wonder Woman, who usually appeared in the intro and often in the finale of JSA stories during this period, is not only listed on the splash, but is shown on this page and the next. (She was not seen in any of the tiers of the concluding chapter which had come to light.)

In panel 6 Dr. Mid-Nite offers Johnny a vitamin tablet—the only time in the entire series he gives a fellow member any medicine! A proofing note directs DC's production department to "Fix it so J. Thunder's balloon is read first," as the script had obviously intended.

Surprisingly, it turns out that, rather than their having been told of the odd will by the attorney seen in the finale, the JSAers already know about it on their own. In fact, Wilson apparently died "last year," potentially leaving to charity "several million dollars"—so at last we know roughly the size of the inheritance.

Two of the will's "impossible" conditions are related in panel 3:

"a man had to visit the moon" and "another [had] to find a dodo egg."

So it wasn't a piece of lunar *green cheese*, per se, that Johnny had to come up with, but merely a trip to the moon itself that was required. The green cheese was probably just Thunder's way of "proving" he'd been there. Still, it was quite close to what the present writer had guessed—and not as "impossible" a feat as Fox and Mayer had imagined, since in the real world that "giant leap for mankind" would occur less than 2½ decades later!

Also, Hawkman's catch shown in the JSA finale is definitely ID'd as a dodo egg, one of this writer's several surmises. Probably the egg of that extinct bird was the best bet from the start, since the expression "dead as the dodo" was much more common in the 1940s than it is today, when the human race is wiping out species at a much-escalated rate.

On page "C" The Atom makes first mention of "The Star of Scheherazade," giving a name to the jewel he is shown holding in the finale, but which wasn't named (or even depicted) in the surviving solo-chapter panels we printed in *Vol. 1*.

In panel 1, Hawkman's mask is shown at an unusual frontal angle which will be repeated on page "E." (In published work, Naydel drew it that way only in a single panel in *All-Star* #32.) It makes him look as if his beak is grinning!

At what is clearly their first meeting, the attorney (who is not named here) gives the six JSA males—they apparently left Wonder Woman back at HQ, as usual—the full list of six items that must be obtained to fulfill the will's terms. Opposite panel 4, a handwritten note indicates that the word "something" should be re-lettered "heavy"—i.e., bold.

Storywise, it must be said that this intro chapter is fairly thin, repetitious, and padded. First the heroes mention three of the will's provisions—then the lawyer repeats those and adds the other three. By the end of page "C," the dodo egg and trip to the moon have been mentioned no less than *three times!* Unlikely as it seems, one is almost tempted to suspect the intro was originally scripted to be just three pages long, and was later expanded, since everything done in its five pages could easily have been accomplished in three—and that's counting the splash!

On page "D" we learn that only three days remain to perform the "impossible" tasks and earn a fortune for charity. The JSAers sure took their time getting worked up about William Wilson's well-publicized will, didn't they?

We learn that the Star of Scheherazade belongs to "the emir of Saudi Arabia" (but wouldn't the proper term even in the mid-1940s have been "king"?). Scheherazade, of course, was the young bride in *A Thousand and One Arabian Nights* who told the caliph of Baghdad stories every evening to keep her head on her shoulders.

Nice touch, having the attorney say that the authenticity of Genghis Khan's sword, if retrieved, "will be judged by experts." Apparently, with that much money at stake, not even the word of The Flash could be taken as gospel! And Abel Northrup is revealed to

have been a recluse for a quarter of a century, and to be a "violent man"—and indeed, he'll later confront Dr. Mid-Nite with a shotgun. Still not much of a hint, though, as to whether there was some real-life model for Northrup.

A chalice by Cellini.

A seal by Cellini.

The attorney also adds details about the goblet, although the reference to "the Cardinal of Ferrara" isn't repeated in the panels we have of the GL chapter.

It will come as no surprise to anyone who knows of writer Gardner Fox's lifelong love of history that the "famous" goldsmith/sculptor Benvenuto Cellini actually did have dealings with one "Cardinal d'Este of Ferrara"—a city in northeastern Italy—who

got Cellini released from prison in 1539. Though the tempestuous sculptor had previously killed a rival metalsmith and had once wounded a notary, this time he was in the slammer merely for embezzlement. In 1540, doubtless in gratitude, he created for the Cardinal an *objet d'art*—though a seal, not a goblet. I found no reference to any of Cellini's work being "lost at sea," but hey, give Gardner a little artistic license!

Johnny Thunder, as per usual, has volunteered for a mission before thinking about it—in this case, going to the moon. Actually, he'd already been all the way to the planet Mercury in 1942's *All-Star* #13, from which his personified Thunderbolt had easily flown him back… and that's probably how Johnny reached Earth's satellite in his missing solo chapter. (Hmm…wonder if JT was thinking about this trip a bit later when, in issue #33, he wondered what "the man in the moon" might do with the captured monster Solomon Grundy. Had he perhaps met even *that* legendary lunar gent in "Will"? We wouldn't be surprised.)

Dead As A Dodo

This flightless bird was first sighted on an island in the Indian Ocean circa 1600—and was declared extinct in 1681 due to overhunting. Now that's progress!

Hawkman, with his bird connections, volunteers to find the dodo egg—and indeed, as drawn by Martin Naydel, the beak on his helmet looks as much like that of a dodo as it does a hawk's.

Two words on this page—the second "extinct" in panel 3, and "succeed" in panel 4—are marked to be "strengthen[ed]." The "C's" in the latter do seem a bit thin. And, in the final panel, the word "Still" was to be replaced by three hyphens, which actually would have made for a slightly more awkward phrasing.

On this page occurs the first reference to the "Alfred Fiddle" who will inherit Wilson's fortune if the JSAers fail in their missions. In the finale, as printed in *Vol. 1* of this series, "Fiddle" will appear in the flesh, only to be exposed as "William Wilson"—as well as the heroes' earlier foe, the original Psycho-Pirate!

This splash panel, drawn by Chester Kozlak, goes with the 2⅓ pages' worth of other Atom artwork that was printed in 2000's *All-Star Companion*. How 2/3 of the page from which this art was taken escaped the chopping block is not known—but then, the preceding five JSA pages and at least one Dr. Mid-Nite page had been left totally intact. Perhaps they were liberated from the DC offices long before Marv Wolfman was given his execution orders.

Below is clearly the bottom row of panels from page 4 of the Dr. Mid-Nite chapter. Since the medical manhunter hasn't yet even bearded Abel Northrup in his lair, there were clearly at least two more pages of this chapter to come. Of course, there's always the very *slight* possibility that this chapter, and not Hawkman's, was the one that was seven pages long….

These two rows of panels are from the Flash chapter, which is the most nearly complete of the various solo segments. Indeed, only its splash panel and a single tier remain to be located, if they still exist.

In the two panels below, from the bottom of page 2 of that episode, The Flash has arrived in the late 12th century on his "impossible" mission to retrieve "the sword of Ghenghis Khan" and spots a lone man being chased by two armed Mongols on horseback. For an instant he hesitates to let anything turn him aside from his quest—but then he realizes that, with his super-speed, it won't be a very *long* detour. So he leaps into action….

Below is the top tier of page 3 of the Flash segment. If Gardner Fox had indeed described the Fastest Man Alive as reaching around from behind to smite his foe, as we see below, he gave Martin Naydel a difficult thing to draw. But of course he may merely have directed the artist to have the hero hit the second Mongol, and the precise way it was done—even the symbolic stars over the rider's head—may have been Naydel's own idea.

A sword of Temujin, a.k.a. Genghis Khan

As shown in the panels printed in our first volume, Flash quickly learns that he has rescued a man named Temujin, son of Yesukai the Valiant—and the speedster is enough of a history buff to know that one day Temujin will become none other than Genghis Khan, the very man whose sword he has come into the past to seek!

The final tier of "The Will of William Wilson" which has come to light to date is the middle panels on this page, page "Y" of the story. It replaces the row of panels which we had put there on page 129 of *All-Star Companion, Vol. 1*, where the top and bottom rows of this page were originally printed. We've reprinted those tiers here, as well, for context.

The two panels directly above, of course, constitute a brief flashback related by The Psycho-Pirate to his captors, the six male JSAers, on the second-from-last page of the story. The handscrawled note in the right margin—probably written by editor Shelly Mayer—indicates that the words "my money…which I acquired honestly…as a bait!" are to be changed to: "the money I acquired honestly as a bait!" A small but real distinction, admitting that some of Psycho-Pirate's riches were gathered by extra-legal means.

The remainder of this page is as per *Vol. 1* of this series.

Until the flashback panels printed on the preceding page came to light, Ye Editor thought that perhaps the above tier belonged in the middle of page "Y"…but now it is clear that it actually constituted the first 3 panels of page "Z." We put these panels in the proper order on this page to show you how they would have appeared if the story had been printed.

Several words were crossed out in panel 1 because a DC editor (Mayer?) didn't care much for the sentence fragment: "I thought, if I can only keep *one* of you from achieving the impossible!" If any phrasing was to have replaced it, it has been lost—or perhaps that dialogue balloon would simply have been shortened.

So there you have it—the final page of "The Will of William Wilson," as it would have been printed—if it had been printed at all!

This caricature of "Will" artist Martin Naydel was sent some years back by Alex Toth to fellow artist Irwin Hasen. See the full image in Alter Ego #63. [© Estate of Alex Toth.]

SHANE FOLEY 2005 — AFTER JOHN BUSCEMA 1968 — inspired by JOE GALLAGHER 1945.

"The Mystery of the Forgotten Comic Cover"

Naturally, if we had other art from "The Will of William Wilson" on hand, we'd print it—but we don't. However, on reading in All-Star Companion, Vol. 1, that in 1967 Roy Thomas had artist John Buscema draw the cover of The X-Men #43 (April 1968) utilizing a layout similar to the one Joe Gallagher had employed on 1945's All-Star Comics #25 (maybe the first issue of that mag Ye Editor ever saw), Australian collector and artist Shane Foley found himself wondering what the JSA and their red-hooded foe would've looked like drawn by one of Marvel's greatest illustrators—so he created his own version thereof. The art for All-Star #25 was done in the same general period that "Will" was drawn, with Gallagher redrawing GL and Flash over other heroes done by Naydel. Great job, Shane! [JSA & All-Star Comics logo TM & © DC Comics.]

One key question from the first page of this article that remains unanswered is:

In a day after DC's comics had shrunk from 64 to a "mere" 48 interior pages, counting ads, as they had by the time of *All-Star* #20 (Spring 1944), precisely where would it have been possible to print a 48-page JSA story?

One possibility, perhaps unlikely, is that the publishers had decided to expand *All-Star* into a regularly-scheduled, 80-page comic (84 with covers) along the lines of DC's *World's Finest Comics* and All-

American's *Comic Cavalcade*. A 48-page "Justice Society" adventure would've made a good lead story for such a mag.

Or, "Will" may have been prepared for a one-shot comic even thicker than *WF* or *CC*. Here the template would've been AA's 128-page *Big All-American Comic Book* (1944), an anthology (now on view in the hardcover *DC Comics Rarities Archives, Vol. 1*) which sported solo tales of every regular or honorary JSAer in the AA stable except Dr. Mid-Nite.

A third possibility was posited by Dennis Mallonee on p. 19: that Gardner Fox's script for "Will" was prepared for a regular issue of *All-Star*, but a bit earlier than the clearly circa-1945/46 artwork would indicate—that it may have been written when the interior page count of DC/AA comics was briefly 56 pages, as it was in *All-Star* #18-19 in early 1944. According to this theory, two other JSAers in the original script were rewritten into Flash and Green Lantern. Together, Mallonee and the recorded 48-page length of the illustrated story make a good case for that hypothesis.

But—if someone went to all the trouble of editing the script thus, almost certainly before the tale was illustrated (since Ye Editor and other experts see no evidence of redrawing in the extant Flash and GL art)—why was it only *after* it was drawn that anybody noticed that, at 48 pages, the story was too long to squeeze into an issue of *All-Star?*

Was some editor asleep at the switch—or is there, indeed, a real possibility that "Will" was once slated for a thicker-than-usual DC/AA comic mag?

We'll probably never know.

It'll have to suffice that—in this day when all 55 Golden Age Justice Society tales have finally been reprinted by DC Comics in 11 beautiful hardcover volumes—a 56th authentic JSA adventure, or at least nearly half of it, has been discovered and preserved.

No, "The Will of William Wilson" may not exactly rank with the Biblical Apocrypha or a lost concerto by Mozart in terms of importance to the cultural history of mankind.

But, to those comic art historians who feel that *All-Star Comics* was—and *remains*—one of the most important series in the history of the field, the piecing together of the artistic shards of this story represents the culmination of nearly four decades of striving by the late Mark Hanerfeld and the present writer, with the aid of several generous researchers and collectors.

It is only to be wished that Mark, to whom *All-Star* enthusiasts owe so much, were around to enjoy seeing so much of that tale finally reprinted between two volumes of *The All-Star Companion*… and that perhaps one day DC Comics will print all the surviving material, in four fabulous colors.

Meanwhile, the good "Will" hunting goes on… as long as even one tier of art and story may be "out there" somewhere....

THE CASE THAT EVEN BATMAN COULDN'T SOLVE!

by Craig Delich

Unsolved Mysteries

Comics have provided a world of entertainment to many people down through the years, but to the serious student of Golden Age comics, there is frustration, as well, especially when it comes to identifying the artists of those bygone years.

I grew up on comics, mainly because of my brother David, who loved Batman and the Captain Marvel characters of Fawcett. One day, perhaps in 1955, I asked David who did the great Batman art that I was gawking over, and he said, "Look on the first page... his signature is there." I did so and saw the name "BOB KANE" in a box... and so I thought for the next 25 years. (That particular story happened to have been drawn by the late Dick Sprang.)

Most of us today have learned about the efforts of Dick Sprang, Jerry Robinson, Lew Sayre Schwartz, Jim Mooney, Winslow Mortimer, Charles Paris, Jack Burnley, Stan Kaye, Sheldon Moldoff, and others who *really* drew many of the early stories of our favorite Caped Crusader. But there is still one mystery, as yet unsolved, which involves Batman and one of my favorite magazines, *All-Star Comics*—and in particular, issue #36 of that title.

The 1947 classic "5 Drowned Men!" was the only issue that prominently guest-starred two of the Justice Society of America's longtime honorary members: Superman and Batman, who had last been seen (very briefly) in *All-Star* six years earlier, in the conclusion to issue #7's tale, "$1,000,000 for War Orphans!"

#36's mysteries begin with the *writer*, as yet totally unknown, although its de facto editor Julius Schwartz has stated that its Flash chapter was at least *re*-written by the late Robert Kanigher, who was then Julie's fellow story editor under line editor Sheldon Mayer. The rest of the script? That's an issue I won't deal with here, but interested parties should take a peek at the extensive coverage of the possible writer(s) in the *first* volume of *The All-Star Companion*.

No, the unsolved mystery *I* want to touch on concerns the *artwork* for this particular issue, which seems in places to be a jumble of styles and many different hands—something which is known to have happened in comics stories at DC, Timely, and elsewhere during the 1940s. My views on this situation will be complemented by those of Jerry Bails and Roy Thomas, who'll give their take on a mystery which, I believe, couldn't fully be solved even by Batman—or by Sherlock Holmes, for that matter.

We haven't reprinted many panels from *All-Star Comics* #36 on these pages, because it is assumed that anyone reading this piece owns copies of both *The All-Star Companion, Vol. 1*, and *All-Star Archives, Vol. 8*, which reprints issues #34-38—even though #36, unfortunately, was reprinted in the latter book from an old set of proofs done circa 1980, on which some of the linework was retouched rather poorly.

Raising Kane
When David Delich first pointed out Bob Kane's trademark signature with the big "O" to his younger brother Craig in 1955, 'twas on a Batman story actually drawn by Dick Sprang. The bogus "Kane" credit was also affixed to the work of many other artists, such as this splash from Batman #92 (June '55), which was in fact penciled by Sheldon Moldoff (and probably inked by Charles Paris). Bob Kane (see photo) had a million of 'em—ghost artists, that is. [Batman art © DC Comics.]

Chasin' Hasen

One oddity of "5 Drowned Men!" is the lack of a typical splash page. Instead, the story sports first a three-page "Prologue," which is very dark and ominous. Irwin Hasen signed the piece, but the inking is heavy and dark, unlike the rest of the art in the issue done by Hasen alone. This suggests that someone other than Hasen inked it—possibly one of Hasen's common inkers, such as John Belfi or Bob Oksner. Coupled with this is the Prologue's opening—we'll call it a "banner"—which features paste-up head views of Superman, Batman, Green Lantern, Flash, Hawkman, Dr. Mid-Nite, and Wonder Woman, illustrated by various artists. Strangely, there is no mention whatever here of The Atom or Johnny Thunder, who are regular JSA members at this time.

Following the Prologue comes the story's usual JSA chapter, featuring five of the regular JSAers. This introduction, apparently illustrated solely by Hasen, goes on to give weak excuses as to why Johnny and The Atom can't be present at this meeting. This is so irregular for an *All-Star* tale that one wonders what is happening. Well, the answer seems to be—more than meets the eye. Or perhaps it *does* meet the eye, coming as it does with the inconsistencies in the issue's artwork—something else highly irregular for a JSA tale.

To see these inconsistencies elsewhere, one must first take note of artistic styles in the introduction (which runs from page "A" through "D"). Notice how *well-drawn* Superman's chest "S" is, as well as his belt and buckle. Look how Batman's utility belt is portrayed: wide, with a hole showing through the buckle, and prominent pouches on that belt. And finally, on page "A," notice Wonder Woman's face...

then compare it to her face as drawn through the rest of the introduction. There *is* a big difference.

Before we tackle the rest of the story, let me mention up front that several chapters in "5 Drowned Men!" appear to be the work of just *one* artist: the Flash segment by Lee Elias, Dr. Mid-Nite by Frank Harry, and Hawkman by Joe Kubert (though the panel of Wonder Woman on page 6 is *not* by Kubert, but appears to be Hasen's work, as seen throughout the issue—logical, since by that time Hasen had become the cover artist on most issues of *Wonder Woman*).

Going To Bat

The first solo chapter of this story, although now starring Batman, was, as Jerry Bails first pointed out, probably originally written for The Atom. I would have to agree: in his five pages, Batman does nothing out of the ordinary, nothing typical of his modus operandi in his own series... no ropeline, no gas capsules from the utility belt, nothing to even suggest that the writer (or editor) cared enough to rewrite this chapter to accommo-date the unique talents of Batman.

When I wrote the *All-Star Comics Revue* back in 1976, I attributed the art in this chapter to Irwin Hasen. Although both the first volume of *All-Star Companion* and *All Star Archives, Vol. 8*, list the artist(s) as "unknown," I firmly believe, as does Jerry Bails, that Hasen *did*, in fact, pencil these five pages. Typical Hasen-style pointy chins abound—the Batman poses are very consistent with what Hasen did in the introduction—and check out the face of the guy on the right on page 1, panel 4. If we're correct on them, then the $64,000 question is: who did *inking touch-ups* throughout this chapter?

Batman Goes Atom

(Above:) A panel from the 3rd page of the Batman solo chapter in All-Star #36 (artists unknown, though Craig votes for Hasen as penciler)—juxtaposed with the same panel as altered by Al Dellinges, with The Atom in for Batman, since both Craig and Jerry Bails believe that segment was originally scripted for the Mighty Mite. [© DC Comics.]

From Lucky Starr to All-Star?

A panel from "The Man Who Could Not Die!" in World's Finest Comics #32 (Jan.-Feb. 1948), drawn at roughly the same time as All-Star #36. Officially penciled by Bob Kane (but actually by Lew Sayre Schwartz), this tale introducing the villain Lucky Starr has been ID'd by as having been inked by Ray Burnley, whom Craig suspects of also inking the Batman episode in "5 Drowned Men!" This story was reprinted in Batman: The World's Finest Comics Archives, Vol. 2. [© DC Comics.]

Possibilities abound, like those pointy chins, to be sure. I considered Bob Oksner at one time, since he often inked Hasen. But I've come to reject that notion. Possibly Winslow Mortimer, who had a hand in #36's cover, may have added a friendly brush here and there to keep that "Batman look." While not totally rejecting that possibility, several art inconsistencies lead me to believe that touch-ups were made in the DC editorial offices by a regular Batman inker of that time, who currently was very busy in all three titles in which Batman was then appearing: *Batman*, *Detective Comics*, and *World's Finest Comics*: Ray Burnley.

There are particular panels touched up that bear all the earmarks of Burnley inking Batman. For example, see panels 3 and 4 on page 2, where Bruce Wayne looks almost like a Dick Sprang rendering of that character. That is the way Ray Burnley (brother of one-time *Batman* comic strip artist Jack Burnley) made Wayne look in other titles of that time. Also, check out Batman's face on page 4, panel 6, and on page 5, panel 2: more ink re-touches that fit Ray Burnley's style. Add to that Batman's utility belt... not the typical Hasen wide belt with belt hole in buckle and prominent pouches... no... a thin belt with no buckle and virtually *lines* for pouches at that belt! This is also the way Ray Burnley inked his Batman stories.

It's A Bird... It's A Plane...It's *Thunderbolt!*

Let's now move on to the Superman chapter, again generally credited totally to Irwin Hasen as artist. Again, I agree that Hasen penciled this chapter and probably did some inking, as well. *But* I see another mysterious inker at work, one who has touched up the Superman figure here and there. Go back and review what I said about Hasen's Superman in the JSA introductory chapter: well-defined chest "S" and belt with buckle. Now, check out the *thin* belt, which rarely has any buckle, and the chest "S," which is *not* the same as in the introduction, and even varies from panel to panel! Was Hasen *that* inconsistent? I hardly think so.

On top of that, look carefully at the five pages of the Superman chapter, and you'll notice that, the longer the story goes on, the more *cartoony* the Man of Steel and the secondary characters become! Then look at page 5—which, incidentally, the eighth volume of the *All Star Archives* incorrectly lists separately on the credits pages, as

[continued on p. 40]

SIDEBAR 1: Jerry G. Bails

[*The following is excerpted and edited from e-mails sent by JGB in early 2001 to fellow fan/collector Bob Hughes, and to the present author. It expands the debate over the possible writer(s) of* All-Star Comics #36 *a bit beyond what was set down in the first* Companion *volume, as well as commenting further on that issue's controversial Batman chapter and cover. Comments between brackets are Ye Editor's.*]

In February 1961, when I was visiting the DC offices, editor Julie Schwartz introduced me briefly to Bob Kanigher, then told me that they had "co-edited" some titles when they were both working under editor Sheldon Mayer [from 1946-48]. Each was editing different stories for the same issue of the 1940s *Green Lantern*, and only rather later did they discover they were using similar villains. I gathered they were talking about *GL* #31 with both The Harlequin and The Fool [see below], but this may just be a supposition I made 40 years ago. Julie suggested they were sharing responsibilities on other books, probably Westerns, in the same way....

While I place high reliance on [comics historian] Martin O'Hearn's judgment in ID-ing comics writers by analyzing their scripts, I think he is simply mistaken about *All-Star* #36. I am still placing my money on Gardner Fox as the writer of the original script. It has just too many Fox features and is not a typical John Broome story. I think it is one of the four "mystery [*All-Star*] scripts" written by Fox, severely rewritten. If it *is* a Fox story, then by the process of elimination it can only be the one he called "Men of Magnifica."

As for that issue's cover featuring Superman and Batman, that's clearly a "sham jam." There is no reason to believe [as some do] that Johnny Thunder and The Atom were ever in that scene. Someone, probably a production artist, was instructed to pluck these figures from various places and put them together. Hell, whoever did it was not a very experienced artist, because Hawkman's wing tip and foot should be *behind* the staff that Wonder Woman is carrying. One clearly sees the work of numerous artists in this composite. To attribute it to one person is, frankly, pushing the envelope too far.

Chad [Grothkopf]'s tendency to swipe Creig Flessel figures [in *Sandman* stories] fooled me for years. The greatest mistake I made in ID-ing pencilers was to be fooled by concentrating too much on the main figures. Secondary figures can reveal when the art has been tampered with or that the main figures are swipes. That's why the Batman figures in *All-Star* #36 are

Clowns To The Left Of Me, Jokers To The Right...

Julie Schwartz (left) and Irwin Hasen ham it up with "Clark Kent" in a 1992 photo taken in the DC offices. Both Julie (as story editor) and Irwin (as artist) contributed to All-Star Comics #36. Photo from the Julius Schwartz Collection, with thanks to Robert Greenberger.

In February 1961, Julie told Jerry Bails that he and Robert Kanigher "co-edited" certain titles under Shelly Mayer, although RK later vehemently insisted they never co-edited "anything." Still, two editors having separately commissioned stories for the same issue would account for Green Lantern #31 (March-April 1948) sporting both a cover story starring the jester-like Harlequin and the somewhat similarly-themed Fool. Hasen drew (or at least penciled) the Harlequin story, Alex Toth the other. Thanks to Michelle Nolan for the art. [Art © DC Comics.]

such a bug. The Batman figures and the secondary figures are by different artists. I sure wish I knew the story of how Win Mortimer was roped in on that book.

I'm more convinced than ever that #36 is "Men of Magnifica." There's just no other possibility that explains all the anomalies.

SIDEBAR 2: Roy Thomas

I've no firm opinion on the matter of the writing of *All-Star Comics* #36, but I concur with Jerry that it makes little sense to continue to count Winslow Mortimer as the sole artist of its cover. He may well have penciled (or at least inked) the Batman figure, perhaps even some of the others (such as Superman and Flash)—but the Wonder Woman figure is clearly by H.G. Peter or someone virtually tracing him.

I suspect Irwin Hasen (who by this point was drawing covers for *Wonder Woman* and *Sensation Comics*) of doing the WW figure—and the Green Lantern and Dr. Mid-Nite figures are almost certainly either drawn by him or virtually traced by another artist. To me, Hasen has always seemed a more logical choice for penciler of the *All-Star* #36 cover than Mortimer.

The Hawkman figure, however, I strongly suspect of being done by Joe Kubert especially for that cover. Until a decade ago, I owned copies of all Joe's Golden Age Hawkman work, and I don't recognize the pose as being one of his that another artist could have swiped. Both the general look of that hero's figure on #36's cover, and even more so its inking, seem at variance with the style in which the other six heroes are done. I suspect editor Mayer had Kubert draw the Winged Wonder—either over an earlier pose done by the cover's main artist, or else on a separate sheet, with someone then pasting it onto the cover, correctly hiding part of Hawkman's left wing behind GL's cape but getting careless with his right wing and foot, as Jerry notes.

Kubert drawing Hawkman on a cover otherwise done by another artist, after all, seems to have happened on at least two other occasions. As reported in *All-Star Companion, Vol. 1*, he once told Craig Delich he felt he had redrawn the wings on Hawkman's helmet on the cover of *All-Star* #31—and, as I realized only recently, there is a Kubert Hawkman head on another cover which is otherwise wholly Hasen's: that of issue #49, "Invasion from Fairyland."

The Write Stuff—For All-Star Comics

Not counting editing changes, the Wonder Woman chapter rewritten by Dr. William Moulton Marston in All-Star #13, and probable re-scripting on Sandman chapters in several issues by Joe Simon and/or Jack Kirby, these three gents between them scribed all 55 Golden Age JSA sagas (l. to r.): Gardner Fox... John Broome... Robert Kanigher. But which one (or more) of them had a hand in "5 Drowned Men"? We'll probably never know. 1940 photo of Fox courtesy of Creig Flessel; 1946 Broome photo from the Julius Schwartz Collection; RK photo courtesy of Mike Catron.

[*continued from p. 38*]

if it were part of the upcoming JSA conclusion, which it definitely is *not!* Clearly, this page is marked "5," not by a letter of the alphabet as in the JSA introductions and conclusions; it is clearly part of the Superman chapter.

On this fifth page the entire Justice Society is shown, and there are many art inconsistencies that reveal this same "mystery inker" at work. One such involves Hawkman: notice his helmet with the lower face bare and its wings straight up, much the way Kubert did them in the Hawkman chapter.

But—and here's the clincher!—look at Hawkman's *shadow* in the final panel [see following page]—and you'll see there the outlines of the helmet closer to the way Hasen had drawn it in the introduction, with the tiny back-swept wings (although no sign of the helmet's lower beak, which was seen on pages "A" through "D"). Clearly, someone redrew Hawkman's helmet in the color art, but neglected to retouch the shadow on the wall!

In addition, look at the cartoony aspect to the JSAers on this final page of the Superman chapter, especially at Superman himself and Green Lantern. GL has a very cartoony face, not unlike that drawn by Bob Oksner in the third chapter of *All-Star Comics* #38 (also reprinted in *All Star Archives, Vol. 8*). Jerry Bails has said he doesn't think the inker was Oksner, because in later stories Hasen gave Green Lantern wavy hair and Oksner followed suit. *But*, in this story, Hasen draws GL's hair more straight-back; the inker would naturally follow that, for all intents and purposes. The super-cartoonish look to characters on this page leads me to the conclusion that a "cartoony" inker was at work, at least over Superman and Green Lantern, and I believe that inker to be Oksner.

A Final Plea

Next comes Green Lantern's solo chapter, and there is no problem with it (as far as identifying the artist, Irwin Hasen, is concerned)—until we get to page 4. Note that in its final panel we have returned to Hawkman's full-face helmet with the flat head and tiny, back-swept wings, which we did *not* see in the Superman chapter. In this segment Hasen pencils all the art... but his art was tampered with by the inker, not only in the Superman chapter but in the upcoming JSA finale, as well.

Finally we come to that concluding chapter, which was definitely penciled by Hasen. However, there are subtle changes by an inker to suggest that Hasen did *not* do *all* the inking here. Most, yes, but not all. Look at Dr. Mid-Nite... notice that the crescent moons on the helmet and vest now face in the same direction, unlike in the introduction. While Batman's utility belt is now once again wide, with belt hole in the buckle and prominent pouches... and the Man of Steel's chest "S" and belt/buckle are once again superbly drawn... we note that Hawkman's helmet is no longer the full Hasen version: it doesn't cover the whole face; the wings go up and then back (the way Hasen drew them in the intro)... well, you get the idea. Who can this inker be? There might be some Oksner, maybe Mortimer, and/or others.

Now you know why I titled this piece "The Case That Even Batman Couldn't Solve!"

Most likely, no one will ever pinpoint every artist involved in this story. But I believe that this should stop no one from ever trying to do so, and I will continue on in this pursuit. I welcome all the help I can get, and would appreciate hearing from all JSA fans out there on this can of worms that has been opened up—by people like me.

CRAIG DELICH has taught social studies in the public schools of Kansas City, Kansas, for more than a third of a century. As a member of Jerry Bails' advisory board for *The Who's Who of 20th Century American Comic Books*, he specializes in Golden Age DC art credits and is a consultant on DC's Archives series. In 1977 he wrote and edited the *All-Star Comics Revue*, which was published by his brother David.

Craig Delich   **David Delich**

Winsome WIN MORTIMER

Exhibit "A" (For "All-Star")

(Left:) The bedeviling cover of All-Star Comics #36. Whodunnit? Contrary to the received wisdom at the time of Vol. 1, Winslow Mortimer may have had less to do with it than we thought. Thanks to Bob Hughes. [© DC Comics.]

(Above:) This photo of artist Win Mortimer appeared in the 1975 Mighty Marvel Comic Convention program book. At that time, WM had recently drawn stories for such Marvel titles as Spidey Super Stories, Supernatural Thrillers, and Night Nurse. We regret neglecting to print it with his brief bio in Vol. 1.

The Doctor Is Still In

The figure at far left on the cover of All-Star Comics #36 is very much an Irwin Hasen figure, even if perhaps traced. Above is a quick convention sketch done by Hasen for collector Todd Franklin at a 2002 comicon. [© DC Comics.]

Shadow Of A Doubt

Sadly exemplary of the careless retouching done for the 1980 reprinting of "5 Drowned Men" in DC Special Blue Ribbon Digest #3 is this final panel from the Superman chapter (seen at bottom left). In it, the retouch artist didn't even try to match Irwin Hasen's linework on Hawkman's wings—or on much of anything else, come to that. Hawkman even lacks a mouth. Also, someone decided that the caption should be replaced by an extension of the art. Unfortunately, that art was basically re-reprinted in 2002's All Star Comics Archives, Vol. 8, and was not up to the current standards of DC reprint work.

However, another minor mystery from the same chapter dates from 1947. Notice (at center left) that the shadow of Hawkman's helmet on the wall doesn't match the headgear he's actually wearing—or even the twin-beaked helmet depicted by Hasen in the JSA intro. It comes closer to the (also-Hasen-drawn) helmet shown in the finale, which has only an upper beak and the small head-wings Irwin gave the Winged Wonder at that time. Something decidedly weird was going on with All-Star Comics #36! [© DC Comics.]

CHAPTER VII

THE MYSTERY OF THE DOPPLEGANGER DETECTIVES

Unmasking The Super-Sleuths Of All-Star Comics' Final Issue

by Mike W. Barr

For Vol. 1 of *The All-Star Companion*, editor Roy Thomas asked me to identify the fictional detectives on whom were based the equally fictitious sleuths who were kidnapped in *All-Star Comics #57*'s "Mystery of the Vanishing Detectives!" For this

volume, Roy asked me to supply a bit of information as to how I concluded which sleuth was modeled after which.

John Broome, who wrote that JSA story in 1950, seems a perfect fit to have crafted a script built around pastiches of famous fictional sleuths. He would later scribe *The New Adventures of Charlie Chan* for DC Comics (based on the TV series of the 1950s) and the *Nero Wolfe* newspaper comic strip, featuring the character created by Rex Stout. In 1998, Peg Broome recalled that she and hubby John had even met Stout in his home in Brewster, New York, to discuss the strip.

Identifying the sleuths after whom Broome's first three *All-Star #57* creations were modeled was, to coin a phrase, "elementary":

Inspector Drew Dawes, though hailing from Scotland Yard, seems, from his speech pattern and appearance, to be inspired primarily by Sir Arthur Conan Doyle's **Sherlock Holmes**, certainly the most famous fictional detective of all

SHERLOCK HOLMES

THE DEADLY INHERITANCE

Holmes and Watson attend a séance to help two brothers settle a dispute over their father's will. The séance produces a cryptic message

. . . and murder. But before Holmes can decipher the riddle or solve the slaying, he himself faces death from the claws of ferocious dogs!

THE TUNNEL SCHEME

Holmes is convinced that the accidents delaying completion of the cross-channel tunnel are really the work of saboteurs . . .

. . . and behind it all is the sinister hand of the master of the London underworld, his deadliest, most dangerous foe!

Elementary, My Dear Wonder Woman!

(Above:) "Inspector Drew Dawes" of Scotland Yard in All-Star Comics #57 (Feb.-March 1951)—a moment before revealing himself to be The Key in disguise. But also behind Dawes' mask, in another sense, stood the iconic Sherlock Holmes. Art in the JSA intro and conclusion of the issue is credited to Frank Giacoia. [© DC Comics.]

(Below:) Giacoia was also the artist of record of the Sherlock Holmes newspaper comic strip—yet this mid-1950s daily was sent to us by Joe & Frank Giella as an example of the former's ghosting done for Giacoia on the feature, as detailed in Alter Ego #52 (Sept. 2005). [© N.Y. Herald Tribune, Inc., or its successors in interest, & Estate of Sir Arthur Conan Doyle.]

(Left:) The inside front cover of Dell/Western's New Adventures of Sherlock Holmes #1169 (April-May 1961) previewed that issue's two stories, both penciled by Mike Sekowsky. Inker uncertain, but may be Frank Giacoia. "The Tunnel Scheme" showcased Holmes' nemesis Dr. Moriarty, "the Napoleon of Crime." All-Star #57's evil mastermind The Key seems to have been intended as a Moriarty type. Thanks to Mike W. Barr. [©1960, 2006 Estate of Sir Arthur Conan Doyle.]

HARRY WAN, DISDAINING TO HUNT FOR CLUES, RELIES ON HIS IMAGINATION...

THIS UNWORTHY POLICE OFFICER WISHES TO OFFER THEORY! PERHAPS THIEVES DISGUISED SELVES AS CITY HEALTH INSPECTORS THEN PRETENDED TO GIVE PILLS FOR NEW EPIDEMIC --INSTEAD GAVE KNOCKOUT DROPS!

ALL AROUND THE HUGE STAGE-SET POWERFUL LIGHTS SUDDENLY BURN WITH INTENSE BRIGHTNESS...

I'm Ready For My Closeup, Mr. Giacoia!

(Left:) Of the quartet of super-sleuths in All-Star #57, only Harry Wan of the Honolulu Police merited a full panel to himself in the introductory chapter. Art credited to Frank Giacoia. [© DC Comics.]

(Center & right:) Cover and interior illo from Charlie Chan Mystery Magazine, Vol. 1, #1 (Nov. 1973). Cover art signed by a Bill Edwards. [Art ©1973, 2006 Renown Books, Inc.]

time, and perhaps the world's most famous fictional character, period. Doyle (1859-1930) based Holmes' world-famous powers of deduction on those of one of his teachers at medical school, Dr. Joseph Bell. Although Holmes is a "consulting detective," the concept of an "alternate-Earth" equivalent of Holmes who worked for Scotland Yard is oddly intriguing, and it may be a shame that Dawes never appeared again.

Harry Wan of the Honolulu Police is perhaps the most transparent alias of the four, having obviously been based on **Charlie Chan**, also of the Honolulu Police. Earl Derr Biggers' (1884-1933) Asian sleuth, arguably the most famous fictional detective created in the 20th century, was conceived when Biggers realized that evil "Orientals" had been done to death, but that a sympathetic Asian character would be a new twist; Chan was based on real-life Chinese investigator Chang Apana. No new material about Chan has been presented in several years, but the literally dozens of movies about the character still pop up frequently on the classic movie channels, and the portly detective is still a household word, having appeared in a long-running comic strip by Alfred Andriola; several comic book incarnations; a Hanna-Barbera animated series (*The Amazing Chan and the Chan Clan*); and his own mystery magazine. The latter two surfaced in the 1970s. Hard to believe that all those appearances sprang from a mere six novels by Biggers, beginning with *The House without a Key* in 1925.

Though **Jacques Durand of the Paris Sûreté** at one point speaks of himself in the third person, in the manner of Agatha Christie's Hercule Poirot, Durand is most likely based on **Inspector Jules Maigret**, the creation of Belgian author Georges Simenon (1903-1989). Judged to be one of the most prolific authors of the 20th century, Simenon wrote over 450 novels and novelettes, 80 of them about Maigret. The Miagret stories lean more toward the psychological than do most mysteries, dealing more with the psyches and

motivations of their characters than the manipulation of physical clues and running around in dark houses at night. Maigret is a highly intuitive policeman, basing most of his sleuthing on his knowledge of human nature.

In 1973 Holmes, Chan, and Maigret, with nine other fictional hawkshaws, were depicted on postage stamps issued by the government of Nicaragua to celebrate the 50th anniversary of Interpol.

With the sources of those three detectives run to ground, that left only the Turkish detective **Mustapha Hakim** to be identified. I came up blank when it came to this character, so it fell to J. Randolph Cox, comics fan and fictional detective aficionado, to point out that this character may have been inspired by **Inspector Chafik J. Chafik** of the Baghdad CID. The creation of "Charles B. Child" (the pseudonym of Claude Vernon Frost, 1903-1993), based on his experiences with British counterintelligence in the Middle East, Chafik stories appeared for years, beginning in 1947, in the pages of the famous *Collier's* magazine, and were later reprinted in *Ellery Queen's Mystery Magazine*, then followed there by a series of new stories. The hero is showcased in *The Sleuth of Baghdad: The Inspector Chafik Stories*, a recent collection from publisher Crippen & Landru. (**www.crippenlandru.com**). Thanks also to Doug Greene, editor at Crippen & Landru, for his help in this matter.

This, it must be admitted, is the loosest "fit" of the four detectives. It is entirely possible that Broome and/or *All-Star* editor Julius Schwartz were familiar with the Chafik stories, which had first appeared only a few years before—or perhaps they simply wanted to add a fourth detective from another part of the world. Chafik is described as "a dapper little man...who wore on his sleek head the black *sidarah* of the modern Iraqi" (a *sidarah* is a characteristic Iraqi headgear, apparently named after an area in Iraq), while Hakim seems somewhat portly and wears a fez. Further emphasizing the distinction, Hakim hails from Turkey, not Iraq, though Turkey and Iraq share a common border.

Since everyone involved with the production of *All-Star* #57 is deceased, the truth may never be known. Yet I think that both John Broome and Julius Schwartz, who always liked to keep their readers guessing, would be pleased that "The Mystery of the Vanishing Detectives!," the final Golden Age appearance of the Justice Society of America, leaves as its legacy one final, unsolved mystery.

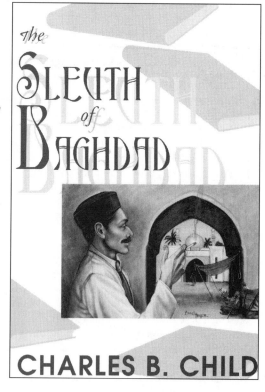

From Paris to Istanbul—Or Even Baghdad—On The Orient Express

(Clockwise from above left:)

Jacques Durand and fez-wearing Mustapha Hakim, both under the mesmeric command of The Key, are disarmed by Green Lantern in the climax of All-Star #57, repro'd here from the original comic. Art credited to Frank Giacoia. [© DC Comics.]

In renowned French director Jean Renoir's 1932 film adaptation of Simenon's La Nuit du Carrefour, Pierre Renoir (his older brother) played Inspector Maigret. Simenon reportedly considered this the definitive portrayal. To date, some 26 actors have portrayed Maigret! [© the respective copyright holders.]

"J'accuse!" Respected actor Jean Gabin, who portrayed Inspector Maigret in several French films in the 1960s, points an accusatory finger at a suspect. [© the respective copyright holders.]

The cover of The Sleuth of Baghdad, the recent book from publisher Crippen & Landru (www.crippenlandru.com) which collects 15 of the 34 tales of the Iraqi police inspector Chafik J. Chafik written by "Charles B. Child" between 1947 and 1969. Was this detective the source of Mustapha Hakim? [Art © Crippen & Landru.]

A portrait by artist John Pike of the detective from Collier's magazine for June 21, 1947, which featured "The Inspector Is Discreet," the first of the Chafik stories. With thanks to J. Randolph Cox. [© the respective copyright holders.]

MIKE W. BARR, longtime comics writer, has published short stories in anthologies and magazines, including *Noir*, *Hot Blood*, *Path of the Bold* (which won the 2005 Origin Award, given by the Academy of Adventure Gaming Arts and Design, for "Best Fiction Publication"), *Star Wars Insider*, and *Kolchak: The Night Stalker Chronicles*, an anthology based on the 1970s cult TV show. He has revived his Eisner- and Harvey-nominated comics series *The Maze Agency* for IDW, and also writes the Internet fantasy comic strip *Sorcerer of Fortune* and manga for TokyoPop.

CHAPTER VIII

"FASCINATING, YET SIMPLE EXPERIMENTS *YOU* CAN DO!"

When The JSAers Donned Lab Coats Over Their Costumes

by Roy Thomas

In the first volume of this series, we pointed out that each of the last ten issues of *All-Star Comics* (#48-57) contained a full- or partial-page feature entitled "The Justice Society of America Laboratory Notes." In these, one (or occasionally two) JSAers detailed basic experiments the reader could perform. These pages were not reprinted in volumes of the *All Star Comics Archives*.

The lab notes were almost certainly the brainstorm of *All-Star Comics* editor Julius Schwartz, who had been a science-fiction fan virtually his entire life, and who believed in at least small doses of didactic material in his comics, as did his JSA writer during this period, John Broome. Chances are that Schwartz wrote these pieces himself, although, when asked about them, he did not specifically recall doing them.

The tentative art IDs on the following pages were made by Craig Delich, who's been studying and researching DC art and art credits for decades. To show how difficult this area is, Jerry Bails, the other major early editor/publisher of books/indexes related to *All-Star*, had this slightly alternative view about giving art IDs in this area:

"[The 'Lab Notes'] appear to be handled in the production dept., and swipes of characters were used. The general art isn't up to either Peddy or Hasen standards. I do see the scratchy inking characteristic of Oksner…. It seems unfair to tag Hasen and Peddy with these very crude steals."

To which Craig D. responds: "I found the exact panels where the art was taken from," so he feels the art IDs are "…okay. I did mention that production did a bit of altering, such as an arm, mouth, etc. But most are exact repros from the art in the stories. I know, as I looked each one up." Matter of fact, Craig kindly send us his list of which published panels he feels were used for each "JSA Lab Notes" art spot, so we've added that information between brackets after each notation below... and even printed the proposed source-panels.

Since even two experts of the caliber of Craig Delich and Jerry Bails cannot quite agree on all points with regard to the art, I've opted to print Craig's IDs below—however, with the advance caveat that, when names like Peddy, Hasen, Giacoia, Sachs, and Oksner, are listed, the reader may wish to mentally add the phrase: "or someone imitating his/their art style." Thanks to both Craig and Jerry for their input. *Vol. 1* featured the first and last of the "Lab Notes," but this is the first assembling of all ten in one place. All art in this chapter is, of course, © DC Comics:

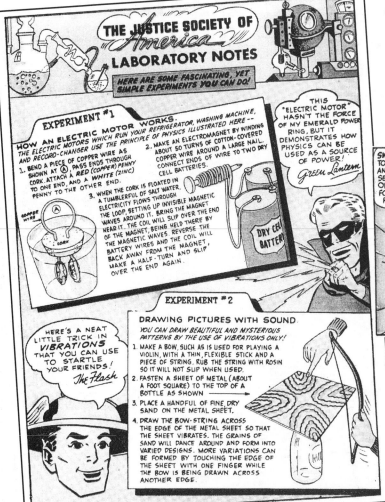

Panels from All-Star #46. All art in this chapter is reprinted from the original comics.

(Left:) The Flash and Green Lantern introduced the feature in All-Star #48. The accompanying GL art was by Arthur Peddy (pencils) and Bernard Sachs (inks)… Flash art apparently by Irwin Hasen (penciler) and Bob Oksner (inks). [Craig feels the Green Lantern art came from All-Star #46, p. 21, panel 3—and the Flash drawing came from that same issue, p. 3, panel 1, with a retouch on the mouth and eyes.]

From All-Star #47.

(Left:) In the second of the series, in All-Star #49 (Oct.-Nov. 1949), JSA chairman Hawkman did the honors, as drawn evidently by Hasen (p) and Oksner (i). [Craig says the Hawkman art originated in All-Star #47, p. 12, panel. 2.]

Irwin Hasen (left) with another 1940s All-Star artist, Carmine Infantino, at a recent New York comicon. Thanks to Keif Simon & Jim Murtagh.

(Right:) From All-Star #50 (Dec. 1949-Jan. 1950). Wonder Woman's experiment shared the page with an ad for Nestlé's Crunch. Art apparently by Hasen (p) & Oksner (i). [Craig says this is the one piece of art he couldn't find a second time; he says it might be a retouch of All-Star #44's cover figure, or come from anywhere in #44-46.]

From All-Star #50.

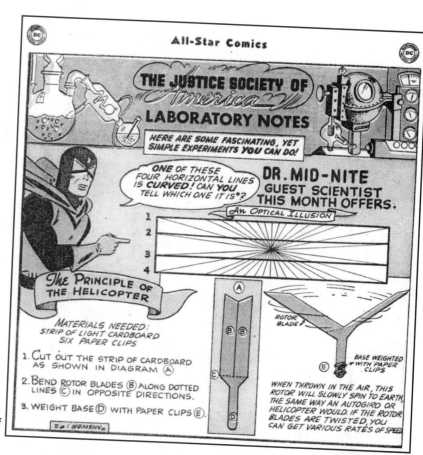

(Right:) Dr. Mid-Nite did the honors in All-Star #51 (Feb.-March 1950), courtesy apparently of Peddy (p) & Sachs (i). [Craig tells us the illo of Doc came from All-Star #50, p. 17, panel 5, with a retouching of the mouth and a finger.]

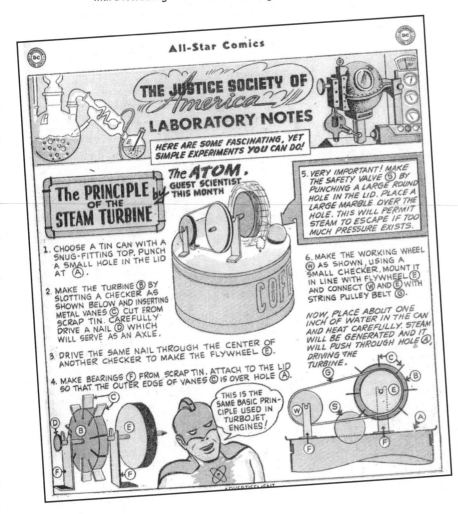

From All-Star #46.

(Left:) The Atom may well have been drawn by Hasen (p) & Oksner (i) on the lab notes for All-Star #52 (April-May 1950). [Craig says he found this art in All-Star #46, p. 8, panel 2, but that heavy retouching was done to the mouth and front of the Mighty Mite's cowl, with the chest symbol added. Gotta admit, this ID looks a bit "iffy" to Ye Editor, but....]

From All-Star #47.

(Left:) The Flash, in All-Star #53 (June-July 1950), had the artistic earmarks of his regular artists— Arthur Peddy and Bernard Sachs. [The Flash art, Craig says, came from All-Star #47, p. 18, panel 1.]

From All-Star #47.

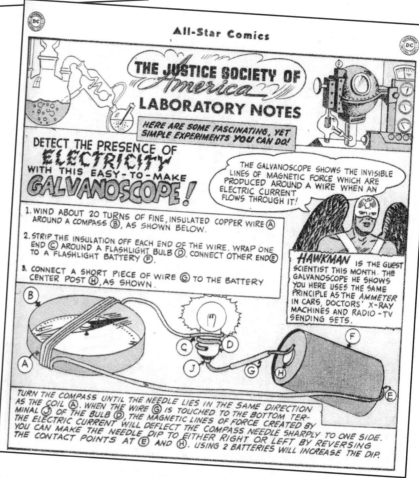

(Right:) Hawkman was back in All-Star #54 (Aug.-Sept. 1950), though the colorist forgot to add the red in the hawk-sigil on his cowl. Art may be by Hasen (p) and Sachs (i). [Craig located this art in All-Star #47, p. 27, panel 1. But, based on the art lines in the neck and collarbone area, it seems less than a perfect fit to Ye Ed.]

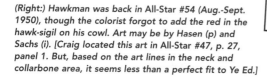

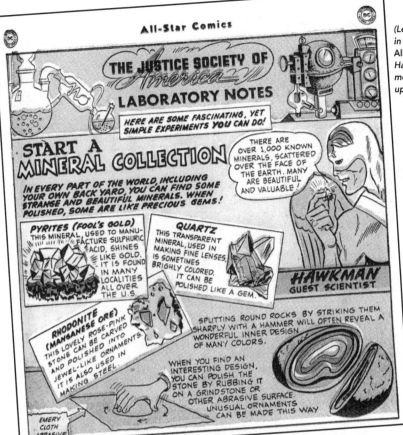

(Left:) Surprisingly, Hawkman returned for a second issue in a row—his third appearance in the lab-notes pages—in All-Star #55 (Oct.-Nov. 1950). Perhaps apparent artists Hasen (p) and Sachs (i) just liked drawing him? [Once more, Craig Delich feels there was a slight "cowl touch-up," this time to art from All-Star #47, p. 12, panel 1.]

From All-Star #47.

From All-Star #54.

(Right:) It was, perhaps, only fitting that Dr. Mid-Nite, who would have been blind during daylight hours without his special glasses, conducted an experiment in the synthesis of light in All-Star #56 (Dec. 1950-Jan. 1951). [Here, with what Craig Delich finds is an evident touch-up to the mouth, the art looks to him like the work of new JSA artist Frank Giacoia, in a reversed figure from All-Star #54, p. 6, panel 2. What do you think?]

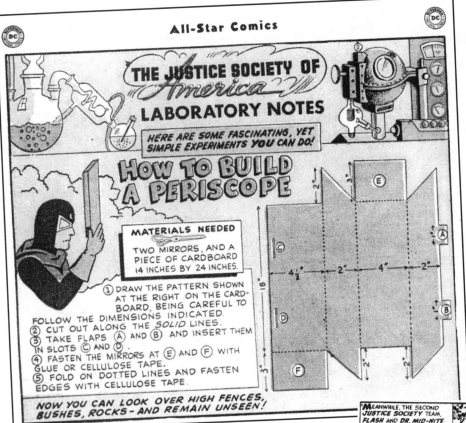

THE JUSTICE SOCIETY OF *America*
LABORATORY NOTES

HERE ARE SOME FASCINATING, YET SIMPLE EXPERIMENTS *YOU CAN DO!*

HOW TO BUILD A PERISCOPE

MATERIALS NEEDED

TWO MIRRORS, AND A PIECE OF CARDBOARD 14 INCHES BY 24 INCHES.

① DRAW THE PATTERN SHOWN AT THE RIGHT ON THE CARD-BOARD, BEING CAREFUL TO FOLLOW THE DIMENSIONS INDICATED.
② CUT OUT ALONG THE *SOLID* LINES.
③ TAKE FLAPS Ⓐ AND Ⓑ AND INSERT THEM IN SLOTS Ⓒ AND Ⓓ.
④ FASTEN THE MIRRORS AT Ⓔ AND Ⓕ WITH GLUE OR CELLULOSE TAPE.
⑤ FOLD ON DOTTED LINES AND FASTEN EDGES WITH CELLULOSE TAPE.

NOW YOU CAN LOOK OVER HIGH FENCES, BUSHES, ROCKS — AND REMAIN UNSEEN!

(Above:) Dr. Mid-Nite made his third appearance in All-Star #57 (Feb.-March 1951), to close out the series—as well as the JSA itself. Art again has the look of Peddy and Sachs—which was only fitting, since they'd been the mag's main art team for its last two-plus years. [Craig feels this art spot was reversed from All-Star #49, p. 17, panel 1—with an arm added, and some retouching.]

From All-Star #49.

Arthur Peddy in the US Army, 1944. With thanks to his son-in-law, Michael Posner.

The lab page in *All-Star* #57 closed out both that feature—and the Justice Society itself. For reasons unknown, The Black Canary was the only contemporary JSAer who never conducted an experiment. Maybe Julie figured that boys wouldn't want non-Amazonian females telling them about science?

With the 58th issue, two months later, the title of the magazine was changed to *All-Star Western*. Apparently The Trigger Twins had little interest in scientific experimentation.

CHAPTER IX
THE *OTHER* HEROES OF ALL-STAR COMICS
These Madison Avenue Madcaps Might Have Given The Justice Society A Run For Its Money!

by Roy Thomas

another ALTER EGO SPECIAL

featuring: CAPTAIN TOOTSIE, VOLTO *from* MARS, THOM McAN, BAZOOKA, "U.S." ROYAL, OLD NICK *and* "R.C."

Superman! Batman! Wonder Woman! Green Lantern! Flash! Hawkman! Golden Age DC's six most popular costumed characters, plus Dr. Mid-Nite, were featured on the cover of *All-Star Comics* #36 in 1947 (see p. 41). A true parade of super-stars—even though, as was noted in *Vol. 1* of this series, it was a parade that didn't really lead anywhere, since the *World's Finest* duo never again appeared in the JSA's mag.

But there were several additional colorful heroes who also appeared in *All-Star* during the 1940s, on comics-format ad pages

sandwiched in between the chapters of the JSA stories. These commercially conceived cut-ups might have been assembled into quite a super-group themselves, had anybody cared to do so. So, just for a lark, we invited Australian collector/artist Shane Foley to utilize the layout of that classic *All-Star* cover to showcase the most flamboyant of them. Turn the page to see them in all their Madison Avenue-spawned magnificence…! [Art © Shane Foley; characters TM & © the respective copyright holders.]

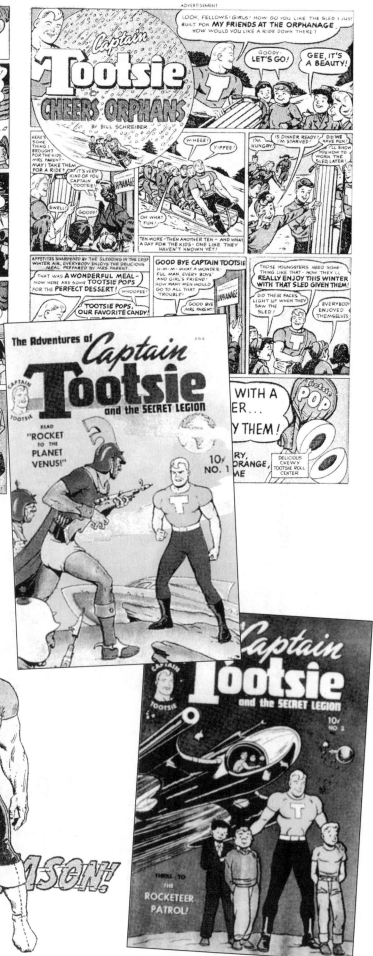

Captain Tootsie

If this guy looks a lot like a blond Captain Marvel, it's because most of his Tootsie Roll-sponsored ad pages were drawn by (and duly credited to) C.C. Beck, original artist/co-creator of the World's Mightiest Mortal. Some of the later strips were done by Beck in tandem with fellow Fawcetteer Pete Costanza; and the bylined early scripter was Rod Reed, who wrote and briefly edited for Fawcett. In the mid-'40s strips, Tootsie, whose crimson shirt and yellow chest insignia and top-flap boots underscored his resemblance to the Big Red Cheese, even had a nemesis, Dr. Narsty, who looked a lot like Doc Sivana!

The tornado-taming sequence above, which of course (like all the ads in this chapter) also appeared in other DC titles, is reprinted here from All-Star #41 (June-July 1948). The strip at top right is from #57 (Feb.-March 1951), with art by Bill Schreiber. The latter's only known comic book credit is—are you ready for this?— Captain Tootsie and the Secret Legion, a Toby Press title that ran for two issues in 1950, as per covers at far right. [© the respective copyright holders.]

Roy Thomas and penciler Herb Trimpe utilized Captain Tootsie (with a touch of Captain Marvel) as the visual inspiration for Doc Samson, the green-haired super-shrink they created for The Incredible Hulk #141 (July 1971); see figure at right. Inks by John Severin.
[© Marvel Characters, Inc.]

Volto From Mars

Forget J'onn J'onzz, Manhunter from Mars! More than a decade before that green-skinned gumshoe debuted in Detective Comics #225, General Foods introduced its own red-and-blue-clad Martian with magnetic powers in full-page ads for Grape-Nuts Flakes cereal. These strips, the first two of the series, appeared in All-American Comics #63 & #64 (Jan. & March 1945); Volto starred in several more over the next couple of years.

Actually, we fudged a little on this entry, since for some reason no Volto ad was ever actually printed in All-Star, perhaps because of its then-quarterly status. But, of course, JSAers Green Lantern and Dr. Mid-Nite shared space with him in All-American. It's been reported that Frank Robbins (or was it Frank Thorne?) and other well-known artists may have drawn the strip at one time or another. [© General Foods Corp. or its successors in interest.]

Volto breaks free of a trap, ready to go into action, in this panel from the "Volto from Mars" page in All-American #68 (Sept.-Oct. 1945).

TUNE IN **HOP HARRIGAN** BLUE NETWORK MON. THRU FRI.

Thom McAn With His Magic "Bazooka-Shoes"

The word "bazooka" was a buzzword during World War II, because of publicity about the newly-developed tube-shaped rocket launcher of that name. The latter was christened a "bazooka" after a humorous musical instrument invented and played by swing musician Bob Burns in the 1930s and '40s (see opposite page).

But there was little that was humorous about the one-page adventure at left from All-Star #26 (Fall 1945), as Thom McAn—a young hero who shares the name of the well-known shoe manufacturing company—retrieves an American-invented earthquake machine stolen by the "Japs" (shades of All-Star #12!), then torches their fabled paper houses just for good measure. The second strip, from All-Star #27, is less bloodthirsty. Doubtless many a moppet was as disappointed as Ye Editor by a trip to a Thom McAn shoe store, when he learned his parents couldn't really buy him a pair of "Bazooka-Shoes" that would propel him through the air!

The identity of the strip's artist(s), alas, is unknown. But one nice touch was Thom's impish little pal "H." Why were his squarish balloons always empty? "Because," a caption invariably explained, "he's like the 'H' in 'Thom McAn'—always silent! (The 'H' is silent, but the value speaks out loud!)" [© the respective copyright holders.]

In All-American Comics #75 (July 1946), Thom used his bazooka-shoes' super-magnetic powers to divert a runaway steamroller from crashing into a crowd of people. [© the respective copyright holders.]

The Guy Who Started It All

Musician Bob Burns with his "bazooka," in an NBC-radio photo taken in the late 1930s.

Bazooka – The Atom Bubble Boy

See? We told you the word "bazooka" was big in the 1940s! Long before Bazooka Joe became the bland face of the Topps Chewing Gum Co.'s major product (besides sports cards, that is), Bazooka the Atom Bubble Boy was forever blowing bubbles that transported him through the air—and lowered him to Earth when he said "Bazooka" backward.

Both these strips seem to have been at least penciled by Irwin Hasen, and appeared in All-Star #41-42 in 1948—at a time when Irwin was also penciling chapters of Justice Society stories! Others drew the ad pages later. [© the respective copyright holders.]

Maybe He Should've Eaten More Wheaties

(Above:) The Flash and fiancée Joan Williams are prisoners of the future-criminal Dmane in Irwin Hasen's one solo Flash story, from the 1946 Wheaties giveaway comic... done around the time he began drawing JSA material with All-Star Comics #31 & 33. [© DC Comics.]

Old Nick

Old Nick was the personification of a candy bar from the same company that produced the better-known Bit-O-Honey. He seems to have been visually inspired by such movie stars as Monty Woolley, or maybe Edmund Gwen in Miracle on 34th Street. He only starred in a few ads, however, such as this one from All-Star #41. An ad-strip in #43 featured instead a heroic girl (named Bit-O-Honey!) who saved a little boy and his puppy from being run over by a fire engine, and the senior citizen merely made a cameo appearance at the bottom of the page to plug "his" candy bar. Artist unknown. [© the respective copyright holders.]

"R.C." And Quickie

You saw other specimens of this long-running Creig Flessel-drawn series on p. 12, but since he's in Shane Foley's group drawing, here's another nice sample—this one from All-Star #36 (Aug.-Sept. 1947), with Hopalong Cassidy himself joining the pitch. [© the respective copyright holders.]

"U.S." Royal With His Jet-Propelled Bike

"U.S." Royal was named after the bicycle tires made by the United States Rubber Company, as per the ad to the right from All-Star #53 (June-July 1950). Apparently he was a "deputy" of some sort, and his bike was said to be "jet-propelled"—but except for its expelling little puffs of smoke while captions related that he "jets off" to do something-or-other, he was left pretty much under-developed. This page was probably drawn by Golden/Silver Age Superman artist Al Plastino. [© the respective copyright holders.]

Howard Duff as radio's
Sam Spade.

The Adventures Of Sam Spade

(Left:) The great Lou Fine drew numerous comics-style ad pages featuring Sam Spade, hero of Dashiell Hammett's 1929 novel The Maltese Falcon. After the success of John Huston's 1941 film version starring Humphrey Bogart and a perfect cast and screenplay, the San Francisco private eye became the hero of a popular radio series starring Howard Duff—until Hammett ran afoul of the House Un-American Activities Committee in 1951, and the ensuing bad publicity led to its demise. Ironically, this page shows Spade capturing a "Red" saboteur! According to Creig Flessel, some of Fine's "Sam Spade" pages were inked by others...but they were often the best-looking art in the comic book in which they ran. This mini-adventure appeared in All-Star #50 (Dec. 1949-Jan. 1950).

(Below:) Although Sam Spade's name inspired radio/TV detectives like Richard Diamond, Private Eye and comic book shamuses like Sam Hill and even Harry Trump in the Thomas-Giordano Jonni Thunder, a.k.a. Thunderbolt in the 1980s, oddly, there was never a full-scale attempt to do a Sam Spade comic. But the novel which had introduced him was adapted into a one-shot comic book in 1946, with art by Rodlow Willard. [© the respective copyright holders.]

Lou Fine in the early 1940s. Photo probably taken by fellow artist Tony DiPreta.

Various comics stars from other media appeared on occasion in *All-Star*, as well, including but not limited to:

Straight Arrow *had his own radio show from 1949-51, and starred in a Magazine Enterprises comic book from 1950-56 (and even had his own short-lived newspaper strip, written by JSA co-creator Gardner Fox). This ad, sponsored by Shredded Wheat cereal, appeared in All-Star #52 (April-May 1950). Artist unknown; Fred L. Meagher, John Belfi, and others drew him in the comic. [© the respective copyright holders.]*

Red Ryder, *writer/artist Fred Harman's popular comic strip cowboy. Strangely, as per this ad from All-Star #44, circa 1948-49 the cowpoke's long-term licensee Daisy Air Rifles reprinted adventures of Red Ryder (who then appeared in Dell comics), Fawcett's Captain Marvel and Ibis the Invincible, and DC's Robotman and Boy Commandos—all in the same black-&-white Daisy Handbook #2! All this, while DC was suing Fawcett over trademark infringement re: Superman and Captain Marvel! [Red Ryder TM & © the respective copyright holders; Capt. Marvel, Ibis, Robotman, & Boy Commandos TM & © DC Comics.]*

Oh yeah—and Chester Gould's top cop, **Dick Tracy,** *popped up in a couple of ads, as well—for "two-way wrist radios" and toy tommyguns! This panel's from All-Star #38. [© Tribune Media Services, Inc.]*

Tom Mix, *movie cowboy who didn't let a little thing like dying in a 1940 auto accident stop him from appearing in this comics-style ad for Ralston cereals' Tom Mix Commandos Comics in All-Star #14 (Oct. 1942-Jan. 1943)—fighting the Axis this time instead of Western outlaws. Matter of fact, Mix would continue on radio for years (played by actor Curley Bradley) and in the Fawcett comic Tom Mix Western from 1948-53. This art is by Fred L. Meagher & Bill Allison, with thanks to Jim Harmon for the art IDs. Mix's image also appeared in All-Star #50, advertising the "Tom Mix super-magnetic Compass Gun and signal whistle – they glow in the dark"! Ralston Whole Wheat Cereal eventually evolved into today's Wheat Chex. [© the respective copyright holders.]*

CHAPTER X

THE MYSTERIOUS CASE OF THE JJSA MEMBERSHIP KITS

Some Answers—And Many More Questions—About The Junior Justice Society of America!

by David Studham

INTRODUCTION: *The first volume of this series contained a 6-page chapter on the Junior Justice Society of America, the JSA "fan club" which readers could join through the mail. That piece was adapted from an article and photos in Craig Delich's* All-Star Comics Revue, *utilizing some materials provided by Jerry G. Bails. The JJSA itself was first announced in* All-Star Comics #11, *and membership solicited in #13-22, with a revised version (during the period when All-American had severed all apparent ties with DC) in #24-26, then a revamped kit in most issues between #37-52. Few of the images relating to the JJSA that appeared in the* Companion, Vol. 1, *are repeated here... but, as David Studham informed us from Australia, there is a bit more to the story than was told there. All art in this chapter except the Captain America/Sentinels of Liberty badge © DC Comics.*

During research for a website about the Junior Justice Society of America (the JJSA, for short), I encountered two membership kits which show new (or at least variations of) items not listed in *The All-Star Companion, Vol. 1* (2000), or in its 1977 predecessor *The All-Star Comics Revue*. These include membership certificates, welcoming letters, notes on changes to the membership badges, and various wartime propaganda pamphlets.

The JJSA has interested me as long as I have read comics about the Justice Society. Indeed, the first Golden Age JSA story I read concluded with the JJSA assisting the "Big Boys"—and Wonder Woman—in apprehending the leader of the *Injustice* Society, The Wizard (*All-Star Comics #37*, reprinted in Australia in *Giant Superman Album #30*, Dec. 1975). Dedicated JSA fan that I am, I even established a JJSA website [**www.vicnet.net.au/~dstudham**] and, having learned the JJSA secret codes, I constructed a dozen homemade decoder wheels for online friends.

I live in Australia and I have never seen an actual JJSA membership kit offered for sale here. During much of the period of the club's operation in the 1940s, American comics and magazines were banned from sale here in order to assist Australia's wartime balance of trade accounts; therefore, I doubt that many would have made it into the country at the time or been imported by collectors since then. My knowledge of the JJSA membership kits developed through secondary sources, such as those listed in the bibliography at the end of this article, but mainly through the two sources listed in the first paragraph above. These publications listed three distinct variations of the kit—1942, 1945, and 1947 (the latter advertised then, but not released till 1948). A number of JJSA items have been sold on eBay and other online auction sites, allowing a wider audience to observe and catalogue the items on the market. In recent years, I have also

The first ad for the Junior JSA, which ran in All-Star Comics #13-14, *was a two-page spread which you had to turn the comic sideways to read. This is the "bottom" half of that spread; the "top" part was seen in Vol. 1. This half showed the four honorary JSAers.*

had the opportunity to make contact with some original members of the JJSA and compare their holdings. This has proved most revealing.

The 1943 membership kit – helping date some changes and additions to the original membership package. *The JJSA membership badge changed to an embroidered patch as supplies of metal diminished due to the World War II effort. This led to the first change in the membership kits.*

I will never forget the day I was first able to examine a JJSA membership kit. It belongs to a JSA fan living in New England who possesses a treasure trove of JJSA items. Some of these are not shown or listed in either the *Revue* or *Companion*, and as the owner of these rare and valuable items he wishes to retain his anonymity. "Mr. Z" is a charter member of the JJSA, having joined when he was ten years old. We had met online (where he posts as Zatarro) and corresponded for over a year before I was lucky enough to spend the day with him during a trip to North America in October 2000. We talked about comics and other common interests and even visited the old store where he had purchased his comics, and I picked a couple off the same wooden racks that had been in use when he was a child.

The day's highlight came when he produced his JJSA kit—still stored in its original envelope. Mr. Z first encountered *All-Star Comics* with issue #14 (cover-dated Dec.1942-Jan. 1943). He has no recollection of how or why he acquired this, but remembers being swept away by issue #15, which was:

"...bought for me by my mother when I was in hospital having my tonsils out. It is likely that I would have sent for my kit in the early months of 1943. That would correspond to the age on the certificate. I had sent for the Supermen of America kit two years earlier, so the idea of a comic book club was exciting to me, but not new by the time of the JJSA. I am pretty sure that the ad I responded to in joining the JJSA promised the badge, and the patch arrived as an unexpected substitution."

The *Revue* and *Companion* list the 1942 kit as containing the envelope and seven items: the certificate; badge; welcome letter; decoder wheel; *Victory Club* pamphlet; 4-page *Minute Man Answers the Call* strip; and a Defense Stamp album. Mr. Z's kit has all of these, except that the metal badge was replaced by the patch. He continues:

"My JJSA kit contains not only the pamphlet indicated in *Revue/Companion* as *How to Organize a Victory Club at Your School* but a pamphlet *Youth and the War Effort*, identified by *Revue/Companion* only as part of the 1945 kit and listed there as 'not available for photography.' In my kit, the pamphlet is described as:

A Radio Address of M.C. GAINES
President of All-American Comics, Inc.
Originator of and U. S. Treasury Representative in the Comic Magazine Field.

From the Columbia Broadcasting System Series
'Children Also Are People'
April 22, 1942.

"It is a glossy 8½ x 11 inch sheet folded into thirds and printed in six columns. Obviously, the 'Youth' pamphlet was distributed long before the 1945 kit."

Mr. Z points out that the address given on both the *Victory Club* and *Youth and the War Effort* pamphlets is that of All-American Comics' office at 225 Lafayette St, New York, even though the welcoming letter from Diana Prince has the DC offices address: 480 Lexington Ave. He added: "I have not seen specific mention of the fact that her welcoming letter 1a refers to a number of comics, including *Fun* rather than, correctly, *More Fun*." He continues:

"The other unusual enclosure in my kit is a blue piece of pulp paper, 3¼ x 5½ inches, with this text in a black border. It reads:

Notice!
Applications for membership in the Junior Justice Society of America have come in so fast that supply of membership pins has become exhausted.
As you realize, all metal is vitally needed for munitions, planes and tanks to be used by our brothers, uncles and fathers in the armed forces.

This house ad for both All-Star Comics #37 and the JJSA ran in various DC comics in 1947.

Since we do not want to use metal which is so necessary for victory, we are sending you this beautiful woven label instead of the pin.
This label can easily be sewed to your sweater, coat or jacket without any trouble, and can be taken on or off each garment without any damage.

"I have never seen any mention of this insert."

It is indeed a rare treasure, not referred to in any published items listed in the bibliography. It is also a useful one for helping to date the changes and supplying membership numbers. Because his kit contains the cloth badge—and explanatory note—instead of the metal one, we know that Mr Z was not one of the earliest members of the club. However, Jerry Bails, the famous comic book collector and historian, *was*. Jerry wrote off for JJSA kits as soon as they were advertised, sometimes signing up in his brothers' names or using fictitious ones, as in his childhood naiveté he thought multiple orders would not be allowed. Jerry's early kits contained the metal badge with the certificate, such as the example from his collection numbered 6955 that is displayed in both the *Revue* and *Companion*.

Mr. Z's certificate has the number 25849 typed in. It is in the original style, the same as Jerry's and the one on page 238 of *All Star Comics Archives, Vol.3*. So if DC first advertised the JJSA in *All-Star Comics #13* (when Jerry first applied) and Mr Z joined after receiving #15, then over 25,000 applications were received in the first four to six months (assuming, of course, that the certificates began with #1 and were numbered consecutively)! The club was indeed proving popular!

In summary, Mr Z has a variation of the 1942 kit listed in the *All-Star Revue* and *Companion*. From his personal information we can date this kit as having been sent to new members in early 1943, and perhaps we can therefore list this in future as comprising "The 1943 JJSA kit" or "The 1943 Variation," as it was not a total redesign.

The Supermen of America club predated the JJSA by a couple of years, as per this DC house ad. The Captain Marvel Club beat it to the punch, as well. Shown re: the latter is its mailing envelope. Note that, even in those days, Fawcett knew the potency of the magic word "Shazam"!

YOUTH
AND THE
WAR EFFORT
★

A Radio Address of
M. C. GAINES
President of All-American Comics, Inc.
Originator of and
U. S. Treasury Representative
in the Comic Magazine Field

From the
Columbia Broadcasting System Series
"Children Also Are People"
April 22, 1942

FROM: Educational Department
ALL AMERICAN COMICS, INC.
225 Lafayette St., N.Y.C.

SCHOOL DEFENSE CLUBS FOR VICTORY

The people in America are uniting, banding together, to do the many tasks that fall to them in the war program. In every state, in every county, in every town, in every block, this spontaneous and directed organization is taking place. In one branch of our society, such unification is of utmost importance. THIS IS IN THE SCHOOLS.

For not alone does a "School Defense Club for Victory" assist in the sale of stamps, in salvage work, in other departments of civilian participation, but the molding of students into a conscious, active group, is one of the best protections possible in case of direct attack by our enemies.

Because we felt that information on how to organize defense activities in the schools was extremely important and deserving of wide distribution, we sponsored a contest at the Samuel J. Tilden High School in Brooklyn, New York, on "How to Organize A Defense Club in Your School".

Tilden High School was chosen because of its well-known and splendid work in the matter of national defense, and with the cooperation of its principal and faculty advisors, three thousand students participated. The outline and essay attached were the prize winners in this contest, and each winner, as well as the School Defense Fund, received a $25 Defense Bond, offered by ALL-AMERICAN COMICS, Inc.

These Defense Bonds were presented to the winners and to the school at a special Defense Assembly of the School on March 6, by Miss Alice Marble, former tennis champion and now Assistant Director for Physical Fitness in the U.S. Office of Civilian Defense.

We send you this prize-winning outline and essay with the hope that they will be helpful to you in forming a Defense Club for Victory in your school.

We will be glad to send additional copies of this defense bulletin to other teachers and school officials requesting them, FREE OF CHARGE.

Very sincerely

ALL-AMERICAN COMICS, Inc.

M. C. Gaines

M. C. Gaines, President

(Far left:) The front of the Youth and the War Effort *pamphlet that reprinted a 1942 radio address by Maxwell Charles Gaines, co-publisher of All-Star Comics and related titles.*

(Left:) A letter from Gaines entitled "School Defense Club for Victory." How was this different from the 4-page pamphlet mentioned in Vol. 1 of this series by Craig Delich, entitled How to Organize a Victory Club at Your School?

a distinct certificate. But more appear to have been produced or used in advertising for the club. One collector's recently-acquired kit revealed a variation on the first certificate.

In July 2001 I received an e-mail from an online colleague and fellow JSA fan Scott Maple informing me of his good fortune in winning a JJSA membership kit on eBay. He knew my JJSA web site had been in touch with JJSAer Mr Z and thought that I would be interested in his new acquisition. Was I ever! Scott said that he had waited years for the opportunity to purchase a JJSA kit, and this was the best buy of his life. The kit had belonged to a David Leonard of 910 Northwood Ave, Fort Dodge, Iowa, who was member #53415. Scott generously scanned a few pieces from his collection for me to add to my JJSA site. These included the envelope and welcoming letter, as well as the certificate. All three proved to be significant items.

The envelope in which the kit was posted is of the same design as both the one belonging to Mr Z, and the one missing from the 1942 kits photographed in the *Revue* and *Companion*, but shown on page 80 of *Comic Book Marketplace #69* (July 1999) in J.C. Vaughn's article "Join the Jr. JSA." The only difference is that this one had a typed postage label attached, whereas Mr. Z's and the one pictured in *CBM* are handwritten.

The welcome letter in Scott's kit is not displayed or discussed in the *Revue*, *Companion*, or *CBM* article. It differs from the original letter in only one sentence, the start of the third paragraph. It reads, "I know that you will be proud to wear this beautiful four color JUNIOR JUSTICE SOCIETY emblem…" while the original had begun, "I know you will be proud to wear this beautiful silver-plated JUNIOR JUSTICE SOCIETY emblem…." The same paragraph was later incorporated into the welcome letter of the 1945 kit. Surprisingly, the new letter—let's call it Welcome Letter 1b—retains the error in the title of *More Fun Comics*. This letter alone makes Scott's kit of interest; however, it was the scan of the unnumbered

The 1943 JJSA membership kit variation (an example owned by Mr. Z)

Items included are

1. The 1st envelope (not shown in *Revue* or *Companion*)
2. Welcome letter 1a
3. Membership certificate 1a
4. Cloth patch – **New**, replacing silver-plated badge of 1942 kit
5. 1st Secret Code wheel
6. *Victory Club* pamphlet
7. *Minute Man Answers the Call* message strip
8. Defense Stamp album
9. Note on change of badge to patch - **New**, addition to kit (not shown in *Revue* or *Companion*)
10. *Youth and the War Effort* pamphlet – **New**, issued earlier than previously thought (not shown in *Revue* or *Companion*)

On a personal level, Mr. Z's kit revealed that my homemade decoder wheels were twice as large as the originals! Having no real concept of the actual size, I was way off. While the wheels may have been made small for little hands, I had just assumed that everything for a child would be big and bright. I am not the only one with these thoughts. Mr. Z himself reminisced that "at this point in my life I am convinced that the nearest equivalent to being ten and holding an original Golden Age comic is being myself now and holding one of the oversize *Famous First Editions*."

The 1944 membership kit – the members receive a new certificate. *The certificates were a key item of the Junior Justice Society of America membership kits. But how many variations were produced? The main sources on the subject point to three distinct variations of membership kit, each with*

When the metal JJSA badge "marched off to war" alongside the "Lucky Strike Green" color on cigarette packs, to be replaced by a cloth badge, so did the metal badge for Timely's Sentinels of Liberty Club, which sported an image of Captain America. But Timely/Marvel simply discontinued the badges completely! [Capt. America TM & © Marvel Characters, Inc.]

certificate that had first caught my eye and which raised the most interest.

My references showed three variations of the JJSA certificate—one from 1942, another from 1945, and a third from 1947 (although not appearing until 1948). Scott's certificate is not one of them. However, it was familiar, and I had seen one before, offered for sale on eBay in 1999. My computer records the date I copied the JPG file from the auction listing as 12 March 1999. It is a low-resolution scan of the certificate, quite blurry but readable. It was issued to nine year-old Glenn C. Kuebeler of Sandusky, Ohio. Glenn had written in "82538" as his membership number. The image contains the same cameo pictures of the JSA members and the DC address for All-Star headquarters as the original 1942 certificate, which is referred to above in Jerry Bails and Mr. Z's kits. However, the wording is clearly different. The "his or her" reference to the member has been changed to just "his," there are two numbered pledges for the new member, and the final oath begins with two extra lines affirming the member's belief in democracy and winning the war—lines which had been included in the main paragraph of the 1942 certificate.

At the time I wanted to ask questions about this "new" certificate, such as "Why the changes?" and "When was it issued?"—but I didn't know whom to ask. So I just placed the 1999 scan on my website side-by-side with the original 1942 certificate which I had seen in the *Revue* and *All Star Comics Archives, Vol. 3*. To continue the existing numbering, I called them "Membership Certificate Type 1a & 1b." "1b" was the variant certificate, so I'll refer to it by that designation for the rest of this article.

With other things on my plate, I forgot all about the certificate and was only reminded of it when Scott forwarded the new scan. I checked my most up-to-date source book, the JJSA section of *All-Star Companion, Vol. 1*, and found that it also did not show, or mention the certificate I called "1b." I delved around and undertook some more research, and instead of answers I came up with even more questions.

In early 2001, while pursuing a local antiquarian bookstore here in Melbourne, I had found a copy of Robert Lesser's 1975 book *A Celebration of Comic Art and Memorabilia*. I had bought the book after spotting a color reproduction of the JJSA code wheel and cloth patch, but had not had time to have a serious look through the whole book, and it had moved down towards the bottom of my "to read" pile. I quickly checked it now, and while there was no in-depth analysis of the JJSA there was a section on "decoders and their manuals" with a brief (and incomplete) list of membership items on page 266 in Lesser's "suggested list of collectibles." This chapter also shows a black-&-white photograph of a JJSA code wheel and certificate on page 278. It is another unnumbered example of 1b.

By this time I had encountered Jerry Bails through e-mail, and Craig Delich had come across my site and e-mailed me some suggested corrections. I assumed that Craig, Jerry, Roy, and others had already discussed the questions I was starting to raise. However,

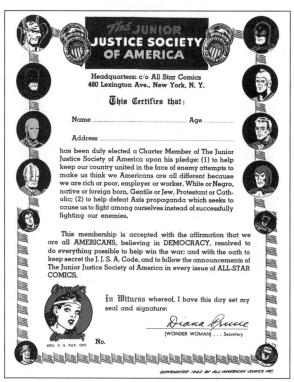

David Studham refers to this version of the JJSA certificate as type "1b," a variant of the type "1a" sent out earlier and depicted in Vol. 1 of this series; see the latter to compare the wording of the two versions. Among other things, this one lists two numbered pledges the prospective member was to make. (Type 1a was seen in Vol. 1 of this series.)

if they had not, what was the harm in raising the issue with them now? If it had been discussed in print somewhere in the past, I could add to my JSA fanzine section or the bibliography section of my JJSA site. So I typed up my questions and sent off an e-mail to Craig and Jerry, attaching two scans of certificate 1b (the one from eBay in 1999 and Scott's copy).

Their responses were prompt, and both were only too willing to help where they could. Craig preferred to defer to Jerry, as the latter had provided most of the material illustrated in the *Revue* and later reproduced in the *Companion*. Unfortunately, they were unsure as to when certificate 1b came out and as part of which kit. The *Revue* and *Companion* state that the patch was introduced in 1943, and while they initially wondered if the certificate could have been introduced at the same time, due to the new welcoming letter, Mr. Z's kit proves that this was not the case. Scott Maple revealed further evidence when he forwarded me a JJSA house ad from *All-Star Comics* #21 (Summer 1944). It shows the patch accompanied by the original certificate. (The patch was reproduced without identification on the inside back cover of *CBM* #69.) So certificate 1b was introduced at a later period than the cloth badge, and we know there are advertisements showing both the cloth patch and the original certificate (1a) issued in early-to-mid 1944, when *All-Star* #21 was released.

Later, in December 2001, another copy cropped up for sale on eBay. Perhaps certificate 1b was not that rare, after all!

A copy belonging to a "Jack Harris, age 12," was auctioned at that time, and it has "1945" written in ink on the top right corner of the certificate. Another Harris-owned certificate in the style from circa 1947/48 was auctioned at the same time and has "1948" written in the corresponding spot. Whether this relates to the date it was received by the owner, or notes the different version, is unclear. Perhaps it shows that 1b was still being issued until early in 1945.

I asked if there could be any JJSA adverts that show certificate 1b, and if so, "would this help provide a firmer date for the introduction of the certificate?" Jerry and Craig did not know of any, and Scott could not find one in his run of *All-Star Comics*, although an advert may have run in any other comics published by DC or AA.

Until evidence is found to date the introduction of certificate 1b, we can only make assumptions. The reference to the war on the certificate, the fact that the cloth badge was being issued in the same kits, and the ad in *All-Star* #21 all point to the new certificate and welcoming letter most probably dating from early 1944. If this is the case, it can be suggested that a further variation of the kit was issued to members who joined in 1944. Since the packaging and designs were roughly the same as the original 1942 kit, for convenience we can call this "the 1944 membership kit variation." It appears to have continued through to the start of 1945, when the revised 1945 kit was briefly issued by All-American Comics after its apparent split with DC. Therefore it appears that there were three variations of what was known in the past as the first JJSA kit of 1942.

The 1944 JJSA membership kit variation (an example owned by Scott Maple)

Items contained are:

1. The 1st envelope (not shown in *Revue* or *Companion*)
2. Welcome letter 1b – **New** revised letter (not shown in *Revue* or *Companion*)
3. Membership certificate 1b – **New** revised certificate (not shown in *Revue* or *Companion*)
4. Cloth patch
5. 1st Secret Code wheel
6. *Victory Club* pamphlet
7. *Minute Man Answers the Call* message strip
8. Defense Stamp album
9. *Youth and the War Effort* pamphlet (not shown in *Revue* or *Companion*)

So that tells us roughly when this kit came out. But what of my other question: "Why the changes?" The alteration in material for the membership emblem due to the metal shortage is understandable. Lesser discusses the same thing for the Captain Midnight Club, where the metal decoder was replaced by an embroidered patch. But why change the wording of the certificates, especially of the new 1b, carried over to the 1945 certificate?

Jerry offered a plausible explanation. He thought that the changes in certificate 1b were most likely made at the suggestion of the US Office of War Information (OWI), "which clearly was involved in encouraging and probably reviewing such efforts." Jerry also thought the switch in the 1945 certificate, No. 2, from "Axis" to "enemy" appears to be another "official" suggestion, but made later:

"I doubt it was something that would originate in Gaines' office, but that's possible. The Italian Fascists had been defeated by the time of the Wildcat/Mr. Terrific kit, I believe, and Germany was scheduled for defeat next, so references to 'Axis' would be stricken from advisories from the War Information Office. That's just reasonable supposition on my part. I have not seen any OWI documents. Such documents would surely be an interesting backdrop for your explorations."

Very sound advice from Jerry. However, as I'm a long way from the USA, the OWI records at the US National Archives are not readily accessible at the moment. The Archives website lists: **Records of the Office of War Information [OWI] (Record Group 208)** including "**Error! Reference source not found.** Records of the Book and Magazine Bureau." It would be interesting to see the effect of the Office's operations on the comic industry as a whole, not just on the JJSA certificates! I wonder if any historians amongst readers of this article would be able or interested in checking this out?

Other certificate variations – what the adverts reveal.

Jerry's reference to the rare 1945 certificate, No. 2, led to further research. This certificate was recently reprinted in color in *All-Star Comics Archives, Vol. 6* (p. 223), and the black-&-white images in the *Revue* and *Companion* are identical to it. I encountered a copy of that certificate on eBay in mid-1999, copied the scan, and added it to my website. The 1945 kit's certificate, No.2, has similar wording to 1b, with one slight variation: the 1945 certificate reads, "(2) to defeat enemy propaganda..." while 1b reads, "(2) to help defeat Axis propaganda....." Both the *Revue* and *Companion* point out a JJSA

The "welcome" letter sent along with the "1a" certificate, in the membership kit today owned by collector Scott Maple.

THE JUNIOR JUSTICE SOCIETY OF AMERICA

Headquarters, c/o All-Star Comics,
480 Lexington Ave., N. Y. C.

Dear Member:

I am glad to welcome you as one of the charter members of the JUNIOR JUSTICE SOCIETY OF AMERICA!

In this envelope, you will find your Membership Emblem, Certificate and Code Card as well as the War Savings Stamp Album, "The Minute Man Answers the Call" and "How to Organize A Victory Club in your School".

I know you will be proud to wear this beautiful four color JUNIOR JUSTICE SOCIETY emblem, and that you will read over carefully and take to heart your pledge on the Membership Certificate!

Study your Code Card carefully so you will know how to decipher the special code messages which are being published every month in "ALL-STAR", "ALL-AMERICAN", "FLASH" and "SENSATION COMICS", as well as "ALL-FLASH" and "GREEN LANTERN", "FUN" and "ADVENTURE COMICS".

And be sure to follow the announcements of our activities in every issue of "ALL-STAR COMICS"!

Very sincerely,

Diana Prince

(Wonder Woman), Secretary

P.S. I think it would be nice if you would bring "The Minute Man Answers the Call" and "How to Organize A Victory Club in Your School" to your teacher — she'll be interested in them, I'm sure!

advertisement in *All-Star* #24 which shows a design variation on the 1945 certificate, but the same wording as 1b. This "hybrid" JJSA certificate is also shown on page 44 of *All Star Archives, Vol. 6*. The graphic design differs dramatically from certificates 1a, 1b, and 2. The DC heroes seem to have been taken off the certificate, and some rushed redesign has taken place as deadline for publication approached. Both Craig and Roy have asked any readers owning a copy of a certificate with that design to contact them, as none seem to be known to exist.

However, when I absorbed the sixth volume of the *All-Star Archives*, I noticed there was a further variation shown in the JJSA advertisements from *All-Stars* #25 & 26 (reprinted on pp. 91 & 122). The design is exactly the same as the main 1945 certificate; however, the wording is also the same as on certificate 1b. It reads "Axis" in the adverts, where the actual certificate reads "enemy." I wondered if AA printed any certificates with the earlier wording, and if there could be two additional variations of the 1945 certificate.

So, more questions: "Does anyone own any certificate like that shown in *All-Star Comics* #25 and #26, or did this form of certificate just appear in the house adverts, as is believed to be the case with the certificate shown in *All-Star* #24?" Jerry and Craig did not know of any, and they support the view that they were never produced. If this is the case, could there have been an advert in *All-Star* or other AA comics for the JJSA that showed the wording as it actually appeared on certificate 2? As with 1b, none exists in *All-Star* itself, but perhaps some other AA publication may have included one.

Finally, the circa 1947/48 certificate also has a minor variation. The first reproduction of this certificate that I saw was Roy Thomas' copy, reproduced in *All-Star Squadron* #39 (1984). Roy is member #193328. He has confirmed to me that the version there is not a

100% accurate color reproduction, as the reprint shows the flag border in black-&-white, while on the original the flag border is red, white, and blue. A more accurate copy of the true coloring of Roy's certificate is printed on p. 207 of *All-Star Comics Archives, Vol. 8*. The copy issued to a Robert Hall of Akron, Ohio, #170967, is shown on the back inside cover of *CBM #69*. It also is a truer representation, with the flag border in color.

Intriguingly, it also shows a copyright notice under the border. While slightly too small to be read clearly with the naked eye, under magnification the fuzzy words appear as "Copyright 1948 National Comics Publications Inc." Neither of the copies in the *Revue* and *Companion*, nor the Jack Harris copy #169559 which was sold on eBay in December 2001, shows any copyright marking. So was this added or dropped at some stage? Does anyone else own a copy of this certificate with a copyright marking? To quote the words that Craig and Roy have used before me, "We ask anyone owning such a certificate to contact us at once!" More questions awaiting more research and, hopefully, more answers.

Conclusion? Or, we now know more, but there is more work to be done.

So where then does all of this new information and analysis leave us on the query of what was issued as JJSA membership kits and certificates? It appears there were five different membership kits issued throughout the existence of the JJSA. Three were quite distinct from each other, while the other two, offering new or different items, were variations of the first—a membership kit for 1943, and another for 1944. Four of the kits offered different certificates— 1a, 1b, 2, and 3 (and possibly a fifth if more copies of the 1948 copyright certificate with the copyright line are revealed). While two variations of certificate 2 appeared in JJSA advertisements, neither of these appears to have actually been issued.

Overall, there are at least 22 items that were issued as part of the JJSA membership kits between 1942 and 1950, with 19 previously listed in the *All-Star Comics Revue* and *All-Star Companion*, and the three previously-unlisted items contained in kits owned by Mr. Z and Scott Maple. With a rising interest in comic book collectibles and broader access to items through online fan clubs and sales or auctions through the Internet, comic collectors and historians are likely to discover more information on the JJSA in the future.

Bibliography

All-Star Comics. New York: National Periodical Pub./All-American/DC Comics, 1940-1951.

All Star Comics Archives, Vol. 3, 6, & 8: New York: DC Comics, 1997, 2000, & 2002.

All-Star Squadron. New York: DC Comics 1981-1987.

Delich, David. *All-Star Comics Revue*. Kansas: David L. Delich, 1977.

eBay – various auctions of JJSA artifacts.

Lessor, Robert. *A Celebration of Comic Art and Memorabilia*. New York: Hawthorn, 1975.

Scans of membership kits items supplied by Scott Maple and Mr. Z from their personal collections.

Thomas, Roy. *The All-Star Companion (Vol. 1)*. Raleigh, NC: TwoMorrows, 2000.

Tollin, Anthony. "Badges, Buttons, and Secret Codes, Too… Just 10¢ to Cover Postage and Handling" in *Amazing World of DC Comics*, No. 8, Sept 1975.

Vaughn, J.C. "Join the Junior JSA! All You Need Is a Badge and Decoder" in *Comic Book Marketplace #69*, July 1999.

This version of the "welcome" letter to JJSA members, included in the 1945 kit, has dropped the reference to "Victory Clubs," but does refer to Gaines' old radio address on Youth and the War Effort.

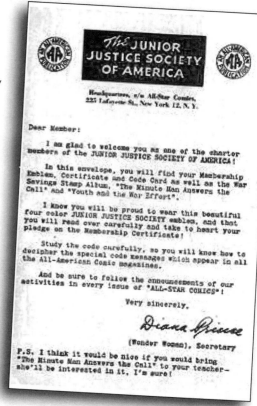

Appendix 1

List of Junior Justice Society items issued in membership kits:

1st envelope – 1942-1944 kits
Welcome letter 1a – 1942-43 kits
Membership certificate 1a –1942 kit
1st silver plated membership badge – 1942 kit
1st Secret Code wheel – 1942-1944 kits
Victory Club Pamphlet – 1942-44 kits
Minute Man Answers the Call message strip – 1942-45 kits
Defense Stamp album –1942-45 kits.
Membership cloth patch – 1943-1945 kits
Note on change of badge to patch –1943 kits
Youth and the War Effort – 1943-45 kits
Welcome letter 1b – 1943/44 kit
Membership Certificate 1b – 1943/44 kit
2nd envelope – 1945 kit
Welcome Letter 2 – 1945 kit
Membership certificate 2 – 1945 kit
2nd Secret Code wheel – 1945 kit
3rd envelope – 1948 kit
Welcome letter 3 – 1948 kit
Membership certificate 3- 1948 kit
2nd silver-plated badge – smaller lettering – 1948 kit
Secret Code chart – 1948 kit

DAVID STUDHAM was introduced to DC characters through their Australian reprints. Among the first he received, at the age of five, was *Mighty Comics #74*, containing "The Stormy Return of The Red Tornado," a story set entirely on Earth-Two that featured a band of heroes known as the Justice Society. Intrigued, enthralled, and inspired, he has been hooked on their adventures ever since. David works as a librarian (an enjoyable way to finance his comic collecting) and lives in Melbourne, Australia. He can be reached via e-mail at dstudham@bigpond.net.au.

CHAPTER XI

"OUR SLIP IS SHOWING!"

Corrections And Additions To The All-Star Companion, Vol. 1

by Roy Thomas

Whoever said that nothing is certain in life but death and taxes didn't get it *entirely* right. There are a *third* and even a *fourth* certainty: namely that, no matter how hard you try to get everything right in a book, you'll have to correct some errors when you come out with a second edition—and that even then, you'll miss a couple of things.

We corrected a number of errors both large and small in the first (2000) volume of this series when we reprinted it in 2004. Because of that fact, we have not noted those mistakes below. If you want our best thinking as of 2004, afraid you'll have to pick up a copy of the second edition, which is still in print from TwoMorrows... or at least read the corrections we listed in *Alter Ego*, Vol. 3, #7, 8, & 10.

Mid-Nite Special

Doc may not have been a major DC super-hero, but his begoggled costume has intrigued many artists—including Marvels and Kingdom Come illustrator Alex Ross. This tight-pencil character study appeared in the Kingdom Come: Revelations volume published in 1997 by DC Comics & Graphitti Designs, and is repro'd here from a photocopy of the original art, courtesy of Keif A. Fromm. [© DC Comics.]

"Be Sure To Get..."

Above is the only JSA "story page"—if as such it can be counted—from the original 55-issue Golden Age run which was not reprinted in the 12 volumes of DC's All Star Archives. This page comes at the end of the JSA tale in All-Star Comics #7—and was repeated as the splash of #8, two months later, when Dr. Mid-Nite and Starman were inducted. The only differences between the two pages are the final paragraph of copy beginning "Be sure to get..." and the white-on-black "on sale" ribbon at the very bottom of the page. Archives, Vol. 2, accidentally printed #8's splash page copy twice—including at the end of issue #7. Thanks to Jerry G. Bails. [© DC Comics.]

However, we missed a few things even there—and have come into possession of a few additional facts—and those we *are* noting here. We haven't bothered to include illustrations of most of the items, though, since often a mere glance at either *Companion V1* or the proper volume of *All Star Comics Archives* is all that is called for.

Oh, and the reason for our quoted title above: that once-risqué phrase must've been used a zillion times back in the 1940s, as well as before and since, when a newspaper or magazine had to acknowledge an error it had committed. So, in honor of *All-Star Comics*, which ran from 1940-51, we thought it was worth one more usage.

Now, onward. The bold page numbers refer to pages in *Companion V1*....

P. 15: Craig Delich, who's been going over the art credits for *All-Star Comics* with a fine tooth comb ever since *Companion V1* came out, feels that "the *All-Star* #1 Sandman story is *all* Chad Grothkopf... pencils, inks, and lettering," though probably not the writing.

P. 16: Craig adds that he believes, upon due consideration, that "the Sandman story in *All-Star* #2 is [Creig] Flessel pencils and

It's A Crime!

As noted in Vol. 1, EC's International Crime Patrol, a loosely-organized multi-national assemblage of non-super-powered law-enforcers, was M.C. Gaines' post-AA answer to the JSA he had published from 1940-45. The group was still a (barely) going concern in Crime Patrol #7 (Summer 1948), wherein Van Manhattan, The Chessmen, and the French operative Madelon appeared in separate stories; their shared villain was a mad rocket scientist. They mostly communicated with each other via messages, as per the Chessmen panel at top left. Martin O'Hearn says Gardner Fox wrote most of the scripts; the Chessmen artist is unidentified. The Madelon story (above) was drawn by early-'40s Hawkman artist Sheldon Moldoff.

#8 (Fall 1948) featured the final Crime Patrol tales: one of Madelon, and one featuring Igor the Archer (left), who hailed from an unnamed USSR. The two battled piratical villains called The Kraken and The Octopus, respectively. The Igor art, according to Russ Cochran's hardcover Crime Patrol, Vol. 1, is by Ann Brewster of the Iger (not Igor) comics shop. After #8, Crime Patrol became just another imitation of Biro and Wood's Crime Does Not Pay—till it morphed into the slightly more memorable Tales from the Crypt! [Art © William M. Gaines, Agent, Inc.]

Grothkopf inks & lettering." So the fabulous Mr. Flessel *did* make it into *All-Star*, after all, if never actually on the Justice Society!

Next comes not a correction so much as new information, courtesy of Kevin Wilkens. He noticed, upon publication of first *Comic Cavalcade Archives, Vol. 1*, then *All Star Comics Archives, Vol. 0*, that the Red, White, and Blue story that had appeared in *All-Star Comics* #2 was reprinted, but with odd *alterations*, in *Comic Cavalcade* #1: "What really piqued my interest was the art change in panel 16, making the arson victim's discovery less 'gruesome' [when reprinted] in *CC* #1. That's when I started a panel-by-panel comparison. The changes in text/dialogue were suddenly obvious; I guess, in hindsight, I thought Doris' swearing in panel 13 was a bit odd given that 1940s-era women wouldn't normally be depicted as swearing. Then I noticed the more subtle changes, like concealing Doris' stocking in panel 13 so that her fall was more 'modest.' I then noticed the discrepancies in credits and even the story titles."

P. 26: We asked Craig Delich why, in his 1977 *All-Star Comics Revue*, he had credited letterer Howard Ferguson with some inking on the Simon & Kirby-drawn Sandman chapter in *All-Star* #14. Craig's response: "Jack Kirby made mention of it somewhere, and that is what verified it for me. However, it was a rarity, as he was primarily a letterer." That's good enough for us! And, *à propos* of no particular pages, Craig adds: "[Artist] Bernard Baily lettered the Hour-Man stories in *All-Star* #1-7, and the Spectre stories in #1-10, 12, 14, 16, and 18." We didn't try to establish lettering credits for *All-Star*, but are happy to include them where they're vouched for by an expert like our Kansas City cohort.

P. 29: According to Robin Snyder, editor/publisher of *The Comics!*, a

monthly "oral history" of the field, Jon Chester Kozlak was born "either in 1917 or 1918." Our bio read "circa 1917." Robin also reports that the artist's Social Security card, issued in his native Minnesota, records him as "Chester Jon Kozlak." An error? Or was his first name actually Chester, not Jon? He was, after all, nicknamed "Chet."

P. 54: Rich Morrissey, an inveterate comics researcher, supplied additional information before he passed away, far too young, in 2001: "Not only was EC's International Crime Patrol reminiscent of a non-powered JSA; it was produced mostly by the same people! Gardner Fox wrote all the stories that Martin O'Hearn [an expert in identifying comic book writers' styles and thus in attributing unsigned stories] has seen, and the artists were largely 'JSA' veterans Sheldon Moldoff, Stan Aschmeier, and Joe Gallagher.... I wouldn't be at all surprised if [publisher] M.C. Gaines deliberately tried to keep together what had been a successful team at AA for the intended flagship of his new EC series."

P. 60: It was Chad Grothkopf, not Paul Norris, who drew the Sandman story (in *Adventure Comics* #69, Dec. 1941) in which that hero first sported a purple-and-yellow costume. Norris penciled the following two Sandman tales, in #70-71 (though Jerry Bails suspects Chad may have *inked* them), after which Joe Simon & Jack

It Pays To Advertise

One of the last full-page DC house ads that pushed the JSA as opposed to the JJSA was this one for All-Star Comics *#34, which featured panel art from various chapters. The Johnny Thunder and Wonder Woman illos came from the JSA finale. Art by Joe Kubert, Frank Harry, Lee Elias, Paul Reinman, Harry Lampert, and Irwin Hasen. Thanks to David Studham.* [© DC Comics.]

Kirby took over the feature. *Vol. 1* had the order of the two artists reversed. Our main point was to correct the oft-recurring misstatement that it was S&K who gave Sandman a tight-fitting super-hero outfit and introduced Sandy the Golden Boy into the feature. 'Taint so… though they did immediately lose Sandman's cape.

P. 61: Fan/collector Dan Makara noted that the Sheldon Moldoff Hawkman figure on the cover of *All-Star* #11 "is actually a re-pasted photocopy of the [Hawkman figure on the earlier] cover of *Flash Comics* #27 (March 1942)." On the earlier cover, Hawkman is felling a thug; on *All-Star* it's a Japanese soldier, but the Winged Wonder's pose is the same. If it wasn't a photocopy, it was at least

a tracing.

Also on that page, it's said that movie star Carole Lombard died in a plane crash in Feb. 1942. That tragic accident actually happened in January.

P. 65: Murray Ward reminds us that, when mentioning Edgar Rice Burroughs' influence on JSA stories, we might have added that Hawkman's belt of "Ninth (later Nth) Metal was probably inspired by the Eighth Ray (in addition to the seven rays of the spectrum) of Barsoom." Barsoom is ERB's name for the planet Mars in his John Carter novels.

P. 73: Golden Age artist Sheldon Moldoff informs us: "The Hawkman splash panel [in *All-Star* #17] was done by me, pencil and ink… and *exactly* as it is reproduced. It drove [editor Sheldon] Mayer nuts when I deviated from the script and broke up the pages, or combined panels. [Writer Gardner] Fox loved my handling of his scripts, but Mayer did not appreciate being usurped. Walking around the office in his riding boots and carrying a crock… Mayer's personality is something that has nothing to do with his accomplishments in the early days of the comic book. However—don't underestimate M.C. Gaines' influence in comics."

Thanks, Shelly—and we assume that when you refer in your first sentence to the "splash panel," you mean the entire splash *page*. We had wondered in *Vol. 1* if perhaps those pages were repasted *after* being drawn, with some material omitted in order to combine 2 or 3 pages into one and thus shorten the chapter from 6 or 7 to what became only four in the printed version, when *All-Star*'s page count abruptly dropped by one "signature" (16 pages) beginning with #17. Any telescoping was surely at editor Sheldon Mayer's direction. We added a short form of this correction to the second edition of *Vol. 1*, but wanted to quote Moldoff at greater length here.

P. 132: An addition to our info. Craig Delich writes: "Tom Orzechowski [major Marvel letterer for many years] has identified the entire JSA story in *All-Star* #33 as being lettered by Gaspar Saladino."

P. 134: Rich Morrissey informed us that comics writer Cary Bates once gave The Wizard's real name as "Frederick P. Garth" in a JLA story. Interesting, though of course that has no bearing on whether, in 1946-47, Gardner Fox intended "W.I. Zard" to be that villain's actual monicker or (more likely) merely an alias.

We Had Faces Then

Above: Barry Fitzgerald (wearing specs) from the Hawkman/Wonder Woman chapter of All-Star Comics *#44—juxtaposed with a photo of Fitzgerald.*

At right: Jane Wyman, who was married for several years to an actor named Ronald Reagan who eventually made something of himself. [Art © DC Comics.]

Written Off—But Now Written About

These two panels, penciled by Golden Age All-Star Comics artist Carmine Infantino, are from the original art of a never-published Green Lantern story, most likely done in 1948—one of those "written off 9/30/49," as noted on p. 25—and probably lopped off from the rest of the page in the late '60s. Inker uncertain. Other panels from this story have appeared in Alter Ego magazine. Thanks to Joe and Nadia Mannerino of (what else?) All Star Auctions. [© DC Comics.]

P. 139: Longtime comics writer and editor Mike W. Barr says that, until he read its plot summary in the *Companion*, he had never considered "a possible source of inspiration—and therefore author-ship" of the controversial *All-Star* #36. "5 Drowned Men," he says, with its "frat brother... who vowed revenge for a college prank [is] very similar to the springboard of the plot for Rex Stout's 1935 novel *The League of Frightened Men*," the second Nero Wolfe outing, in which "the alleged motivation for the killer is having been crippled in a college prank by other students. Years later, the 'other students' start showing up murdered."

As Mike notes, the similarities could be mere coincidence, and in any event prove nothing about the scripter of *All-Star* #36, even though ofttimes JSA scripter John Broome later wrote the *Nero Wolfe* comic strip, since Stout's work was very popular in the '30s and '40s: "Gardner Fox is known to have been an avid fan of John Dickson Carr, and might also have read Stout. Even curmudgeonly Bob Kanigher, who's admitted to liking Clint Eastwood movies, may have read Stout." Even so, it's interesting to know of a possible source of the plot idea for that most problematical JSA adventure.

P. 145: Although the cover of *All-Star* #39 was indeed at least penciled (and perhaps inked) by Irwin Hasen, we don't know how we failed to notice, all these years, that the Hawkman head thereon was definitely totally redrawn, either by Joe Kubert or by someone carefully tracing him. It has quite a different look there from the Winged Wonder's head on the splash and in the rest of the issue. (See p. 40 of this volume for more on Kubert's clandestine cover work.)

P. 155: Craig Delich now feels that Chapter 2 of *All-Star* #44 was penciled by Irwin Hasen rather than Arthur Peddy, and that Bernard Sachs' inking made the two art styles look more similar.

P. 156: We listed one-panel cameos in *All-Star* #44's "Evil Star over Hollywood" by unidentified movie stars Humphrey Bogart, Lauren

Bacall, Bob Hope, Bing Crosby, James Stewart, Peter Lorre, and Cary Grant (plus another actress we thought might be his then-wife Betsy Drake)—but we totally forgot to mention Arthur Peddy's nice likeness of Barry Fitzgerald on p. 17 of that issue! Fitzgerald is best remembered for playing priests in films, especially opposite Bing Crosby in *Going My Way*.

And "Mad Mona," one of our regular correspondents, writes: "I believe that's *Jane Wyman* rather than Betsy Drake with Cary Grant! In 1948 Jane Wyman won an Academy Award for *Johnny Belinda*. She was married to Ronald Reagan at one time, and had that style hair for her character in that movie." You may well be right, Mona.

Also, it seems a bit less certain now than originally thought that Chapter II of *All-Star* #45 was penciled by Arthur Peddy. Craig Delich thinks it, like the other two chapters, may have been penciled by Irwin Hasen… yet Jerry Bails feels it was indeed Peddy. You might wanna put a question mark after that one….

P. 157: The cover of *All-Star* #46, Craig Delich now believes, was penciled by Irwin Hasen rather than Arthur Peddy.

P. 159: And Craig D. feels certain now that Hasen, not Peddy, penciled both the cover and lead splash page of *All-Star* #48. He says that Hasen himself verified that it was his work. Peddy penciled the rest of Chapter I in that issue.

P. 160: For reasons spelled out in the corrections below re pp. 161-162, you should probably just take a big black marker and cross out the entire "Artist Note" that says Irwin Hasen's last *All-Star* work appeared in #48. 'Twould seem the future artist of the newspaper strip *Dondi* did some penciling for #49-50, as well, making the latter his final bow in the JSA's mag. Read on….

P. 161: Everyone's had a change of heart about the penciler of the cover of *All-Star* #49, seen on p. 32 of *Vol. 1* of this series. Both Craig Delich and Jerry Bails (who till recently owned the original art) have had second and even third thoughts about attributing the pencils to Arthur Peddy. Delich says: "I'm almost certain now that [Irwin] Hasen penciled and [Bernard] Sachs inked. The Flash's helmet wings are Hasen's style, not Peddy's. If you compare The Flash's helmet wings in this story [as penciled by Peddy], you'll note they are large; then, if you look at Hasen's art on Flash in #48, [those wings] are, for the most part, narrow, like on #49's cover."

Bails agrees with Delich's conclusion, but has his own reasons: "The evidence of the penciler is best drawn from the poses of the figures and the layout. That GL figure is Hasen's. Smaller details, like the size and shape of wings on the helmet, may reflect an inker's preference, especially if he handles the character on a regular basis. Ears, insignia, belts, and things like that are clues to the inker, whereas the larger features are indications of the penciler."

As one who has long wondered if Hasen might have penciled #49's cover, the present author seconds (or rather, thirds) the above opinions. Please mark your copies of *Vol. 1* accordingly.

P. 162: Craig D. believes on closer inspection that the cover of *All-Star* #50 was inked by Joe Giella, not Bob Oksner. When Ye Editor e-mailed Craig that he wondered if the *penciler* of that cover was not Arthur Peddy, as listed, but Irwin Hasen, Craig said he had come to believe the same thing: "The cover to #50 has Hasen's Wonder Woman and Hawkman... positively. The fact that Giella did the inks makes one *have* to look at Green Lantern, and that GL figure *with* the Giella inks is Hasen. In fact, I'll go you one better than that. Chapter III is *not* penciled by Peddy—it is penciled by Irwin Hasen. One clue I just noticed is the wings of Flash's helmet... very small, just the way Hasen does them... Peddy always does them much larger (look at Chapter I, for example, that Peddy did). The faces in Chapter III are Hasen's, as well. So—cover and Chapter III: Hasen pencils and Giella inks." So be it, C.D.!

P. 163: In November of 2005, Craig Delich wrote to say: "I discovered two oddities in *All-Star* #50. In chapter 1, Mr. Alpha is shown with short sleeves. The other two chapters show him with full-length shirtsleeves. The other concerns Wonder Woman's footgear. On the cover and in chapters 1 & 2, she is shown with her [new] sandals. However, in chapter 3, she has her old boots on."

P. 166: Here's a generations-spanning error! Very soon after DC's *All Star Archives, Vol. 11* came out in 2005, we received a letter pointing out that pp. 16 & 17 of the reprint of *All-Star Comics* #53 were *reversed*. We naturally assumed it was an error made by DC's Archives department—till we checked our copy of the original #53, and discovered those two pages were reversed *there*, as well! Somehow, they even got *misnumbered* back in 1950—probably because both are pages on which Wonder Woman and Dr. Mid-Nite fight the forces of Attila the Hun. If we'd ever noticed that over the past half century plus, we'd totally forgotten it! We just wish we hadn't lost the name of the sharp-eyed reader who sent us that e-mail, 'cause we owe him a copy of this book!

P. 168: Craig Delich assures us that, though Frank Giacioa may be credited with the rest of Chapters I-II in *All-Star* #55, the splash page is the work of Arthur Peddy (pencils) and Bernard Sachs (inks).

While concurring with Ye Editor that Prof. Napier in *All-Star* #55 was almost certainly named after Edgar Rice Burroughs' hero Carson of Venus, whose real monicker was Carson Napier, Rich Morrissey noted that both John Broome and even ERB might have taken it from "Jack Napier... the actual name of the Scottish mathematician who invented logarithms and a calculation device with the delightfully Jokerish name of 'bones.'" Rich also observed that The

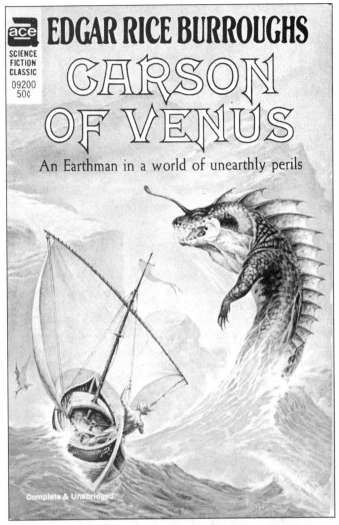

Venus, If You Will...

Undoubtedly the best art that ever graced Edgar Rice Burroughs' novels about Carson Napier was Frank Frazetta's cover for Carson of Venus, *a paperback issued by Ace Books in the 1960s. [Carson of Venus TM & © Edgar Rice Burroughs, Inc.]*

Joker was named Jack Napier in the 1989 *Batman* movie and the 1992 animated series, "but that name more likely came from the word 'jackanapes,' the fact that a Jack (like a Joker) is a playing-card, and/or the name of the actor in the role, Jack Nicholson."

P. 169: Re those "in-joke" posters in the background of two panels in *All-Star* #55, Murray Ward asks, "Could 'Ira Knox' be a reference to DC letterer Ira Schnapp, who might even have lettered that story?" Could be.

P. 171: Craig Delich and Roy Thomas both feel that the splash page of the JSA story in *All-Star* #57 is by Peddy (p) and Sachs (i), although the rest of the first chapter is credited to Frank Giacoia.

Rich Morrissey again, this time re *All-Star* #57: "Ironically enough, [scripter] John Broome would in a few years have the opportunity to write the adventures of the 'real' Charlie Chan... in a short-lived DC title." See Mike W. Barr's article on pp. 42-44.

P. 189: Re *Justice League of America* #123-124, we wrote in *Vol. 1* that the "evil Cary Bates" forced the Injustice Society to attempt to kill the JSA. Actually, he compelled the *JLA* to try to kill the JSAers, who were *disguised* as the Injustice Society at the time. A small but real distinction, pointed out by Tim Scotty.

Silver Years, Bronze Decades
The Justice Society In The 1960s & 1970s (Mostly)
by Roy Thomas

Though we're saving our gala coverage of DC's 1963-1985 Justice League-Justice Society team-ups and the 1970s JSA revival for the third and final volume of this series, we wanted to at least touch on those two blockbuster blocs of tales—if only to remind us all of what came in between the demise of the Golden Age *All-Star Comics* at the turn of 1951 and *All-Star Squadron*'s debut thirty years later. (Yes, we realize the last few JLA-JSA get-togethers occurred *after* the Squadron came along, but we think those annual confabs should still be treated as a unit.)

Actually, as we pointed out back in *Alter Ego* V3 #9 (July 2001), if the JSA hadn't lost its berth in the early 1950s, it might well have eventually inducted a few other DC heroes and wound up a more interesting organization than ever.

With that in mind, collector Michael Dunne recently commissioned an illustration by Golden/Silver Age Aquaman artist Ramona Fradon of what one version of such a 1950s Justice Society might have looked like—with regulars Green Lantern, Flash, Dr. Mid-Nite, and The Atom welcoming fellow DC stalwarts Aquaman and Green Arrow—not to mention Blackhawk, who became a DC hero at the start of 1957 when the Quality Comics Group went out of business. Just for the heck of it, Michael asked Ramona to toss in Dr. Fate, who even by 1951 had been in limbo for over half a dozen years. The result, we think, is an intriguing vision of what might have been….

RAMONA FRADON

[Characters © DC Comics.]

With that tantalizing glimpse of not-quite-history out of the way, it's time to whet your appetite for the goodies to come in *All-Star Companion, Vol. 3*, in the autumn of 2007. Here are a few key pages of Silver and Bronze Age wonderment, with art by some stellar talents, beginning with…

THE JUSTICE LEAGUE–JUSTICE SOCIETY TEAM-UPS

Since it was the first "two-Flashes" story, in *The Flash* #123 (Sept. 1961), that had ushered in the classic concept of Earth-Two, where the JSAers lived on a world parallel to that inhabited by the JLA—and since it was in *Flash* #137 (June 1963) that the JSA returned from limbo as a group—it seemed only fitting to begin this truncated section with a scene from *Justice League of America* #22 (Sept. 1963)—more or less.

Here, the Green Lanterns of two worlds rescue the Flashes of two worlds, as scripted by Gardner Fox, penciled by Mike Sekowsky, inked by Bernard Sachs, and edited by Julius Schwartz. This page, however, is reproduced from the *Mexican* edition of that story, which appeared in— *Batman* #239 (published for "8 de octubre de 1964"). As related by Fred Patten in *Alter Ego* #43 (Dec. 2004), the comic starring "El Hombre Murciélago" was then a *weekly* South of the Border, and alternated the contents of US issues of *Batman*, *Detective Comics*, *World's Finest Comics*, *The Flash*, *Green Lantern*, and *JLA*.

[© DC Comics.]

Although Mike Sekowsky was the original penciler of *Justice League of America* and drew the feature for its first eight years, it was his replacement, longtime *Blackhawk* artist Dick Dillin, who in the end would illustrate more issues of DC's flagship super-group than any other artist, beginning with *JLA* #64 (Aug. 1968).

(Right:) The original Green Lantern in a solo fight page from a JLA-JSA team-up in Justice League of America #73 (Aug. 1969). Script by Dennis O'Neil, art by Dick Dillin & Sid Greene. Repro'd from a photocopy of the original art, courtesy of Jerry G. Bails. [© DC Comics.]

Say "Big Red Cheese!"

(Left:) Who was left to have taken this "photo" of the Justice Society and other super-heroes of two worlds except Captain Marvel? The peerless Neal Adams, who contributed the classic cover for the JSA's belated origin tale in 1977's DC Special, Vol. 7, #29, had drawn the massed JSA once before—on the wraparound cover of DC 100-Page Super-Spectacular #6 (1971). Here's the back cover of that reprint issue, repro'd from a photocopy of the original art. Somehow, though, non-JSAers Johnny Quick, the second Red Tornado, and the Mrs. Peel-style Wonder Woman of Earth-One showed up here, while Dr. Mid-Nite, JSA/JLAer Black Canary, and the Earth-Two Wonder Woman sneaked onto the front half. Repro'd from a photocopy of the original art; donor, alas, unknown. [© DC Comics.]

Section B
ALL-STAR COMICS & THE JSA: THE 1970S REVIVAL

When writer/editor Gerry Conway revived *All-Star Comics* with a #58 having a Jan-Feb. 1976 cover date, the original penciler was Ric Estrada. The engaging Mr. Estrada did the commission drawing of Dr. Fate at left for collector Michael Zeno a few years back, and we thank them both for generously sharing it with us.

[Dr. Fate TM & © DC Comics.]

Estrada's two issues were inked by the legendary Wally Wood, and when Ric moved on after #59, Wally remained to embellish the pencils of newcomer Keith Giffin in #60-61. The splash at right is from #60 (May-June 1976).

The longest-running scripter of the 1970s JSA revival was Paul Levitz, now president and publisher of DC Comics—and the longest-running artist was Joe Staton, whom we saw selling pencils recently outside the Heroes Con in Charlotte, NC. No, just kidding—Joe's doing great, and looks back on his JSA stint with fondness. In fact, since he was the first artist ever to visualize the Levitz-conceived Huntress, daughter of Earth-Two's Batman, here's a sketch he did of her at that con in 2005 for the aforementioned Michael Dunne:

This page from *All-Star Comics* #68 (Sept.-Oct. 1977) by Levitz, Staton, and inker Bob Layton looks almost like a sequel to the Dillin/Greene sequence from *Justice League of America* #73 that we saw just two pages ago! At least, Green Lantern is again wielding a giant Power Ring-forged sword, even if this time it's against fellow JSAer Dr. Fate. Thanks to Brian H. Bailie for a photocopy of the original art.

See you in The All-Star Companion, Vol. 3!

CHAPTER XIII
WHO WAS WHO IN THE ALL-STAR SQUADRON (1941-1945)

ONLY THEIR BEST FRIENDS— AND WORST ENEMIES— KNOW FOR SURE!

Main Text by Pedro Angosto

Captions & Added Input by Roy Thomas

Appearance Info from Jerry G. Bails' *Collector's Guide: The First Heroic Age* (1969)

Jerry Ordway's cover of All-Star Squadron #31 (March 1984)—repro'd from a photocopy of the original art, courtesy of Jerry. [© DC Comics.]

*V*olume One of the Companion *featured mini-bios (with Golden Age appearances) for all 18 heroes of the 1940-1951 Justice Society of America (including one-timer Mr. Terrific and non-member Red Tornado). Those entries were written by those who knew the JSAers best: their confidants, paramours, spouses, and the like. This time around, we're listing the 70 stalwarts who appeared in* All-Star Squadron *and/or* The Young All-Stars *(since only a few characters were unique to the latter), plus a handful of heroes who—as Ye Editor should know, if anyone does—were mentally slated to appear eventually in one series or the other but never quite made it before the sands ran out. Most of the material in these bios is taken from their original 1940s appearances, but a few particulars have been added, where it made sense, from their exploits recorded in 1960s comics and later. We've tried, when possi-* ble, to include additional or qualifying information in the captions *that accompany the art. The majority of the characters for whom there are entries were published by DC/AA in the 1940s, but we have noted where described heroes were originally published by Quality, Fawcett, and even Charlton. —Roy.*

AIR WAVE

I'm **Static**, the pet parrot of the hero known as Air Wave. Give me a cracker, and I'll tell you his secret origin! *Mmmm...* yummy! Okay, here goes: **Larry Jordan** was a law clerk who decided he needed to do more to fight crime in New York City. He made a special helmet and belt that gave him electromagnetic powers. He could even ride the telephone wire lines with his rollerblades. In the long run, though, he went further in his law career, becoming District Attorney, than in his masked life as Air Wave. Give me another cracker, and I'll tell you about his son!

GOLDEN AGE APPEARANCES:

Detective Comics #60-137 (Feb. 1942 - July 1948) - no origin story

Air Wave and Static, from Detective Comics #118 (Dec. 1946). Though he showed up for a couple of meetings, Air Wave never played an active part in any All-Star Squadron adventures until #59-60. Art by Lee Harris. [© DC Comics.]

AMAZING-MAN

Dr. Terry Curtis here—maybe you know me better as the infamous **Cyclotron**. I've made lots of mistakes in my life, but in hiring **Will Everett** as janitor of my lab, I took the first step toward redemption. Will was a young athlete who, along with Jesse Owens, had won medals in the 1936 Berlin Olympics, putting Hitler's "Aryan supermen" to shame. My ill-fated alliance with The Ultra-Humanite resulted in an an electrogenerator giving Will the power to absorb the properties of any substance he touched. As Amazing-Man, he fought on Ultra's behalf till he realized the error of his ways and joined the All-Star Squadron instead. Several months later, his powers somehow mutated into magnetic ones. My little friend Al (Atom) Pratt's powers mutated, too... but that's another story....

GOLDEN AGE APPEARANCES:
None - first appearance and origin in *All-Star Squadron* #23 (May 1983)

Amazing-Man Times Two—Plus One!

(Left:) Bill Everett's hero of that name debuted in Centaur's Amazing-Man Comics #5 (Sept. 1939); seen here is the writer/artist's best (and final) cover for that mag, #11 (April 1940). The All-Star took his code name from the earlier character. [© the respective copyright holders.]

(Center:) Terry Curtis as Cyclotron in All-Star Squadron #21. Art by Jerry Ordway & Mike Machlan. [© DC Comics.]

(Above:) Roy Thomas christened the 1980s Amazing-Man Will Everett, in honor of his friend Bill E., who died in 1973. Co-creator Jerry Ordway provided photocopies of his original art for the 1980s Who's Who in the DC Universe. [© DC Comics.]

The Sub-Sea Supermen

(Above left:) Bill Everett's Timely origin of Prince Namor, the Sub-Mariner, premiered in Marvel Comics #1 (Oct. 1939)—or, likely, slightly earlier in the black-&-white giveaway Motion Picture Funnies Weekly #1. Figure from Human Torch #3 (Winter 1941), repro'd from photocopies of the original art. [© Marvel Characters, Inc.]

(Above center:) Another sub-oceanic stalwart, The Shark, first surfaced in Centaur's Amazing-Man #6 (Oct. 1939)—the same month as Sub-Mariner's four-color debut. Thanks to creator/writer/artist Louis Glanzman for art from A-M #10 (March 1940). [© the respective copyright holders.]

(Right:) Aquaman, scripted by Mort Weisinger and drawn by Paul Norris, didn't appear till two years after the preceding pair—but, to date, he's proven to have even better sea legs than Namor! DC's sea king never played an active part in any published All-Star Squadron tale. In Adventure Comics #120 (Sept. 1947) he went off to college—and took along a few finny friends. Art attributed to Louis Cazeneuve, script to Joe Samachson. In 1959 he was given a second, quite different origin (which, oddly, closely paralleled Subby's of 1939!) and the name Arthur Curry; but no birth-name was ever given for DC's "Earth-Two" Aquaman. [© DC Comics.]

AQUAMAN

I'm the **Captain** of a ship torpedoed by a Nazi submarine—the first surface-person to ever meet Aquaman and learn of his incredible origins. He told me his father was a famous undersea explorer who discovered a sunken city he identified as the fabled Atlantis. He made a water-tight home in one of its palaces and studied the records and devices of the extinct race's marvelous wisdom. From them he learned how to teach his son to live under the ocean, using the power of the sea to make him wonderfully strong and swift. Unfortunately, I never learned either Aquaman's real name, nor his father's.

GOLDEN AGE APPEARANCES:
More Fun Comics #73-107 (Nov. 1941 – Jan.-Feb. 1946) – origin in #73

World's Finest Comics #6 (Summer 1942)

Adventure Comics #103-117, 119-152, 154, 156, 158, 160, 162, 164, 167-68, 170-206+ (April 1946 – Nov. 1954+)

THE BLACK CONDOR

I am **Father Pierre**—or rather, I am the *spirit* of Father Pierre. As a missionary, I found the most amazing "noble savage" ever recorded. The infant **Richard Grey, Jr.**, was the only survivor of his parents' expedition to the Mongolian mountains. He was reared by wild black condors—who, even more incredibly, taught him to fly! (Maybe he really *was* a mutant, as some later chroniclers believe.) I found him and brought him back to civilization. Perhaps by divine design, I was killed soon thereafter, a crime which inspired him to become The Black Condor to avenge my death. You think you've heard it all? On his way to America, Richard discovered he bore a striking resemblance to a murdered US Senator, **Thomas Wright**, so he adopted his identity—and even his girlfriend, Wendy Foster. Only Wendy's father is in on his secret. Richard/Thomas flies through the clouds, so high that one day he'll reach Heaven.

GOLDEN AGE APPEARANCES:
Crack Comics #1-31 (May 1940 – Oct. 1943) – origin in #1
Uncle Sam Quarterly #2 (Winter 1940) – cameo in Uncle Sam

Fly Like An Eagle
Splash panel of a Golden Age Black Condor story from Hit Comics #6 (Nov. 1940)—drawn by Lou Fine, under Quality Comics' house name "Kenneth Lewis." [© DC Comics.]

BLACKHAWK (& THE BLACKHAWKS)

I'm **Blackie**, pet mascot of the Blackhawks. No, I wasn't a talking hawk, but if you can believe a man was taught to fly by condors, you should be able to believe a hawk can speak! **Blackhawk** (even *I* don't know his *real* name) was an aviator in the Polish Air Force at the time of the 1939 Nazi invasion. After his brother and sister died when a German plane bombed their farm, he formed a volunteer group of fighter pilots, composed of his fellow Pole **Stanislaus**, an American called **Chuck**, **Olaf** from Norway, Frenchman **André**, and **Hendrickson** from the Netherlands—with **Chop-Chop** gatecrashing from China a bit later. During World War II they operated out of the secret Blackhawk Island off the European coast in specially modified aircraft.

GOLDEN AGE APPEARANCES:
Military Comics #1-43 (Aug. 1941 – Oct. 1945) – origin in #1;
  [title changed to:] *Modern Comics* #44-102 (Nov. 1945 – Oct. 1950)
Blackhawk #9-107+ (Winter 1944 - Dec. 1956) – from #108 [Jan. 1957]
  on, title published by DC instead of Quality
Hit Comics #26 (Feb. 1943) – cameo with Kid Eternity

Fly Like A Hawk

Blackie the Hawk, a DC addition to the fabled aerial squadron, is seen above from Blackhawk #111 (April 1957); thanks to Michelle Nolan. However, all seven of the series' human aviators debuted in the feature's first year at Quality, as per the cover at left from Military Comics #17 (March 1943). From left to right are Blackhawk (grappling with Japanese soldier), Chop-Chop, Olaf, Hendrickson, Chuck, André, & Stanislaus. [© DC Comics.]

The Blackhawks' first identifiable fighter planes (seen at right as traced by Al Dellinges) were replaced by Saber-type jets after the end of World War II. The photo Al sent shows the experimental fighter craft on which they were based: the Grumman XP-50 Skyrocket, which never actually flew in combat. This model was the XF5F-1. [Blackhawk art © DC Comics; photo © the respective copyright holders.]

Captain Marvel splash page with character origin summary:

CHOSEN TO RECEIVE THE POWERS OF SIX MIGHTY ELDERS, YOUNG NEWSCASTER BILLY BATSON HAS ONLY TO SPEAK THE NAME OF THE ANCIENT WIZARD...

SHAZAM!

AND IN A FLASH OF LIGHTNING, HE IS TRANSFORMED INTO THE WORLD'S MIGHTIEST MORTAL...

CAPTAIN MARVEL!

SOLOMON-WISDOM
HERCULES-STRENGTH
ATLAS-STAMINA
ZEUS-POWER
ACHILLES-COURAGE
MERCURY-SPEED

I AM MR. TAWNY, THE *TALKING TIGER!* AND BELIEVE IT OR NOT, IT'S BECAUSE OF ME THAT CAPTAIN MARVEL IS BATTLING THE MOST INCREDIBLY POWERFUL VILLAIN OF HIS CAREER!

YOU SEE, THAT MAN DISCOVERED A *SECRET* ABOUT ME--ONE THAT WAS PARTICULARLY DANGEROUS --SINCE EVEN I MYSELF DID NOT KNOW...

The Secret of Mr. Tawny

E. NELSON BRIDWELL WRITER
DON NEWTON, PENCILLER
KURT SCHAFFENBERGER, INKER
SHELLY LEFERMAN LETTERER
ADRIENNE ROY COLORIST

Captains Courageous—And Outrageous

At right, Captain Nazi shows why he hates the Big Red Cheese, in Fawcett's Captain Marvel Adventures #22 (March '43). Script by Otto Binder, art by C.C. Beck, from the 1943-45 "Monster Society of Evil" serial, as reprinted in part in the hardcover Shazam! from the 30's to the 70's.

Above is the more realistically-drawn version of Cap published by DC in World's Finest Comics #259 (Oct.-Nov. 1979), which influenced his guest turns in the 1980s All-Star Squadron. The Don Newton art is repro'd from a b&w Australian reprint comic; thanks to Mark Muller. [© DC Comics.]

CAPTAIN MARVEL

It was late at night. Young **Billy Batson** was still on the streets selling newspapers when I beckoned him to follow me down into an abandoned subway station. There, a special train took us to a cavern where he was welcomed by an old man on a marble throne. When Billy uttered the old man's name—*Shazam*—magic lightning struck the boy, turning him into Captain Marvel. The lad soon had to use his newfound powers as Captain Marvel (Solomon's wisdom, Hercules' strength, Atlas' stamina, Zeus' power, Achilles' courage, and Mercury's speed) to battle Dr. Sivana. Billy himself got a job as a radio reporter. He was never a member of the All-Star Squadron, but did join them for an adventure or two from his own parallel world, known as Earth-S. As for who I am, I am only—a **Stranger**. (Though there are those who claim I was actually old Shazam himself—and I'm far too polite to argue with them.)

OWW! MY WRIST! MEN! MEN! *DO SOMETHING,* FOOLS! HE'S AMPUTATING MY WRIST---OWWW!

LONG TIME NO SEE, CAPTAIN NAZI! TELL ME, ABOUT YOURSELF!

GOLDEN AGE APPEARANCES:

Whiz Comics #2 (actually the first issue)-155 (Feb. 1940 – Jan. 1953) - origin in #2
Special Edition Comics (1940)
Captain Marvel Adventures #1-150 (1941 – Nov. 1953)
Captain Marvel Thrill Book #1 (1941)
America's Greatest Comics #1-8 (1941 – Summer 1943)
Master Comics #21 & #50 (Dec. 1941, May 1944)
Marvel Family #1-89 (Dec. 1945 – Jan. 1954)
Captain Marvel Miniature (Wheaties giveaway, 1946)
Whiz Miniature (Wheaties giveaway, 1946)
Captain Marvel Dime Action Book (1941) (similar to Big Little Books)
Gift Comics #1-4 (1941-49 – reprints)
Xmas Comics #1-7 (1941-52 – reprints)
Holiday Comics #1 (1942 – reprints)
Fawcett Miniatures (c. Jan. 1943 – reprints)
Captain Marvel (miniature) (c. Jan. 1943, reprints)
Captain Marvel Story Book #1-4 (Summer 1946 – 1948)
Daisy Handbook #2 (1948 – reprints)
Captain Marvel and the Good Humor Man (1940)
Captain Marvel and the Lieutenants of Safety (1950-51, two issues).

CAPTAIN MARVEL JR.

I am **Albrecht Krieger**, proudly christened **Captain Nazi** by Adolf Hitler himself. This is a story with a clear moral: never leave your business unfinished. I was fighting Captain Marvel when he knocked me into the sea. Saved by an old man, I killed him in "thanks" and crippled his teenage grandson for life. That was my *big* mistake, because Captain Marvel took young **Freddy Freeman** to the wizard Shazam and, though the old mage was unable to heal him, he gave him the power to become Captain Marvel Jr. by shouting aloud his hero's name: "Captain Marvel!" But he soon proved he wasn't a match for me, as he needed the help of Bulletman to defeat me. He never really got to join the All-Star Squadron, either. *Hah!*

GOLDEN AGE APPEARANCES:

Whiz Comics #25 (Dec. 1941) – origin in #25 in Captain Marvel story
Master Comics #23-133 (Feb. 1942 – April 1953)
Captain Marvel Jr. #1-119 (Nov. 1942 – June 1953)
All Hero Comics #1 (March 1943)
America's Greatest Comics #8 (Summer 1943)
Marvel Family #1-89 (Dec. 1945 – Jan. 1954)
Gift Comics #? (reprints)
Xmas Comics #? (reprints)
Fawcett Miniatures c. Jan. 1943 (reprints)
Captain Marvel Jr. c. Jan. 1943 (reprints).

Shazam, Jr.

Captain Marvel Jr., drawn by Mac Raboy, from an early-'40s Fawcett story reprinted in the 1977 hardcover book Shazam! from the 30's to the 70's. [© DC Comics.]

CAPTAIN TRIUMPH

I'm **Kim Meredith**, fiancée of **Michael Gallant**. Michael was a pilot during World War II and had a twin brother, **Lance**. On their fateful 23rd birthday in late 1942, Michael perished when his hangar was sabotaged. Lance and I were horrified. Lance swore vengeance, and soon the ghost of his dead brother showed him how to obtain it. By touching the mysterious T-shaped birthmark they shared, Lance could merge their spirits, turning into the powerful Captain Triumph. Later, I discovered the strange destiny of my dead lover and I helped him, as did his friend Biff, a circus clown. Captain Triumph never got any closer to membership in the All-Star Squadron than having his photo lying on a table on a comic book cover, but if their stories had ever reached the point of late 1942, I'm sure he'd have been ready and willing!

GOLDEN AGE APPEARANCES:
Crack Comics #27-62 (Jan. 1943 – Sept. 1949) – origin in #27

Triumph And Tragedy

(Left:) A Golden Age Captain Triumph splash—with art by the great Reed Crandall, or else by someone who'd learned to swipe his style cold! Actually, All-Star Squadron ended its run before CT's late-1942 debut allowed this Quality hero to make an appearance—but he was seen in a "photo" on the cover of issue #1. Repro'd from an Oz b&w reprint, thanks to Michael Baulderstone. [© DC Comics.]

CAPTAIN X OF THE R.A.F.

Hey, dudes, I'm **Ronnie Raymond**, better half of the hero you knew as Firestorm. And no, *I* wasn't a member of the All-Star Squadron, either. But guess what? My *grandfather* may have been! **Richard "Buck" Dare**, a reporter for the *Tribute*, an American newspaper published in England, became an aviator for the secret organization called The Group, because he was intent on helping the British before the USA entered the war. As Captain X, he fought Nazis in top-secret missions behind enemy lines, flying his experimental plastic plane christened *Jenny*, which was always ready, thanks to his grease-monkey Stuffy. Perhaps his as-yet-unpublished diaries will reveal that some of those missions were alongside the All-Star Squadron.

GOLDEN AGE APPEARANCES:
Star Spangled Comics #1-7 (Oct. 1941 – April 1942) – no origin

"X" Marks the Spot

(Center right & near right:) Captain X goes into action—and so does his "plastic plane" Jenny—in Star Spangled Comics #6 (March 1942), in a tale that pre-dated the Japanese attack on Pearl Harbor that brought America into World War II. Thanks to Bob Hughes for the scan. [© DC Comics.]

(Far right:) Those real-life aviator heroes the RAF (Royal Air Force) fought the Battle of Britain in 1940, flying Hurricanes and Spitfires. The Spitfire Mark XII, seen here, had a more powerful Rolls-Royce engine than earlier models, plus other features to improve its performance between 5000 to 18,000 feet. [Photo © the respective copyright holders.]

SORRY... I'M NATTERING AWAY...JUST A BIT NERVOUS...

BY THE TIME I RETURN TO LONDON, I'M SURE WE'LL BE FAST FRIENDS.

COMMANDER STEEL

This is **Winston Churchill**, Prime Minister of Great Britain from 1940-1945, speaking to you from the Beyond about Steel the Indestructible Man—a tale of triumph and tragedy. It is by people such as he that the war was won. His tragic origin is recorded in his secret journal: Biology student **Hank Heywood** joined the US Marines after Germany invaded Poland. While fighting saboteurs trying to blow up his camp's ammunition dump, he was caught in a terrible explosion. His mentor Dr. Gilbert Giles used their joint discovery, the "Bio-Retardant," to surgi-cally replace his damaged limbs and organs with steel alloy tubing, micro-motors, and an artificial lung. And so the super-hero called Steel was born. When he saved my life *twice* after joining the All-Star Squadron, my good friend President Roosevelt promoted him to "*Commander* Steel." I really should have mentioned him in my monumental multi-volume work *The Second World War*, but so much about him is still classified.

GOLDEN AGE APPEARANCES:

None –*Steel the Indestructible Man* #1-5 (March-Nov. 1978) – origin in #1

Blood, Toil, Sweat, And Steel

(Above:) Winston Churchill has popped up in many a comic book since 1940. Here, he charms Miss America as Captain America and The Human Torch look on, at a June 1942 rendezvous with President Roosevelt, in Giant-Size Invaders #2 (2005). Art by Lee Weeks; script by Roy Thomas. [© Marvel Characters, Inc.]

(Right:) Along with Captain America, one visual influence on Steel's costume may have been that of Simon & Kirby's mid-1950s Fighting American. [© Joe Simon & Estate of Jack Kirby.]

(Top right:) Steel in his pre-"Commander" days, from Steel the Indestructible Man #1 (March 1978). Art by Don Heck & Joe Giella; script by Gerry Conway. [© DC Comics.]

THE CRIMSON AVENGER & WING

The Martians are coming! ... Got you again, eh? This is **Orson Welles** speaking to you, likewise from the Beyond. On the infamous night of Oct. 30, 1938, while I was terrifying America with my "War of the Worlds" radio broadcast, *Daily Globe-Leader* publisher **Lee Travis** attended a Halloween costume party dressed in slouch hat, mask, and trenchcoat. When armed robbers killed one of the guests, Travis, a veteran of the Spanish Civil War of 1936-39, brought them to justice, aided by his faithful Oriental valet **Wing**. The Crimson (as he was originally called) became one of the very first masked mystery-men; later he donned a form-fitting costume and joined both the Seven Soldiers of Victory and the All-Star Squadron. I enjoyed writing and playing his role on the *Crimson Avenger* radio program... until I had to resign to work on a film project. Its name? *Citizen Kane.*

GOLDEN AGE APPEARANCES:

Detective Comics #20-29, 37-89 (Oct. 1938-July 1939; March 1940-July 1944) – no origin story - new costume in #44 –Wing becomes C.A.'s costumed aide in #59

World's Best Comics #1 (Sept. 1941)

World's Finest Comics #2-5 (Summer 1941 – Sept. 1942) – Wing in #4-5

Leading Comics #1-14 (Winter 1942 – Sept. 1945) as members of Seven Soldiers of Victory

THE CRIMSON RETURNS THE GANG'S FIRE WITH ACCURATE SHOTS AT THE TIRES.

WE NO TAKE HAND, WE GIVE FOOT!

THE AVENGER'S FLAMING SWORD, PRODUCED BY A SPECIAL CHEMICAL, STRIKES PANIC INTO THE HEARTS OF THE STARTLED THUGS!

HEY-- WHAT...

Martians And Masked Men

(Above:) Orson Welles as Brutus in Julius Caesar, 1937. For Halloween of the next year, he and his Mercury Theatre on the Air scared much of the nation with their ultra-realistic radio broadcast about invaders from Mars.

(Above right:) The "Green Hornet" phase of The Crimson Avenger, from Detective Comics #22 (Dec. 1938). He was even on that issue's cover—and Batman was still five months away! Art by Jim Chambers. [© DC Comics.]

(Bottom right:) The costumed Crimson Avenger and Wing attack, in Detective #78 (Aug. 1943). The "flaming sword" insignia was a temporary gimmick. Art by John Lehti. [© DC Comics.]

DR. OCCULT

I am **Zator**, disciple of The Seven, a brotherhood of mystics. On New Year's Eve, 1899, I rescued two infants being sacrificed to the evil entity Koth and took them to the secret citadel of The Seven, where they were reared and their mystic potential developed. In 1935 they returned to civilization as **Dr. Richard Occult** (some accounts say his real name was Osgood Armsby) and Rose Psychic, opening a detective agency specializing in the paranormal. "The Ghost Detective" battled vampires, ghosts, zombies, werewolves, and mystical cults, but his greatest battle was against Koth. At that time, The Seven gave him a costume and sword, and he became perhaps the first "costumed hero." He always triumphed over evil with the help of Rose and the powerful amulet of The Seven.

GOLDEN AGE APPEARANCES:
New Fun Comics #6-7 (Oct. – Nov. 1935) – no origin
More Fun Comics #8-33 (Dec. 1935 – July 1938)

Fighting Evil Till Their Heads Hurt

Dr. Occult and his mystic mentor Zator, in a panel from a late-1930s issue of More Fun Comics. Script by Jerry Siegel; art by Joe Shuster. [© DC Comics.]

These Heroes Don't Shrink From Danger

(Above:) The original size-shrinking comics hero was Tiny Tim, in a newspaper strip begun in 1933 by Stanley Link; seen here is the cover of a 1937 Big Little Book that adapted one of his adventures. [© the respective copyright holders.]

(Right:) Quality's Doll Man packed a mean punch even when pint-sized. This 1940s story was reprinted in Australian b&w comics in the '70s from earlier DC reprints—with thanks to Michael Baulderstone. [© DC Comics.]

THE DOLL MAN

I, **Professor Roberts**, was an amazed witness to the birth of the diminutive Doll Man. I suggested to chemist **Darrell Dane** that he might use *aqua regia* to reduce a formula he had discovered to a fluid state. Little did I dream he'd try it on himself, and be shrunk for brief periods to under a foot in height, though with the strength of twenty men! He was briefly disoriented, but was soon returned to his senses by his fiancée, my daughter Martha. He devoted himself to a crusade against crime and became a member of the All-Star Squadron during the war. Some years later, my dear Martha tried the shrinking formula, too, becoming Doll Girl and sharing his adventures—which were many, for Doll Man was only small in size, not in courage.

GOLDEN AGE APPEARANCES:
Feature Comics #27-139 (Dec. 1939 – Oct. 1949) – origin in #27
Doll Man #1-47 (Fall 1941 – Oct. 1953)

THE FIREBRAND

You can call me **Slugger**—everybody does, since even before I became a prize-fighter. Hey, don't run away—I'm not gonna tell ya sad stories about washed-up boxers dyin' in back alleys. I got lucky and left that life for a better one as the gofer of **Rod Reilly**, who was born with a silver spoon in his mouth—plus a knife and fork to go with it! After that playboy made me teach 'im how to fight, he spent his spare time as a masked character called The Firebrand, battlin' crooks just for the thrill of it! But his career got cut short when he was wounded durin' the Japanese attack on Pearl Harbor. His sister Danette took his place—and then some! Later he recovered and joined the All-Star Squadron and the Freedom Fighters, but if ya ask me, the only time we had fun was when we ran into Wildcat. That guy really knows how ta throw a right hook!

GOLDEN AGE APPEARANCES:
Police Comics #1-13 (Aug. 1941 – Nov. 1942) – no origin story

Fire When Ready!

The original Firebrand appeared in Quality's Police Comics; Reed Crandall art at left from #6 (Jan. 1942), repro'd from AC Comics' America's Greatest Comics #9 (2004). Above, Rod Reilly and Slugger Dunn in US Navy uniform, in Police Comics #10 (Feb. '42), in a story attributed to Lee Ames, as per AC's Men of Mystery Comics #23 (2000). [Firebrand TM & © DC Comics.]

FIREBRAND (II)

Time is like dominos: hit one and all the rest will fall. No one knows this better than I, **Per Degaton**. I've tried to conquer the present by changing events in the past, only to be defeated time and time again. Once, the JSA lay defeated at my feet, yet there was a domino I had failed to reckon with: **Danette Reilly**, vulcanologist sister of Rod Reilly, the original Firebrand. In December 1941, Destiny placed her on the volcanic island where I'd set up a hidden base. My lackey Wotan knocked her into molten lava with a magic bolt. Some combination of those two things caused her, days later, to burst into flame, even to fly. She assumed her wounded brother's identity as a new, super-powered Firebrand, and joined the alliance of heroes that my schemes of world conquest had unwittingly helped assemble: the All-Star Squadron. But now that I know their origins from these pages, I'll discover what events I must change to prevent their ever joining forces. This Degaton swears!

Come On, Baby, Light My Fire!

GOLDEN AGE APPEARANCES:

None – debut (as Danette Reilly) in *All-Star Squadron Preview* in *Justice League of America* #193 (Sept. 1981); becomes Firebrand in *All-Star Squadron* #5 (Jan. 1982)

(Above:) In All-Star Squadron #2, Danette Reilly gained power over flame, and assumed her wounded brother's code-name. Script by Roy Thomas; art by Rich Buckler & Jerry Ordway. [© DC Comics.]

(Right:) The original four-color flamethrowers: The Human Torch and Toro, as drawn by creator Carl Burgos in HT #4 (Spring 1941). Repro'd from Photostats of the original art. [© Marvel Characters, Inc.]

FLYING FOX

From the Land of the Hunt That Does Not End, I, **Arak, Son of Thunder**, son of He-No the Sky Father, warrior of Charlemagne, still watch over my vanished tribe, the Quontauka. When the Nazis came to our lands, in the country known as Canada, and killed the chief of the tribe to which I had belonged centuries before, I chose my descendant, the chief's son, to be the defender of our people as **Flying Fox**. He was given the mantle of that beast, a fox emblem was painted onto his chest, and he gained powers over the wind. He helped The Young All-Stars, a youthful band within the All Star Squadron, to defeat the evil Axis Amerika. By sword or by magic, my descendants will remain among the defenders of the mortal world until the end of times.

GOLDEN AGE APPEARANCES:

None – first appeared in *The Young All-Stars* #1 (June 1987) – origin in #20 (Jan. 1989)

Return Of The Native (Americans)

(Center:) Arak lived and fought at the turn of the 9th century AD, as per the cover figure from Arak, Son of Thunder #1 (Sept. 1981; art by Ernie Colón & Dick Giordano)—while Flying Fox (center right) debuted in The Young All-Stars #1 (June 1987), with art by Brian Murray & Malcolm Jones III. Script for both by Roy Thomas. [© DC Comics.]

(Bottom right:) RT's inspiration for introducing a hero called Flying Fox to replace Batman in the post-Crisis, no-WWII-Batman DC Universe was the fact that a "flying fox" is a type of bat, and that name had once been used as a secret ID by a young Bruce Wayne in a Batman story. But DC's first "Flying Fox" was an aviator (real name, Rex Darrell) who soared in More Fun Comics #37 (Nov. 1938) and four more stories over the ensuing six months. This art, from one of those tales, is by Terry Gilkison; thanks to Jerry G. Bails & Hames Ware. [© DC Comics.]

FURY

Enter Hades, O mortal, and hear a story that began long before the Trojan War. We are the ancient goddesses **Alecto**, **Megaera**, and **Tisiphone**—**The Furies** who punish deeds of evil. The young Greek girl **Helena Kosmatos** came to the Aeropagus, crying out to us for revenge upon her brother, who had collaborated with the Nazi invaders of her land. The touch of Tisiphone's scythe turned her into our armor-covered mortal incarnation. But her vengeance came at a price—for now, in moments of wrath, she became possessed by the unstoppable death-lust of that Blood Avenger. Helena was taken back to America by Johnny Chambers and Libby Lawrence, where she joined The Young All-Stars. Yet she was taken over by Tisiphone time and time again. Little happiness shall she find in her life, for the touch of The Furies is one that reaches out across generations.

GOLDEN AGE APPEARANCES:

None – first appeared (with origin) in *Secret Origins* #12 (March 1987)

Hell Hath No Fury... Or Maybe It Does

(Left:) This 4th-century BC Greek amphora illustrates a scene from Sophocles' tragedy *Electra*, wherein a sister and brother slay their mother—but only after she killed their father. Fair is fair! Flanking the top of the pillar, above the three human figures, float two of the three Furies. (You guess which two!) The vase itself is flanked above by Helena Cosmatos as Fury—and on the right by the blood-mad Tisiphone whom she turned into in moments of extreme stress or wrath. Art by Brian Murray & Malcolm Jones III, from *The Young All-Stars* #3 (Aug. 1987); and by Howard Simpson & Malcolm Jones III from #13 (June 1988), respectively. [Comic art © DC Comics.]

THE GAY (OR IS IT GRIM?) GHOST

My name was... *is* **Deborah Wallace**, and I have lived two lives by that name—or so my phantom lover says. Born Keith Everet, Earl of Strethmere, in Ireland, he was killed by rogues in 1700 while on his way to meet an ancestor of mine who shared my name. His spirit haunted Connaught Castle until, in 1941, I inherited it and visited it with my fiancé **Charles Collins**. Sadly, Charles was killed by Nazis who hoped to use it as their base. Keith's ghost entered his dying body and felled the spies, taking the name The Gay Ghost—though some later preferred to call him the very opposite of that: The Grim Ghost. In America, I learned I was a reincarnation of his long-dead beloved. He may even have helped the All-Star Squadron in some adventures; but, since he was invisible and immaterial, perhaps they never suspected!

GOLDEN AGE APPEARANCES:

Sensation Comics #1-33, 38 (Jan. 1942 – Feb. 1945)
  – origin in #1
Comic Cavalcade #4 (Fall 1943)

The Ghost Goes To DC

(Left:) Many plot elements for The Gay Ghost's origin had their inspiration in the 1936 United Artists film *The Ghost Goes West*, a fantasy comedy starring Robert Donat, directed by René Clair from a script by playwright Robert E. Sherwood. [© United Artists or its successors in interest.]

(Right:) The Gay Ghost goes grimly into action in *Sensation Comics* #1. Script by Gardner Fox, art by Howard Purcell. [© DC Comics.]

THE GHOST PATROL

Heil Hitler! This is **Captain Buehler**, reporting to the Nazi Office of Paranormal Studies. Three pilots of the French Foreign Legion—**Fred, Pedro, and Slim,** by name—died to prevent the bombing of some native villages in North Africa that I had ordered. Incredible as it may seem, since their deaths, there have been many reports of paranormal activities and of poltergeists fighting against the Army of the Third Reich, somehow connected to the spirits of these three dead airmen. Please send one of *Der Führer's* occult specialists to investigate the truth of this reports and counteract them, if possible.

GOLDEN AGE APPEARANCES:

Flash Comics #29-65, 69-104 (May 1942 – Feb. 1949) –
   origin in #29
Comic Cavalcade #1-2 (Winter 1943 – Spring 1943)
Big All-American Comic Book (1944)
Flash Comics Wheaties Giveaway (6½" x 8¼" giveaway) 1946.

Chasing Adolf

The Ghost Patrol from Flash Comics #40 (April 1943). Art by Frank Harry; script was by sometime AA (and All-Star) story editor Ted Udall. RT never quite got around to featuring them in Squadron. [© DC Comics.]

Slings And Arrows

(Above left:) Even though its title character was the villain, the 1940 Green Archer movie serial of 1940 was probably the inspiration for The Green Arrow—along with Robert Louis Stevenson's novel The Black Arrow and maybe a friendly traffic light. [© the respective copyright holders.]

(Above right:) GA and Speedy tackle crooks with trick arrows in this (circa 1950?) panel from an Oz b&w reprint comic, sent by Mark Muller. Art by George Papp? [© DC Comics.]

GREEN ARROW & SPEEDY

Holy copycats! It's **Robin** here, the original Boy Wonder! After I started fighting beside Batman, a legion of boy sidekicks were acquired by other mystery-men of the day. But two of them went too far! We had the Batmobile, so they had the Arrowplane (which was actually just a car); we had the Batplane, so they turned the Arrowplane into a *real* plane; and so it went, right down the line! Millionaire **Oliver Queen** found young **Roy Harper** stranded on the Lost Mesa with his servant Quoag, after a plane crash. Queen was looking for Native American artifacts, but instead he found crooks searching for a gold mine. He and Harper defeated them with bows and arrows and have kept on fighting crime as Green Arrow and Speedy. Batman and I have yet to run into them outside an All-Star Squadron meeting—but when we do, we'll show them who're the originals, and who're the copycats!

GOLDEN AGE APPEARANCES:

More Fun Comics #73-107 (Nov. 1941 – Jan-Feb. 1946) – no origin
   for GA till 1950s; origin of team in #89
Leading Comics #1-14 (Winter 1942 – Spring 1945) as members of
   Seven Soldiers of Victory
World's Finest Comics #7-70+ (Feb. 1942-May-June 1954+)
Adventure Comics #103-205, 207+ (April 1946 – Dec. 1954+).

THE GUARDIAN

Ladies and gentlemen, I'm **Anthony Rodriguez**, often addressed as **"Big Words"** by my quasi-literate companions, the remainder of the Newsboy Legion. They hawk newspapers all day on big city street corners, but clearly they rarely try *reading* one! I am present and accounted for to elucidate about the bemasked hero who constantly watches over our lives, keeping us out of harm's way: The Guardian. We suspect him of being our actual *legal* guardian, police officer **Jim Harper**, who (we believe) has adopted a costumed identity so he can better fight dastardly dealings in our underprivileged neighborhood, popularly known as Suicide Slum. You need not be a boy genius such as myself to notice that The Guardian's shield is shaped like a police badge!

GOLDEN AGE APPEARANCES:

Star Spangled Comics #7-57 (April 1942 – June 1946), #59-63
   (Aug. 1946 - Dec. 1946) – origin in #7
Boy Commandos #1 (Winter 1942-43) – cameo in BC story

Accompanied By A (Foster) Parent Or Guardian

The Newsboy Legion act "The Proud Poppas" to a sick pal as The Guardian looks on, as per the Joe Simon & Jack Kirby cover of Star Spangled Comics #35 (Aug. 1944). Big Words, of course, is the kid with the glasses; the other three, from left, are Scrapper, Gabby, and Tommy. [© DC Comics.]

YES, THAT'S WOO WOO BALI-- SHE WAS A SOUTH SEA ISLAND DANCER BEFORE SHE GOT TOO PLUMP AND LOST HER JOB!

A Hop Across The Ocean

(Left:) The most famous comic strip aviator was Smilin' Jack, created by Zack Mosely in 1933—a feature which lasted 40 years! [© Chicago Tribune-New York News Syndicate, or its successors in interest.]

(Below:) Hop Harrigan (at the controls) and his mechanic Tank Tinker track a "sea serpent" in All-American Comics #84 (April 1947). Art (and probably story) by the characters' creator, Jon L. Blummer. Odd that Hop had his own radio show for years, but DC/AA never tried him out in his own solo comic. RT had unrealized plans to turn him into the All-Stars' pilot—but only managed to shoehorn him into The Young All-Stars #8. [© DC Comics.]

WOW! FULL THROTTLE! LET'S SEE...

IT-IT **IS** A SEA SERPENT! LOOK AT IT COIL, UNCOIL AND STRIKE WITH ITS BEAK! THE NAGANTIC'S STOVE IN!

HOP HARRIGAN

I'm **Prop Wash**, a pilot. I knew young teenage whiz kid **Hop Harrigan**, son of Col. Harrigan, who had died in a plane crash. Poor Hop was raised by cruel farmer Silas Crane. But he soon taught himself how to fly and streaked off in his dad's old biplane. He saved mechanic Tank Tinker, and they both became my friends. Soon we founded our own airplane construction company. Hop had lots of airborne adventures and was a pilot for the USA during World War II. He even briefly took the costumed identity of The Guardian Angel, and may even have joined the All-Star Squadron on a secret mission or two, for all I know. Nobody tells me anything!

GOLDEN AGE APPEARANCES:

All-American Comics #1-99 (April 1939 – July 1948) – origin as Hop in #1 – becomes *The Guardian Angel* #25-28

World's Finest Comics #4 (Winter 1942)

Green Lantern #8-11 (Summer 1943 – Sept. 1944)

Comic Cavalcade #3-9, 11-26 (Summer 1943 – April-May 1948)

Big All-American Comic Book (1944)

Flash Comics #66-68 (Aug.-Sept. 1945 – Dec.-Jan. 1946-47)

Also appeared in text stories in early issues of *Green Lantern*, *All-Star Comics*, *Wonder Woman*, et al.

POLICE COMICS   PAGE 57

THE HUMAN BOMB

Bomb's Away!

Splash page from Quality's Police Comics #21 (Aug. 1943). "Paul Carrol" was a pen name of artist Paul Gustavson, who earlier had co-created The Angel at Timely/Marvel and The Fantom of the Fair at Centaur. [© DC Comics.]

THE HUMAN BOMB

Hey, I'm **Hustace Throckmorton**, the famous sidekick of The Human Bomb. Well, at least *one* of them, if you count those kids, the Bombardiers. **Roy Lincoln** was a chemist who assisted his father in developing the explosive labeled 27-QRX. When foreign agents tried to get hold of the compound by killing his father, Roy swallowed it. His hands began to glow, and he could cause anything he touched to explode. He defeated the Nazis and designed gloves of fibro-wax to contain his power. Adding a full suit and helmet, he became The Human Bomb. Later on, I got to acquire the same powers—not in my hands, but in my *feet!* So I got a *kick* out of fighting crime!

GOLDEN AGE APPEARANCES:
Police Comics #1-58 (Aug. 1941 – Sept. 1946) – origin in #1

WILDFIRE
BY JIM MOONEY AND ROBT. TURNER

DURING A GREAT FOREST FIRE THAT KILLED HER PARENTS CAROL VANCE RECEIVED FROM THE GOD OF FIRE, THE POWER TO COMMAND AND CONTROL ALL FLAMES. ADOPTED BY MR. AND MRS. JOHN MARTIN, SHE NOW GOES FORTH SECRETLY AS WILDFIRE, PRINCESS OF FLAMES, TO USE HER GREAT POWERS TO FIGHT THE FORCES OF EVIL!

IT IS NIGHT OUTSIDE THE SMALL TOWN OF PLEASANTVILLE. "MEN OF THE FIRE CULT IT IS TIME TO STRIKE!"

"WE ARE READY, MASTER!"

THEN INTO THE ARMORED TRUCK AND PREPARE THE FLAME-THROWER!

INSIDE THE HUGE ARMORED TRUCK.

THE FEED-FURNACE IS WELL STOKED!

THEN START THE TRUCK AND LET'S ROLL INTO PLEASANTVILLE!

THE INVISIBLE HOOD

I'm **Wildfire**, one of that scarce species, a super-heroine of the Golden Age. I never got to join the All Star Squadron (I suspect Firebrand kept me out because I'm so much like her!)— so I'm here to tell you about another hero who didn't "appear" there too often, either: The Invisible Hood, a.k.a. Invisible Justice. **Kent Thurston** donned a hooded robe treated with a secret chemical that allowed him to become invisible and fight crime. But his career was cut short, and anyway he would probably never have amounted to much, since invisibility isn't much of a power compared to Superman, The Spectre, and company!

NOW TO TURN OFF THE POWER—HOPE CHUCK IS DOING HIS PART!

GOLDEN AGE APPEARANCES:
Smash Comics #1-32 (Aug. 1939 – March 1942) – origin in #1 – called "Invisible Justice" in early issues, later changed to "Invisible Hood."

Flames And Phantoms

(Left:) Wildfire was the self-styled "Princess of Flames" in Quality's Smash Comics #25-37 in 1941-42. This Jim Mooney-drawn splash is from #31 (Feb. 1942), as reprinted with retouching and gray tones added in AC's Men of Mystery #29 (2001). [Retouched art © AC Comics.]

(Above right:) This Quality hero was still called Invisible Justice in Smash Comics #9 (Feb. 1941). [© DC Comics.]

"IRON" MUNRO

I, **Hugo Danner**, was born the world's first recorded super-human, after my father injected my expectant mother with an experimental serum. My titanic strength brought me only grief, so I staged my own death and hid out in a lost world on a South American plateau. But my earlier one-night liaison with my college sweetheart Anna Blake Munro led to the birth of **Arnold (Arn) Munro**, who inherited half my strength and invulnerability. When "Iron" Munro was eighteen, he saved the kid super-hero Dyna-Mite from Nazi saboteurs and joined him and others as that All-Star Squadron appendage, The Young All-Stars. He even found my diary, learned his origins, and tracked down myself and the natives I had turned into my powerful Sons of Dawn. The latter perished in an Armageddon against the All-Star Squadron. I faked my death again and disappeared, plotting from the shadows the true destiny of my heir....

KKRAAKSH!

SKRRJTCH

GOLDEN AGE APPEARANCES:
None – first appeared in *The Young All-Stars* #1 (June 1987) – origin told in #11

Men Of Iron And Steel

(Above right:) Arn Munro stops a car the hard way in The Young All-Stars #1. His name was derived from the hero of John W. Campbell, Jr's, 1934 "future superman" novel The Mightiest Machine, first serialized in Street & Smith's Astounding science-fiction pulp magazine. That Munro (whose first name was spelled "Aarn") had great powers on Earth because he'd grown up in the terrific gravity on Jupiter! Later, S&S used the name Iron Munro for a space-opera feature in its Army and Navy Comics. (Yes, you read right!) Art by Michael Bair, Brian Murray, & Malcolm Jones, III.

(Bottom right:) Hugo Danner was the super-powered protagonist of Philip Wylie's 1930 novel Gladiator, which circumstantial evidence suggests was an influence on Siegel & Shuster's Superman. This art, by Lou Manna & Bob Downs, is from YAS #28. Script by Roy Thomas. [© DC Comics.]

SURE I WILL. WHY SHOULDN'T I?

IT'S HUGO DANNER!

NEXT: GLADIATOR AND SONS!

YOWWWW!

THOSE BRICKS HURT YOUR HAND? YOU SHOULD HAVE USED YOUR HEAD!

THE JESTER

I'm **Bobo Benetti**, but you better not call me that. Me, I've fought against lotsa Golden Age heroes, but The Jester was one'a the few I fought alongside. He was just a rookie cop in New York City, name of **Chuck Lane**, who decided to dress up like a medieval court jester and fight crime, using comedy routines. Some of them crooks nearly died laughing! He never did much funny the only All-Star Squadron meeting or two he showed up for, though.

GOLDEN AGE APPEARANCES:

Smash Comics #22-85 (May 1941 – Oct. 1949) – no origin story

Jester Closer Walk With Thee

The Jester, in a Quality panel reprinted in AC's Men of Mystery Comics #46 (2004). Artist unknown. [Jester TM & © DC Comics.]

JOHNNY QUICK

Hey, folks! This is a very special newsreel by your favorite cameraman, **Tubby Watts**, so sit back and enjoy your popcorn. Professor Gill deciphered an ancient Egyptian math formula that turned him into a super-fast "master of time and space." Before he died, he passed on that "magic formula" to his young ward, my buddy **Johnny Chambers**, who memorized it and adopted the masked identity of "Johnny Quick." Whenever he muttered "3X2 (9YZ) 4A," he'd move through space like time had stopped, even *flying* due to his speed (which The Flash couldn't do—so how come *he's* the more famous one?). Johnny soon trusted me with his secret, and I've helped him lots of times; he's saved me once or twice, too. Lately he's busy being a member of the All-Star

YOUR PIE—

YOUR SANDWICH—

YOUR SOUP—

SORRY—WITH JOHNNY QUICK SERVING— WE'RE ALL OUT OF FOOD! THERE'S NOTHING LEFT TO EAT.

AND ME STILL WAITING FOR A MEAL! MAYBE YOU COULD RUN OUT AND GET ME ONE, JOHNNY.

ME? WHO DO YOU THINK I AM—JOHNNY QUICK?

Squadron and the bridegroom of Libby Lawrence, alias Liberty Belle. Not many women in the group, but you can bet Johnny would get the prettiest one. He isn't called "quick" for nothing, you know?

GOLDEN AGE APPEARANCES:

More Fun Comics #71-107 (Sept. 1941 – Jan.-Feb. 1946) – origin in #71
Adventure Comics #103-204, 206-207 (April 1946 – Dec. 1954) – origin retold with new details in #159

Quick As A Wink

(Above:) Johnny Quick is a one-man restaurant crew in "Mayhem in the Meal-O-Mat" in Adventure Comics #127 (April 1948). (Left:) At story's end, Johnny Chambers gives the comic book hero's customary wink at the reader, following a remark by Tubby Watts. Art by the marvelous Mort Meskin. [© DC Comics.]

JUDO MASTER

JUDOMASTER

Sergeant Rip Jagger was an athlete and boxer before he joined the military. While serving in the Pacific during World War II, he led a group of soldiers to an island, where he saved my grand-daughter from a native sniper. Then their company was attacked and he was the only survivor. In gratitude, as **leader of our tribe**, I taught him the physical and spiritual secrets of judo. He used this knowledge to liberate our island, and from then on he was know as Judomaster. He was later joined by a young sidekick, known as Tiger. He teamed up with the All-Star Squadron some time after the extant stories were recorded.

GOLDEN AGE APPEARANCES:

None – first appeared in *Judomaster* #80 (May-June 1966)

Kids—Don't Try This At Home!

The Charlton series' artist/creator Frank McLaughlin drew the pic accompanying his hero's entry in Who's Who: The Definitive Directory of the DC Universe #2 (1985). Judomaster, all of whose stories were set during World War II, never appeared in All-Star Squadron, though it was Roy Thomas' intention to utilize him eventually. His image did appear in the All-Star Squadron entry in Who's Who. [© DC Comics.]

THE KING

Hello. I'm **The Witch**, beautiful gangster and nemesis of The King, master of disguise. **King Standish** began his crime-fighting career after surviving a shooting, thanks to his bulletproof vest. At first both criminals and cops thought he was on the opposite side, but it was soon clear he was one of the so-called "good guys." (It all depends on your point of view, after all.) He always left behind his calling card, which featured a crown insignia. I often matched wits with him, always trying to find out what disguise he was using this time. *I'm* a master of disguise, too, so we had a great time playing cat and mouse… and maybe more.

Who Was That Masked Man?

(Left:) The Phantom Detective was the longest-lived pulp magazine which starred a continuing hero, and featured a crimefighter called The Phantom—but Thrilling/Nedor Publications must've felt they needed to add the word "Detective" to the title to avoid running afoul of the comic strip Phantom. The pulpster was a master of disguise. [© the respective copyright holders.]

(Top right:) The King, drawn by Flash co-creator Harry Lampert, in a splash from an issue of Flash Comics. He was slated to one day join the All-Star Squadron, but....! [© DC Comics.]

GOLDEN AGE APPEARANCES:

Flash Comics #3-37 (March 1940-May 1943; titled *King Standish* #3-15)

World's Best/World's Finest Comics #1-5, 8 (Spring-Summer 1941-Winter 1943)

Comic Cavalcade #3-4 (Summer 1943-Fall 1943)

All-Flash #3 (Winter 1944)

LIBERTY BELLE

I'm the ghost of **Tom Revere**. Before I was murdered by Baron Blitzkrieg, I was custodian of the Liberty Bell here in Philadelphia—and the only non-super-hero who knew the secret of the heroine the Bell inspired. When I met **Libby Lawrence**, she was already a celebrity, having swum the English Channel to escape the Nazi assault on Dunkirk in 1940 and become a radio newscaster to warn America of the threat of Hitler. When she visited the Liberty Bell, we discovered that her bell-shaped pin—an athletic prize made from a fragment of it—vibrated in resonance when the Bell rang. Taking on the identity of Liberty Belle, she soon became a charter member of the All-Star Squadron, and even its chairwoman. Whenever the need arose, I rang the Bell—and, wherever she was, she felt energized. After she developed sonic powers, she became even more the living incarnation of the Liberty Bell, and of America's fight for freedom.

GOLDEN AGE APPEARANCES:

Boy Commandos #1-2 (Winter 1943 – Spring 1943) – origin in #1

Star Spangled Comics #20-68 (May 1943 – May 1947)

Give Me Liberty

Tom Revere rings the Liberty Bell—Libby Lawrence's pin vibrates—and Liberty Belle goes into action against spies, in panels from Star Spangled Comics #35 (Aug. 1944). Don Cameron wrote and Chuck Winter drew this series from start to finish. For her appearances in All-Star Squadron, she was given a mask, a jagged crack drawn on her Liberty Bell chest symbol, and—perhaps less advisedly—a sometime cape and tighter pants. [© DC Comics.]

LITTLE BOY BLUE & THE BLUE BOYS

I'm **Dan Rogers**, District Attorney. When the gangster Boss Lupo kidnaped the only witness against his protection racket, my young son **Tommy** decided to dress up as a "mystery man," joined by his pal **Tubby**. They ended up finding the gangsters hiding in their clubhouse, and with the help of another boy, **Toughy**, defeated them and Boss Lupo, who was convicted. Just a stroke of luck—well, one of many more to come—even if the All-Star Squadron never invited them to join....

GOLDEN AGE APPEARANCES:

Sensation Comics #1-34, 37-83 (Jan. 1942 – Nov. 1948) – origin in #1
Big All-American Comic Book (1944)
Flash Comics #81 (March 1947)

Come Blow Your Horn—On The Piano

Little Boy Blue, Tubby, and Toughy (the latter two didn't have any individual names as Blue Boys) give piano lessons to a couple of hoodlums in this previously-unpublished panel from a story written off for tax purposes on Sept. 30, 1949. Art by Frank Harry. Thanks to Marv Wolfman. [© DC Comics.]

He Must Have Animal Magnetism

Magno confronts a spy in Quality's Smash Comics #9, in a story drawn by Paul Gustavson. What really impresses us is that the bad-guy recognized such an obscure hero! By the way, a pic of entry-presenter Spider Widow appears on p. 93 of this volume. Panel provided by Jim Amash. [© DC Comics.]

MAGNO

I, **Spider Widow**, have been chosen to tell you the origin of another lesser-know hero: Magno. **Tom Dalton** was a lineman for an electric company who was electrocuted by 10,000 DC volts of electricity. One of his buddies thought that perhaps an equal current of AC voltage would shock Dalton back to life. Not only did he come back from the dead, but he gained super-powers, to boot: now he can attract and repel objects like a magnet, melt objects, and give an electric shock with his punches. And if he runs out of power, he can recharge himself just by sticking his fingers into a socket. Hey, kids—don't try this at home!

GOLDEN AGE APPEARANCES:

Smash Comics #13-21 (Aug. 1940 – April 1941) – no origin story

MANHUNTER (I)

I'm **Police Chief McGonigle**, boss of patrolman **Dan Richards**, who adopted his Manhunter identity to clear a fellow officer framed for a crime he didn't commit. Alongside his German shepherd dog Thor, he fought crime in both his identities (I pretended not to know anything about Manhunter). I've heard his mutt turned out to be a robot or something—but I don't think I believe it.

GOLDEN AGE APPEARANCES:

Police Comics #8-101 (except #90, 92) - (March 1942 – Aug. 1950) – origin in #8

A Manhunter's Best Friend

The Quality Comics hero called Manhunter made his debut in comics cover-dated exactly one month before the DC version. He and his dog Thor outlasted the latter by more than half a decade. Art by John Cassone. [© DC Comics.]

MANHUNTER (II)

Nobody escapes the Manhunters! I'm the **Grandmaster** of the Manhunters, and I'm here to tell you how detective **Paul Kirk** decided to adopt a masked identity and join our order, after the villainous Vulture killed Police Chief Donavan. Paul became a second hero called Manhunter only a few weeks—if *that* long—after Dan Richards took the same identity. He lived many lives, but the first one, even if he didn't suspect anything, was at our service. This dread secret was discovered only in the 1980s.

***GOLDEN AGE
APPEARANCES:***

Adventure Comics
#73-92 (April 1942 –
June-July 1944) –
origin in #73

Hunting License

(Above:) The Grandmaster was the leader of the alien Manhunters in the DC weekly super-series Millennium *in 1987. This panel, with art by Joe Staton & Ian Gibson and script by Steve Englehart, is from issue #1. The Manhunters' blue-visaged outfits were based on that of a 1970s Jack Kirby hero, which in turn was based on:*

(Right:) The Simon & Kirby Manhunter of the early 1940s. This symbolically huge drawing of the hero is from Adventure Comics #75 (June 1942), as reprinted in the 1970s. [Both panels © DC Comics.]

Mary, Mary...

Only moments after Mary Batson first says the magic word "Shazam!" and turns into Mary Marvel, she fells criminals who've captured her brother Billy and Freddy Freeman. Art by Marc Swayze (writer uncertain), from Captain Marvel Adventures *#18 (Dec. 1942), as reprinted in the hardcover* Shazam! *from the 30's to the 70's—now on view in color in* The Shazam! Family Archives, Vol. 1*. [© DC Comics.]*

MARY MARVEL

We are the goddesses **Selena, Hippolyta, Ariadne, Zephyrus, Aurora,** and **Minerva**. By shouting the magic word "Shazam!" young **Mary Bromfield** can become Mary Marvel. When Mary B. was interviewed by kid radio reporter Billy Batson, they discovered they had matching pieces of a broken locket—and that they were twins, separated at birth. Learning that her brother could become Captain Marvel, she tried in a moment of crisis to see if she could summon the same great power—and we turned her into the World's Mightiest Girl. But while Billy turned into an adult when he became Captain Marvel, Mary Marvel stayed the same age. Perhaps that was just us goddesses' way of giving her an extra gift of youth. But even *we* could never get her more than a guest appearance with the All-Star Squadron.

GOLDEN AGE APPEARANCES:

Captain Marvel Adventures #18-19, 37, 43 (cameo) (Dec. 1942 –
 Feb. 1945) – origin in #18
Wow Comics #9-58 (Jan. 1943 – Sept. 1947)
Mary Marvel #1-25 (Dec. 1945 – June 1948)
Marvel Family #1-89 (Dec. 1945 – Jan. 1954); *Master Comics* #118
 (Oct. 1950)
Xmas Comics (#s?) (reprints)
Gift Comics #4 (1949) (reprints)

MIDNIGHT

Hi! I'm **Gabby**, the intelligent talking monkey of Doc Wackey, villain turned eccentric scientist. Don't ask! We are usually allies of Midnight, whose real name is **Dave Clark**. Dave started as a boxer, later worked as a radio announcer. One day he played the voice of a radio serial about "The Man Called Midnight." When he was witness to the collapse of a building where he couldn't save everybody, he decided to become an incarnation of the radio character and expose the crooked constructor. That was the beginning of a successful crimefighting career—even if he did look an awful lot like another crimefighter, called The Spirit!

GOLDEN AGE APPEARANCES:
Smash Comics #18-85 (Jan. 1941 – Oct. 1949) – origin in #18

Getting Into The Spirit

Quality publisher Busy Arnold wanted a clone of Will Eisner's Spirit (above), so he had Plastic Man writer/artist Jack Cole create Midnight (left). Ironically, Cole later worked on the Spirit Sunday feature, as well. The Eisner art is reprinted from a 1940s contents page in Warren Publications' Spirit magazine #12 (Feb. 1976); Cole's cover for Smash Comics #47 (Oct. 1943) shows Gabby and Doc Wackey, to boot. [Spirit TM & © Will Eisner Studios, Inc.; Midnight TM & © DC Comics.]

MISS AMERICA

I, **Prof. Mazursky**, am head of the secret Project M, hidden beneath the Statue of Liberty. **Joan Dale** was a reporter we captured and subjected to experiments. Thinking we had accidentally destroyed her mind, we left her on a bench on Liberty Island. There she dreamed that the Statue of Liberty came to life and endowed her with super-powers. Awakening, she discovered she could alter matter and fire energy bolts from her hands. Ere long, she donned a costume and took on a secret identity—surprise, surprise. Wonder if she'll ever discover the true source of her powers—and, in fact, we're not even positive that the source of her powers was our own experiments. Maybe she really *did* get her powers from Lady Liberty herself....

GOLDEN AGE APPEARANCES:
Military Comics #1-7 (Aug. 1941 – Feb. 1942) – origin in #1 – costume in #3

Here She Comes, Miss America—Both Of Them!

Quality's Miss America gained a costume only in her third story—but she still beat out Wonder Woman by a couple of months in the red-white-and-blue-costumed-female sweepstakes. Art top right from Military Comics #4 (Nov. 1941) is by either Elmer Wexler or Tom Hickey. The panel directly above, from her retro-fitted origin in Secret Origins #26 (May 1988), shows Prof. Mazursky; art by Grant Miehm, script by Roy & Dann Thomas. [© DC Comics.]

(Left:) After that Miss A.'s series was dropped, Timely/Marvel came up with a super-heroine of their own by that name. This one wore glasses (at least in later stories) to shield her secret identity—nor is the ID of the artist who drew this chapter of the All Winners Squad tale in All Winners Comics #19 (Fall 1946) known to us. Maybe Pauline Loth? [© Marvel Characters, Inc.]

MR. AMERICA

Me? I'm **Bob Daley**, better known as **Fatman**, the faithful companion of Mr. America. **Tex Thomson** left his oil business to live out many adventures alongside me and his manservant Gargantua Potts. While escorting a shipment of food to Europe, he was thought dead when the ocean liner was sabotaged by Nazis. But he survived and adopted the patriotic costumed identity of Mr. America, master of the whip. After Pearl Harbor, he changed his name to the even more patriotic **"Americommando"** and fought the Nazis as an undercover agent on occupied soil.

GOLDEN AGE APPEARANCES:

Action Comics #1-74 (June 1938 – July 1944) – series titled "Tex Thomson" with no secret identity #1-32; Tex becomes Mr. America in #33 (Feb. 1941) – no origin story; Tex & Bob (Fatman) become The Americommandos in #52 (Sept. 1942)

There He Goes—Mr. America!

Tex Thomson—Mr. America—Americommando—this hero drawn by Bernard Baily changed both modus operandi and name, depending on which way the sales winds were blowing. Not that that's a bad thing. Art from Action Comics #33 (Feb. 1941). [© DC Comics.]

Bob Daley as Fatman.
[© DC Comics.]

NEON THE UNKNOWN

I'm **The Unknown**. No, not Neon, but another super-hero who's even *less* well known. **Tom Corbet** (no relation to the later TV Space Cadet) was a Foreign Legionnaire stationed in Africa, who was ordered to cross a desert to check on a tribe of restless natives. His company got lost and everyone else died of dehydration. Finding a glowing oasis filled with phosphorescent water, Tom drank—and suddenly his torn uniform was replaced by a colorful costume, and he was filled with fantastic energy. He discovered he could fly and shoot neonic energy bolts from his hands, which is better than dying of thirst in the desert, right?

GOLDEN AGE APPEARANCES:

Hit Comics #1-17 (July 1940 – Nov. 1941) – origin in #1
Uncle Sam Quarterly #2 (Winter 1940) – cameo in Uncle Sam

Neon Lights

Neon was drawn not by "Tagor Maroy" but by Alex Blum in Quality's Hit Comics #17 (Nov. 1941); this story was reprinted in AC Comics' Men of Mystery Comics #46 (2004). [Neon the Unknown TM & © DC Comics.]

Hawkman's VOYAGE TO VENUS!

NEPTUNE PERKINS

A man of many names, I was born **Arthur Gordon Pym**. In my Antarctic explorations I found a lost civilization called The Dzyan, masters of the Vril, a mysterious energy I soon mastered—or perhaps it mastered me, since it magnified my evil tendencies. As "Captain Nemo," I built the submarine *Nautilus*. Decades later, visiting the USA under the name "Perkins," I fathered a son named Ross. I used my mobile war-island to sink the *Titanic* and seize its gold. When Ross tracked me down and married one of the survivors, he and his wife conceived a child under the rays of the Vril, hoping their offspring would bring about my defeat. Their mutant son **Neptune** was born with webbed hands and feet and fabulous swimming prowess, though a deficiency in bodily sodium salts forced him to live close to salt water. When his parents were killed by Nazis, this "human dolphin" became a marine explorer and participated in adventures with the All-Star Squadron, later joining The Young All-Stars. He and the latter saved the Vril from falling into the wrong hands, thus redeeming the man he'd been conceived to defeat—myself. May he enter the history books and make my legacy even more glorious!

GOLDEN AGE APPEARANCES:
Flash Comics #66, 81 (Aug.-Sept. 1945, March 1947) – origin in #66.

By Neptune's Trident!

(Above:) The amphibious Neptune Perkins appeared twice in Golden Age Hawkman stories—his second outing being this cover shot from Flash Comics #81, wherein he and the Winged Wonder were transported to the planet Venus. Art by Chester Kozlak.

(Right:) After a couple of "retroactive continuity" appearances in All-Star Squadron, he graduated to co-star status—and a full costume—in The Young All-Stars #1. Pencils by Michael Bair & Brian Murray; inks by Malcolm Jones III. [© DC Comics.]

NEAR SANTA BARBARA, CALIFORNIA, THREE RUGGED BITS OF LAND JUT PROUDLY SKYWARD.

LINKED AT LOW TIDE, THEY ARE KNOWN AS ANACAPA ISLAND.

THIS LATE APRIL NIGHT, A RED-CLAD YOUTH LEAPS DOLPHINLIKE BETWEEN THE TWIN WORLDS OF FROTHING SEA AND DRIVING RAIN.

HIS NAME IS NEPTUNE PERKINS.

STARMAN

PHANTOM LADY

Hello, I'm **Starman**, a.k.a. **Ted Knight**. Heroism runs in the Knight blood, as witness what happened to my cousin **Sandra**: she was waiting for her father, Senator Henry Knight, on the steps of the US Capitol Building when they were attacked by two kidnappers. Sandra defeated them easily and hid before my uncle knew who had saved him. When she discovered a black light ray developed by one Prof. Davis, she decided to use it to fight crime by temporarily blinding criminals, in her disguise as The Phantom Lady. Believe me, it's a pity that the villains never get to see my cousin Sandra in that yellow swimsuit...!

GOLDEN AGE APPEARANCES:
Police #1-23 (Aug. 1941 – Oct. 1943) – origin in #1

Feature Comics #70 (Aug. 1943) in crossover with Spider Widow.

[**NOTE:** "Phantom Lady" was revived in her own book and with a new color scheme at Fox Comics in 1947, but there is no real continuity with her original Quality appearances; that version was also briefly revived in 1955.]

PHANTOM LADY

FRANK M. BORTH Feature

Duel Heroines

Even after he ceased being cover-featured on Adventure Comics, Jack Burnley's Starman was seen in a head shot in the top corner—in this case, now looking down as his retconned cousin Phantom Lady (right) duels with fellow Quality heroine Spider Widow in a rare crossover story from Police Comics #21 (Aug. 1943), while the costumed Raven looks on. [© DC Comics.]

PLASTIC MAN

I am a **monk** from Rest-Haven, who found the criminal **Eel O'Brian** unconscious near our monastery. He had fled here from the police after they had interrupted his and others' attempted robbery of a chemical plant. Eel, in his flight, got doused in a strange acid from a toppling vat. He soon discovered the acid had turned his body into some kind of rubbery flesh. He adopted the secret identity of Plastic Man to fight against his old gang, although eventually he gave up being Eel O'Brian entirely.

GOLDEN AGE APPEARANCES:

Police Comics #1-102 (Aug. 1941 – Oct. 1950) –
  origin in #1
Plastic Man #1-2 (1943 & 1944 issues);
Plastic Man #3-64 (Spring 1946 – Nov. 1956)

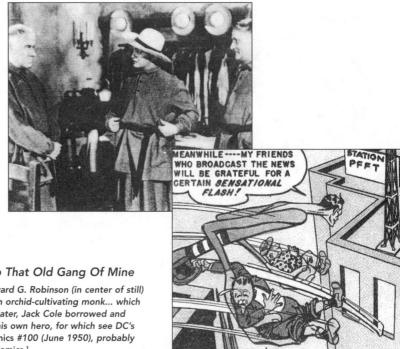

Those Monastery Bells Are Breaking Up That Old Gang Of Mine

In the 1940 Warner Bros. film Brother Orchid, Edward G. Robinson (in center of still) was transformed from hardboiled racketeer into an orchid-cultivating monk... which put him at odds with his mob of criminals. A year later, Jack Cole borrowed and mutated elements of that movie for the origin of his own hero, for which see DC's Plastic Man Archives, Vol. 1. Panel from Police Comics #100 (June 1950), probably by Cole. [Film still © Time-Warner, Inc.; art © DC Comics.]

QUICKSILVER

I'm **The Flash**, Fastest Man Alive—but that doesn't mean I can't appreciate another speedster like Quicksilver. Little is known about him—not even his real name, assuming he has one. He's a former acrobat turned crimefighter, and seems to operate out of a hidden laboratory—oh yes, and he was an avid comic book reader. Guess I'll have to wait to see if Johnny Quick and I can give this new guy a run for his money. Everybody wants to get into the act!

GOLDEN AGE APPEARANCES:

National Comics #5-71, 73 (Nov. 1940 – Aug. 1949) –
  no origin story
Uncle Sam Quarterly #2 (Winter 1940) – cameo in Uncle Sam

Quick As A Flash?

Maybe The Flash (as per cameo by E.E. Hibbard for alternating covers of Flash Comics) is smiling at the sight of Quicksilver in action because he knows that the latter, fast as he is, is no threat to him in terms of miles per hour (or nanosecond). The Jack Cole art is from an issue of Quality's National Comics, as restored for AC Comics' Men of Mystery Comics #23 (2000). [Flash & Quicksilver TM & © DC Comics.]

THE RAY

I, **Dr. Styne**, invented a new type of hot air balloon. Reporter **"Happy" Terrill** (whose real name was apparently Lanfor—no wonder he used his nickname!) was coming along for the inaugural ride when we were caught in an electrical storm that struck him, giving him the power to fire blasts of light and heat, to fly, and become a creature made of light itself. Still, those great powers depend on the amount of light, and he can lose them if he stays too long in the dark, like a human solar battery.

GOLDEN AGE APPEARANCES:

Smash Comics #14-40 (Sept. 1940 – Feb. 1943) – origin in #14
Uncle Sam Quarterly #2 (Winter 1940) – cameo in Uncle Sam

Ray Of Hope

The Ray, in a Smash Comics panel drawn by the great Reed Crandall for Quality Comics Group. [© DC Comics.]

THE RED BEE

I am **Baron Blitzkrieg**, living symbol of the scientific power of the Third Reich. I have tangled with several American heroes, and some of them paid the highest price for daring to interfere my plans. One of these was The Red Bee. **Rick Raleigh** was an Assistant District Attorney in Superior City, Oregon, who decided to take direct action against the gangster "Boss" Storm. He used trained bees as his weapons—the most faithful of them being named Michael and kept in in his belt. Well, enough of this nonsense—it wasn't too long before The Red Bee felt my own deadly sting.

GOLDEN AGE APPEARANCES:

Hit Comics #1-24 (July 1940 – Oct. 1942) – no origin story
Uncle Sam Quarterly #2 (Winter 1940) – cameo in Uncle Sam

Don't Let A Name Bug You

The name of many an early super-hero was inspired by radio's (and the comics') Green Hornet, seen above left on the cover of Harvey's Green Hornet #13 (July 1943 – artist unidentified). Among these was Quality's Red Bee, drawn by the legendary Lou Fine on the cover of Hit Comics #1. [Green Hornet art © the respective copyright holders; Red Bee TM & © DC Comics.]

THE RED TORPEDO

We are the **inhabitants of Merrezonia**, a sub-oceanic civilization not related to the Atlantis of Aquaman fame. Our world was discovered by the adventurer called The Red Torpedo. **Jim Lockhart** was a Navy captain who built a submarine he likewise christened the *Red Torpedo*. The sub was also capable of flying and had two frontal energy beams. He saw himself as the "Robin Hood of the Deep." Most of his adventures pitted him against The Black Shark. We're not sure what ever happened to him, or if he was actually killed by that Japanese kamikaze pilot who rammed his sub. Sure *hope* not!

GOLDEN AGE APPEARANCES:

Crack Comics #1-20 (May 1940 – Jan. 1942) – origin in #1

Can You Hit A Shark With A Torpedo?

Red Torpedo and Black Shark in Quality's Crack Comics #17 (Oct. 1941); art by Henry Kiefer. Thanks to Bruce Mason. [© DC Comics.]

I Robot—You Jailbird

In these panels from Star Spangled Comics #7, Chuck Grayson, jailed for allegedly murdering scientist Bob Crane, is startled to confront him in the flesh—or rather, in a rubberized mask, with the new name Paul Dennis—and Crane/Dennis soon goes into action as Robotman to clear his assistant's name. Script by Jerry Siegel, art by Ed Dobrotka and perhaps others of the Joe Shuster studio. [© DC Comics.]

ROBOTMAN

I'm **Chuck Grayson**—cousin of you-know-who—but I'm fairly well-known myself. I was the assistant to **Dr. Robert Crane**, who developed the first mechanical body able to sustain the life of a human brain. Ironically, he was shot by criminals trying to steal his design; to preserve his intellect, I had no choice but to transplant his still-living brain into a metal body he had constructed. But the ironies didn't end there, as I was accused of murdering my friend! Thank God the experiment worked, and Bob created for himself the identity of **Paul Dennis**—hiding his metal features under a rubber mask. He quickly captured his own "killers" as the new mechanical hero, Robotman. "Paul" adapted very well to his new life, was a founding member of the All-Star Squadron, and later even built himself a robotic dog he named Robby.

GOLDEN AGE APPEARANCES:

Star Spangled Comics #7-82 (April 1942 – July 1948) –
 origin in #7
Detective Comics #138-154, 156-202 (Aug. 1948 – Dec. 1953) –
 origin retold in #138

SARGON THE SORCERER

I am **The Ruby of Life**. In 1917 I was found by archeologist Richard Sargent, who gave me as a present to his wife. When their son **John Sargent** was born, I was the first thing he touched—so, once he grow up, he discovered that, using my magical power, he could control any substance. He adopted the guise of Sargon the Sorcerer and battled evil. When World War II began, he joined the All Star Squadron like many other heroes. There he met fellow mystics, including Zatara. But he remained ignorant of the true power he wielded and the price of using it. He thought he was using me, but in truth was I was using him! But that's another story....

GOLDEN AGE APPEARANCES:
All-American Comics #26-50, 70 (May 1941 – June 1943, Jan.-Feb. 1946) – origin in #26
Comic Cavalcade #3-6, 14 (Summer 1943 – Spring 1944, April-May 1946)
Big All-American Comic Book (1944)
Sensation Comics #34-36, 52-83 (Oct. 1944-Dec. 1944, April 1946-Nov. 1948)
Green Lantern #37 (March 1949)

Don't Keep Things Bottled Up
Trapped inside a large bottle, Sargon had only to touch it—and it came to life and liberated him. This panel is from an unpublished late-'40s story, probably drawn by Arthur Peddy (pencils) and Bernard Sachs (inks). With thanks to Tom Horvitz.
[© DC Comics.]

THE SHINING KNIGHT

Past, present, and future are as one to **Merlin the Magician**. Let me relate the legend of the noblest Knight of the Round Table, **Sir Justin**. On his way to fight the ogre Blunderbore, he freed me from the tree where the evil Morgan Le Fey had trapped me. As a reward, I gave him invulnerable golden armor and an invincible sword, and transformed his steed Victory into a winged Pegasus. From then on, he was known as The Shining Knight. He killed the giant, but in the battle he was encased in an avalanche of ice. However, my final gift was to induce the sleep that preserved him alive, until he was revived in 1941 by Dr. Moresby, curator of a museum. He now warred against the twin evils of crime and fascism. He joined the ranks of a new heroic chivalry, first the Seven Soldiers of Victory—though I cannot fathom why they were christened after Sir Justin's horse—and, later, the All-Star Squadron. May he keep alive the dream of Camelot for many years!

GOLDEN AGE APPEARANCES:
Adventure Comics #66-125, 127-128, 131-132, 137-139, 142-145, 148, 150, 151. 153, 155, 157, 159, 161, 163, 165, 166 (Sept. 1941 – July 1951) – origin in #66

Leading Comics #1-14 (Winter 1942 – Spring 1945) as member of the Seven Soldiers of Victory.

Knighty-Knight
(Above:) The Shining Knight, riding Winged Victory, attacks a criminal in Adventure Comics #120 (Sept. 1947); art by Chuck Winter. Contrary to the intro to DC's Seven Soldiers of Victory Archives, Vol. 1, Sir Justin's secret identity never had the last name "Arthur" (or any other last name we know of) back in the 1940s. Dr. Moresby and others just called him "Justin." Lord knows how he got a Social Security card to work at the museum!
[© DC Comics.]

(Left:) With the help of artists John Verpoorten, George Tuska, and John Buscema, writer/editor Roy Thomas developed the 1960s hero The Black Knight from two earlier Marvel characters of that name, with a nod to Sir Justin. Buscema & Tuska drew this panel from The Avengers #54 (July 1968).
[© Marvel Characters, Inc.]

Alias THE SPIDER

Hello, gentlemen. I'm **The Shade**. You know me as the rogue master of darkness, nemesis to that modern-day Mercury, The Flash. But today I want to tell you about another masked adventurer, **Tom Hallaway**, alias The Spider. He fights crime with bow and arrows, driven in his car The Black Widow by his valet Chuck and using a "spider seal" able to penetrate his enemy's flesh. He is different from all those other valet-driven-playboys-in-tights, in that he's more than willing to kill criminals... so perhaps there's a dark side to this archer, as some later accounts maintain. But why he dubbed himself "The Spider" I'll *never* understand!

GOLDEN AGE APPEARANCES:

Crack Comics #1-30 (May 1940 – Aug. 1943) – no origin story

Along Came A Spider—Or Three

Quality's archer (center, drawn by Paul Gustavson) was a grim character, all right—though we discount later reports that he was in truth a serial killer—and was neither the first nor last hero to call himself "The Spider." The 1930s star of The Spider pulp magazine received a much more arachnid look, webbed cloak and all, when Warren Hull played him in two movie serials in 1938 and 1941 (top right)—and of course Stan Lee & Steve Ditko's Spider-Man (seen at right from The Amazing Spider-Man #11, April 1964) made most of the world forget about both of 'em! [Spider © the respective copyright holders; Spider-Man © Marvel Characters, Inc.]

THE STAR-SPANGLED KID & STRIPESY

Say hello to **Merry, the Girl of 1000 Gimmicks**. Even if you never heard of me, maybe you know my more famous brother, **Sylvester Pemberton III**, a.k.a. The Star-Spangled Kid (not a great name either, I know). He was the only costumed hero whose sidekick was older than he was, since **Pat Dugan**, our chauffeur, donned his "Stripesy" outfit and ran around after my brother to keep him safe, probably so he could hold onto his job! Pat also built their flying car, the Star Rocket Racer. They even fought as a part of the Seven Soldiers of Victory—but I was too young to join, and didn't take on a secret identity until after the war was over. Oh, well, just wait until I convince our *housekeeper* to become *my* sidekick!

GOLDEN AGE APPEARANCES:

Star Spangled Comics #1-86 (Oct. 1941 – Nov. 1948) – origin in #18 (March 1943) – joined by the Girl of 1000 Gimmicks (Mary Pemberton) from #81 (June 1948) – no Stripesy in #83-86
Leading Comics #1-14 (Winter 1942 – Spring 1945)
World's Finest Comics #6-18 (Summer 1942 – Summer 1945)

The Little Sister

The Star-Spangled Kid and Stripesy were a colorful acrobatic team, as per this Star Spangled Comics #35 (Aug. 1944) splash by Hal Sherman—yet by then they'd lost their cover spot to The Newsboy Legion and The Guardian. For young Sylvester, the final ignominy must've been seeing his kid sis Merry, as the masked Gimmick Girl, take over his series totally with #87. Art above left from SSC #90 (March 1949) is by Win Mortimer, script by Otto Binder, as reprinted in Adventure Comics #416 (March 1972). Wonder if Syl sent a sympathy card when his sibling's solo series was dropped after a mere four issues? [© DC Comics.]

TARANTULA

My book *Altered Egos*, if you can find it in a library, tells of the life and times of the costumed heroes of World War II. I know about them—because I was *one* of them. As **Jonathan Law**, I'd already written bestselling mystery novels, but I decided to become the star of my own stories. I trained, developed a "webgun" and suction-soled shoes, and with a not-so-original costume I became The Tarantula— since "The Spider" was already taken, and I didn't like that phrase "spider man" used on some radio reports about me. (Let some lesser hero opt for *that* cornball name!) I soon realized my cape was a hindrance when I was walking upside-down on a ceiling, so my German housekeeper Olga made a new outfit for me, around the time I joined the All-Star Squadron. But, that's enough about me—look up my book and read about *them!*

GOLDEN AGE APPEARANCES:
Star Spangled Comics #1-19 (Oct. 1941 – April 1943) – origin in #1

...Does Whatever A Spider Can!
Tarantula was walking on ceilings years before Spider-Man crawled up his first wall, as per Star Spangled Comics #16 (Jan. 1943); art by Hal Sharp. At far right is Jerry Ordway's art for the Who's Who entry in the 1980s, after he had re-designed Tarantula for All-Star Squadron, so he wouldn't look so much like the post-gasmask Sandman. Repro'd from the original art, courtesy of Jerry. [© DC Comics.]

Save The Tigress! Oops—Too Late!
Liberty Belle and her fellow heroes accepted The Tigress as one of The Young All-Stars two issues after she popped up; the Brian Murray/Malcolm Jones III art above is from YAS #9 (Dec. 1988). But of course she was destined from the first to become the villainous Huntress, the principal late-1940s foe of Sensation Comics' Wildcat, as per art at right by Mort Meskin, who drew the Feline Fury's exploits in #68-70, according to the Grand Comic Book Data Base. Maybe the panel at right is from #68 (Aug. 1947), the lass' first appearance as The Huntress (and first anywhere in Real Time, of course). Repro'd from a photocopy of the original art, courtesy of Ethan Roberts. [© DC Comics.]

THE TIGRESS

I'm **Wildcat**, but maybe I ought to change my name to "Black Cat," since I'm unlucky enough to be the only one of the long-underwear legion whose nemesis, The Huntress, was a masked heroine gone wrong! **Paula Brooks** idolized the famous big-game hunter Paul Kirk (better known to us as Manhunter). She trained herself in archery and jiu-jitsu and donned a tiger suit left over from some "jungle girl" movie serial. As The Tigress, she joined the Young All-Stars to get near Manhunter. But things took a turn for the weird when she was mortally injured fighting Gudra, a Nazified Valkyrie. Like a cat, she had eight lives left, but she came back deranged and turned against her former pals. Maybe if she gets knocked off pulling one of her crazy crimes, she'll come back as a heroine in her *next* life....!

GOLDEN AGE APPEARANCES:
Sensation Comics #68-69, 71, 73, 75-76 (Aug.1947 – April 1948) as The Huntress in all *All-Star Comics* #41 (June-July 1948) as a member of the *In*justice Society of the World

TNT & DAN THE DYNA-MITE

I am **Gudra the Valkyrie**. Here in Valhalla, bards sing the feats of the brave, who died in battle. **Thomas N. ("Tex") Thomas** was a chemistry teacher who was working on an experiment with his star pupil, **Dan Dunbar**. When they accidentally touched each other, they found they'd absorbed the energy of chemicals they'd been handling; afterward, when they clashed their "Dyna-Rings" together, the chemical reaction gave them super-human powers which they used to combat crime as TNT and Dyna-Mite. They joined the All-Star Squadron, but TNT later perished while fighting our glorious Nazi saboteurs. I claimed the fallen warrior's soul. I would have claimed his young ally, as well, if not for the intervention of "Iron" Munro. But the war is still young, and Dyna-Mite, though now able to conjure up his power on his own, may yet join his master in Hela's realm!

GOLDEN AGE APPEARANCES:
Star Spangled Comics #7-23 (April 1942 – Aug. 1943) –
 origin of the team in #8 (May 1942)
World's Finest Comics #5 (Spring 1942)

A Dynamite Duo

TNT and Dan the Dyna-Mite were an explosive act to follow, as per art above from Star Spangled Comics #16 (Jan. 1943), which is attributed to Louis Cazaneuve. But Gudra, a Valkyrie backdated from a post-WWII Wonder Woman story, had her deadly eye on both guys, even if "Iron" Munro managed to save at least Dyna-Mite from going to Valhalla prematurely. Art at right from Young All-Stars #1 by Brian Murray & Malcolm Jones III. [© DC Comics.]

TSUNAMI

I, **Prince Daka**, a.k.a. **Dr. Daka**, am head of Imperial Japanese undercover operatives. In 1942 **Miya Shimada**, code-named "Tsunami" by Admiral Yamamoto himself for her water-manipulative powers, was one of my agents. Her parents were forced to return to Japan under suspicion of being Western spies. Miya was a Nisei (first-generation American), and abandoned our cause after fighting briefly against the All-Star Squadron. After that, she became an impediment to our plans of Empire by joining The Young All-Stars, though she still protested against the internment camps for Japanese and Japanese-Americans in the USA. Those relocation centers show the true face of the American "defenders of liberty," and perhaps it is not too late to manipulate her again into fighting for the Emperor. *Banzai!*

GOLDEN AGE APPEARANCES:
None – first appeared in *All-Star Squadron* #34 (June 1984)

Sweet Tsunami

Dr. (a.k.a. Prince) Daka, as portrayed by J. Carrol Naish, (above), was pulled from the 1943 Columbia movie serial Batman into the pages of All-Star Squadron. Tsunami was originally a loyalist of Imperial Japan, but she soon switched sides. Art by Rick Hoberg & Bill Collins from All-Star Squadron #34. [Art © DC Comics; movie still © the respective copyright holders.]

Say Uncle!

In 1941 Will Eisner introduced a super-hero version of Uncle Sam, seen above left on the cover of Uncle Sam #1 (Fall 1941)—whether drawn entirely by Eisner or in concert with Dave Berg, who did the interior art. The 1942 postcard at right (art accredited to one Walter Munson) utilized the original version of that personification of the US to display American hostility toward the Japanese in those post-Pearl Harbor days. Racism? Perhaps a touch—and any current use of the epithet "Japs" would rightly be considered offensive. Still, many Japanese, in those days, felt much the same about the West. [Uncle Sam cover art © DC Comics; postcard © Tichnor Brothers, Inc., or successors in interest.]

UNCLE SAM

Call me **Buddy**. I'm just an American boy who has the honor to fight side by side with a living legend—literally. In 1777 a patriot named **Samuel** (his last name is lost to history) volunteered to distract British troops from attacking Yankees carrying supplies for George Washington's troops. He fulfilled his mission, but perished in so doing. Sam's spirit rose from his body and merged with the spirits of Freedom and Liberty—and thus was born Uncle Sam, living symbol of the United States of America. In 1940, Uncle Sam merged with another man—this one named **Samuels**—who was fighting against the Nazi Black Legion. The Nazis didn't fare any better than the Redcoats had!

GOLDEN AGE APPEARANCES:
National Comics #1-45 (July 1940 – Dec. 144) – origin in #1
Uncle Sam #1-8 (Fall 1941 – Fall 1943) – origin expanded in #1

THE VIGILANTE

Hiya, hombres! I'm **Billy Gunn**, but everybody calls me Pop. I've shared many early escapades with **Greg Sanders**, "The Prairie Troubadour," who became the modern masked cowboy called Vigilante to avenge his father's death at the hands of "stagecoach bandits." Greg grew up admiring the legendary cowboys of the Old West: Johnny Thunder, Nighthawk, and the like. He fashioned himself after them, but in place of a faithful horse he rode a motorcycle. During one foray in Chinatown he met his later young companion, Stuff. Vig was one of the Seven Soldiers of Victory and had lots of adventures just like his Western idols, when he wasn't singing or making movies.

GOLDEN AGE APPEARANCES:
Action Comics #42-198 (Nov. 1941 – Nov. 1954) – origin in #42 – Billy Gunn intro'd in #43, Stuff intro'd in #45
Leading Comics #1-14 (Winter 1942 – Spring 1945) as a member of the Seven Soldiers of Victory
Action Comics Miniature (1947) (all-Vigilante issue published in conjunction with *Vigilante* movie serial)
Western Comics #1-4 (Jan.-Feb. 1948 – July-Aug. 1948) (Oddly, the Vigilante stories in *Western* were set in the Old West!)

Ever Vigilant(e)

Mort Meskin drew Vigilante, the hero he had originated with writer Mort Weisinger, in solo chapters in early issues of Leading Comics. This panel of Vig and sidekick Billy Gunn from #2 (Spring 1942), with scripting attributed to Bill Finger, is repro'd from The Seven Soldiers of Victory Archives, Vol. 1. [© DC Comics.]

THE WHIP

I'm **Marissa Dillon**, journalist for the *Seguro Sentinel*, the newspaper of a little New Mexican town where the Association of Ranchers was oppressing the poor peons. In our local church, **Rodney Elwood Gaynor** (a playboy visiting from the East) and I discovered the legend of *El Castigo*, a masked caballero (descended from the Grandes de España) who fought 100 years ago to protect peons from wealthy Mexican land-owners. That night, when the ranchers tried to lynch a poor man guilty of no more than stealing something to eat, El Castigo—The Whip—rode again in defense of the weak and helpless. I soon suspected who was behind his mask, but kept his secret so he could keep fighting the good fight.

GOLDEN AGE APPEARANCES:

Flash Comics #1-55 (Jan. 1940 – July 1944)
 – origin in #1
Big All-American Comic Book (1944)
Sensation Comics #43 (July 1945).

Zorro Whips It Up

The masked, black-clad, whip-wielding Zorro (Spanish for "Fox") first made a splash in cold print in 1919—and became a cultural phenomenon when Douglas Fairbanks starred in the film The Mark of Zorro the very next year. The hero appeared in his first movie serial in 1937; the still at left is from the second one, Zorro's Fighting Legion (1939). [© the respective copyright holders.]

Many were the descendants of Zorro—and indeed, even Superman and especially Batman can be partly considered as such. But DC went all-out with The Whip, phony Spanish accent and all, as in the Homer Fleming-drawn panel below from Flash Comics #40 (April 1943). [© DC Comics.]

(Left:) In the 1950s, Golden Age Green Lantern/JSA artist Alex Toth drew several Zorro comics for Western, adapting the popular Disney TV series. This 1992 drawing was done for a fellow artist, and appeared in one of Manuel Auad's indispensable Toth volumes. [Art © Alex Toth; Zorro TM & © the respective copyright holders.]

★ READ ZATARA'S MAGIC WORDS BACKWARD.

ZATARA THE MASTER MAGICIAN

Ym tnadnecsed, **Innavoig "Nhoj" Arataz**, si osla dednecsed morf a suoirolg enil fo snaicigam: lemalF, ortsoilgaC, sumadartsoN dna flesym, **Odranoel Ad icniv**. Sih rehtafdnarg saw a egats naicigam ohw evag eht gnuoy innavoiG a xob lluf fo sporp os eh dluoc trats sih nwo reerac. Tub t'nsaw litnu eh dnuof eht neddih yek ni ym tseret sgnitirw taht eh derevocsid taht, yb gnikaeps sdrawkcab, eh dluoc redro lla ytilaer ot yebo mih. Eh desu sih dnuofwen srewop ton tsuj sa a egats naicigam tub sa a "oreh-repus."

GOLDEN AGE APPEARANCES:

Action Comics #1-132, 136, 138, 141 (June 1938 – Feb. 1950) –
 no origin story
New York World's Fair Comics (1939 & 1940 issues)
World's Best Comics #1 (Spring 1941)
World's Finest Comics #2-45, 47-51 (Summer 1941 – April-May 1951).

Do You Believe In Magic?

(Above right:) Mandrake the Magician by writer/creator Lee Falk and artist Phil Davis was one of the most popular adventure comic strips of the 1930s. Here, Mandrake gestures hypnotically, as he's done for most of his career, and the bad-guy sees him in triplicate! [© King Features Syndicate.]

(Above left:) Zatara continued the tradition of mustachioed magicians wearing top hats and tails, but performed real magic by speaking words backward. In Action Comics #92 (Jan. 1946), he wants to learn certain truths about a ham actor, so figures he'll ask "his most intimate companion, the one who sees him most often"—namely, his mirror. Nice touch! Art credited to W.F. White. [© DC Comics.]

PEDRO ANGOSTO has written for fanzines, Spanish editions of Marvel Comics, *The Jack Kirby Collector*, et al. His comic book credits include the Spanish super-hero group *Circulo Justiciero*, as well as a few US comics stories. He dreams of "writing the JSA and a couple of thousand other super-heroes."

CHAPTER XIV

ALL-STAR SQUADRON

Issue By Issue

by Roy Thomas & Kurt Mitchell

Introductory Note

67 issues of *All-Star Squadron* were published between 1981 and 1987, in addition to the 16-page *Preview* insert in *Justice League of America* #193, three *All-Star Squadron Annuals*, and three crossovers with the modern-day JLA and JSA in *Justice League of America*. Following is an issue-by-issue listing of those 74 comics, with pertinent information on the Golden Age DC, Quality, and Fawcett heroes who appeared in them (see abbreviations in the Key below), the creative teams, brief synopses of the stories (plus titles and page counts), plus noteworthy points, oddities, and historical context concerning the issues. Kurt Mitchell wrote most of the story synopses and contributed other tidbits of information. Further facts about the background of the stories or art have been added either under the sections headed "NOTES," or in captions accompanying the various art spots.

FOLEY '04
after
ANDERSON
after
? HIBBARD

With Apologies To Frank Brunner Dept.:

Australian collector/artist Shane Foley drew this homage to a certain comic book cover that shall remain nameless, utilizing key members of the All-Star Squadron. [Heroes TM & © DC Comics; All-Star Squadron logo is a trademark of DC Comics.]

KEY:
AM = Amazing-Man	CT = Captain Triumph	HB = Human Bomb	MH = Manhunter (DC hero)	RB = Red Bee	ST = Stripesy
AQ = Aquaman	DD = Dan the Dyna-Mite	HG = Hawkgirl	MH/Q = Manhunter (Quality hero)	RM = Robotman	SU = Superman
AT = Atom	DF = Dr. Fate	HM = Hawkman	MI = Miss America	RO = Robin	SY = Speedy
AW = Air Wave	DL = Doll Man	HO = Hour-Man	MM = Mary Marvel	RT = Red Tornado	TA = Tarantula
BC = Black Canary	DM = Dr. Mid-Nite	HU = Huntress	MN = Midnight	SA = Sandman	TB = Thunderbolt
BH = Blackhawk	DO = Dr. Occult	IH = Invisible Hood	MT = Mr. Terrific	SD = The Spider	TNT = TNT
BL = Black Condor	FB = Firebrand (Danette Reilly)	JE = Jester	MI = Miss America	SG = Sargon the Sorcerer	TS = Tsunami
BM = Batman	FB/M = Firebrand (Rod Reilly)	JQ = Johnny Quick	MN = Midnight	SK = Shining Knight	US = Uncle Sam
CA = Crimson Avenger	FL = Flash	JT = Johnny Thunder	NE = Neon the Unknown	SM = Starman	VG = Vigilante
CJ = Captain Marvel Jr.	GA = Green Arrow	LB = Liberty Belle	NP = Neptune Perkins	SN = Sandy the Golden Boy	WC = Wildcat
CM = Captain Marvel	GL = Green Lantern	LBB = Little Boy Blue & The Blue Boys	PG = Power Girl	SP = Spectre	WH = The Whip
CS = Commander Steel	GU = Guardian	MA = Mr. America	PL = Phantom Lady	SS = Star-Spangled Kid	WI = Wing
		MG = Magno	PM = Plastic Man		WW = Wonder Woman
			RA = The Ray		ZA = Zatara

SPECIAL ALL-STAR SQUADRON PREVIEW, in JUSTICE LEAGUE OF AMERICA #193

(Sept. 1981)

COVER (of *Preview*): Rich Buckler (p) & Dick Giordano (i)

STORY: (no title besides *All-Star Squadron* logo; no splash) 14 pp.

ARTISTS: Rich Buckler (p) & Jerry Ordway (i)

STARRING: WW, FL, GL, WC, SA, ST, JT (w/TB), DF, SP, SU, BM, RO, HM, DM, AT. (Cameos:) CA, VG, GA, SY, SS, ST, SK, JQ (as Johnny Chambers), LB (as Libby Lawrence), FB/M (as Rod Reilly), PM (unidentified, in shadow), RM (ditto).

SYNOPSIS: Five JSAers—plus honorary members Green Lantern, Flash, Superman, and Batman, as well as Robin and Wonder Woman—are captured on Dec. 6, 1941, by anachronistic villains Wotan, Solomon Grundy, Sky Pirate, and Professor Zodiak. But Hawkman, Dr. Mid-Nite, and Atom defeat the equally out-of-time entity called The Monster. President Roosevelt fails in attempts to contact the JSA so they can foil Japan's plan to attack Pearl Harbor.

(The final page of this 16-page insert is a full-page house ad for *All-Star Squadron* #1, announcing the issue will be on sale June 18, 1981.)

NOTES:

- Instead of Starman, the *Preview* "cover" depicts The Shining Knight, who was never a member of the JSA as were all the other heroes shown.

- Roy Thomas worked with editor Len Wein and letterer Gaspar Saladino on the logo, using as a model the one appearing on *All-Star Comics* #43-57. Roy made certain a hyphen was inserted in "*All-Star*"—not that that's always stopped other writers and editors from leaving it out. The only change ever made in the logo was that, starting with #4, the "S" in "Squadron" had a more curved look; before that, it had resembled a backward "Z."

- The USO gig of Superman, Batman, and Robin was inspired by the cover of *World's Finest Comics* #6 (Summer 1942—cover artist uncertain). It's on view in the first volumes of both the *Superman* and *Batman* editions of the *World's Finest Comics Archives*.

- In one panel, Buckler drew Robotman looking at the famous statue of the US flag-raising on Iwo Jima—but that statue was based on a photo that wouldn't be taken till 1945! Thomas had Ordway alter it to the Washington Monument.

- Roy goofed, as well, in that same panel. A caption says the figure in a hat and overcoat was "braced against the chill late-autumn winds." Robotman would hardly have been bothered by even a stiff breeze, let alone the cold!

Bonus Points

In the early 1980s, DC Comics often introduced new magazine series by including a 16-page insert in the middle of an ongoing comics title, without raising the cover price. All-Star Squadron, quite fittingly, was folded into Justice League of America #193. [© DC Comics.]

- By and large, the super-heroes were drawn and colored in *All-Star Squadron* very much as per authentic 1941-42 comics, except for Hawkman's 1946-era helmet (a personal quirk of RT's), the red rather than orange lapels on The Atom (at the insistence of editor Len Wein), Liberty Belle's added mask (RT didn't feel her Veronica Lake peekaboo hairstyle would really hide her secret ID), Dr. Mid-Nite's copper-colored gloves and boots (which he did sport occasionally in the '40s, instead of the usual gray), and The Shining Knight's hawk chest-insignia (which was dropped after early stories).

- Detailed articles by RT on the *Preview* and #1 are still available in *Alter Ego* (Vol. 3) #6, 8, 12, 14, & 21—containing far more background info than we've room for here!

Preview Of Coming Attractions

The All-Star Squadron (left) and Bloodwolf, Son of Thunder (above).

Coming Soon To This Comic Book Store

(Left:) The cover of DC's 4-page Coming Attractions for May 1981, a pamphlet published for retailers, trumpeted Roy Thomas' two forthcoming new DC creations upon leaving Marvel after 15 years. At this point, the series destined to become Arak, Son of Thunder was still titled Bloodwolf; pencils by co-creator Ernie Colón. RT later heard unofficially that All-Star Squadron #1 sold a then-hefty 250,000 copies, Arak #1 only slightly less. [© DC Comics.]

(Right:) Hal Schuster's news fanzine Comics Feature (#11, Aug. 1981), edited by Richard Howell & Carol Kalish (who interviewed Roy Thomas therein), threw a spotlight on those two upcoming series. Bill Black, today the publisher/editor of AC Comics, drew the cover art shown at right. [All-Star Squadron © DC Comics.]

Winning By A, Er, Nose

The March of Dimes charity race in JLA #193's Preview (seen at right), wherein not-yet-JSAer Wonder Woman outstripped Flash and Green Lantern, was inspired by the above wraparound cover for Comic Cavalcade #1 (Dec. 1942-Jan. 1943), which is attributed to artist Frank Harry. In the 1981 tale,

though, Wildcat was present only as a judge, and The Ghost Patrol, et al., weren't on hand at all—unless they were in the audience. Presumably, the "photo" of that photo finish was taken some time before it was used as a comic cover. The CC art was restored for DC's Comic Cavalcade Archives, Vol. 1. Preview interior art by Rich Buckler & Jerry Ordway; script by Roy Thomas. [© DC Comics.]

"This Means War!"

(Above:) On the final story page of the JLA #193 Preview: on the night of Dec. 6/7, 1941, President Franklin Delano Roosevelt and special assistant Harry Hopkins receive the decoded text of a secret Japanese message, and FDR is reported to have said the three words quoted above. (But—"readed"?!) In our world, Hopkins was not present at this moment. FDR's addressing him as "Harry" led some readers to believe the man with him was Harry Truman; but Senator Truman only became FDR's Vice President in early 1945. [© DC Comics.]

(Right:) Though FDR and Hopkins had a close professional and personal relationship all during the 1930s New Deal and World War II, there are very few photos of the two men together.

The Evil That Men Do Lives After Them...

Each of the JSAers' attackers on Dec. 6, 1941, in the Preview was a time-displaced villain, seen below in panels from 1981 and the 1940s. 1981 art by Buckler & Ordway: [All art © DC Comics.]

(Above:) Solomon Grundy premiered in All-American Comics #61 (Oct. 44), where GL's ring had no effect on the swamp monster. Script by Alfred Bester, art by Paul Reinman.

(Above:) Wotan's first face-off with Dr. Fate had occurred in their mutual debut in More Fun Comics #55 (May 1940); script by Gardner Fox, art by Howard Sherman—soon on view in DC's hardcover Golden Age Doctor Fate Archives, Vol. 1. In All-Star Squadron, Degaton had rescued Wotan from limbo in "the late '40s."

(Above:) Post-WWII baddie Sky Pirate's final Golden Age match-up with GL took place in Comic Cavalcade #25 (Feb.-March 1948), in a tale penciled by Irwin Hasen.

(Below:) The Monster and Prof. Zodiak (a.k.a. The Alchemist) would take their first bows in All-Star Comics #20 & #42, respectively. To see them in their only 1940s appearances, see appropriate volumes of the All Star Comics Archives.

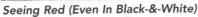

Seeing Red (Even In Black-&-White)

Rod Reilly (the original Firebrand) and his sister Danette did a cameo in the Preview. Danette was the birth-name of Roy's then-bride Dann Thomas, likewise a redhead. [© DC Comics.]

A Cast Of Characters

The team supreme on the Preview. (Clockwise from top left:)

Len Wein (editor) entered the field as a writer in 1971. Wrote major titles for both DC and Marvel during that decade, but most noted for his work with artist Bernie Wrightson on DC's Swamp Thing.

Roy Thomas (scripter) became writer and assistant editor at Marvel in 1965, noted especially for The Avengers and the Conan titles before moving to DC at the end of 1980.

Rich Buckler (penciler) became a professional artist in the early '70s for DC and Marvel, working on such major titles as Fantastic Four and Avengers. Seen at right is a 2006 sketch of Johnny Quick done by Rich for Keif Simon, who snapped the photo.

Jerry Ordway (inker, pp. 2-14) debuted as a pro on All-Star Squadron, soon becoming penciler of first that mag, then Infinity, Inc. His 1988 Liberty Belle sketch is courtesy of the artist.

Len's pic is from the 1975 Marvel Convention program book... Roy's 1980s mug shot is courtesy of Jennie-Lynn Falk... Rich's was taken at a 2005 New York comics convention by Keif Simon & Jim Murtagh... and Jerry's likeness was snapped at the 1997 Fandom Reunion Luncheon in Chicago by J.E. Smith. [Heroes in art TM & © DC Comics.]

The Main Event!

The final, 16th page of the Preview was a house ad for All-Star Squadron #1, on sale a few weeks later. Incidentally, DC's powers-that-be had originally wanted all JSAers downplayed in the series, but Roy argued persuasively for utilizing a nucleus of Hawkman, Dr. Mid-Nite, and The Atom—in reality, mostly just as a matter of personal preference. [© DC Comics.]

[© DC Comics]

ALL-STAR SQUADRON #1
(Sept. 1981)

COVER: Rich Buckler (p) & Dick Giordano (i)

[**SPECIAL NOTE ON COVER:** HM, DM & AT are shown standing amid a table and wall which feature color photos of SK, GA, PL (mostly obscured), JQ, BM, RO, SS, ST, VG, RM, DF, SA, SU, FL, CT, TA, LB, PM, CA, JT (w/TB), SP, GL, WW.]

STORY: "The World on Fire!" – 25 pp.

ARTISTS: Rich Buckler (p) & Jerry Ordway (i)

STARRING: HM, PM, SK, FB/M (as Rod Reilly), DM, AT, JQ, LB, RM. (Cameos:) FL, GL, WW, SU, BM, RO, DF, SP, SM, SA, JT (w/TB).

SYNOPSIS: Hawkman and Plastic Man battle King Bee's Insect Men. Shining Knight and vulcanologist Danette Reilly are captured at Per Degaton's Pacific island HQ. Pearl Harbor is attacked on Dec. 7, 1941, and Lt. Rod Reilly is badly wounded. Hawkman, Plas, Dr. Mid-Nite, Atom, and non-JSAers Robotman, Liberty Belle, and Johnny Quick respond to FDR's call; the President dubs them the All-Star Squadron.

NOTES:

- The only Dec. 1941 JSAer not shown on the cover is Starman.
- "The World on Fire" was the title of a song popular in December 1941. A recording of it was apparently on the jukebox at the Pearl Harbor PX at the time of the attack, and, while it was probably not playing while the bombs were falling as in *All-Star Squadron #1*, it has been reported that it was played over and over that night: "*I don't want to set the world on fire/I just want to start a flame in your heart.*" It was, and remains, astonishing to Roy Thomas that no one has ever written a history of World War II bearing that title.

Joyful DICK GIORDANO

Dick Giordano (inker of the covers of both #1 and the Preview in JLA #193) has been a comic artist since the early 1950s, and was also a DC editor in 1981, soon becoming the company's managing editor; he was noted particularly for his inking of Neal Adams on Green Lantern/Green Arrow and "Batman." Photo from the 1975 Marvel Convention program book

- Hawkman appeared on the splash because he's always been RT's favorite JSA (and Golden Age) hero—and because he was the only JSAer who was featured in every one of the group's 1940-51 adventures. RT intended the Feathered Fury to make at least a cameo appearance in every issue of *Squadron*—and he came within one of pulling it off!

- In 1941-42 Plastic Man's adventures were published by the Quality Comics Group; he only became a DC hero decades later.

- Along with brief origin recaps for several All-Stars, this issue reprised events in *All-Star Comics* #10 & #35. The latter, of course, introduced Per Degaton; his *All-Star Squadron* appearances occurred between #35 and his membership in the first *In*justice Society of the World two issues later, which would be explained in the later limited series *America vs. the Justice Society*.

- The issue contains a one-page text piece by RT detailing the creation of *All-Star Squadron*.

Poor Little Lost Bird-Man?

As Jerry Ordway revealed in Alter Ego #14, Buckler's original pencil art for "the first 14 or so pages" of All-Star Squadron #1 was lost in transit by Federal Express, so DC gave Jerry "poor photocopies to ink over, on vellum"... which was "a nightmare." Not that you could tell from the finished product by Rich Buckler and "Jeremiah Ordway"! [© DC Comics.]

Bee Prepared

(Above:) Hawkman tackles King Bee—who's now on view in All Star Archives, Vol. 4, reprinting All-Star Comics #18 (Fall 1943), which took place nearly two years after events in All-Star Squadron #1. ("Lucky Lindy" is Charles Lindbergh, who in 1927 became the first aviator to fly the Atlantic to Paris.) [© DC Comics.]

The most famous comics characters with insect names have been The Green Hornet, Blue Beetle, and The Fly (spiders aren't insects!), but let's not forget Bee-Man, that campy Harvey hero from Double Dare Adventures in 1966-67. Or maybe we should. With thanks to the aptly-named "Gone and Forgotten" website. [© the respective copyright holders.]

Homage Sweet Homage

(Left:) Dick Giordano—who apparently was once slated to be the original editor of All-Star Squadron and inked Buckler's cover for #1—drew this gala transmutation of that cover for Alter Ego #32 (2004), utilizing Golden Age Timely/Marvel heroes instead. It's a beauty! [© Marvel Characters, Inc.]

(Above:) Artist Al Bigley drew this commission illo for collector Brian S. Carney, substituting likenesses of newspaper comic strip heroes—which included Superman and Batman! [Art © Al Bigley; Superman & Batman TM & © DC Comics; other characters TM & © the respective trademark and copyright holders.]

"Live In Infamy"

Though many Americans had no idea on Dec. 7, 1941, where Pearl Harbor was, the attack by Imperial Japanese planes brought the US into what was now, beyond doubt, the Second World War. This photo of the USS Arizona's forward magazine exploding was taken from the hospital ship Solace. On Earth-Two, the doomed Arizona—which sank with 1000 men aboard—was the battleship of Ensign Rod Reilly and seaman Slugger Dunn; they were strafed trying to reach it during the assault.

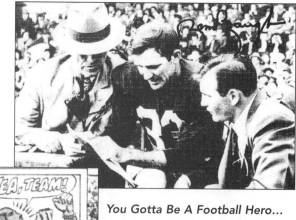

You Gotta Be A Football Hero...

Yes, Virginia, there was a Washington Redskins football game on the afternoon of Sunday, Dec. 7, 1941. Legendary quarterback Sammy Baugh was indeed playing, as various military personnel were paged from their seats to learn of the attack on US bases in Hawaii. On Earth-Two, Dr. Mid-Nite and The Atom were among the crowd. (P.S.: We didn't print a photo here of FBI Chief J. Edgar Hoover, who also appeared in #1, because we ran one of him in Vol. 1.) Comic panels by Thomas, Buckler, & Ordway. [Comic art © DC Comics.]

Three From Column A...

...plus three from column B, and one from column C. A trio of JSAers... another of DC non-JSAers... and a dash of Quality. That became the makeup of Squadron. By Buckler, Ordway, & Thomas. [© DC Comics.]

Meeting Cute

Johnny (Quick) Chambers and Libby (Liberty Belle) Lawrence encounter each other for the first time just outside the gates of the White House on Dec. 7, 1941. By Thomas, Buckler, & Ordway. [© DC Comics.]

Okay, Axis, Here We All Come!

(Right:) In the earlier Marvel WWII comic developed by Roy Thomas, The Invaders take their name from a comment by British Prime Minister Winston Churchill, whom they'd rescued from Master Man, in Giant-Size Invaders #1 (June 1975). Script by RT, pencils by Frank Robbins, inks by Vince Colletta. Thanks to Bruce Mason for the scan. [© Marvel Characters, Inc.]

(Above:) In All-Star Squadron #1, it's President Roosevelt who christens the DC group. Script by Thomas, art by Buckler & Ordway. (In 1977's DC Special #29, it had been Superman who named the 1940 Justice Society of America... in FDR's presence.) [© DC Comics.]

☆★

ALL-STAR SQUADRON #2
(Oct. 1981)

COVER: Joe Kubert

STORY: "The Tyrant Out of Time!" – 26 pp.

ARTISTS: Rich Buckler (p) & Jerry Ordway (i)

STARRING: HM, DM, AT, PM, RM, LB, JQ, SK, PL. (Cameos:) SA, SM, DF, SP, JT (w/TB), GL, FL, SU, BM, RO, WW.

SYNOPSIS: Seven All-Star Squadron heroes head West, as Degaton launches Japanese Zeros from his special sub. He reveals to Shining Knight and Danette Reilly that he's come from 1947 via Prof. Zee's time machine to carve out an empire, by maneuvering the US into abandoning its "Germany First" plan following Pearl Harbor so that neither Germany nor Japan is defeated by the Allies. Sky Pirate leads the Zeros in a raid on San Francisco; Phantom Lady joins in foiling it.

NOTES:

- The impromptu singing of the National Anthem outside the White House fence is based on fact.

- One sharp-eyed reader pointed out later that #2 had the All-Stars flying in a B-29 bomber, an aircraft which didn't go into service until 1944. RT responded that he had noticed that when Buckler's pencils came in, but there wasn't time to have it redrawn—but later US bombers in the series were usually B-17s or B-24s.

- #2's Fact File on Per Degaton gave his height as 5'4". He'd been drawn as if taller in #1, but his proportions were soon brought into line. In *All-Star Comics #35,*

he had clearly been modeled in part after Napoleon. Script by RT; art by Buckler & Ordway.

- As per the story, there was a natural, powerful desire on the part of many Americans to engage Japan first, not Germany—but US leaders knew that would be both impractical and bad strategy.

- The issue includes a one-page text piece by RT on the historical background of the series and the All-Stars' first comic book appearances.

Just A Guy Named Joe

Starting with #2, Joe Kubert (seen above in the 1970s) became the artist of many of the mag's covers. At right is the (autographed) splash of the first story he ever drew: "Volton," from Holyoke's Cat-Man #8 (Feb. 1942), done when Joe was around 15. Thanks to Mike Bromberg's Volton Fanzine #1; check out MB's full-color Golden Age reprints at mike@designbymike.com. [Art © the respective copyright holders.]

Westward Bound

(Left:) On their way to Pearl Harbor by plane, the All-Stars exchanged origin stories—and even secret identities! Repro'd from a photocopy of the original Buckler/Ordway art, courtesy of Rick Shurgin; script by RT.

(Above & right:) Panels from Liberty Belle's origin in Boy Commandos #1 (Winter 1942-43), in which she's swimming the English Channel from Dunkirk to escape the Germans, and later dons her costume (but no mask!) for the first time. Her origin was backdated to December 1941 because All-Star Squadron needed super-heroines. Script by Don Cameron, art by Chuck Winter. [© DC Comics.]

ENEMY PLANES OFF FRISCO

Formations Lose Way as Radio Stations Quit Air; Craft Get Close to Golden Gate

The Rising Sun By Night

(Clockwise from top left:) The first wave of Japanese warplanes takes off from a carrier 200+ miles north of Honolulu on the day that was, in Japan, already Dec. 8, 1941.

On the morning of Dec. 8 in the USA, many San Franciscans—thanks to a long night of sirens—believed enemy aircraft had flown over their city the night before, as per this headline from a Dec. 9 Buffalo, NY (!), newspaper.

Lt. General John L. DeWitt (commanding officer, Fourth Army and Western Defense Command—seen here with San Francisco mayor Rossi) told newsmen that "Japanese planes... were over our community for a definite period.... Why no bombs were dropped, I do not know. It might have been better if some bombs had dropped to awaken the city." He hadn't "any doubt the planes came from a carrier." In our world, it was just war nerves; on Earth-Two, the Zeros were launched from Degaton's special sub/carrier. So DeWitt was right on one world, anyway!

Even so, this newspaper map captioned "Enemy Planes Reported Over Coast" showed paths allegedly taken by two squadrons of Japanese planes on Dec. 7. All-Star Squadron #2 made them a reality. [© the respective copyright holders.]

I Left My Headlights In San Francisco

Phantom Lady, in 1941 a heroine published by the Quality group, helps restore order to a panicked San Francisco—and becomes an All-Star—in issue #2. In retrospect, Roy Thomas feels perhaps it might have been a better idea to leave Quality's heroes on the Earth-X created by All-Star Squadron editor Len Wein. Repro'd from a photocopy of the original art, courtesy of Rick Shurgin. [© DC Comics.]

ALL-STAR SQUADRON #3
(Nov. 1981)

COVER: Rich Buckler (p) & Dick Giordano (i)

STORY: "The Dooms of Dark December!" – 27 pp.

ARTISTS: Rich Buckler (p) & Jerry Ordway (i)

STARRING: HM, RM, JQ, PM, AT, DM, LB, PL, SK, SA, BM, RO, WW, FL, SM, JT, SU, DF, SP, GL.

SYNOPSIS: The initial All-Star Squadron heroes (now including Phantom Lady and Shining Knight) defeat Degaton and his forces and free the captive JSAers, Robin, and Wonder Woman. By a fluke of the time machine, the heroes forget the anachronistic villains they fought—and even precisely what happened to them.

NOTES:

• Joe Kubert drew a cover for #3 with a similar scene, but Rich Buckler convinced editor Wein that, as interior penciler, he should do all the covers. RT utilized Kubert's unused cover, with the artist's blessing, as a story page in the 1988 *Young All-Stars Annual #1*; it became the only page RT has ever scripted featuring the art of Kubert, his favorite comic artist. It was later used as the cover of the trade paperback *Alter Ego: The Comic Book Artist Collection*.

• In *All-Star Comics* #42 (1948), Prof. Zodiak's "alchemically-powered plane" did not work properly and crashed, but it functions well in this later/earlier tale.

• Degaton's flashback details why Solomon Grundy was shown returning from exile on the moon in 1965's *Showcase* #55, when the lunar denouement to 1947's *All-Star* #33 had been superceded by Grundy's fourth and final Golden Age appearance, in *Comic Cavalcade* #24 (Dec. 1947-Jan. 1948), wherein GL buried him deep in the Earth. It also explains away Grundy's greater intelligence in the *CC* story.

• Degaton's troops are revealed to have been mesmerized by the same drug used to turn men into human robots in the GL solo story in *All-Star* #2.

• To get past the fact that speaking or writing the initials of "All-Star Squadron" could be awkward, Superman says one must be "careful how you abbreviate it." Of course, the proper abbreviation of that actually-*two*-word name would be "AS" anyway.

• The issue contains a one-page Super-Villain Fact File with info on Grundy, Zodiak, Wotan, and Sky Pirate. All such pages through #8 feature art penciled by Bucker and inked by Ordway in advance of *All-Star Squadron #1*, with script by RT.

The First Lady

On the evening of Dec. 7, The Spectre conjures up an image of a slightly earlier radio address by Eleanor (Mrs. Franklin) Roosevelt. Though a reference to the All-Star Squadron was added in the comic, that speech actually occurred. A photo of the wartime First Lady is below. [© DC Comics.]

Hail, Hail, The Gang's All Here!

The JSA and All-Stars get together for the first time near the end issue #3. [© DC Comics.]

ALL-STAR SQUADRON #4
(Dec. 1981)

COVER: Rich Buckler (p) & Dick Giordano (i)

STORY: "Day of the Dragon King!" – 27 pp.

ARTISTS: Rich Buckler (p) & Jerry Ordway (i)

STARRING: Same heroes as #3, plus TB, minus PL & PM.

SYNOPSIS: 17 All-Stars arrive at devastated Pearl Harbor, determined to carry the war to Japan. Danette Reilly is reunited with her wounded brother Rod. The mysterious Dragon King technologically magnifies the power of the Spear of Destiny and Holy Grail (Grailstone) to give the Axis control of any magic-based beings who encounter their aura—including Superman (because of an unknown Kryptonite component)—thereby forcing America's most powerful heroes to keep out of Axis-held territory.

NOTES:

- Was it on purpose or by accident that one Wein-written blurb on the cover reads: "A Climax You'll Never Forget!"?

- Johnny Thunder's Thunderbolt makes his first appearance in the series (not counting the *Preview* in *JLA* #193); as an entity subservient to JT, he was never officially a member of either Squadron or JSA.

- The Shining Knight notes that Danette Reilly seems "warmer to the touch than you should"—a harbinger of issue #5's revelations. (It also underscores the fact that, from #1, Justin and Danette seemed destined for a romance.)

- Slugger Dunn, Rod Reilly's confidant, is seen on crutches.

- As DC wished to avoid the racially-charged word "Japs," which was in common usage in America during WWII, the first few issues use the equally authentic term "Nips," a milder (though still somewhat loaded) term which is short for "Nippon," the Japanese name for their land.

- Superman's musings on how, only three years earlier, he'd been "the *only* guy with such fantastic powers on the *whole* planet" is a nod to the fact that all comic book super-heroes are ultimately derived from his debut in 1938's *Action Comics* #1.

- Mention is made of near-simultaneous Japanese attacks on Wake Island, Guam, and the Philippines as well as on Hawaii, but not of those on British colonies such as Thailand and Mayala.

- This issue features the series' first letters column, titled "All-Star Comments." RT wrote and signed all LPs, under Len Wein from #1-18. Most issues had letters sections.

Dragon His Feet

The Dragon King, an agent of the Japanese Empire, vows further action—but never again appeared in All-Star Squadron. Roy Thomas had other things vaguely in mind for him, but never quite got around to realizing them. [© DC Comics.]

Hickam Field On Earths-Two & -Prime

At left, the All-Stars land at the US Army's Oahu airfield on Dec. 8, 1941. The photo shows a makeshift observation post at Hickam, formed of sandbags, furniture, and a wrecked airplane engine. [Art © DC Comics.]

" WHEN, AS THEY ARE SCHEDULED TO DO MERE SECONDS FROM NOW, THOUGH SEPARATED BY THOUSANDS OF MILES--

"--REICHSFÜHRER HITLER AND PREMIER TOJO PERFORM CERTAIN RITES, SPEAK CERTAIN WORDS OVER THEIR TWIN TALISMANS--

"--THEIR ACTIONS WILL MAKE BOTH HITLER'S FORTRESS EUROPA AND OUR OWN GREATER EAST ASIA CO-PROSPERITY SPHERE TOTALLY IMPREGNABLE TO COUNTERATTACK BY AMERICA'S MOST POWERFUL COSTUMED CHAMPIONS!

The Spears and Grailstones Of Outrageous Fortune

(Left:) In #4, Nazi Germany's Adolf Hitler and Japan's war minister Gen. Hideki Tojo (see photo in Vol. 1) brandish twin talismans. The Spear of Destiny is making a reappearance from 1977's DC Special #29. The Holy Grail is postulated in All-Star Squadron #4 to be "a cup carved wholly of stone—and graven with ancient mystic runes." In his poem Parzival, the German writer Wolfram von Eschenbach (1170-c. 1220) proposed that the Grail was not a chalice but a gemstone; later writers linked this with Moldavite, a mineral found in a meteorite crater in Czechoslovakia and reputed to have spiritual powers. (You can buy a chunk of it now over the Internet!) Roy T. wished to minimalize the Holy Grail's legendary origins as the cup from which Christ drank at the Last Supper. The reason for the use of the two talismans in different hemispheres was to provide a rationale for why the most powerful All-Stars (The Spectre, Superman, et al.) didn't simply invade Germany and Japan and end the war soon after Pearl Harbor... though, in retrospect, RT feels he handled it a bit clumsily by forcing the whole story into a single issue. [Comic art © DC Comics.]

(Above right:) Trevor Ravenscroft's bestselling 1972 book The Spear of Destiny popularized myths about the shaft which had allegedly pierced the side of Christ on the cross. The Spear was brought into the DC Universe in Weird War Tales #50 (Jan.-Feb. 1977) by writer Steve Englehart and artists Dick Ayers & Alfredo Alcala; a few months later, scripter Paul Levitz utilized it in "The Untold Origin of the Justice Society" in DC Special #29.

ALL-STAR SQUADRON #5
(Jan. 1982)

COVER: Rich Buckler (p) & Romeo Tanghal (i)

STORY: "Never Step on a Feathered Serpent!" – 27 pp.

ARTISTS: Rich Buckler (p) & Jerry Ordway (i)

STARRING: HM, DM, SM, AT, JT, SP, SA, DF, RM, JQ, LB, SK, FB (intro), HG (as Shiera Sanders). (Cameos:) GL, FB/M (in photo).

SYNOPSIS: The JSA disbands so all its regular members except Spectre (a ghost) can join the US armed forces in their civilian identities. Robotman and Johnny Quick save the Statue of Liberty from saboteurs. Danette Reilly discovers she's gained power over flames and becomes the new Firebrand. She and seven other All-Stars head for Mexico to locate Shiera Sanders—and find her a captive of Nazi agents and the masked villain called The Feathered Serpent.

What's Hot—And What Was Not

The original Rich Buckler/Romeo Tanghal art for the cover of All-Star Squadron #5 is seen here obscuring most of the cover as published—because, due to a glitch, only the word "FIREBRAND!" was printed in the arrow at its upper left. Roy T. printed the full copy in the next issue's LP. Thanks to Rick Shurgin. [© DC Comics.]

NOTES:

- The scene in this issue of FDR giving his "date which will live in infamy" speech to a joint session of Congress on Dec. 8, 1941, matches one (also written by RT) in *Giant-Size Invaders* #1 in 1975—but, in the earlier story, RT accidentally wrote "day" instead of "date."

- Danette's fiery new powers are indicated to have been generated by a combination of scientific and magical factors.

- The term "Quisling" refers to Vidkun Quisling, a Norwegian leader infamous for having helped deliver his country to the invading Germans in 1940. The word swiftly entered the English language, referring to one who betrays his own people to an enemy.

- The Feathered Serpent asserts that he intends for his own native-born cult, not the Nazis, to rule Mexico after the USA is defeated by the Axis.

- A reference by the Serpent to Hitler's quest for "the still-lost Ark of the Covenant" is, of course, a nod to Steven Spielberg's block-buster 1981 film *Raiders of the Lost Ark*.

(Armed) Service With A Smile

Splash of #5, repro'd from a photocopy of the original art, courtesy of Rick Shurgin. The opening pages of the issue retold events from the JSA intro in 1942's All-Star Comics #11, which nowadays is on view in All-Star Archives, Vol. 3. [© DC Comics.]

Even Marilyn Monroe Had The Radio On

In this photocopy of the original art of issue #5, p. 16, we see Danette taste-fully "nude" in shadow, as per Buckler & Ordway. Staffer Carl Gafford was instructed to add underwear lines on this and another page before sending it to the Comics Code—a dirty job, but somebody had to do it. Panel 1 is ill-aligned because Roy T., who always indicated copy on the original art in those days, added the caption above the penciled area, and shaved a matching area off the bottom; the production dept. later pasted a Photostat of the panel into place. Art courtesy of Rick Shurgin. [© DC Comics.]

Remember The North Atlantic!

According to Green Lantern #4 (Summer 1942) by writer Bill Finger and artist Mart Nodell, the Nazis planned to attack the cities of America's Northeast via an experimental aircraft carrier on Dec. 8, 1941, the day after the Pearl Harbor raid—but ran afoul of the Emerald Gladiator. This sequence was redrawn by Buckler & Ordway in All-Star Squadron #5 (top right). 1942 cover by Irwin Hasen.

On our Earth, the Germans may not even have had advance notice that the Japanese were about to launch that assault. Fortunately, Hitler did the USA the unintended favor of declaring war on it on Dec. 11; otherwise, it's problematical whether FDR would've been able to persuade Congress to open hostilities with Nazi Germany (which after all hadn't attacked America—and isn't even mentioned in his "infamy" speech to Congress on Dec. 8), even though the US and Germany had been fighting a virtual undeclared naval war in the Atlantic, as FDR tried to give "all aid short of war" to the beleaguered British. Seen in the photo is a German U-boat, type VII-A, which one historian calls "the scourge of Britain's seas in those hard months of 1940 and 1941." [Art © DC Comics.]

☆☆☆☆☆☆☆☆☆☆☆☆☆☆☆☆☆☆☆☆☆☆☆☆☆☆☆

Altared Plans

Rich Buckler's pencils for #6's cover are his last work for All-Star Squadron, done before he left the series in a dispute with DC prior to beginning penciling the issue. Oddly, the title of #5's story, "Never Step on a Feathered Serpent," was used as the topline on this cover a month later.
[© DC Comics.]

ALL-STAR SQUADRON #6
(Feb. 1982)

COVER: Rich Buckler (a) & Jerry Ordway (a)

STORY: "Mayhem in the Mile-High City!" – 27 pp.

ARTISTS: Adrian Gonzales (p) & Jerry Ordway (i)

STARRING: HM, SK, HG, AT, DM, JQ, FB, LB, RM.

SYNOPSIS: The All-Star Squadron disrupt the alliance between The Feathered Serpent and the Nazis meant to conquer Mexico for the Axis. Shiera goes into action as Hawkgirl. The Feathered Serpent is revealed to be a German who intended to carve out a Latin American empire of his own, independent even of Hitler.

NOTES:

• There's another mention of Quisling, and also a disparaging reference to Marshal Petain, revered French general of World War I, who tarnished his reputation with the British and Americans by heading the government of "Vichy France" from 1940-44. Vichy became the capital of the one-third of France which, though unoccupied after the German conquest in June 1940, became politically subservient to the Third Reich. If you've seen the 1942 film *Casablanca*, you don't need to hear any more.

Gonzales Is Piped Aboard

Adrian Gonzales, All-Star Squadron's second penciler (#6-18), who later moved on to Arak, Son of Thunder, also drew such heroes as Superman, Batman, and Sgt. Rock for DC. He passed away on Oct. 23, 1998, of an aneurism. Our thanks to his widow Luz Gonzales for the photo. For a sample of Adrian's pencils, see p. 140.

- The Feathered Serpent mentions that both the [real-life] scientist J.L. Stephens and his own contemporary, "Prof. Indiana Jones," had searched for the Lost Pyramid of Kulklan—another nod to *Raiders of the Lost Ark*.

- One panel shows a detailed drawing of the front of the National Palace, home of Mexico's President and of its own "Liberty Bell," first rung in 1810 to announce the country's independence from Spain.

Aztecs, Mayas, and Nazis

The plumed/feathered serpent of stone above, in the Mexican National Museum, may represent Quetzalcoatl, the Aztec equivalent of the Mayan deity Kulkulkan. Nearly a decade and a half before All-Star Squadron *#5-6, Marvel's* The X-Men *#25 (Oct. 1966) had introduced a super-villain sporting the latter name, as per the panel at right by Werner Roth & Dick Ayers from the b&w* Essential Classic X-Men, Vol 2. *It's hardly a coincidence that Roy Thomas, who scripted all the above issues, had spent a month driving around Mexico in 1964. [Art © Marvel Characters, Inc.]*

Kulkulkan Kayoed

This Gonzales/Ordway panel from #6 is repro'd from a photocopy of the original Gonzales/Ordway art, minus dialogue, courtesy of veteran comics writer & editor Paul Kupperberg. [© DC Comics.]

¡Viva Avila Camacho!

Manuel Avila Camacho, President of Mexico from 1940-46, makes a prominent appearance in issue #6, where the All-Stars protect him from The Feathered Serpent and the Nazis. After two of its ships carrying oil were sunk by German U-boats, Mexico declared war on Germany on May 22, 1942.

★★★★★★★★★★★★★★★★★★★★★★★★★★★★★★

ALL-STAR SQUADRON #7
(March 1982)

COVER: Joe Kubert

STORY: "Carnage for Christmas!" – 27 pp.

ARTISTS: Adrian Gonzales (p) & Jerry Ordway (i)

STARRING: AT, HG, LB, JQ, RM, FB, SK, PM. (Cameos:) HM, JT, SA, SP, DM, SM, AT, DF, SU, BM, FL, GL, CS (unidentified, in shadow).

SYNOPSIS: Baron Blitzkrieg captures British Prime Minister Winston Churchill, who's come to America for a Christmastime war conference with President Roosevelt. Plastic Man takes FDR's place, surviving the explosion of a "Churchill robot," and the All-Stars rescue Winnie himself.

NOTES:

• As a letter-writer in #11 would point out, #7's cover "photo" of the JSA includes Hourman (no longer a member) and Sandman in his early gasmask outfit. Clearly, the *Washington World* used a file photo from months before, which showed all ten charter members except The Spectre.

• On p. 3 we glimpse a poster for the MGM film *Nazi Agent*, which would be released a month later, on Jan. 21, 1942. By an ironic coincidence, since *All-Star Squadron* #7 involved a robot doppleganger for Churchill, Conrad Veidt plays German twins, one a Nazi (and Baron!), the other a refugee who detests the Nazis.

• Churchill arrived in the US on the battleship *Duke of York* on Dec. 22, 1941, and was later met at the Washington, DC, airport by FDR himself. In the comic, FDR greets Churchill as "Former Naval Person," the PM's code name in their correspondence that began in 1940…and Churchill addresses Roosevelt as "POTUS," short for "President of the United States."

• Although the JSA/All-Stars several times encounter FDR in his wheelchair, most of the American public was unaware of just how handicapped the President was, as he generally appeared in public standing with the aid of another, or with heavy metal braces on his legs.

• The story closes with excerpts from Churchill's speech given on the White House lawn on Dec. 24, that "strange Christmas eve": "Let the children have their night of fun and laughter…. Let us grown-ups share to the full in their unstinted pleasure, before we turn again to the stern task and the formidable years that lie before us, resolved that, by our sacrifice and daring, these same children shall not be robbed of their inheritance, or denied their right to live in a free and decent world. And so, in God's mercy… a Happy Christmas to you all!" To which The Atom whispers: "Amen."

It's A Dog's Life

In the image at left, The Atom pays a late-night call on President Roosevelt and his famed Scottish terrier Fala (seen in photo with FDR above left); script by Thomas, art by Gonzales & Ordway. [Art © DC Comics.]

Computer artist Alex Wright composed the fictitious Life magazine cover seen above especially for this volume. Despite its cover date, it shows not the JSA's disbanding but its formation in November 1940, as per 1977's DC Special #29—with Starman, Wildcat, Dr. Mid-Nite, and Wonder Woman added to the mix. [Heroes TM & © DC Comics; Life name & logo are trademarks of Time-Warner, Inc.]

Winston Looks Good—Like A Prime Minister Should

(Left:) Winston Churchill, arriving in the United States for his December 1941 conference with FDR, is startled to find himself face to face with Baron Blitzkrieg— and a robot double of himself! Script by RT, art by Gonzales & Ordway. The Baron and his assistant Zwerg (the word means "dwarf" in German) first appeared in the tabloid-sized 1978 comic All New Collectors' Edition, Vol. 7, #C-54 ("Superman vs. Wonder Woman," set in mid-1942), written by Gerry Conway and drawn by Jose Garcia Lopez & Dan Adkins. All-Star Squadron #7 takes place half a year earlier. [© DC Comics.]

(Center:) In this photo with FDR taken when Churchill arrived at the White House after dark on Dec. 22, he looks weary—understandable, after a long sea voyage and a night flight, even without the added menace of Baron Blitzkrieg! But he still found energy for a long evening of dinner, drinks, and a private confab with the President.

For Churchill's arrival on that same date in a 1975 Marvel comic and his initial encounter with Captain America, Human Torch, and Sub-Mariner, see p. 109.

☆☆☆☆☆☆☆☆☆☆☆☆☆☆☆☆☆☆

flashback recounts Steel's origin and his being sent by Churchill in 1940 to kidnap Hitler. Several All-Stars prevent Kung, the Assassin of a Thousand Claws, from killing Churchill on a train taking him back to Washington, DC.

NOTES:

• The Black Assassin, who tries to shoot Churchill on p. 1, is a one-shot villain, never seen again.

• Canadian Prime Minister William Lyons MacKenzie King is referred to in a caption, but is not depicted in the story.

• A Face File page features Buckler/ Ordway illos of and info on The Shining Knight, Robotman, & Johnny Quick.

Script by RT.

• On the LP, RT says that few heroes had been proposed for membership in the All-Star Squadron by as many letter-writers as Steel.

ALL-STAR SQUADRON #8
(April 1982)

COVER: Joe Kubert

STORY: "Afternoon of the Assassins!" – 24 pp.

ARTISTS: Adrian Gonzales & Don Heck (p) & Jerry Ordway (i)

[**NOTE:** "Steel" flashback scripted by Gerry Conway]

STARRING: SK, LB, CS (intro, as Steel), HG, AT, FB, FM, JQ, RM. (Cameo: HM.)

SYNOPSIS: Steel the Indestructible Man joins forces with Shining Knight and Liberty Belle in Canada to protect Churchill. A

A Speaker For All Occasions

(Left:) On Dec. 30, 1941, Churchill addressed the Canadian Parliament, and delivered the lines quoted in this panel by scripter Roy Thomas; art by Gonzales & Ordway. At the time, we didn't run across any photos of that event (though we're sure there were many)—and thus this layout of the chamber resembles that of the US Congress more than it does that of the British-style Canadian Parliament.

(Above:) Just a few days earlier, on Dec. 26—what the English call "Boxing Day"— Churchill had addressed a joint session of the US Congress, saying: "Prodigious hammer strokes have been needed to bring us together again!"

Another *Man Of Steel*—
Another Star-Spangled Avenger

(Above:) #8-9's flashback featuring the super-hero called Steel was originally intended to be part of the late-1970s series Steel the Indestructible Man. When that mag was cancelled after five issues, much of the unpublished #6 was printed in the privately-circulated Cancelled Comic Cavalcade, and Roy Thomas decided to incorporate much of Don Heck's penciled art and Gerry Conway's script into All-Star Squadron. Inking by Jerry Ordway. [© DC Comics.]

(Top right:) RT and editor Len Wein agreed that every good WWII group needed a "Captain America type"—and Steel was it! Here, Cap wades into German spies in Captain America Comics #11 (Feb. 1942), with pencils by Al Avison (inking by Al Gabrielle and/or Syd Shores). [© Marvel Characters, Inc.]

(Right center:) Gerry Conway & unidentified friend in a recent photo. The writer and editor of many DC and Marvel comics between 1968 and the late 1980s, GC is currently co-executive producer of the popular TV series Law and Order: Criminal Intent.

Kung? Foo!

Wonder Woman #228-242 featured tales of the Amazon set in 1943. In #237 (Nov. 1977), she faced the assassin Kung, as per this page from a b&w Australian reprint, sent by Mark Muller. Script by Gerry Conway; art by Jose Delbo & Vince Colletta. All-Star Squadron #8 backdated Kung to December 1941 and had the Japanese shape-shifter working hand in glove with the off-panel Baron Blitzkrieg. [© DC Comics.]

"At This Theatre Next Week"?

Pro artist Dusty Abell (Green Lantern Corps, et. al.) prepared this concept sketch for DC several years back, treating a suggested Justice Society 6-issue series as if it were a movie serial. The designated writer was to be Howard Chaykin. Along with Hitler and Blitz, it featured a likeness of Robert J. Oppenheimer, the scientist who headed the Manhattan Project that developed the atomic bomb. The limited series, however, never came to fruition. Thanks to Scott Maple for the scan, and to Dusty for permission to print it. [Green Lantern, Hawkman, & Baron Blitzkrieg TM & © DC Comics.]

ALL-STAR SQUADRON #9
(May 1982)

COVER: Joe Kubert

STORY: "Should Old Acquaintance Be Destroyed…" – 26 pp.

ARTISTS: Adrian Gonzales & Don Heck (p) & Jerry Ordway (i)

[**NOTE:** "Steel" flashback scripted by Gerry Conway]

STARRING: Same as #8 plus HM.

SYNOPSIS: At a New Year's gathering at the White House, FDR promotes the newest All-Star to "Commander Steel." A flashback reveals the failure of Steel's plan to snare Hitler and his own capture. Steel, obeying subconscious hypnotic orders from Baron Blitzkrieg, tries to kill FDR and Churchill, but is freed from their influence by the heat of Firebrand's flame.

NOTES:

• On the splash page, where Roosevelt and Churchill toast the newly-promoted Commander Steel, the British Prime Minister refers to the then-King of England as "George V," instead of the correct "George VI." RT would write in a later LP that he had noted the error (based on his own typo) when proofing the issue, but somehow the change hadn't gotten made at the DC offices. (He added the extra "I" in his own copy of the issue before it became part of a bound volume.)

• Pp. 5-14 of this issue are also taken from the unpublished *Steel* #6 by Conway and Heck, and show Steel stripped to his shorts in a Nazi concentration camp.

Commander Decision

(Above:) RT got the notion of promoting Steel to "Commander" rank from the name of a World War II Canadian super-hero whose adventures he'd read in a late-'60s reprint; he figured there were already enough "Captains" running around. The original Commander Steel was drawn by Ed Furness, who also illustrated wartime Captain Marvel tales for Canada's Grand Slam Comics. [© the respective copyright holders.]

[© DC Comics]

Steel Vs. Steel…

(Right:) Robotman against the post-hypnotically-controlled Commander Steel, at the climax of issue #9. Repro'd from a photocopy of the original art, courtesy of Rick Shurgin. [© DC Comics.]

A Couple Of Fun Guys

The flashback in All-Star Squadron #9 is composed of more Conway-Heck material from the unpublished Steel the Indestructible Man #6, inked by Ordway. In its final panel, at left, Nazi Führer Adolf Hitler and S.S. chief Heinrich Himmler arrive at the concentration camp. Above, on our Earth, Hitler and Himmler walk together at a conference. [© DC Comics.]

Hide In Plain Sight

In our continuum, Churchill emerged from his bath in the White House one morning to find an embarrassed FDR waiting to talk to him. On Earth-Two, The Atom and Liberty Belle were with the President. Churchill's first line in the fourth panel shown, uttered on both worlds, was priceless and deserved quoting. [© DC Comics.]

ALL-STAR SQUADRON #10
(June 1982)

COVER: Joe Kubert

STORY: "If An Eye Offend Thee…!" – 24 pp.

ARTISTS: Adrian Gonzales & Jerry Ordway

STARRING: HM, SM, SK, JQ, HG, FB, DM, AT, LB, RM, CS.

SYNOPSIS: Hawkman and Starman go into action when a "Flying Eye" aircraft causes B-17s to fall from the sky, while Johnny Quick, Shining Knight, and Hawkgirl defend the Washington Monument. On the Eastern Front, German and Soviet troops are blasted by the Eye—which soon lands on the White House lawn. An emerging spaceman announces he is Aknet from the twin star Proxima Centauri, come to annex this planet for the Binary Brotherhood.

NOTES:

- Robotman and Commander Steel begin a friendship, having in common the fact that both are, in their different ways, "men of steel."

- As a later letter-writer noted, word balloons for the Soviet and German tank commanders somehow got switched around, so that the German was spouting Russian, and vice versa. (See below left, panels 1-2.)

- The Fact File page contains info on and Buckler/Ordway illos of Starman, Liberty Belle, and The Atom. Script by RT.

- The issue's LP tells interested readers that "circumstances" made even a guest appearance by any of The Marvel Family "impossible" at that time. (Licensee DC, which wouldn't purchase the rights to Fawcett heroes outright for several more years, had to pay a pro-rated fee for any comic in which they appeared. Shortly afterward, however, the powers-that-be relented and allowed the Marvels to appear in a few issues)

- The LP announced that, because it had been pointed out that the use of the term "Nips" for Japanese was still a somewhat offensive one, its use would be curtailed in future issues.

Even Worse Than "General Winter"

On Earth-Two, the Flying Eye appeared over the scene of heavy fighting between the German Wehrmacht (army) and Soviet troops in the USSR region of Feodosiya and Kerch (trust us on this—we looked it up). At right, German troops use shovels and picks to try to dig out a Panzer (Panther) tank which has become stuck in the snow despite having cleated tracks.

I Come In Peace—Not!

(Left:) "Akhet of Proxima Centauri" claims our planet for the Binary Brotherhood in All-Star Squadron #10. Incidentally, the symbol on his flag is based on an old alchemists' symbol from the Middle Ages, representative of "The Spirit of the World." [© DC Comics.]

(Right:) In The Invaders #30 (July 1978), Komtur, the Teutonic Knight, piloted his flying saucer-like Fliegentod (Flying Death) against Captain America, Sub-Mariner, Human Torch, Union Jack, and Spitfire. Script by RT, cover art by Joe Sinnott. Komtur, though, was an avowed Nazi, not an alien, real or fake. Thanks to Greg Fischer, Barry Pearl, & Gregg Whitmore for the scan. [© Marvel Characters, Inc.]

(Below:) In the 1951 film classic The Day the Earth Stood Still, the alien Klaatu (Michael Rennie) emerged from a flying saucer to address a nervous crowd on a sandlot baseball field in Washington, DC. This half-sheet poster also shows the giant robot Gort that came along as backup. Earlier, RT had adapted Harry Bates' short story "Farewell to the Master," on which the movie was based (and in which the robot was named Gnut), in an issue of Marvel's Worlds Unknown. [© 20th Century-Fox.]

ALL-STAR SQUADRON #11
(July 1982)

COVER: Joe Kubert

STORY: "Star-Smasher's Secret!" – 25 pp.

ARTISTS: Adrian Gonzales & Jerry Ordway

STARRING: RM, JQ, FB, CS, HG, SK, AT, LB, HM.

SYNOPSIS: The All-Stars from last issue (joined midway by Hawkman) battle the Flying Eye. Captured, Hawkgirl and Atom discover Akhet is a robot created by Hawkman's old enemy, Dr. Hastor—who has captured numerous brilliant scientists and imprisoned them, unconscious, in transparent tubes.

NOTES:

• Adolf Hitler is shown in his East Prussian commander bunker called *Wolfsschanze (Wolf's Lair)*, raging against the failure of German forces to totally defeat the USSR since the June 22, 1941, invasion.

• Churchill refers to his famed "blood, toil, sweat, and tears" speech to the British House of Commons on May 13, 1940—often misquoted as simply "blood, sweat, and tears."

• Garrett Owens, the "pioneer bio-chemist" who is an early captive of Dr. Hastor (and a fatality) is a wholly fictitious character created for this story arc.

• Dr. Elwood Napier—the last scientist to be captured by Hastor—debuted as a key character in *All-Star Comics #55* in 1950, where the "eminent physico-mathematician" is called a "close friend" of the JSAers; see *The All-Star Companion, Vol. 1,* for more details.

• Dr. Hastor was the first foe ever fought by Hawkman—in *Flash Comics #1* (Jan. 1940). He was a reincarnation of the ancient Egyptian priest Hath-Set. That story is currently on view in DC's *The Golden Age Hawkman Archives, Vol. 1.*

Eye'll Be There!

Along with FDR, Churchill, and Hitler, the other major world leaders of the day—Stalin, Chiang Kai-Shek, Mussolini, and Gen. Tojo—also receive visitations from the Flying Eye. [© DC Comics.]

We All Wear Many Masks

(Above & below:) Hawkgirl confronts various specimens of Hawkman's headgear that he'll wear between 1940-48. This was a bit of fun on RT's part, of course, as it was unlikely Carter Hall would have fashioned all these masks by late 1941. For authentic repros of all models, see Vol. 1 of this series. On p. 19 Hawkgirl muses on the simple yellow cowl with the red hawk sigil at far right, of which Hawkman is alleged to have said: "The day I start wearing that one, you'll know I'm about ready to retire!" Another in-joke, since he would don that mask (and Shiera a similar one) for Flash Comics #98-104, his final seven solo stories, as well as in All-Star Comics #42-57. Shown below is the Kubert splash from Flash Comics #98 (Aug. 1948); thanks to Al Dellinges. [© DC Comics.]

Marshall Arts

General George C. Marshall, US Army Chief of Staff (seen at right in photo), briefs FDR, Churchill, and several All-Stars in issue #10. Marshall is credited as the architect of much of the successful American victory strategy—but ironically is mostly remembered today because of the Marshall Plan of the late 1940s, which helped rebuild Western Europe. In truth, however, the "Marshall Plan" would be largely the brainchild of President Harry Truman. [Art © DC Comics.]

☆☆☆☆☆☆☆☆☆☆☆☆☆☆☆☆☆☆☆☆☆☆☆☆☆☆☆☆☆

ALL-STAR SQUADRON #12
(Aug. 1982)

COVER: Joe Kubert

STORY: "Doomsday Begins at Dawn!" – 25 pp.

ARTISTS: Adrian Gonzales & Jerry Ordway

STARRING: Same as in #11.

SYNOPSIS: Dr. Hastor is utilizing the work of captive scientists, especially Dr. Elwood Napier, to power the Flying Eye and make the Earth believe it is under attack. But where Napier hoped to unite mankind against "aliens," Hastor plans pure conquest—until the All-Stars defeat him.

NOTES:

• On his own volition, Jerry Ordway penciled and inked a proposed cover for this issue, showing the All-Stars attacking Akhet on the White House lawn; but editor Len Wein opted for another cover by Kubert. Ordway's cover was printed as a pin-up in issue #65 (see p. 220).

• Several pages in #12 retell events from the first Hawkman tale, in *Flash Comics* #1 (Jan. 1940). Although, in his first few stories, Hawkman's helmet sat high on his head and didn't cover his face, it's shown used as a mask in this issue's flashback, in which Hawkman's wings are their original color (light blue).

• Roy Thomas took the basic idea for this story arc from a radio drama he heard in the late 1940s or early '50s, in which an apparent invasion from outer space aliens is actually just the brainstorm of some idealistic scientists who wish to force the oft-quarrelsome nations of the Earth to band together. (Anybody out there know what radio program that might've been?) RT has Dr. Hastor taking control of those scientists and warping their plans to suit his own ambitions.

• The Flying Eye was inspired by the great Eye of Horus, which flew around devastating the world in ancient Egyptian myth. RT had used that theme, in more authentic form, in the second comic book story he ever wrote—Charlton's *Blue Beetle* #54 (Feb.-March 1966)—and would later do a sequel to that story in *Infinity, Inc.* #44 (Nov. 1987).

The Shape Of Things That Didn't Come

(Left:) Dr. Anton Hastor, like most pre-WWII pundits, was certain the "next war" would be fought with dirigibles and poison gas. But by that time, dirigibles were largely obsolete as weapons of war—and poison gas was considered such an undependable agent that it was little used from 1940-45. [© DC Comics.]

Hawks And Jackals

(Left:) In Flash Comics #1, the ancient Egyptian "hawk-god" is called Anubis—but there, writer Gardner Fox erred. The hawk-headed god of that place and time was Horus; Anubis, often an evil-doer, bore the head of a jackal. Both these images are from the Egyptian Book of the Dead.

(Above right:) Hawkman and Hawkgirl combine mental wills, through the Blade of Hath-Set, to battle that evil ancient-Egyptian priest psychically as Prince Khufu and Princess Shiera, reflecting events in Flash Comics #1. In truth, Hastor/Hath-Set never appeared in a second Golden Age story. [© DC Comics.]

★★★★★★★★★★★★★★★★★★★★★★★★★★★★★★

ALL-STAR SQUADRON #13
(Sept. 1982)

COVER: Joe Kubert

STORY: "One Day, during the War…" – 25 pp.

ARTISTS: Adrian Gonzales (p) & Mike DeCarlo (i)

STARRING: Same as in #11-12, plus Rod Reilly (but not as FB/M). (Cameos: BM, SP, SU, WW, FL, GA, SY, VG, SS, ST, CA, MT, WC, AW, TNT, DD, MA, MH/DC, PM.

SYNOPSIS: Liberty Belle is elected to chair the Squadron. Commander Steel tells his old girlfriend that Hank Heywood (his alter ego) is dead. Robotman learns a shyster lawyer is trying to have him declared a public menace and turned into scrap metal. Shining Knight returns to England as Churchill's bodyguard, while Belle, Johnny Quick, and Firebrand entertain wounded servicemen in a hospital.

NOTES:

• The early pages of #13 are used to strengthen the series' concept and to work in some personal bits. Roy Thomas believed, as Stan Lee had often told him, that you can get away with

Photo Graphics

A photocopy of the original art for Joe Kubert's cover for issue #13 (a strikingly effective montage of art and photos) was provided by Tom Ziuko, longtime pro colorist who also added tones to this book's cover. [© DC Comics.]

Remembering Pearl Harbor—And The Philippines

(Above:) Like many Americans in 1941-42, Firebrand gets hot under the collar about the recent sneak attack, spouting the J-word. Though DC policy was generally to avoid that term, writer Roy Thomas convinced the powers-that-be that an exception should be made in this case, in the interest of authenticity. Art by Adrian Gonzales & Mike DeCarlo. [© DC Comics.]

(Right center:) War in the East led to racially-inflamed hatreds, as evidenced by this British graphic which was used to illustrate a 1943 article in the New York Times Magazine.

(Bottom right:) And the Japanese returned the favor. In this cartoon from the Osaka Puck, a bayonet skewers a caricature of a horned Churchill (standing in for John Bull, the British equivalent of Uncle Sam). The shackled figures represent the masses of the Orient, which the Japanese claimed to be liberating into their "Greater East Asia Co-Prosperity Sphere."

having a bunch of super-heroes just standing around talking for a few pages, if you need to, because they look interesting in their costumes.

- A marquee touts the new movie *The Fleet's In*, starring Dorothy Lamour and William Holden.

- The "Sabatini Bros. Furniture" sign on a truck is a takeoff on a real New York company named Santini Bros.—and Rafael Sabatini, author of such swashbuckling novels as *Captain Blood*, *Scaramouche*, and *The Sea Hawk*.

- The scene between the lawyer and Robotman is adapted from *Star Spangled Comics* #15 (Dec. 1942); further expansion on that story would come in *All-Star Squadron* #17.

- Danette Reilly begins to rethink her hatred of all Japanese when her brother Rod reveals that he and Slugger, wounded at Pearl Harbor, were rescued by a soldier who was killed moments later by a strafing Zero: "That soldier's name was Ken Hosokawa. He was born in California— but both his parents were born in Japan. And he died, giving his life for a country that denied those parents citizenship. Well? Still think they're all 'dirty yellow scum'?"

The Face Of War

(Above:) In issue #13, Liberty Belle, Johnny Quick, and Firebrand visit survivors of the Pearl Harbor attack in a Stateside Naval hospital ward. In the panels that follow, Brandy is reunited with her brother Rod, and the heroes entertain the patients with a super-stunt display. Repro'd from a photocopy of the original art, courtesy of Rick Shurgin. [© DC Comics.]

Homeward Bound

(Above photo:) In mid-January 1942 Churchill returned to England aboard a Boeing Flying Boat, which he piloted for a short time on the hop to Bermuda, a British possession.

(Center:) In The Invaders #4 (Jan. 1976), Churchill's flight was the cue for U-Man, a Nazi takeoff on DC's Aquaman, to try to kill the PM. Of course, The Sub-Mariner was there a couple of panels later to stop him. Art by Frank Robbins & Vince Colletta; script by RT. Thanks to Chris Fama & Gregg Whitmore for the scans. [© Marvel Characters, Inc.]

(Right:) In All-Star Squadron #13, Churchill persuades The Shining Knight to return with him as his personal bodyguard and "a living incarnation of Great Britain's illustrious traditions." (After all, Sir Justin had been a Knight of the Round Table!) Arriving over London, the Knight fights off attacking German planes. Art by Gonzales & DeCarlo; script by RT. [© DC Comics.]

☆ ☆

ALL-STAR SQUADRON ANNUAL #1 (1982)

COVER: Jerry Ordway

STORY: "The Three Faces of Evil!" – 38 pp.

ARTISTS: Adrian Gonzales & Jerry Ordway

STARRING: GL, WW, FL, WC, GU, AT. (Cameos:) HM, JQ, FB, LB, RM, CS, SK, HG (as Shiera Sanders).

SYNOPSIS: GL, Wonder Woman, and Flash are attacked by Wildcat, Guardian, and Atom. The latter three discover that the same man, Joe Morgan—who had earlier helped hone their physical skills—is behind their hypnosis. Morgan, in turn, was controlled by an evil Globe Being which (though the heroes never learn this) was exiled to the Earth-Two dimension eons before by the Guardians of the Universe.

NOTES:

• This *Annual* saw the first published cover totally penciled and inked by Jerry Ordway—with, happily, many more to come.

• An added scene in The Guardian's origin flashback is inspired by a similar one in the 1956 film *Somebody Up There Likes Me*, featuring Paul Newman (as boxer Rocky Graziano) and Sal Mineo as his doomed boyhood chum. The latter comic character's name "Leo" was taken from Leo Gorcey, leader of the East Side Kids/Bowery Boys in a popular series of movies.

• In the Guardian flashback, both hero and captured crook use the term "super-hero," quoted from the Simon & Kirby story in *Star Spangled* #7. This may have been the first time that expression appeared in a comic book (or much of anywhere else)—though Jerry Siegel & Joe Shuster had used it, hyphen and all, to describe Superman in a 1936 concept sketch, as seen in Les Daniels' 1998 hardcover *Superman: The Complete History*.

• Musing by The Atom ties the *Annual* in to the monthly series by relating what Johnny Quick, Liberty Belle, Firebrand, Robotman, Commander Steel, The Shining Knight, and Hawkman are currently up to.

• It's never spelled out if there's any connection between this issue's Globe Being from space and the ones featured in *All-Star Comics* #31 (Oct.-Nov. 1946).

• There are four Fact File pages—on Wonder Woman, Flash, and Green Lantern with Buckler/Ordway art, and on The Guardian (and Newsboy Legion) with Ordway's first interior penciling-and-inking. Script by RT.

• There is no text page in this issue. No room!

Love On A Tightrope

(Left:) The splash of All-Star Squadron Annual #1 shows the scene from the cover of Comic Cavalcade #2 (Spring 1943); the original version is on view in Comic Cavalcade Archives, Vol. 1. Art by Gonzales & Ordway; script by Thomas. The two-dozen-plus CC cover drawings of Wonder Woman, Green Lantern, and The Flash having fun together influenced RT to make them good friends in All-Star Squadron, starting with their first get-together in the All-Star Squadron insert in Justice League of America #193. [© DC Comics.]

(Above:) This is probably as good a place as any to mention that Carl Gafford, who in 1981 had become Len Wein's assistant editor just in time to color the Preview in JLA #193, colored all the early issues of All-Star Squadron, and quite well, too. He'd also been the first colorist of the All-Star Comics revival of the 1970s. Gaff left Squadron after #17, but returned near the end of the run. When asked for a photo of himself, he sent the above "self-portrait" instead. [Art © Carl Gafford.]

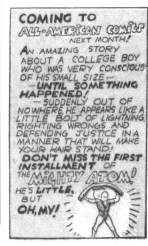

Atom And "Evil"

(Above left:) "The Three Faces of Evil!" (which took its name from the popular book and film The Three Faces of Eve) recaps the origins of Atom, Wildcat, and Guardian. Turns out that the same man, under different names, had acted as trainer to all three super-heroes as civilians—although, as a letter-writer would point out, Joe Morgan did appear in an Atom story or two after the Tiny Titan's origin, contrary to a statement in the Annual. By Gonzales, Ordway, & Thomas.

Above right is an ad from All-American Comics #18 (Sept. 1940) which heralded the next-issue debut of "The Mighty Atom"; it appeared as the final panel of a different series, with the Atom's shirt colored green and his mask and cape yellow! Thanks to Bob Hughes for the scan. [© DC Comics.]

Where Is The Magic?

The Annual's final page revealed that The Guardians of the Galaxy from the Silver/Bronze Age Green Lantern series were at the root of the issue's situation. In GL #112 (Jan. 1979), they had attempted to expel all magic from the continuum in which they and Earth-One existed into an "alternate cosmos"—which turned out to be that of Earth-Two. This Annual thus features the first crossover in All-Star Squadron between the Schwartz/Fox-created parallel worlds; yet, by coincidence, a full-scale collision of the twin Earths would occur in the next two issues of the monthly mag. [© DC Comics.]

Maybe You Can Go Home Again

Adrian Gonzales & Jerry Ordway captured the feel of Suicide Slum (The Guardian's beat) and Williams' Gym (named after the famous Stillman's) in splashes to these two team segments. Script by RT. [© DC Comics.]

JUSTICE LEAGUE OF AMERICA #207

(Oct. 1982)

COVER: George Pérez

STORY: "Crisis Times Three!" – 23 pp.

WRITER: Gerry Conway (Roy Thomas, plot consultant)

ARTISTS: Don Heck (p) & Romeo Tanghal (i)

STARRING: (JLA:) Superman, Zatanna, Hawkman, Firestorm, Aquaman; (JSA:) GL, DF, SM, Power Girl, Huntress; (All-Star Squadron:) FB, JQ, LB, RM, CS. (NOTE: The five All-Stars appear only in the final panel of the issue.)

SYNOPSIS: When five 1982 Justice Leaguers try to teleport five JSAers to Earth-One for their annual get-together, what materializes instead is the evil Crime Syndicate of America (from Earth-Three): Superwoman, Power Ring, Owlman, Ultraman, and a criminal Johnny Quick. The CSA manage to exile both hero teams to limbo. Escaping, the JSAers find Earth-Prime in ruins from atomic warfare that occurred years earlier—while the JLA discover a 1982 Earth-Two ruled by Per Degaton. When Superman takes his group to the Earth-Two of 1942 to learn what happened at that time, they are startled to encounter five of the All-Star Squadron entering JSA-HQ.

NOTES:

- This issue begins the longest of any of the 23 JLA-JSA teamups of 1963-1985. This five-issue story arc has the overall title "Crisis on Earth-Prime!" and leapfrogs between three issues of *Justice League of America* and two of *All-Star Squadron*.

- Despite RT's repeated requests, Commander Steel is listed as merely "Steel" on the covers of all five issues.

- The idea for the storyline arose because the year was 1982, and *All-Star Squadron* was set in 1942. Splitting the difference gave them 1962—the year of the Cuban Missile Crisis. The fact that the titles of many of the JLA-JSA teamups contained the word "Crisis" was just the icing on the four-color cake.

- It was decided at the outset there'd be no overlap in personnel between the 1982 JSAers and the 1942 All-Stars who took part, to avoid having to deal with yet another time paradox. The only "doppel-gangers," after a fashion, were the two unrelated Johnny Quicks.

- RT will reveal in a later LP that, when he decided to have Liberty Belle elected chairwoman of the All-Stars, he was unaware Gerry Conway had just done the same for Zatanna in the JLA.

- When the writers began work, they didn't know that any of the Crime Syndicate of America had appeared in stories since their 1964 debut. Fortunately, being made aware in time of two CSA "breakouts" from their inter-dimensional prison, they were able to account for them.

- As a letter-writer will point out in issue #20, the date on a calendar in JSA-HQ is "July 1942," when it should have been January of that year.

Manhattan, Mon Amour

In JLA #207, five 1982 JSAers find themselves on an Earth-Prime (hitherto DC's version of our super-heroless world) decimated by nuclear war—though they must be quite a distance from ground zero for anything to remain of New York City's buildings. Script by Gerry Conway, art by Don Heck & Romeo Tanghal. [© DC Comics.]

We've Got To Stop Meeting Like This!

Intriguingly, we have two versions of Don Heck's art for the final page of JLA #207—unpublished pencils on the left, and the finished page, as dialogued by Conway and inked by Tanghal, on the right. Why was Heck's first rendering not used? Most likely because of its second panel, which shows the five All-Stars arriving at JSA-HQ. They hadn't been seen previously in the issue, so editor Len Wein probably decided they should be seen only in the final big panel—and coming through the door, not already inside the room. Thanks to Rick Shurgin for both versions—and to R. Dewey Cassell for the 1970s photo of Don Heck, from a Marvel promotion. [© DC Comics.]

ALL-STAR SQUADRON #14
(Oct. 1982)

COVER: Joe Kubert

STORY: "The 'Mystery Men' of October!" – 23 pp.

[NOTE: Gerry Conway, plot consultant]

ARTISTS: Adrian Gonzales & Jerry Ordway

STARRING: Same 15 heroes as Justice *League of America* #207. (Cameos: DM, FL, PL, PM, WW, GL, HM, AT, RM, SK.)

SYNOPSIS: In 1947, Degaton regains his memory of his first encounter with the JSA and sets out to use Prof. Zee's time machine to conquer the world. He frees the Crime Syndicate from limbo and enlists them to help him use the 1962 Cuban Missile Crisis as a means of devastating Earth-Prime. The JLA learn the Earth-Two of 1982 has been ruled by Degaton for four decades. Meanwhile, back in 1942, after battling the

magnetic villain Nuclear, a quintet of All-Stars enter JSA-HQ… and come face to face with five of the JLA.

NOTES:

• The title "The 'Mystery Men' of October!" is a play on the name (*The Missiles of October*) of an historical "docu-drama" made for TV in 1974, based on Robert F. Kennedy's book *Thirteen Days: A Memoir of the Cuban Missile Crisis*. In the 1940s, before the term "super-hero" was in wide usage, costumed heroes were often referred to as "mystery men."

• One day in 1947 Degaton suddenly recalls his previous defeats (a few weeks earlier in 1947, in 331 BC, and in 1941), while his "erstwhile foes" have forgotten them all—and he hopes to use that knowledge to triumph this time.

• Part of RT's influence re this storyline was a well-known literary essay on his favorite novel, *Catch-22* by Joseph Heller, which postulates that the book's events

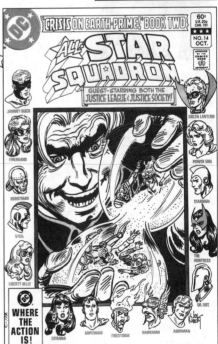

Hourglass Figures

The cover of this issue is an homage to that of 1947's All-Star Comics #35 (see All Star Archives, Vol. 8, or Vol. 1 of this series). Ironically, since earlier Roy Thomas had had two similar homages to that Irwin Hasen illo done at Marvel, this time it was editor Len Wein's idea—and RT couldn't have been happier about it. [© DC Comics.]

are not told chronologically—except for the deeds of the unscrupulous Milo Minderbinder, whose timeline follows a linear path. (This analysis has since been shown to be not 100% accurate, but that's neither here nor there.)

- The Crime Syndicate of America had debuted in the JLA-JSA team-up in *Justice League of America* #29-30 (Aug-Sept. 1964). Since then, Ultraman had fought and been re-imprisoned between dimensions by the Supermen of Earths One and Two in *DC Comics Presents Annual* #1, which was just going on sale …while three of the group had briefly escaped in *Secret Society of Super-Villains* #13-14 (March & April-May 1978).

- Nuclear, the magnetic villain the All-Stars encounter in the issue, had appeared in only one published story, in *Wonder Woman* #43 (Sept.-Oct. 1950); see p. 137 of this volume.

The Day That Dropped Back Into Time

(Above:) A 1947 nightmare about the All-Star Squadron restores Per Degaton's memory of his first set-to with the Justice Society, as recorded in All-Star Comics #35, "The Day That Dropped Out of Time." Script by RT, art by Gonzales & Ordway. Repro'd from a photocopy of the original art, courtesy of Michael Dunne. [© DC Comics.]

Isn't This Where We Came In?

(Above:) The final page of Squadron #14 showed the same scene as that of Justice League of America #207—but this time from the All-Stars' angle. Art by Gonzales & Ordway, script by RT. Repro'd from a photocopy of the original art, courtesy of Rick Shurgin. [© DC Comics.]

(Right:) Hawkman is the Silver Age-born hero whose costume most resembles the Golden Age version—so having him in this five-parter was almost like having the 1940s Winged Wonder on the scene. This commission sketch of the hero by Hellboy creator Mike Mignola is used courtesy of the artist. Thanks to Robert Knist. [Hawkman TM & © DC Comics.]

"The Triple Pillar Of The World"— October 1962

Though US President John F. Kennedy, Cuban Premier Fidel Castro, and Soviet Premier Nikita Khrushchev had only a few lines of dialogue each in the five-part JLA-JSA-Squadron story arc, they were depicted as the central players in the October 1962 Cuban Missile Crisis. The photo of JFK was taken April 3, 1963, during a news conference in which he confirmed that 4000 Soviet troops had left Cuba. Still, in the photo at right taken in Cuba in 1964, Castro and Khrushchev could still smile for the cameras despite their frayed relationship. [Photos © the respective copyright holders.]

☆☆☆☆☆☆☆☆☆☆☆☆☆☆☆☆☆☆☆☆☆☆☆☆☆☆☆☆☆

JUSTICE LEAGUE OF AMERICA #208

(Nov. 1982)

COVER: George Pérez

STORY: "The Bomb-Blast Heard 'Round the World!" – 23 pp.

WRITER: Gerry Conway (Roy Thomas, plot consultant)

ARTISTS: Don Heck (p) & Sal Trapani (i)

STARRING: Same JLA, JSA, and All-Star Squadron heroes as *Justice League of America* #207

SYNOPSIS: As the JLA and All-Stars meet with FDR, Degaton demands that all major leaders on Earth-Two surrender, or he'll bombard their nations with atomic missiles stolen from Cuba in the year 1962. On 1982 Earth-Prime, the JSA quintet learn that the USA and USSR went to war over Cuba there in 1962, resulting in a nuclear holocaust. In 1942, the JLA, All-Stars, and 1982 JSA are reunited, as Degaton prepares to strike.

NOTES:

- Images of FDR, Harry Hopkins, John F. Kennedy, Robert F. Kennedy, Nikita Khrushchev, Fidel Castro, and Ronald Reagan all appear in the issue, along with those of other 1942 world leaders. Those of the Kennedys, Hopkins, and Reagan are not particularly recognizable. FDR's dog Fala comes off okay, though.

- A key part of Degaton's plan is that, by having the CSA steal atomic missiles from the Cuban site in 1962, the suspicions of JFK and Khrushchev that each is lying to the other about where the weapons are will lead to nuclear war. On Earth-Prime, this has led to atomic holocaust—on 1982 Earth-Two, the nations of the Earth had surrendered to him in 1942.

- Degaton detonates an A-bomb in 1942 to demonstrate his power—3+ years before two would be exploded over Japan and end World War II. Some circles have criticized President Truman's 1945 decision to use the bomb immediately as a weapon, rather than find a way first simply to "demonstrate" its power to the resisting Japanese. It is this writer's humble opinion that those critics are wrong.

- When Hopkins says that the futuristic "television receiver" (actually a 1980s VCR) delivered by Degaton to the White House bears the label "Made in Japan," Robotman remarks, "We had no idea their science was so advanced!"

It's A Blast!

To establish his bona fides to FDR when he announces his nuclear blackmail, Degaton mentions "General Groves," "Dr. Oppenheimer," and "the Manhattan Project"—all of which Per himself certainly knew about by 1947. However, in actuality (though not in the comic), his words would have mystified the historical Roosevelt, as "the Manhattan Engineer District" (the official name of what became known after 1945 as "the Manhattan Project") wasn't established until August of 1942—and Brigadier General Leslie Groves of the Army Corps of Engineers, the military man in charge of the program, didn't meet scientist J. Robert Oppenheimer and recommend that he head the group's scientific activities at a still-unchosen site till October of that year. The above photo of Oppenheimer (left) and Groves was taken at the site of the first A-bomb test in the New Mexican desert in summer of 1945, only weeks before the weapon was used against Japan.

ALL-STAR SQUADRON #15
(Nov. 1982)

COVER: Joe Kubert

STORY: "Master of Worlds and Time!" – 23 pp.

[**NOTE:** Gerry Conway, plot consultant]

ARTISTS: Adrian Gonzales & Jerry Ordway

STARRING: Same 15 three-Earth heroes as in *Justice League of America* #207-208. (Cameos: SK, HM in flashforward to 1980s)

SYNOPSIS: In 1942, FDR gives the 15 heroes five hours to stop Degaton, or he must resign the Presidency in favor of the arch-villain. The heroes split into teams, three of which battle Ultraman in space, Superwoman on a Pacific isle, and Power Ring in the American Midwest. Degaton vows he'll triumph yet—"or there will be no Earths—anywhere!"

NOTES:

• When Liberty Belle says that the super-heroes have to make certain atomic explosives are "never used by anyone," fellow team members Starman and Aquaman decide not to enlighten her with their 1982 insight. "It'd just depress her," says the Sea King.

• Starman and Aquaman also withhold further information when Belle overhears them mention "Jimmy Doolittle" and his "bomber raid"—a reference to the morale-boosting attack by US Gen. Doolittle and sixteen B-25 bombers on Tokyo in April 1942—three months in the future, as far as Belle is concerned.

[© DC Comics]

A Pair Of Missile "Silos"

(Above:) Perhaps the touch scripter RT most enjoyed adding to this story arc was the disguising of Degaton's stolen missiles in actual farm-type silos—when, in our world, we've been used for decades to speaking of "missile silos" of a slightly different kind. In All-Star Squadron #15, the CSA baddie Power Ring activates one of the hidden missiles. Art by Gonzales & Ordway. [© DC Comics.]

(Right:) Photo of a Titan II missile in its 146-foot-deep silo, surrounded by work platforms.

Kale And Hearty

(Above:) Degaton rages as he prepares to begin the final round—while two of his minions whisper. If their dialogue at right sounds familiar, it's because RT lifted it, word for word, from the original King Kong—except for substituting the name "Kale" for "Captain." In the 1933 movie, the exchange is between crewman Bruce Cabot and the captain of the "moving picture ship," concerning moviemaker Carl Denham, played by Robert Armstrong. Right-hand man Kale had first appeared in All-Star Comics #35. Art by Gonzales & Ordway. [© DC Comics.]

☆ ☆

JUSTICE LEAGUE OF AMERICA #209

(Dec. 1982)

COVER: George Pérez

STORY: "Let Old Acquaintances Be Forgot…" – 23 pp.

WRITER: Gerry Conway
[Roy Thomas, plot consultant]

ARTIST: Don Heck

STARRING: Same 15 three-Earth heroes as in previous two *JLA* issues.

SYNOPSIS: One hero-team defeats the evil Johnny Quick. Then the entire group tracks down Degaton and Owlman, who have their hideout beneath the site on which the Pentagon is being built in 1942. The Crime Syndicate are returned to inter-dimensional limbo. Degaton is restored to 1947 as Prof. Zee's lab assistant yet again, with no memory of what has occurred—nor do the heroes retain any recollection of it, as they're sent their separate ways in time and space.

NOTES:

• On p. 3 of *JLA* #209, Harry Hopkins has charted the five JLA-JSA-All-Star teams, their destinations, their CSA opponents, and the whereabouts of the 27 purloined atomic missiles on a White House blackboard. Gerry Conway and RT did much the same thing in the former's office on Ventura Boulevard in L.A., where they co-plotted much of the series.

• In a flashback showing the zombie-like inhabitants of Manhattan in a post-nuclear-war, Dr. Fate refers to "a war in which the survivors envy the dead"… a paraphrase of a statement made in the early 1960s by Soviet Premier Khrushchev.

• Although he can't speak for Gerry Conway, and is aware that some have criticized the length and complexity of the five-issue series, Roy Thomas has always considered "Crisis on Earth-Prime" one of his favorite *All-Star Squadron* storylines.

[© DC Comics]

It's Déjà Vu All Over Again—Or Did We Say That Before?

One of RT's quirky delights in Degaton stories—and apparently he passed it on to Gerry Conway, as well—was to keep showing the final scene of All-Star Comics #47 over and over, drawn by different artists. (Some have said that Roy was bitten by an Alain Resnais movie at an impressionable age.) Here, clockwise from far left, are: (a) the 1947 panel by Irwin Hasen, scripted by John Broome, repro'd from the comic, not the Archives edition… (b) the corresponding panel from All-Star Squadron #3 by Buckler & Ordway… (c) ditto from All-Star Squadron #14, by Gonzales & Ordway (only the name of the time-travel element RT had invented was "Chronium," not the typo'd "Chromium")… (d) its final appearance (through 1982, anyway!) from Justice League of America #209. RT & GC inadvertently changed "tubes" to "test tubes," however. [© DC Comics.]

☆☆☆☆☆☆☆☆☆☆☆☆☆☆☆☆☆☆☆☆☆☆☆☆

ALL-STAR SQUADRON #16
(Dec. 1982)

COVER: Joe Kubert

STORY: "The Magnetic Marauder" – 24 pp.

ARTISTS: Adrian Gonzales (p) & Rick Hoberg (i)

STARRING: RM, CS, LB, FB, JQ, WW. (Cameos: GL, FL, WC, AT, GU, HM.)

SYNOPSIS: The five All-Stars enter JSA-HQ, in a sequence that repeats the ending of issue #14—but this time they find Wonder Woman there, wounded by Nuclear, The Magnetic Menace. The six track the magnetic villain to his hideout beneath the home of his alter ego, Percy Playboy (nee Plazchek), where Nuclear appears to perish in a molten pit. The heroes let his sister Joye believe Percy died a hero.

NOTES:

- This story takes place before Wonder Woman, who only debuted in comics in late 1941, was yet a member of the Justice Society. In this series, she joined the All-Star Squadron before she did the JSA!

- At one point, she says that "for the first time since coming to Man's World," she "needs the help of other costumed heroes!" Either RT or editor Len Wein added an impish footnote: "*Obviously she hasn't read issues #1-3. –Len." At least, Ye Editor *assumes* Len wrote it; RT doesn't remember writing it himself!

- Nuclear's alter ego in 1950's *WW* #43 was too corny—"Percy Playboy"—so RT had his sister Joye explain that the real family name is "Plazchek": "But a gossip columnist once called Percy that—and out of spite, he changed it legally to Playboy." A

Déjà Vu—Or Is It "Presque Vu"?

On the p. 2 splash of issue #16, their memories of the "Crisis on Earth-Prime" erased, five super-heroes again enter JSA-HQ—but this time, instead of facing a quintet of Justice Leaguers, they confront a bruised and battered Wonder Woman! Note the "photo" on the wall of the first meeting of the JSA in 1940; it's dated "11-22-40," which by an astonishing coincidence happens to be the birthdate of writer Roy Thomas. Art by Adrian Gonzales (pencils) & Rick Hoberg (inks). Repro'd from a photocopy of the original art, courtesy of Jerry G. Bails. [© DC Comics.]

The Nuclear Option - 1982

In 2003, collector Joel Thingvall even turned up a copy of the entire script for the unpublished 1940s Wonder Woman story "Nuclear, the Magnetic Menace" and sent Ye Editor a copy. Part of one script page was printed in Alter Ego #23, though it's not certain if it was written by regular WW writer/co-creator William Moulton Marston, who died in 1947. Did one or both Nuclear stories sit on a shelf for three years, before only the second one was published?

Naturally, since Roy Thomas had no access to either script or art of the earlier tale in 1982, his story could only build on the flashback panels in the one printed in 1950. Besides, this was an All-Star Squadron saga, so five other All-Stars were written in—as per this page from the issue's climax, drawn by Gonzales & Hoberg. Want to know more? Order back-issue copies of Alter Ego #5 & #23. You won't regret it! [© DC Comics.]

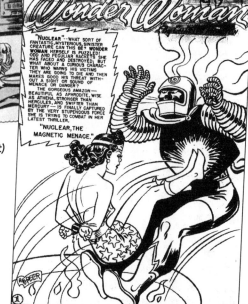

bit convoluted, perhaps, but Roy got a kick out of doing it. The name "Plazchek" was taken from the name of Billy Placzek, a young Chicagoan he'd met in 1964, who had been written up in newspapers for having been given a thousand Golden Age comics by a family friend.

Going Nuclear (& Clockwise From Top Left)

All-Star Squadron #16 is basically an intended "prequel" to the only Nuclear story ever printed—in *Wonder Woman* #43 (Sept.-Oct. 1950), with art by H.G. Peter. That story's title, however, was "Nuclear Returns!" Along with action such as the panel at top left, there was a flashback (above) to an earlier tale in which the Amazon fought magnetic marauder. That one, however, has never been published! (By the way, in the 1950 episode, Nuclear's armored outfit was colored quite differently from the way it appeared in the 1982 comic, despite RT's best efforts.)

It was later learned that the first of the two stories featuring this villain, titled "Nuclear, the Magnetic Menace," had lain on a shelf for years for reasons unknown before finally being cut up and disposed of by DC in the late 1960s. The splash page and a number of tiers (rows) of panels survive, however. All art from it then known to exist was published at last in *Alter Ego* #5 & #23; alas, we've no room here to reprint any of that art but the splash (above right). Thanks to Glenn David Gold for a photocopy of the original art.

Amazingly, however, since then, the final two panels of the earlier story have surfaced—and are printed below, for the first time anywhere. Thanks to both Dominic Bongo and All Star Auctions for sending us this fearful finale. Notice that, in the panel where Steve is kissing Wonder Woman, there's an editorial directive to "separate [their] faces"—and the heroine's dialogue and thought balloons were crossed out so they could be rewritten. [All Wonder Woman art © DC Comics.]

Despite his atomic name, however, Nuclear was a magnetically-powered bad-guy, and as such was a non-mutant harbinger of a somewhat more famous positive/negative personage—namely Magneto, who made his debut in *The X-Men* #1 in 1963, with script by Stan Lee and art by Jack Kirby & Paul Reinman. [© Marvel Characters, Inc.]

★★★★★★★★★★★★★★★★★★★★★★★★★★★★★

ALL-STAR SQUADRON #17
(Jan. 1983)

COVER: Joe Kubert

STORY: "To Slay the Body Electric!"

ARTISTS: Adrian Gonzales (p) & Rick Hoberg (i)

STARRING: RM, CS, LB, FB, JQ. (Cameos: WW, SU, HM, DF, SP, DM, SM, JT, SA, AT.)

SYNOPSIS: Robotman is put on trial, in chains, as an inhuman menace to society in a case brought by the lawyer Slattery. At the trial the hero recounts his origins, even revealing he has the brain of the late Dr. Robert Crane. When the courtroom building starts to collapse, he supports it long enough for his fellow All-Stars to help people escape. The case is dismissed.

NOTES:

- The title, of course, comes from a line of poetry by Walt Whitman—"I sing the body electric"—and Ray Bradbury's use of same as the title of a book.

- Adam Kubert, son of cover artist Joe Kubert, lettered this issue; since then, he and his brother Andy have become major artists in the comic book field.

- Carla Conway, then the wife of comics writer Gerry Conway, is the daughter of an attorney, and knew enough about her father's business to offer RT a bit of free expertise concerning the trial of Robotman—and is credited on the splash page for "a bit of extra-legal advice."

- Beginning with this issue, Carl Gafford's job as assistant editor is filled by Nicola Cuti, himself an artist and writer.

- The name of the shyster lawyer was altered from "Sam Slugg" in *Star Spangled Comics* #8 to "Sam Slattery," as being less corny.

- Johnny Quick makes a passing reference to Joe Palooka, the hero of one of the most popular daily comic strips in the country's newspapers during WWII.

- Affidavits from several All-Stars saying Robotman is "as human as themselves" contain the irony that Superman is an outer-space alien.

[© DC Comics]

- In court, Chuck Grayson relates a several-page origin of Robotman—naturally omitting the fact that Dr. Bob Crane is now "Paul Dennis."

- The Brain Wave is introduced in a cameo panel.

- The LP contains a mildly disparaging reference to the "Whatever Happened to…?" backup series running till recently in *DC Comics Presents*. RT had persuaded DC to discontinue the use therein of All-Star Squadron members, since it often revealed facts about their 1980s lives that tied his hands. RT tried, though, to live with what had already been published therein, and would later script the series' entry on The Black Pirate—who wasn't a 20th-century hero, but, as it happened, *would* later appear in an issue or two of *All-Star Squadron*.

- That same LP answer revealed there were two heroes on Earth-Two called Manhunter—the characters published in the 1940s by DC and Quality.

- One letter in #17 is from Fred DeBoom, who's since provided copies of JSA-related and other original art from his collection to the pages of *Alter Ego*.

A Tale Worth The Retelling

Here, for contrast with the cover of All-Star Squadron #17, is the splash of the Robotman story in Star Spangled Comics #16 (Jan. 1943). Art probably by origin artist John Sikela, who was part of the Joe Shuster shop—but it's not known if Robbie's (and Superman's) co-creator Jerry Siegel wrote the story. Squadron #17 basically adapted the 1943 tale. [© DC Comics.]

We, Robots

(Top left:) The plot of the 1943 "Trial of Robotman!" closely echoes that of "Eando Binder's" short story "The Trial of Adam Link, Robot," which had appeared in the July 1939 issue of the seminal science-fiction pulp magazine Amazing Stories. Interior illustration by Robert Fuqua. [© the respective copyright holders.]

Adam Link was a true robot with an artificial mind, not a robot body housing a human's brain—but otherwise the stories are strikingly similar: a metal protagonist is put on trial and in danger of being dismantled when accused of murder of a close associate—he gives an impassioned speech in court about his desire to be treated as a man, not a machine—and he finally wins approval by breaking free to save humans (in Binder's prose tale, a boy on roller skates is about to be struck by a car; in SSC #16, the courtroom itself begins to collapse because of the excessive crowd).

Coincidence? Highly unlikely. "Eando Binder" was Otto Binder, who'd earlier written comics for DC but by 1942 was scripting tales of Captain Marvel, et al., for rival Fawcett. What's more, Binder and (possible) Robotman scripter Siegel had been friends and fellow sf fans since the 1930s; even if Siegel didn't write this Robotman tale, other DC scribes were probably also familiar with Binder and his work. A number of Adam Link stories were published in Amazing between 1939 and the early 1940s; "Trial," the second of them, was trumpeted by name on the pulp's cover.

(Below:) Until 1982, Adam Link even had Robotman surrounded! In EC Comics' 1955 Weird Science-Fantasy #27, Binder scripted an adaptation of the first Link story ("I, Robot") in comic book format; in #28 (March-April 1955) he adapted "Trial." Both featured exemplary art by Joe Orlando; the panels here show Adam saving a young boy's life. Matter of fact, the author re-adapted those Link tales and others in the late 1960s for Warren Publications' black-&-white comic Eerie—and Orlando illustrated those, as well! [Art © William M. Gaines, Agent; Adam Link TM & © Estate of Otto Binder.]

(Below left & left:) In Star Spangled #16, Robotman saves the terrified courtroom crowd on his own—in a panel juxtaposed with a page drawn by Gonzales & Hoberg for All-Star Squadron #17, in which the metal man breaks free of his chains to perform his heroics, while trial attendees Liberty Belle, Commander Steel, Firebrand, and Johnny Quick get people to safety. [© DC Comics.]

ALL-STAR SQUADRON #18
(Feb. 1983)

COVER: Joe Kubert

STORY: "Vengeance from Valhalla!" – 23 pp.

ARTISTS: Adrian Gonzales (p) & Rick Hoberg (i)

STARRING: JQ, FB, LB, RM, CS, TA, SA (in flashback). (Cameos: WW, HM, JT, DM, AT, DF, SM.)

SYNOPSIS: Tarantula, attending his first Squadron meeting, reveals that he and Sandman sport similar costumes because both were both made by Sandman's girlfriend Dian Belmont, who dies in a flash-back. At JSA-HQ, the All-Stars are attacked by "Fairytales" Fenton, who mistakes Tarantula for his nemesis, Sandman. Fenton believes he's the Norse thunder god Thor—and this time he has an electrifying hammer to back up his claim—but is still defeated.

NOTES:

• Tarantula notes to the All-Stars that a radio announcer called him a "spider man"—a reference to his origin in *Star Spangled Comics* #1 (Oct. 1941).

• As related in #18's LP, the 9-page chapter explaining why Tarantula and Sandman wear similar purple-and-gold outfits in the early 1940s had a curious genesis. Earlier, *The Brave and the Bold* editor Dick Giordano had suggested RT script a back-up story for that mag, to be penciled by Adrian Gonzales. Soon after the story was drawn, however, changes were made in *B&B* (perhaps related to Giordano's promotion to managing editor of DC), so it was decided to use the 9-pager in *All-Star Squadron*—and RT wove the rest of the issue around it.

• Later scribes resurrected Sandman's early confidant Dian Belmont, who's killed off in #18—but that "survival" happened after the obliteration of Earth-Two in *Crisis on Infinite Earths*, and those tales have no bearing on the fact that, in the 1982 story, she definitely died—and became Wes Dodd's "ex-girlfriend" in the same sense that the bird in a

A Quick Start To The Story

The splash page of All-Star Squadron #18. Repro'd from a photocopy of the original art, courtesy of Rick Shurgin. [© DC Comics.]

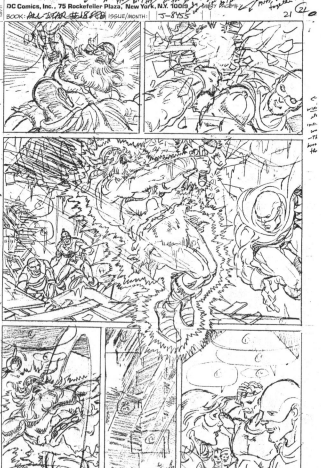

As James Bond Might Say: "Shocking!"

Tarantula tricks "Thor" into getting a heckuva shock by slamming into the building's wiring, as per Adrian Gonzales' pencils for p. 21. Thanks to Jerry Ordway, who was sent photocopies of the pencils of #18 to refer to while he was busy on his debut pencils for #19. "Fairytales" Fenton's trashing of JSA-HQ gave the All-Star Squadron an excuse to move, next issue. [© DC Comics.]

Sure He'th Thor! He'th Got A Hammer, Doethn't He?

Thor, Norse god of thunder, was no stranger to comics in 1982. A few key specimens (clockwise from top right):

Chances are the first comic book Thor was the super-hero in Fox's *Weird Comics* #1-5, who even wielded the hammer Mjolnir at least by this second appearance (May 1940). This splash by artist Wright Lincoln was provided by Will Murray. [© the respective copyright holders.]

The *Sandman* story "The Villain from Valhalla" in *Adventure Comics* #75 (June 1942) introduced the "Fairytales" Fenton version of "Thor," by the team of Joe Simon & Jack Kirby, repro'd here from an Australian b&w reprint of an early-'70s DC reprint—with thanks to Shane Foley. Fenton, according to a cop at story's end, "used to be a professor of metallurgy... or something... before he turned to crime." Sandman pronounced "Thor's hammer" to be "an electrical masterpiece." [© DC Comics.]

Kirby penciled (and Mort Meskin inked) another version of Thor's hammer in *Tales of the Unexpected* #16 (Aug. 1957), as per this page also sent from Oz by Shane Foley. [© DC Comics.]

Jack is back, yet again—in *Journey into Mystery* #83 (Aug. 1962), penciling the Marvel super-hero who's easily the most famous comic book incarnation of the thunder god. Note how much his "uru hammer" resembles the one Kirby drew in 1957, thong and all. Inks by Joe Sinnott, story by Stan Lee, script by Larry Lieber. [© Marvel Characters, Inc.]

Kirby also penciled the covers (but not the interiors) of *The Invaders* #32-33 (Sept.-Oct. 1978), wherein Thor—whom the Germans called Donner, as in "Donner and Blitzen"—was magically conjured up from antiquity by the Third Reich's occult-obsessed Führer in 1942 and conned into

battling Marvel's WWII heroes. The Hitler quote re Richard Wagner's operatic Ring Cycle used on the splash of *All-Star Squadron* #18 was the springboard of this earlier two-parter. Interior story and cover copy by RT; inks by Joe Sinnott. Thanks to Michael Baulderstone, Barry Pearl, & Gregg Whitmore for the scan. [© Marvel Characters, Inc.]

In a 10-page *All-Star Squadron* tale in *All-Star Comics 80-Page Giant* #1 (Sept. 1999), RT unveiled Donar, a DC Teutonic equivalent of Marvel's Thor—in effect, a DC-published equivalent of his own *Invaders* #32-33. Art by Kevin Sharpe & Jason Baumgartner. [© DC Comics.]

famous *Monty Python* sketch was an "ex-parrot."

- The LP says that, at a Creation Convention in San Diego, RT had recently heard a new fan-coined term for what was being done in *All-Star Squadron*: "retroactive continuity." He's always liked that term—and he's gotten used to its short form "retcon"—but he dislikes the later phrase "continuity implant," which sounds like something painful done by a plastic surgeon.

"I Can't Place the Name, But the Costume Is Familiar"

(Above:) Tarantula's flashback in #18 explains why his costume and the Sandman's second one are so similar. (You didn't think RT was gonna say it was just a coincidence, do you—even though in our world it probably was?) This art depicting the two heroes' first encounter is by Gonzales & Hoberg. [© DC Comics.]

(Right:) Sandman's outfit consisting of gasmask, cape, hat, and cape continues to fascinate fans and pros alike, making it an oft-requested subject for commission drawings and convention sketches. Here's a nice 2001 illo of the original Sandman, courtesy of artist Michael Lark and collector Michael Zeno. [Sandman TM & © DC Comics.]

- Tarantula makes a passing reference to Faye Emerson, an actress who, as it turned out, would soon be a daughter-in-law of President Roosevelt.

- In the flashback chapter, Jonathan Law (Tarantula), already a successful writer of mystery novels, interviews Dian Belmont for a book he's writing "on these masked heroes who are popping up all over."

- In 1940s *Star Spangled Comics*, Tarantula's alter ego was called "John Law." But that had specific connotations

as a personification of the police, so RT opted to refer to him as "Jonathan."

- This issue marks Adrian Gonzales' last *All-Star Squadron* work; he moved on to become penciler of another RT co-creation, *Arak, Son of Thunder*.

- With #18, Gene D'Angelo takes over as *Squadron* colorist.

☆☆☆☆☆☆☆☆☆☆☆☆☆☆☆☆☆☆☆☆☆☆☆☆☆☆☆

ALL-STAR SQUADRON #19
(March 1983)

COVER: Jerry Ordway

STORY: "Death, Considered as a State of Mind!" – 23 pp.

ARTIST: Jerry Ordway

STARRING: RM, JQ, LB, CS, TA, FB, HM, JT, SA, SM, WW, DF, AT, DM, SP (the latter actually Brain Wave in disguise).

SYNOPSIS: Summoned to the Perisphere on the grounds of the 1939-40 New York World's Fair, six All-Stars discover eight JSAers held in suspended animation by Brain Wave (pictured only as a giant floating brain). He induces in the JSAers visions of heroic feats they perform in the aftermath of Pearl Harbor, so that he can then make them dream vividly of their own deaths—and thereby lose their combined will to live, if the All-Stars can't save them.

NOTES:

- Johnny Quick's quip on p. 1 reflects the fact that Clark Gable and Spencer Tracy

co-starred in several MGM movies in the 1930s, including *San Francisco* and *Boom Town*.

- While RT sent Jerry Ordway photo reference on the Fairgrounds, Jerry also used some of his own, including for the Four Freedoms statues on pp. 2-3.

- Danette Thomas (Roy's wife, who soon legally changed her name to Dann) and Flo Steinberg ("Fabulous Flo" of mid-1960s Marvel Bullpen Bulletins pages, when she was Stan Lee's corresponding secretary) are listed as "N.Y. World's Fair researchers." Roy and Dann visited the old Fairgrounds, which had also been the scene of the 1964-65 World's Fair, which RT had attended. The only building left from the 1939-40 Fair was now the Queens Museum. Roy also corresponded during this time with Helen A. Harrison, author of the 1980 book *Dawn of a New Day: The New York World's Fair, 1939/40*, which he utilized.

- Tarantula mentions that the Trylon is 610 feet tall, not 700 as per a contemporary article in *Life* magazine (and many sloppily-researched articles since).

- Elektro the Moto Man (robot) actually made appearances at other events after the Fair ended; he wasn't put in mothballs as in issue #19.

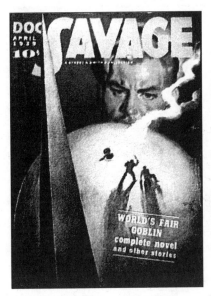

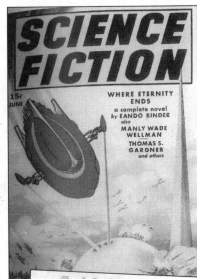

All's Fair...

(Above:) The 610-foot Trylon and the 200-foot Perisphere (both names were coined especially for them) were the "theme" structures at the 1939-40 New York World's Fair. Note the long Helicline people walked down to exit the Perisphere, which housed a model future metropolis called Democracity. Ubiquitous as the Art Deco symbol of the Fair and its "World of Tomorrow" motif, on our Earth these structures were nevertheless demolished in late 1940 for scrap metal, to aid the defense effort—but on the far more imaginative Earth-Two, they still existed in early 1942, and after issue #19 would become the new headquarters of the All-Star Squadron.

(Above center:) On top of the trend was Street & Smith's Doc Savage pulp magazine, whose heroic "Man of Bronze" met a "World's Fair Goblin" in its April 1939 issue—the same month the Fair opened! Cover painting by Emery Clarke. [© Conde-Nast.]

(Top right:) Other pulp mags got into the act, as per this Frank R. Paul cover for a (probably 1939) issue of Science Fiction; photocopy sent by Todd Franklin. It touts stories by Otto ("Eando") Binder, who wrote comics from the early 1940s till the late 1960s, and Manly Wade Wellman, who also scripted a few. [© the respective copyright holders.]

(Right:) Beginning in Centaur's Amazing Mystery Funnies, Vol. 2, #7 (July 1939), a full-hooded hero called The Fantom of the Fair roamed the Fairgrounds in Flushing Meadows, Queens. In Vol. 2, #11 (Nov. 1939), he fights what looks like a rampaging Elektro the Robot (see next page), with Fair buildings as backdrop. Little was ever revealed of his true ID—and RT admits to ambivalence over the fact that, in Secret Origins #7 (Oct. 1986), he turned the character into a super-villain when devising a 1939 origin for Sandman. The "F" spelling was probably to avoid conflicts with the newspaper strip The Phantom; the ultimate source of inspiration, of course, was the Gaston Leroux novel and Lon Chaney film The Phantom of the Opera. [© the respective copyright holders.]

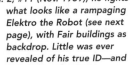

Is This A Dynamic Debut, Or What?

(Left:) The initial page of Jerry Ordway's first penciling job on All-Star Squadron, done for #19. He inked it, as well—and sketched the above self-portrait for a letters page bio. Script by RT. [© DC Comics.]

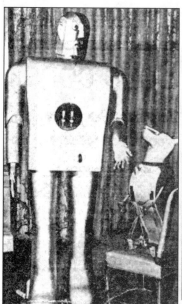

Elektro: Assassin

(Far left:) "Elektro the Moto Man" was a major attraction at the 1939 World's Fair. He was later given a mechanical dog called Sparko (probably the forerunner of Robotman's mid-'40s metal companion Robbie). Elektro did have a few bad habits, though—like smoking cigarettes to amuse the customers at the Fair's General Electric exhibit.

(Left:) Thomas & Ordway gave Elektro another bad trait—namely, trying to kill the All-Star Squadron. Of course, he/it was only following orders; The Brain Wave was the mastermind behind it all. For four Ordway-penciled panels dropped from the published comic for reasons uncertain, see Alter Ego #44. [© DC Comics.]

Fourteen Heroes And A Villain (Hissss!)

Roy Thomas has remarked that it was seeing Jerry Ordway's pencils for the page in which six All-Stars encounter eight captive JSAers (right) that erased any doubts about All-Star Squadron's new penciler. Above, The Brain Wave conjures up lifelike images—but (because, in comics, he wasn't destined to meet any super-heroes till All-Star Comics #15 in 1943) he appeared to the good-guys only as a giant human brain. [© DC Comics.]

To Dream, Perchance To Die

Because the events of All-Star Comics #11, the first issue produced post-Pearl Harbor, were so anti-historical (Starman recapturing Formosa, Hawkman downing Zeros launched from a Japanese aircraft carrier off San Francisco as seen above, etc.), the actions of that 1942 comic were turned in All-Star Squadron #19 into a powerful dream foisted upon the JSAers by Brain Wave. He was merely setting them up for vivid nightmare-images in which they saw their own deaths, as per Starman's at right. [© DC Comics.]

[© DC Comics]

ALL-STAR SQUADRON #20
(April 1983)

COVER: Jerry Ordway

STORY: "…For the Dark Things Cannot Stand the Light…!" – 23 pp.

ARTIST: Jerry Ordway

STARRING: Same heroes as #19, plus GL, SP (real), SU, BM, RO, FL.

SYNOPSIS: Brain Wave causes six All-Stars to dream of their own deaths in war against the Japanese, and they become comatose like the JSAers. An enraged Green Lantern unleashes the full fury of his Power Ring against the Japanese in his own vivid dream, in scenes that foreshadow the atomic blasts to come in 1945. This violent act restores his 14 fellow All-Stars to consciousness—but GL feels like a murderer, even if the world he demolished was an illusory one.

NOTES:

- The letters section of #20 relates a handful of errors that sneaked into Conway & Thomas' five-part "Crisis on Earth-Prime!" Along with the incorrect calendar date in *JLA* #207, there's the fact that, in *JLA* #209, five All-Stars are shown getting out of a cab in Times Square—while in the corresponding scene in the earlier *All-Star Squadron* #14, two of those heroes showed up later. But perhaps those few errors weren't too bad for a 115-page story by two writers and five artists!

Centuries Go By In A Flash

To account for what the JSA's honorary members were up to at roughly the time All-Star Comics #11 hit the newsstands, Ordway redrew scenes from Superman's battle with Luthor (not yet Lex L.) for the Powerstone in Superman #17 (July-Aug. 1942), and Robin's rescue from a Joker-set trap in Batman #11 (June-July 1942), both now on view in Archives volumes—and The Flash was shown in a time-travel sequence from All-Flash Quarterly #4 (Spring 1942); cover pictured at right, though JO & RT didn't involve Father Time, as the earlier story had. (Non-honorary Spectre was shown fighting Kulak, his enemy from All-Star #2, in a new sequence.)

The fourth honorary JSAer had joined the Army in Green Lantern #4 (Spring 1942) and was shown on KP (Kitchen Patrol) duty with his pal Doiby Dickles (center right). As an in-joke, Ordway drew Alan Scott identical to movie actor Alan Ladd, since GL's original writer/co-creator Bill Finger had revealed he'd once considered giving that name to the hero's alter ego as a derivation of "Aladdin," because GL had a magic ring. He decided against it, Finger said, because the name was "too corny." As it happened, this was not long before Ladd became a star following his breakthrough role in 1942's This Gun for Hire, and avoided an awkward situation. [© DC Comics.]

(Left:) Alan Ladd starred in his own DC comic from 1949-51.

Through A Pair Of Glasses, Darkly

In more Brain Wave-induced nightmares, the six All-Stars "perish" attacking Japan to try to save the JSAers. Art by Ordway, script by RT. [© DC Comics.]

- Details of Brain Wave's origins from *All-Star Comics* #15 are related in a thought-flashback.

- Brain Wave's thought-narrative reveals he was behind Dr. Elba's plot to drive men insane in *All-Star* #8. This is "retroactive continuity" with a vengeance, as Elba seems definitely self-employed in the 1941 comic—even though Brain Wave says he'd manipulated him subconsciously. Right after Elba's suicide (seen in a flashback in *Squadron* #20), Brain Wave introduced himself to the JSAers in his civilian identity as "Dr. Henry King."

- In this issue Jerry Ordway gave Luthor (red) hair, even though he'd been bald in the 1942 stories, because it had been established in his appearances in E. Nelson Bridwell's 1970s "Mr. and Mrs. Superman" series that Earth-Two's Luthor always had the red hair he sported in *Action Comics* #23; his baldness in Golden Age comics is presumably the result of garbled transmission between Earth-Two and Earth-Prime.

"I Am Become Death… the Shatterer of Worlds"

The mushroom cloud over Hiroshima, Japan, on Aug. 6, 1945, was the first use in warfare of a nuclear weapon. Green Lantern's Power Ring matched the A-bomb's fury 3½ years earlier, in his Brain Wave-induced dream sequence in All-Star Squadron #20; he was mentally devastated by the experience. The quote he utters is the same that Manhattan Project chief scientist J. Robert Oppenheimer would voice at the first atomic test in July 1945—a line from India's ancient epic, the Mahabharata (in the poem therein known as the Bhagavad-Gita). RT has since felt he dropped the ball by not referring back to GL's torment in later issues, and using it as motivation for Alan Scott to be reluctant to wield his ring's full power. [Art © DC Comics.]

☆☆☆☆☆☆☆☆☆☆☆☆☆☆☆☆☆☆☆☆☆☆☆☆☆☆☆☆☆☆☆

ALL-STAR SQUADRON #21
(May 1983)

COVER: Jerry Ordway

STORY: "A Tale of Three Citadels!" – 23 pp.

ARTISTS: Jerry Ordway (p) & Mike Machlan (i)

STARRING: SU, HM, LB, JQ, JT (w/TB), CS, RM, FB, WW, GL, DM, AT, SM, DF, SA, TA.

SYNOPSIS: The All-Stars decide to make the Perisphere their HQ. At the burning JSA-HQ, Dr. Fate, Hawkman, and Firebrand encounter Cyclotron, who seeks the Hammer of Thor seen in #18. Superman, Liberty Belle, and Green Lantern find the former's secret Citadel commandeered by electric-powered Deathbolt and The Ultra-Humanite, who still inhabits the body of a female movie star and wields the Powerstone, one of three Talismans of Power he/she needs for total domination of the Earth.

NOTES:

- Beginning with this issue, newly-promoted DC managing editor Dick Giordano

arranged for Roy Thomas and a few other writers to become paid editors of comics they scripted. RT had been both a writer and editor at Marvel from 1965-80; that's how he preferred to work, despite his good relationship with original *All-Star Squadron* editor Len Wein (who also became a writer/editor under this system).

- Hawkman says the "Thor's hammer" used in #18 by "Fairytales" Fenton sounds "like a mallet I lost on a case"—the one he'd related in *All-Star Comics* #3. Check it out in the hardcover *All Star Comics Archives, Vol. 1.*

- The two team chapters are mastheaded by small logos from 1940s stories of the individual heroes. Firebrand's was taken from a tale of the male hero; that of The Atom had previously appeared only on a single episode in 1948.

- Firebrand finds she can *absorb* flame, as well as create and hurl it—and that she can fly. Guess she'd been reading *Human Torch* comics.

- The Atom mentions Monogram serials. That company and several other small film studios operated in an area of Hollywood referred to in the business as

Before There Was Atom-Smasher, There Was—Cyclotron

The costume of Cyclotron was, of course, a retconned forerunner of the garb The Atom (whom he's holding aloft on the cover of #21) would adopt in 1948. [© DC Comics.]

[Continued on p. 148]

FASTER THAN A SPEEDING BULLET!

MORE POWERFUL THAN A LOCOMOTIVE!

ABLE TO LEAP TALL BUILDINGS AT A SINGLE BOUND!

LOOK! UP IN THE SKY!

IT'S A BIRD!

IT'S A PLANE!

IT'S SUPERMAN!

Where's Jackson Beck When You Really Need Him?

(Left:) RT asked for this opening splash in #21 so he could utilize the opening narration from the Adventures of Superman radio program he'd loved as a kid in the late 1940s, as the Man of Tomorrow shows up for the first time since issue #4, Earth-Two "S" symbol and all! (Jackson Beck was the later-famous announcer of the radio series, and also shouted out that final immortal line, "It's Superman!" Beck and RT met when they lived in the same apartment building in New York City from 1968-76.) Art by Jerry Ordway (pencils) & Mike Machlan (inks). [© DC Comics.]

Hey, That's What Friends Are For!

1990s photo of Mike & Eve Machlan, courtesy of themselves. Jerry Ordway, too busy to do full art chores on the series after #19-20, got his good friend and fellow Wisconsin artist the job of inking the title, starting with #21. During the 1980s Machlan would pencil and/or ink various DC series, including All-Star Squadron, Infinity, Inc., Blue Devil, and others; in the early '90s he would do some work for Marvel.

THE NAME'S DEATHBOLT!

REMEMBER IT!

NOT "HOW," GIRLIE — "WHO"!

ONLY WHEN MY ELECTRIC BILL'S OVERDUE.

YOU HAVE BUT ONE CHANCE BLUE BOLT!

NO! I WILL NEVER DESERT DOCTOR BERTOFF!

ROY & DANN THOMAS and DELL BARRAS

CAPTAIN THUNDER AND BLUE BOLT

The New Age of Heroes Begins!

Like A Bolt From The Blue

The outfit of the electric-powered super-villain Deathbolt (at left, from the team of Thomas, Ordway, & Machlan) is a green-and-purple/gray version of garb worn by Novelty Press' Golden Age hero Blue Bolt.

Blue Bolt (above) was created by Joe Simon and, starting in Blue Bolt, Vol. 1, #2 (July 1940), was drawn by the brand new Simon & Kirby team. By coincidence, Blue Bolt fought the evil Green Sorceress in a subterranean realm, while Deathbolt is allied with underground creatures ruled by Ultra—who's also a woman at this stage in his career. [DC art © DC Comics; restored Blue Bolt art © Pure Imagination Publishing.]

RT really liked Blue Bolt—both the look and the name. In 1986 (above right), the Novelty hero, rechristened "Vic Volt," appeared as one of the Limbo Legion in the first issue of the First Comics super-hero series of Alter Ego, though he was killed off-panel; art by Ron Harris, who'd later draw The Young All-Stars. [Art © Ron Harris; story © Roy & Dann Thomas.]

And in 1987, for Heroic Publications, RT and wife Dann launched Captain Thunder and Blue Bolt (right), about a father-and-son super-hero team; art by Del Barras. [Alter Ego, Captain Thunder, & Blue Bolt TM & © Roy & Dann Thomas; Alter Ego art © Ron Harris.]

[Continued from p. 146]

"Poverty Row," and had such Western stars as Whip Wilson and Sunset Carson.

• Superman takes GL and Belle to his secret Citadel (forerunner of the Fortress of Solitude), first seen in *Superman* #17 and *World's Finest Comics* in 1942.

• On a wall in the Citadel is a poster announcing the "World Premiere of Superman!!!"—probably an in-joke reference by artist Jerry Ordway to Paramount/Fleischer's *Superman* theatrical animated shorts that debuted in 1941.

Fiorello!

Firebrand and Dr. Fate with Fiorello LaGuardia, legendary mayor of New York City from 1934-45—by Ordway, Machlan, & RT. At right, the real "Little Flower," as he was affectionately known, confers with Eleanor Roosevelt. He is remembered for reading the comic strips over the radio during a newspaper strike—but in issue #21 he's talking to a couple of comic book characters! As seen in Vol. 1 of this series, he appeared in All-Star Comics #5—and was slugged by an angry Sub-Mariner in 1940's Marvel Mystery Comics #7. [Art © DC Comics.]

★★★★★★★★★★★★★★★★★★★★★★★★★★★★★★★★

ALL-STAR SQUADRON #22
(June 1983)

COVER: Jerry Ordway

STORY: "The Powerstone Corrupts—Absolutely!" – 23 pp.

ARTISTS: Jerry Ordway (p) & Mike Machlan (i)

STARRING: SU, GL, LB, JQ, RM, CS, TA, FB. (Cameos:) HM, AT, DF, JT (w/TB), SM, WW, SA, DM.

SYNOPSIS: Ultra-Humanite, Deathbolt, and Cyclotron defeat Superman, Firebrand, and Robotman. Cyclotron reveals to Firebrand that he is actually Dr. Terry Curtis, her former lover. Ultra, now in possession of the Powerstone and the Hammer of Thor, needs only Dr. Fate's original helmet to make his/her power complete.

NOTES:

• Flashbacks deal with the backstories of The Ultra-Humanite and Terry Curtis, based on sequences in *Action Comics* #13, 14, 17, & 19-21 in 1939-40… and with Hawkman's loss of the hammer of Thor in *All-Star Comics* #3. All these stories are on view in DC's *Archives* editions—though, of course, none were in 1983.

• A movie marquee heralds *A Yank on the Burma Road*, a film starring Barry Nelson and Laraine Day, which was released in New York on Jan. 28, 1942.

• With #22, David Cody Weiss, who later often signs his name "Cody," becomes the magazine's regular letterer. Previous to this, John Costanza had lettered the majority of issues.

Forever Female—Not!

Ultra (in a woman's commandeered body) wields the Powerstone, courtesy of Ordway, Machlan, & Thomas. [© DC Comics.]

There'll Be Some Changes Made

With #21, new editor Roy Thomas altered the letters-column title to "All-Star Squadroom," lettered in the same style as the cover logo. [© DC Comics.]

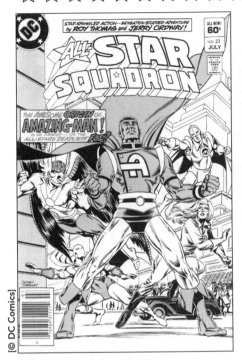

The Quicker Picker-Upper

(Above:) The Atom finds out the hard way that The Amazing-Man has the power to change his bodily structure to that of any substance he touches—in this case, a stone wall! By RT, Ordway, & Machlan. [© DC Comics.]

(Right:) Stan Lee & Jack Kirby's Absorbing Man had the same ability when introduced in Journey into Mystery #114 (March 1965)—plus he could assimilate the power of Thor or his hammer by touching them. Hey, there are just so many super-powers to go around, right? You never noticed that Thor maybe had just a little bit in common with the original Captain Marvel? Inks by Chic Stone; as reprinted in The Essential Thor, Vol. 2. [© Marvel Characters, Inc.]

ALL-STAR SQUADRON #23
(July 1983)

COVER: Jerry Ordway

STORY: "When Fate Thy Measure Takes…!" – 23 pp.

ARTISTS: Jerry Ordway & Rick Hoberg (p) & Mike Machlan (i)

STARRING: GL, LB, JQ, CS, HM, AT, DF. (Cameos: RM, SU, FB)

SYNOPSIS: Dr. Fate says his original helmet was threatening to take posses-sion of him. An African-American who calls himself Amazing-Man arrives at Fate's Salem tower to steal that headpiece for Ultra-Humanite. Defeated by Fate and Atom, he reveals that he is Olympic athlete Will Everett, who now has the power to become any substance he touches. Dr. Fate dons his full helmet again, despite the risk, knowing only its power can hope to defeat Ultra.

NOV 13 1982
JERRY
ORDWAY

NOTES:

- The title "When Fate Thy Measure Takes" (minus the exclamation point) is a quota-tion is from the poem *Epigram* by James Russell Lowell.

- Hawkman and Dr. Fate mention the extreme wartime housing shortage in Washington, DC—already becoming a widely-reported phenomenon even just a few weeks after Pearl Harbor.

- Dr. Fate relates his origin in six panels, and reveals he had to cease wearing his original helmet because it was "trying to take me over, somehow!" This occurred,

That's Amazing, Man!

Jerry Ordway's 1983 concept sketch for Amazing-Man. RT, now editor as well as writer of All-Star Squadron, asked for only one change: to turn that great "A" on his belt into a chest symbol. (Okay, so maybe they should've thought in terms of having him wear a mask.) Apparently Jerry'd sent an earlier sketch which he asked Roy (in a note attached to this one) to disregard—and Roy did—though both guys wish they'd hung onto it! [© DC Comics.]

A Very Special Olympics

(Left:) On Earth-Two, Will Everett had shared glory at the 1936 Olympics with another African-American, Jesse Owens, as seen in the Amazing-Man origin chapter in #23; script by RT, with art by Rick Hoberg & Mike Machlan. [© DC Comics.]

(Above:) On our Earth, Jesse Owens—the son of sharecroppers and the grandson of slaves—demolished Hitler's ideas of using the Berlin Olympics to demonstrate the superiority of the so-called "Aryan race."

he says, right after "the Justice Society adventure the world's not ready to learn about yet"—a foreshadowing of June 1941 events which, a year-plus later, would be related in *All-Star Squadron Annual* #3! Although RT didn't yet have all the details of that story worked out, he already knew that in it he intended to deal with several things that occurred between *All-Star Comics* #7 & #8, such as the change in Fate's helmet and powers, Green Lantern stepping down after a super-brief spell as JSA chairman, and Hourman's abruptly leaving the team.

- The 6-page "Secret Origin of Amazing-Man!" in the middle of the issue represents Rick Hoberg's first penciling on *All-Star Squadron*, and was done to gain Jerry Ordway time as he, Mike Machlan, and RT began work on the new series that would soon emerge as *Infinity, Inc.*

- Will Everett discovers the limitations of his powers: by becoming one with the stones of Dr. Fate's Salem tower, he can pass through its walls—but he can't take the mage's helmet with him.

- When Roy Thomas and Bill Everett had roomed together in New York during much of 1965-67, the creator of the 1939 Amazing-Man had given RT his verbal blessing to develop a new hero of that name, though it took the latter years to get around to it. (RT had feared Stan Lee would feel it was "too corny" a name for

Master Of My Fate

(Above:) The moment many fans had been waiting for since All-Star Squadron began: Dr. Fate dons his original helmet. The half-mask was the one the less-magically-powered Fate wore during the period covered by the comic, but everyone associated with the series preferred that full helmet, too. Jerry Ordway drew it better than anyone before or after, in RT's less than humble opinion. Many artists don't seem to "get" the concept that it's composed of two identical halves, and draw the crest as a third, separate piece. Art by Ordway & Machlan, script by RT. [© DC Comics.]

a Marvel super-hero.)

- The issue's LP contains a letter from Justice Society co-creator Gardner F. Fox, giving his blessing to *All-Star Squadron*.

He quotes All-American co-publisher M.C. Gaines as saying back in the 1940s: "Don't give me Rembrandt, give me production!"

ALL-STAR SQUADRON #24
(Aug. 1983)

COVER: Jerry Ordway

STORY: "The Man Who'll Know Too Much!" – 24 pp.

ARTISTS: Jerry Ordway (p) & Mike Machlan (i)

STARRING: BM, RO, RM, SU, FB, JQ, GL, LB, CS, TA, DF, AT. (Cameos:) JT, SM, WW, DM, SA, HM.

SYNOPSIS: Ultra-Humanite, scheming to put his brain into Robotman's body, capsizes an ocean liner in New York Harbor. Johnny Quick is injured saving workmen, but Green Lantern rights the vessel. Tarantula encounters a costumed man who calls himself Brainwave Jr. and is seeking writer Jonathan Law—Tarantula's other identity. The newcomer says he's the son of the criminal Brain Wave, come from 1983 to warn of danger. In a new costume made by his landlady, Olga, Tarantula hurries to find the All-Stars.

NOTES:

- The title "The Man Who'll Know Too Much!" was adapted, of course, from that of the two Alfred Hitchcock films called *The Man Who Knew Too Much*. And, of course, the JSA story in *All-Star Comics* #29 was titled "The Man Who Knows Too Much."

- Dick Grayson (Robin) and Chuck Grayson (lab assistant to Bob Crane/Paul Dennis/Robotman) are revealed to be cousins.

Me Tarzan—You Batman!

When Jerry Ordway drew this beautiful homage to a classic early Bob Kane Batman pose as the splash of #24 (left), he probably had no idea he was actually channeling master illustrator Harold R. Foster! Jack Bender, the current artist of the long-running Alley Oop comic strip, sent the grouping of three panels above: 1939 Batman panels from Detective Comics #31 & #33, flanking a panel from "Episode #34" of the Foster-drawn comics serialization of Edgar Rice Burroughs' novel Tarzan of the Apes. The latter had run in newspapers in 1929, ten years earlier. Batman #1 (Spring 1940) reprinted the sequence from Detective #33. [All-Star Squadron & Batman art © DC Comics; Tarzan art © Edgar Rice Burroughs, Inc.]

Hollywood At War

Bud Abbott and Lou Costello (seen at right) were the most popular comedy team during WWII, and sold millions of dollars' worth of War Bonds—but, alas, were plagued by tax problems a few years later. In issue #24, Johnny (Quick) Chambers and Tubby Watts film them for the movie newsreels at a War Bond Drive in honor of the late Carole Lombard. That talented film comedienne, the wife of super-star Clark Gable, had been killed in an airplane crash on Jan. 16, 1942 (less than a month before this story takes place), while on a Bond tour. Gable, too, did a cameo in #24. Ye Editor erred in writing in Vol. 1 of this series (which featured a photo of Lombard and Gable) that she died in February of '42. [Art © DC Comics.]

Along Came A Spider

(Near right:) Precisely whose idea it was—Roy Thomas' or Jerry Ordway's—to re-design Tarantula's garb so he looked less like Sandman is lost in the mists of comics history. But Jerry writes that this 1982 front-and-back drawing he dug up for this book was the "first Tarantula sketch by me – brought to NYC when DC flew us all in – you passed on it, and I started afresh." The drawing was a bit too generic— coincidentally, not unlike the rendition Steve Ditko has drawn of Jack Kirby's original Spider-Man costume, as he recalls seeing it in 1962.

(Far right:) There were no doubt intermediate drawings, but here's what Jerry calls his "final sketch, printed in letter col of ish of All Star Squad. DC never paid for it." Yes, it did appear in issue #24—and at least DC coughed up for that flight to New York, Jer!

(Right center:) Tarantula, in his new outfit, confronts Commander Steel in the Perisphere in #24. Art by Ordway & Machlan, script by RT. [© DC Comics.]

Wave To The Nice People, Junior!

(Above:) Brainwave Jr., son of the original Brain Wave, shows up in 1942 from the 1980s in All-Star Squadron #24. He thus became the first of the brand new grouping known as Infinity, Inc., to appear in any comic book; his fellow Infinitors would follow in #25. Hey, it also means that JSAers met him before they met in person their vintage nemesis, his father! Time paradoxes, anyone? (Junior's costume was based on the mentally-induced appearance taken on by his old man in 1976's All-Star Comics #58; see p. 155.)

Roy Thomas postulated that, after WWII, Jonathan (Tarantula) Law would write a book about his fellow super-heroes called Altered Egos. Roy never figured he'd ever be doing anything else with the name of the comics fanzine he'd helped Dr. Jerry Bails launch in 1961! [© DC Comics.]

Lafayette, We Are Here

(Above & right:) In issue #24, Green Lantern saves the French liner Normandie from sinking in New York Harbor while it's being refitted to be an aircraft carrier, after an explosion that, on Earth-Two, was caused by The Ultra-Humanite. On our Earth, the Normandie—which had been rechristened the USS Lafayette—burned all the afternoon of Feb. 10, 1942, having turned on her side. The mysterious blast was believed by many at the time to be an act of Nazi sabotage; but, in retrospect, it appears to have been a tragic accident, caused by a workman dropping an acetylene torch. The ship was never salvaged into war service. [Art © DC Comics.]

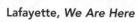

☆☆☆☆☆☆☆☆☆☆☆☆☆☆☆☆☆☆☆☆☆☆☆☆☆☆☆☆☆

ALL-STAR SQUADRON #25
(Sept. 1983)

COVER: Jerry Ordway

STORY: "The Infinity Syndrome!" – 23 pp.

ARTISTS: Jerry Ordway (p) & Mike Machlan (i)

STARRING: HM, SM, SA, WW, JT, DM, BM, RO, CS, GL, AT, LB, TA, FB, RM, SU, GU, PL, AT, AM (as a hero).

SYNOPSIS: When Amazing-Man learns The Ultra-Humanite intends to destroy much of Brooklyn, L.A., and Detroit (Will

Everett's home town), he helps the All-Stars against his former boss. Defense factories in those cities are attacked by teams from a super-powered group called Infinity, Inc., who've come from 1983. The All-Stars defeat the interlopers, but several of the former vanish into thin air upon grasping the Infinitors.

NOTES:

• The figure of the Silver Scarab was added to the upper left of #25's cover at the last minute. *Alter Ego* #44 printed Jerry Ordway's original art, minus the Scarab.

• The Guardian was featured in the story and on the cover because DC (and RT) wanted to protect the company's potential trademark on that name, since Marvel had recently introduced its own Guardian, a member of *Alpha Flight*.

[© DC Comics]

They Also Serve Who Only Stand Around And Wait

One of RT's favorite pages in All-Star Squadron is the splash of #25. Jerry Ordway caught each of the six heroes in a slightly different aspect. Inks by Mike Machlan. [© DC Comics.]

The Old War-Horse

(Above:) Secretary of War Henry L. Stimson and General George C. Marshall. See Stimson photo at right; that of the Army Chief of Staff appeared on p. 124. The scene in which they ask the JSA (known as the Justice Battalion during the early part of WWII) for help leads into events in All-Star Squadron #30. [Art © DC Comics.]

Victory Through Air Power

Above, Batman, Robin, and Tarantula visit a Los Angeles aircraft factory. With them is Sandra Knight, who'll soon be called upon to change into Phantom Lady. At right is a 1942 photo of two young women working on a fighter plane engine at Langley Field, Virginia. During the war, females took over many of the tough jobs it was long thought only males could handle. Art by Ordway & Machlan, script by RT. [Art © DC Comics.]

- Gen. George C. Marshall is startled by Starman's mention of "Ultra"—till he realizes the Astral Avenger is referring to Ultra-Humanite. Clearly the All-Stars hadn't been let in on "Top Secret Ultra," the code name for the British breaking of the German ciphers (especially those created by the ingenious Enigma machine), a feat that Gen. Dwight Eisenhower, commander of Allied forces in Europe, called "decisive" in winning the war. The deciphering of the Nazis' codes wasn't public knowledge before F.W. Winterbotham's 1974 book *Top Secret Ultra*.

- When Belle easily flags down a car to hitch a ride from Queens to Brooklyn, Commander Steel says she's "got Claudette Colbert beat all hollow!" This refers to a famous scene in Frank Capra's 1934 screwball comedy film *It Happened One Night*, in which incognito reporter Clark Gable tries in vain to get a car to stop for him, and Miss Colbert (who plays a rich runaway) then halts one with just a flash of leg and a smile.

- The Newsboy Legion (stars of the *Star Spangled Comics* feature in which The Guardian actually got second billing) appear in a pair of panels.

- Because #24-25 was the first appearance of any of Infinity, Inc., in a comic, the speech patterns of one or two of the young heroes are inconsistent with those in their upcoming series.

- Nothing more than vague hints are given in this issue that the Infinitors are the sons, daughters, and wards of members of the 1980s Justice Society.

- The issue's LP contains a letter from Sheldon Mayer, original editor of *All-Star Comics*, writing about how he and Gardner Fox co-plotted the 1940s Justice Society stories.

ALL-STAR SQUADRON #26
(Oct. 1983)

COVER: Jerry Ordway

STORY: "Talons across Time!" – 23 pp.

ARTISTS: Jerry Ordway (p) & Mike Machlan (i)

STARRING: BM, TA, PL, RO, GU, AM, CS, LB, AT, GL, JQ, FL, WC, RM, SU, FB. (Cameo: HM in flashforward to 1981)

SYNOPSIS: In place of the vanished All-Stars appear 1983 villains Vulcan, The Mist, the 2nd Psycho-Pirate, Rag Doll, Monocle, and the original Brain Wave. Hero teams drive the evil-doers out of the defense factories. Brainwave Jr. rouses Johnny Quick from his hospital bed; they join forces with Guardian, Phantom Lady, Flash, Robin, and Wildcat. He explains that Ultra-Humanite

implanted false memories to turn Infinity, Inc., into his/her agents. The captured Infinitors regain their mobility and memories.

NOTES:

- The Guardian's young buddies, The Newsboy Legion, make another brief cameo.

- Brainwave Jr. makes an oblique reference to a time when the Trylon and Perisphere are no longer standing—but does he mean they'll be eventually melted down for scrap as they were in our world, or to their destruction (albeit in "Civic City") seen in *All-Star Comics* #51 in 1950?

- Phantom Lady reveals that her black-light ray can now make her invisible—a power she didn't have in 1940s Quality comics.

- A thought balloon from Brainwave Jr. reveals for the first time that the other six members of Infinity, Inc., are "the *sons*, the *daughters*, the more or less adopted *wards*" of the JSA in 1983.

- A comment from Junior that "the *simple* plots are all in the *comic-books*" is a bit ironic, considering both this storyline and that of "Crisis on Earth-Prime"!

- The LP announces that, after *Annual #2* (debuting two weeks after #26), Jerry Ordway (then scheduled to ink, not pencil, *Infinity, Inc.*), would be leaving *All-Star Squadron* to draw, as well, an upcoming six-issue *Justice Society of America* mini-series. These plans didn't

"Okay, Ultra—Here We Come!"

The multi-hero word balloon on the cover of #26 was RT's nod to his 1970s WWII-set series, The Invaders. He'd made the battle cry of the Marvel group "Okay, Axis—Here We Come!"—adapted from a wartime house ad, by way of its use by journalist/sf fan Don Thompson as the title of a 1961 article on Golden Age Timely/Marvel. This splash by Frank Robbins (pencils) & Frank Springer (inker), with script by RT, is from The Invaders Annual #1 (1976), reprinted in the 2004 trade paperback The Avengers: Once an Invader. RT has loved seeing several Invaders stories republished of late; hopefully one day there'll be a 500-page Showcase edition or three of All-Star Squadron. [© Marvel Characters, Inc.]

It's Always Foul Weather…

Each of the super-villains who materialized in place of vanishing Infinitors had previously battled JSA heroes between 1941 & 1976. Here are the panels in which they're introduced in #26, followed by their premier appearances (clockwise from top left):

(Top row:) Vulcan, Son of Fire, was created for the revived All-Star Comics #60 (May-June 1976) by writer Gerry Conway and artists Keith Giffen & Wally Wood—while Starman first encountered The Mist in Adventure Comics #67 (Oct. 1941), drawn by Jack Burnley and probably written by Gardner Fox, as reprinted in The Golden Age Starman Archives, Vol. 1.

(Right & below center:) The second Psycho-Pirate took over from the original 1940s version in the Fox-scripted, Murphy Anderson-illoed Showcase #56 (May-June 1965)—while the elder Brain Wave's wearing the costume and physique he "first" sported in All-Star Comics #58 (Jan.-Feb. 1976). Thanks to Bob Cherry for the Showcase scan.

(Left & below left:) Rag Doll initially took on Jay Garrick in Flash Comics #36 (Dec. 1942), with script by Fox & art by E.E. Hibbard—and The Monocle first eyed Hawkman in Flash #64 (April-May 1945), drawn by a teenage Joe Kubert and written by the ubiquitous Gardner Fox. Did Gar ever sleep? Thanks to Al Dellinges for the latter scan
[All art © DC Comics.]

The Lineup

(Above:) Brainwave Jr., IDs his fellow Infinitors for The Flash in All-Star Squadron #26. Repro'd from original b&w art as printed in the comics-news magazine Amazing Heroes #36 (Dec. 1, 1983), not long before Infinity, Inc. #1 hit the comics shops. (It never hit the newsstands at that time, since it was a "direct-only" book.) Script by RT, art by Ordway & Machlan. [© DC Comics.]

Three More Faces Of Evil

(Right:) The Ultra-Humanite started out as a bald evil-scientist type in early Action Comics (a position soon filled by Luthor)—next got his brain transplanted into the body of movie star Dolores Winters (also in Action)—and, in JLA #195-197 (Oct.-Dec. 1981), finally received his, er, ultimate form to date: George Pérez's great white ape. Tossed into limbo at the end of that JLA-JSA crossover, he and five other villains encountered Vulcan and hatched their new plan, involving 1942. In #26, Ordway & Machlan provided this brief flashback to JLA #197; script by RT. [© DC Comics.]

materialize quite as planned.

• The LP says Japan's reputed Black Dragon Society "seems to have been wholly fictitious." RT made this (erroneous) statement before further research made him aware that it had, indeed, existed; what was mythical was merely its rumored involvement in sabotage in the USA.

• Also launched in this LP was a poll, in which readers were asked if they'd like to see *All-Star Comics* #12 fully adapted in *All-Star Squadron*, or just be recounted in a several-panel flashback.

★★★★★★★★★★★★★★★★★★★★★★★★★★★★★★★★★★★

ALL-STAR SQUADRON ANNUAL #2 (1983)

COVER: Jerry Ordway

STORY: "The Ultra War!" – 39 pp.

ARTIST: Jerry Ordway

STARRING: SU, FB, RM, AM, PL, FL, RO, WC, GU, JQ, GL, TA, LB, AT, BM, CS. (Cameos:) HM, SM, JT (w/TB), SA, DM, WW, SP, DF.

SYNOPSIS: Brainwave Jr. and an All-Star team are captured battling Ultra-Humanite's group, which Amazing-Man has rejoined. Five other All-Stars team up with Infinity, Inc., to rescue the captives and stop Ultra from usurping Robotman's body. The heroes save the Supreme Court, Congress, and the White House from the villains. Cyclotron shows Firebrand his infant daughter Terri, then blows himself up to destroy Ultra. All time-displaced persons return to 1983, and Firebrand and Atom vow to rear Cyclotron's infant daughter.

Legislative, Executive, And Judicial—Not Necessarily In That Order

(L. to r.:) US Supreme Court Chief Justice Harlan Fiske Stone (left & photo), Vice President Henry Wallace (who of course presided over the Senate), and FDR represented the three branches of government assaulted by Brain Wave's forces. Only thing is, somehow RT & Jerry Ordway got hold of the wrong reference, since the white-mustachioed "Chief Justice" depicted in Annual #2 (left) in no way resembled the photo of H.F. Stone next to it! Comics material by RT & Ordway. [Art © DC Comics.]

NOTES:

- On the cover, The Brain Wave is drawn in his true "big-headed" aspect, so he won't look nearly identical to his son Brainwave Jr., whom he's battling.

- Ultra's hideout is inside Mount St. Helen's, a mountain in southwest Washington state that, on our Earth, would suddenly erupt as a volcano on May 18, 1980.

- FDR's assistant, Harry Hopkins, remarks on the fact that FDR had poliomyletis some years before, but has overcome it.

- Cyclotron, according to the *Crisis on Infinite Earths* limited series of 1985-86, was thrust forward at some point to that event, then returned to the instant he had left 1942—just in time to die.

- Immediately following the story is Jerry Ordway's own version of the cover of *All-Star Comics* #3; it was seen in *Vol. 1* of this series.

- The issue's final interior page reprints p. "C" from *All-Star Comics* #11 from photocopies of the original art, with script by Gardner Fox and art by Jack Burnley. This is the only page of *published* Golden Age art showing the gathered JSA that is known to exist.

Web-Headache

(Above:) Tarantula considers a time paradox. By Ordway & Thomas. [© DC Comics.]

Life Goes On

(Above:) After Infinity, Inc., go back to 1983, Chuck Grayson and a whole passel of All-Stars—most prominently godparents Atom and Firebrand— gather around Terry Curtis' infant daughter Terri—who'll grow up to be the mother of the Infinitor originally called Nuklon (now Atom-Smasher). [© DC Comics.]

- For *The DC Sampler* of 1983, a promotional summer giveaway provided to comics shops, Jerry Ordway penciled and inked a two-page spread showing the Squadron battling the super-villains who appear in the *Annual*. It was utilized as the wraparound cover of *Alter Ego* #44 (Jan. 2005).

ALL-STAR SQUADRON #27
(Nov. 1983)

COVER: Jerry Ordway

STORY: "A Spectre Is Haunting the Multiverse!" – 23 pp.

ARTISTS: Richard Howell (p) & Larry Houston (i)

STARRING: FB, AT, SU, GL, PL, GU, CS, JQ, LB, BM, TA, AM, HM, SM, DM, SA, JT, WW, SP, DF.

SYNOPSIS: The Atom, irradiated during his battle with Cyclotron, is hospitalized. The JSA, rushing to his side, use Wonder Woman's magic sphere to monitor Dr. Fate's quest for the missing Spectre. The trail leads Fate to the extradimensional tomb of the evil Kulak, where Spectre stands guard. The two heroes clash. Spectre overpowers Fate too late to stop Kulak from awakening and attacking Earth—as the latter's giant hands are seen ripping a gigantic hole in the sky itself, gaining Kulak entrance into the realm of men.

NOTES:

- Some astute readers probably guessed that The Atom's passing out in the hospital was related to his close encounter with Cyclotron—and that it would have a retcon connection with the Mighty Mite's gaining atomic strength in 1948.

- The sidereal domain in which Dr. Fate and The Spectre battle over Kulak has a deliberate resemblance to the other-world realms established by Steve Ditko in Marvel's Dr. Strange series in the mid-1960s.

- Rick Hoberg was announced as scheduled to become penciler of *All-Star Squadron* with #29, with Larry Houston as regular inker. But Hoberg got delayed a bit, and Houston departed after one issue.

What's On The Tube Tonight?

Jerry Ordway's cover for #27, with its Magic Sphere, had a layout suggestive to that of All-Star Comics #48 (1949)—as can be seen in All-Star Companion, Vol. 1, or The All Star Comics Archives, Vol. 10. [© DC Comics.]

- RT explains on the LP his rationale for adding an African-American hero, Amazing-Man, to the series, even though there were no black super-heroes in mainstream American comic books prior to Marvel's Black Panther.

Fated To Draw All-Star Squadron

(Center:) Richard Howell in a debonair photo from a few years back, courtesy of the artist. A graduate of Harvard, class of '76, for years he's been the writer/artist/publisher of the alternative comic Portia Prinz of the Glamazons, and has drawn numerous other comics stories.

(Right:) In issue #27, Dr. Fate manages to get past the sentinel Spectre long enough to learn the secret he's hiding—blue skin, third eye, and all! Script by RT, art by Richard Howell & Larry Houston. [© DC Comics]

ALL-STAR SQUADRON #28
(Dec. 1983)

COVER: Jerry Ordway

STORY: "By Hatred Possessed!" – 22 pp.

ARTISTS: Richard Howell (p) & Gerald Forton (i)

STARRING: HM, WW, JT (w/TB), DM, SM, SA, SP, DF, AT, SG.

SYNOPSIS: As his spell of hate infects all mankind, Kulak sends an ensorcelled Spectre against the JSA and new arrival Sargon, who revives Dr. Fate and sends him back into battle. Defeating Fate, Kulak triumphantly dons the Helmet of Nabu, which reflects the power of his third eye

back upon himself. The resultant backlash sends Kulak, still wearing the helmet, careening helplessly through the dimensions, perhaps forever.

NOTES:

- The issue's inker was Gerald Forton, a prominent French cartoonist.
- A "postscriptum" at story's end announced that, after renouncing it again in #28, Dr. Fate "only regained Nabu's helmet in the early 1960s, just in time for the first of many Justice League-Justice society team-ups." It was promised that this story would be told "someday, somewhere."
- The issue contains a two-page Infinity, Inc., pin-up penciled by Machlan & inked by Ordway. Included with the others are Power Girl and The Huntress (from the 1970s *All-Star Comics* revival) and a new motorcycle-riding character in an orange Wildcat-style outfit referred to as "La Garro" (Spanish for "The Claw").

Do You Believe In Magic?

Only when Sargon the Sorcerer greets them (at left) on a flying carpet in #28 do the Justice Society realize he's more than just another stage magician. Comics wizards like Mandrake, Zatara, and Sargon were to a great extent inspired by the likes of Harry Houdini and Harry Blackstone (1885-1965, seen in photo). Blackstone the Magician has been called "perhaps the most innovational magician since Houdini," and achieved great popularity in the US during the 1930s. He even had his own Street & Smith comic book during the 1940s. [Art © DC Comics.]

--BUT PEOPLE ALL OVER THE PLANET!

IN THE WAR-TORN RUSSIAN SOVIET AND GERMAN SOLDIERS ALIKE STARE UPWARD WITH WIDENED EYES, GAPING JAWS.

AS, ON CORREGIDOR IN THE PHILIPPINES, WHERE DESPERATE AMERICAN FORCES HAVE FOUGHT A LAST-DITCH HOLDING ACTION FOR MORE THAN TWO MONTHS...

GENERAL MACARTHUR-- WHAT'S HAPPENING? THAT HORRIBLE FACE UP THERE--!

IN SINGAPORE, NIGH-EXHAUSTED BRITISH TROOPS WONDER IF, SOMEHOW, THE BESEIGING JAPANESE ARE INDEED THE SONS OF HEAVEN THEY CLAIM TO BE--

WHILE, IN THE SUBURBS OF THE FALLING CITY, THE INVADING ORIENTALS LIKEWISE WONDER WHAT MEANS THIS SIGN IN THE HEAVENS.

--AND THIS IS SOME MYSTIC MANIFESTATION OF SOME HIGHER POWER.

FORGET IT, SOLDIER! IT'S JUST SOME JAPANESE TRICK!

--I HOPE.

"I Shall Return"

Unlike The Flying Eye earlier, Kulak was precisely what he seemed to be when his huge taloned hands tore open the sky. Art by Howell & Forton, script by RT. Kulak was seen all over the Earth at the same time, including by embattled US forces who by February 1942 had spent two months holding off the Japanese on Corregidor, a small rock of an island off Manila in the conquered Philippines. General Douglas MacArthur, seen here in Dec. 1941, would soon be ordered to flee Corregidor for Australia, so that he would not have to surrender along with his surviving troops. [Art © DC Comics.]

ALL-STAR SQUADRON #29
(Jan. 1984)

COVER: Jerry Ordway

STORY: "A Man Called Doome!" – 23 pp.

ARTISTS: Jerry Ordway (p) & Rick Magyar (i)

STARRING: SK, SS, ST, GA, SY, VG, CA, WI. (Cameos:) HM, HG, DM, SM, WW, FB, RM, CS, LB, AT, JQ.

SYNOPSIS: The Shining Knight tells Churchill of the Seven Soldiers of Victory's recent battle with Dr. Doome: Doome brought Alexander the Great, Attila the Hun, Genghis Khan, Napoleon, and Nero forward through time to steal rare metals needed to perfect his "time beam." The Soldiers returned the quintet to their own eras, then pursued Doome to the Trojan War and back. His time machine exploded as he projected himself into the far future. Sir Justin elects to remain in England rather than attend a meeting of the All-Star Squadron.

NOTES:

• The Shining Knight logo that appears on the first page of the story is from one of the hero's later stories, during the period they were drawn by Frank Frazetta.

• Roy Thomas gives the Seven Soldiers their own war cry of sorts: "What do we *want?*" "*Victory!*" "What'll we *settle* for?" "*Victory!*"

• In abridging the story, each of the "solo" exploits of the five heroes or teams is related on a single page.

• The Star-Spangled Kid remarks that, one of these days, they should make the absent Wing "an *official* Soldier of Victory." This is a dig at the fact that, The Crimson Avenger's Oriental aide took part in most of the group's 14 tales in *Leading Comics*, yet was never counted as a member.

• Kurt Mitchell, co-writer of this chapter, points out that Vandal Savage claimed in *Green Lantern* #10 (Winter 1943) to have been Genghis Khan.

Soldier On!

Jerry Ordway generously provided us photocopies of his original art for several All-Star Squadron covers, minus text. Most of these will appear in Alter Ego magazine, but we're printing #29's cover from the b&w art because it sported so little "copy"—just the name of the writer and artists, and the phrase "7 Soldiers of Victory!" The red, white, and blue areas of the American flag were "color-held" on the published version, with the black lines dropped, to make the super-hero septet stand out. [© DC Comics.]

Don't Know Much About History

Dr. Doome greets the five "Tyrants of Time" he has summoned via time beam: Nero... Attila... Napoleon... Genghis Khan... Alexander the Great. This juxtaposed art from Leading Comics (Aug. 1942) and All-Star Squadron #19 shows how a panel by artist Mort Meskin (top left) was adapted by Jerry Ordway (left, with inks by Rick Bryant), four decades later. The entire Golden Age tale is on view in The Seven Soldiers of Victory Archives, Vol. 1—but the '42 panel is reprinted here from RT's copy of the actual comic.

Since the historical Genghis Khan, Alexander, and some Attila-style Huns were pictured in Vol. 1 of this series, because they figured in All-Star Comics #35 & #38, pictured above are Napoleon (in David's famous painting of Bonaparte on horse-back) and the Roman emperor Nero.

Prepare To Meet Thy Doom—Or Is It Doome—Or Doog—Or Droom?

(Above left:) The Ordway/Magyar Dr. Doome in #29 caught the spirit of Meskin's 1942 version. [© DC Comics.] (Above right:) A slightly better-known Dr. Doom, in the first panel Jack Kirby ever penciled of Marvel's most celebrated villain; script by Stan Lee, inks by Joe Sinnott. Coincidentally, both Doome and Doom use time travel in their initial forays, though Victor Von D. in Fantastic Four #5 (July 1962) manipulates the super-heroes themselves. [© Marvel Characters, Inc.]

Oddly, we suspect the evil Dr. Doog in the very first Starman story, in Adventure Comics #61 (April 1941), was scripted to be called Dr. Doom; the "g" in "Doog" looks like poorly-spaced relettering wherever it appears (see The Golden Age Starman Archives, Vol. 1). And, even earlier, according to writer/co-creator Gardner Fox, Dr. Fate was originally slated to be called Dr. Droom, and might easily have been rechristened Dr. Doom for More Fun Comics #55 (May 1940). Why neither of these two became comics' first Dr. Doom is a pair of unsolved mysteries!

Seven Soldiers Assemble!

(Above:) Green Arrow and Speedy gather together the rest of the "Law's Legionnaires" in issue #29, on this page repro'd from a photocopy of the original pencils. Courtesy of artist Jerry Ordway. [© DC Comics.]

ALL-STAR SQUADRON #30
(Feb. 1984)

COVER: Jerry Ordway

STORY: "Day of the Black Dragon!" – 22 pp.

ARTISTS: Mike Machlan (p, pp. 1-13), Richard Howell (p, pp. 14-22) — Sam De La Rosa & Mike Machlan (i)

STARRING: WW, LB, HM, DF, SM, JT (w/TB), SA, AT, DM, SP.

SYNOPSIS: In the Perisphere, Wonder Woman writes up details of the JSA's latest case: Sent against the Black Dragon Society, seven JSAers retrieve or destroy top-secret experimental US weapons stolen by the Dragons and rescue the scientists who invented them. Johnny Thunder wishes himself to the Dragons' secret HQ and is about to be executed, but his Thunderbolt brings the rest of the JSA in time to save him.

NOTES:

- The events transcribed by Wonder Woman in this issue, as secretary of the JSA, are adapted from *All-Star Comics* #12, generally referred to as "The Black Dragon."

- The Hawkman, Atom, and Johnny Thunder solo chapters from the 1942 story are the only ones that receive more than a single-panel recap.

- While not wishing to falsify what had been written in the wartime version, Roy Thomas felt it advisable to omit certain racially offensive remarks and attitudes from the original story, though the word "Jap" was retained in the Atom segment for impact.

- Wandering through the "Japanese sector" of San Francisco, The Atom says he

[© DC Comics]

A Cutting Edge Cover

Jerry Ordway's cover for All-Star Squadron #30 is repro'd below from a photocopy he provided of the original art; you can see the logo and topline copy on the printed version behind it. The artist used Kraftint shading on this cover to get a modeled, moody effect. Incidentally, Dr. Fate is wearing his (incorrect) full helmet here, as a reader pointed out in the LP of #35; RT and Jerry noticed it in time, but Jerry had drawn the cover on a type of illustration board that made it difficult to do corrections—so they let it go. [© DC Comics.]

Race Matters

(Left:) The Atom and a Japanese-born lab assistant in San Francisco tackle the Black Dragon Society. All-Star Comics #12, on which Squadron #30 was based, contained so many racist elements, especially in the Atom chapter, that RT actually had the Mighty Mite apologize to the guy he'd called a "Jap." The assistant in the 1983 comic was named after Morrie Kuramoto, a Japanese-American letterer who'd befriended Roy when he first went to work for Marvel in 1965. Pencils by Richard Howell, inks by Sam De La Rosa. [© DC Comics.]

knows the area "about as well as I know Mars"—foreshadowing *All-Star Comics* #13, not many weeks in his future, when he'll be sent to the red planet in a Nazi rocket.

- The Atom chapter provides definitions of the terms "Issei" and "Nisei" as they relate respectively to Japan-born persons living in the US, and to those born in the US of Japanese parents and thus automatically American citizens.

- Liberty Belle is startled when Wonder Woman finishes writing out her entire account of the case while Belle's still "scribbling away on the same page" of her own All-Star Squadron minutes.

There Are Many Kinds of "Infamy"

As Michi Weglyn, author of Years of Infamy: The Untold Story of America's Concentration Camps (1976), pointed out in her caption accompanying this photo from the National Archives: "Most of the 110,000 persons removed for reasons of 'national security' were school-age children, infants, and young adults, not yet of voting age." As a teenager, Weglyn herself was interned in the Gila Relocation Center in Arizona. The odious comparison with the Nazis' concentration camps, in Ye Editor's opinion, can be overstated; but that the situation was a cruel injustice is undeniable.

At the end of #30, President Roosevelt signed Executive Order 9066, on Feb. 19, 1942, which would soon lead to the establishment of "relocation centers" for Japan-born US residents and even for many Americans born of Japanese parents. More details on this historical tragedy were given in Vol. 1 of this series.

☆☆☆☆☆☆☆☆☆☆☆☆☆☆☆☆☆☆☆☆☆☆☆☆☆☆☆☆☆☆

ALL-STAR SQUADRON #31
(March 1984)

COVER: Jerry Ordway

STORY: "Uncle Sam Wants You!" – 23 pp.

ARTISTS: Rick Hoberg (p) & Mike Machlan (i)

STARRING: MN, HM, HG, RA, BL, LB, SA, SN, WC, PM, SP, SM, TA, GU, AW, JE, RM, BM, RO, SU, DF, WW, DM, JQ, GL, AT, PL, JT, HB, MH, MH/Q, VG, GA, SY, CA, WI, SS, ST, MT, SG, MA, WH, TNT, DD, RB, FB, FL, ZA, CS, US, RE, MG, MI, NE, IH, HO, DL (last panel). (Cameos:) AM, SK, AQ, BH.

SYNOPSIS: The masked man called Midnight, carrying a metal box, is pursued through New York streets by Nazi assassins. At the Perisphere, 47 super-heroes hold the first full All-Star Squadron meeting. Uncle Sam appears and informs them of Earth-X, a world with no super-heroes. Months ago, creating a gateway between Earths, he recruited six super-heroes—Magno, Miss America, Neon the Unknown, Invisible Hood, Red Tornado, ex-JSAer Hourman—to cross over with him to that world. He says those six are all dead, and he's returned to recruit new, more powerful allies. Just then, a wounded Midnight arrives—and collapses. Inside his metal box is an unconscious, perhaps dying Doll Man!

NOTES:
- The cover of #31 is inspired by James Montgomery Flagg's famous 1917 recruiting poster for World War I (which

In The Spirit Of Eisner

Rick Hoberg's splash for issue #31 (far left), featuring the Quality hero Midnight, is an homage to The Spirit—which is only fitting, since in 1941 Quality publisher Busy Arnold had asked writer/artist Jack Cole to create a hero virtually identical to the Will Eisner character, which Arnold co-owned at the time. The background sign is an in-joke refererring to the popular Manhattan Transfer singing group. Inks by Mike Machlan. [© DC Comics.]

At near left is the splash from the weekly Comic Book Section, starring The Spirit, for Nov. 30, 1947, as reprinted by DC in Will Eisner's Spirit Archives, Vol. 15. [© Will Eisner Studios.]

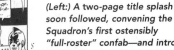

was re-utilized during WWII) of Uncle Sam saying "I Want You"—which in turn was influenced by a *British* poster featuring the historical military leader Lord Kitchener, created earlier in WWI.

• Hawkgirl gives Hawkman a hard time because the JSA never invited her to join—yet the boys "all went *ga-ga* over that upstart Amazon with the star-spangled girdle."

• The two Manhunters—no doubt unaware that on Earth-Prime they are published by two different comics companies—take an instant dislike to each other.

• FDR addresses the assembled conclave "by means of that amazing new invention, television." His speech spells out RT's original rationale for the retcon grouping: "Just as there's one wartime organization for labor, one for industry …so there should be one large, overall group to which all loyal mystery-*men* and *women* belong… namely, the *All-Star Squadron*."

• #31 features Mike Machlan's last inking on the series, as he concentrates on the just-debuting new mag *Infinity, Inc.*

• The LP says that, in a certain sense, the story told in the five-part JLA-JSA-All-Star Squadron crossover earlier is being "continued" in the "first few issues" of *Infinity, Inc.* A better phrasing, perhaps, would've been to call the latter a "sequel."

• A final LP note announces that the storyline begun in this issue was created partly to deal with the conundrum of "Earth-X," the world first seen in *Justice League of America* #107-108 in 1973, on which the Axis had won World War II: "Are there *two* Phantom Ladys, *two* Black Condors," etc.? RT announced he was happy to have the blessing of Earth-X creator Len Wein for this story arc.

Absent Friends

Belle accounts for the whereabouts of Amazing-Man, as well as of The Shining Knight and the Blackhawks, busy fighting the Axis abroad—and Aquaman's image was shown to establish the Golden Age sea king, who wouldn't make an on-stage appearance until #69. [© DC Comics.]

All Present And Accounted For

Never let it be said writer/editor Roy Thomas made it easy on "his" artists—but Rick Hoberg says he actually enjoyed working on this pair of two-page spreads that showed virtually all the then-current DC super-heroes and many of the Quality ones. The Perisphere's circular meeting-room was the space occupied in 1939-40 by the World Fair's Democracity exhibit. Chairwoman Liberty Belle's off-panel reading of the roll call and the attendees' responses were alternately colored pink and yellow for clarity of reading—and RT worked in a few character bits, as well. Great job, Rick—and inker Mike Machlan! It holds up, even a quarter of a century later. [© DC Comics.]

At left are a self-portrait Rick drew for #32 of himself as Johnny Quick—and a photo taken of him on the rim of the N'goro N'goro Crater in Tanzania a couple of years back. Very Frank Buck! Photo by Glenn Koenig. [Art © DC Comics.]

☆☆☆☆☆☆☆☆☆☆☆☆☆☆☆☆☆☆☆☆☆☆☆☆☆☆

ALL-STAR SQUADRON #32
(April 1984)

COVER: Jerry Ordway

STORY: "Crisis on Earth X! The Prequel" – 23 pp.

ARTISTS: Rick Hoberg (p) & Bill Collins (i)

STARRING: DL, PL, WW, GL, US, RA, TA, HB, JQ, HM, BL, DF, PM, FL, SM, AT, FB, SP, SU, BM, LB, WC, MN, DM, SS, JT, RE, MI, NE, IH, MG, HO, SG, CS, RM, GU, DM. (Cameos: SA, RO)

SYNOPSIS: Uncle Sam says that, early on Dec. 7, 1941, his transported "Freedom Fighters" turned back the force that was on its way to attack Earth-X's Pearl Harbor; but a *kamikaze* plane killed all but Sam. After months in a sanitarium, he saw a vision predicting the invasion of California on that parallel Earth, where the US was still neutral. Midnight and Doll Man, following Sam to Earth-X, joined the French Underground but were nearly killed by Baron Blitzkrieg. The Spectre propels seven All-Stars through Sam's gateway into Earth-X, but The Voice that gave Spectre his after-life stops him from entering. Sam and his new Freedom Fighters—Black Condor, Phantom Lady, Doll Man, Human Bomb, The Ray, and Red Bee— arrive on a California coast being attacked by Japanese Zeros and assault boats.

NOTES:

• #32 begins a series of issues inked by Bill Collins, formerly an art assistant to Dick Giordano. Writer/editor Roy Thomas became quite partial to his "mechanical" approach to embellishing.

."X" Marks The Original Art
Jerry Ordway's black-&-white art for #32's cover, courtesy of the artist. [© DC Comics.]

A Living Doll—But For How Long?

(Left:) The All-Stars react in astonishment to finding a badly hurt Doll Man inside a metal box carried by Midnight. Art by Rick Hoberg & Bill Collins; script by RT. [© DC Comics.]

• In this version of the World War II history of Earth-X, the United States remained neutral in December 1941 because the Japanese attack on Pearl Harbor was called off—and, in Uncle Sam's words, "America went on straddling the fence, and the Axis gobbled up even more of Europe and Asia"—with Japan itself spending the next 2+ months preparing for an attack on the US West Coast.

• Doll Man makes a reference in passing to "Ish Kabibble," the stage name of a horn player, novelty singer, and comedic foil in Kay Kyser's big band from 1938-50—while Midnight jokes about "Mr. Moto," hero of 1930s novels by John P. Marquand in which a secret agent of Imperial Japan is a hero. Some of these tales were made into Hollywood movies starring Peter Lorre, before tensions in the Pacific had reached the boiling point.

- As noted in a later LP, Midnight couldn't have known about Baron Blitzkrieg from accounts of his attack on Churchill in #7, since he and Doll Man were on Earth-X by that time. (RT's proofreading note re that caption had been missed by DC's production crew.)
- Don Thompson, co-editor of the *Comics Buyer's Guide*, later pointed out that the term "sci-fi" in #32 is an anachronism, having been coined by *Famous Monsters of Filmland* editor Forrest J. Ackerman in 1957. RT regretted not using instead the truly awful word "scientifiction," coined by *Amazing Stories* editor Hugo Gernsback circa 1930.

"Kamikaze" Means "Divine Wind"

(Photo at left:) In the last year of World War II in the Pacific, kamikaze planes—in which Japanese pilots attempted to crash their aircraft like flying bombs into American aircraft—were a growing threat. This photo of a Zero, set afire by an antiaircraft shell, was taken only a moment before it struck the flight deck of the USS Essex in November 1944. In this case, however, the carrier was only slightly damaged. [Photo © the respective copyright holders.]

(Above right:) Uncle Sam and the super-heroes he recruited encountered a kamikaze attack in late 1941, in a world where Pearl Harbor never happened—but that didn't make the Japanese Zero any less deadly when it struck The Red Torpedo's sub, as related by Uncle Sam in #31, via Thomas, Hoberg, & Collins. [© DC Comics.]

Sure *The Guy's Crazy!* He Claims He's Uncle Sam!

(Left:) Incarcerated as a madman, Uncle Sam was haunted by images of the heroes he felt he had gotten killed. Flashback script from #32 by RT, art by Hoberg & Collins. [© DC Comics.]

☆★☆★☆★☆★☆★☆★☆★☆★☆★☆★☆★☆★☆★☆★☆★☆★☆★

ALL-STAR SQUADRON #33
(May 1984)

COVER: Rick Hoberg (p) & Jerry Ordway (i)

STORY: "The Battle of Santa Barbara—Times Two!"—23 pp.

ARTISTS: Rick Hoberg (p) & Bill Collins (i)

STARRING: SP, US, RE, HB, RA, BL, DL, PL, SM, FB, JQ, LB, NP (intro), HO, HM. (TS as villainess.) (CAMEOS: GL, RM, WW.)

SYNOPSIS: Stuck between Earth-X and Earth-Two, Spectre watches as the Freedom Fighters foil the attack on California. On Earth-Two, Johnny Quick and Firebrand meet the aquatic Neptune Perkins. Starman and Liberty Belle seek Capt. Rick Cannon in a Santa Barbara, CA, warehouse—and encounter Tsunami, a sea-powered agent of Imperial Japan who's trying to turn the local Japanese-American community against the US. During a fight, Tsunami accidentally causes her father's death. The two Earths begin to merge—which will destroy them

both—as Spectre strives to keep them apart. On Earth-X, the FF find Hourman alive, but a hostage of Blitzkrieg.

NOTES:
- This issue features Rick Hoberg's first cover pencils for the title; Jerry Ordway continues to ink the covers.
- Capt. Rick Cannon of G-2 (Army Intelligence) first appeared in Liberty Belle's origin in *Boy Commandos* #1 (Winter 1942-43), there called Ricky. RT planned to eventually give him super-powers and call him "Cap Cannon," à la Doc Savage, but never got around to it.
- Tsunami says she is a "*kibei*"—a term of derision in Imperial Japan, referring to one born abroad of Japanese parents but returning to live in Japan.
- Miya Shimada was given the code-name Tsunami by Admiral Isoruko Yamamoto, the naval commander behind the December 1941 attack on Pearl Harbor. His photo was seen in *Vol. 1.*
- Liberty Belle calls Tsunami "a bargain basement Esther Williams"—referring to the swimming star then starting to make a big splash in MGM movies.

- RT used the phrase "Imperial Japan" (rather than simply "Japan") whenever possible, to distinguish the 1942 military-dominated Axis nation from the stable democracy of 1984, and as a parallel to the terms "Nazi Germany" and "Fascist Italy."

- The LP contains a biographical letter from Green Lantern co-creator Mart Nodell.

Wonder What His Middle Name Is!

(Center:) Neptune Perkins makes his dramatic "1942" debut in issue #33, surprising Johnny Quick and Firebrand, courtesy of Thomas, Hoberg, & Collins.

(Below:) Nep's real-world premiere was in Flash Comics #66 (Aug.-Sept. 1945), in a Hawkman story drawn by Joe Kubert and probably written by Gardner Fox. Thanks to Al Dellinges for the photocopy. [© DC Comics.]

Zero Hour, Man!

(Above:) Hourman makes his first non-flashback appearance in All-Star Squadron—as a captive of Baron Blitzkrieg. Art by Hoberg & Collins, script by RT. [© DC Comics.]

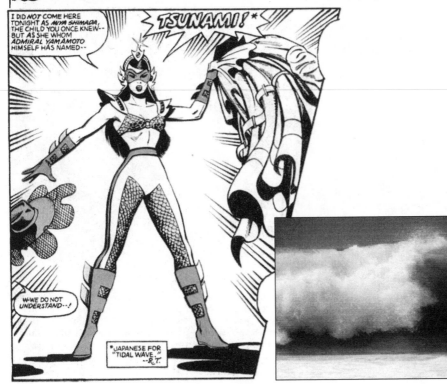

The Name Above The Tidal (Wave)

(Far left:) When Tsunami made her debut in #33, that Japanese word for "tidal wave" wasn't nearly as well known as it is today, hence the footnote. RT recalls spotting the term on a notice in the main L.A. post office, where he drove late at night to mail material to Marvel in the latter 1970s—and it stuck in his mind as a great name for a character. Art by Hoberg & Collins. [© DC Comics.]

(Left:) The word entered Americans' consciousness with a vengeance after the devastating tsunamis of Dec. 26, 2004. Caused by a strong earthquake with an epicenter off Sumatra, they left over 200,000 people dead.

ALL-STAR SQUADRON #34
(June 1984)

COVER: Rick Hoberg (p) & Jerry Ordway (i)

STORY: "The Wrath of Tsunami!" – 23 pp.

ARTISTS: Rick Hoberg (p) & Bill Collins (i)

STARRING: JQ, FB, NP, SP, HO, PL, US, RE, HB, DL, RA, BL, SM, LB. (TS as villainess.) (Cameos: HM, DF, WW, FL.)

SYNOPSIS: As Spectre strives to keep Earths-Two and -X from merging, Johnny Quick and Neptune Perkins are captured by a Japanese sub. On Earth-X, Baron Blitzkrieg defeats The Freedom Fighters and exposes Hourman as being addicted to the Miraclo drug that gives him super-strength for 60-minute periods. On Earth-Two, other All-Stars stop the Japanese sub from shelling the coast and free its captives. The sub explodes. Johnny and Liberty Belle wash up on the beach—to find a tidal wave, mentally controlled by Tsunami, rushing towards them.

NOTES:

- Was it one of the artists or letterer David Cody Weiss who drew a tidal wave inside the letters of the word "Tsunami" in the splash page title? Hmm… does that make it a "title wave"?

- Every *All-Star Squadron* title splash featured a quotation of some kind—in #34, a line from a poem by the earlier Japanese Emperor Meiji, quoted by Emperor Hirohito in 1941 as war with the West drew near: *"Why are waves and winds so unsettled nowadays?"*

- On the LP, a reader from Down Under asks if the All-Stars "could make an appearance in Australia during… the bombing of Darwin and so forth." RT responds he wasn't able to work in a story about the Japanese attack on Port Darwin—"Australia's Pearl Harbor"—on Feb. 19, 1942, but did mention it in #31.

- The LP features a long letter arguing the view that FDR knew about the Pearl Harbor attack in advance. RT, having read most of the books written on the subject over the years, feels that, at the very least, the jury is still out on the matter.

If You Prick Me…

Why was Santa Barbara, California, the site of the Japanese invasion on Earth-X? Because writer/editor Roy Thomas stumbled across an astonishing true story as to why, on our Earth, a small oilfield there was shelled by a Japanese sub on Feb. 23, 1942. As related in this flashback in #34, a Japanese tanker captain really did fall into cactus while visiting it in the late 1930s; he was offended by American workers' laughter. When war came, he commanded a sub and lobbed a few shells at that very oilfield, though they did little damage. That incident also influenced scenes in Steven Spielberg's 1979 comedy film 1941. RT even used the actual name of the man and his vessel: "Captain Kizo Nishino… commander of the submarine I-17, of the [Japanese] Sixth Fleet." Art by Hoberg & Collins. [© DC Comics.]

ALL-STAR SQUADRON #35
(July 1984)

COVER: Rick Hoberg (p) & Jerry Ordway (i)

STORY: "…That Earths May Live!" – 23 pp.

ARTISTS: Rick Hoberg (p) & Bill Collin (i)

STARRING: HO, PL, BL, US, SP, LB, JQ, FB, NP, RA, HB, DL, RE, SM, HM, HG, BM, RO, PM. (TS as villainess.)

SYNOPSIS: Starman and Firebrand rescue Liberty Belle and Johnny Quick; Neptune Perkins takes on Tsunami. On Earth-X, Baron Blitzkrieg tries to force Hourman to reveal the secret of Miraclo. The Red Bee—thought dead in an earlier explosion—perishes distracting Blitzkrieg long enough for the other heroes to break free. Blitzkrieg and three Stormtroopers escape to Earth-Two. With only seconds to right the cosmic balance, Spectre and the others return to their world, leaving Uncle Sam, Black Condor, and The Ray on Earth-X to compensate for the missing Nazis' life energy. Tsunami and Blitzkrieg escape—the latter stricken blind—but the Earths are out of danger.

NOTES:

- Liberty Belle breaks free of an embrace by Rick Cannon, her boyfriend in the *Boy Commandos*/*Star Spangled* series—and at issue's end she and Johnny Quick kiss for the first time.

- More is revealed about Hourman's Miraclo addiction.

- Though Doll Man, Phantom Lady, and Human Bomb return to Earth-Two with Hourman, they're destined to come back to Earth-X and join Uncle Sam's Freedom Fighters—who, after the events of *Justice League of America* #107-108 in 1973, had their own DC comic from 1976-78.

An Army Travels On Its Oil Barrels

The oil that was pumped near Santa Barbara, CA, might have gone, later in 1942, to help the US troops at the bitter battle for the island of Guadalcanal in the Pacific. US Army photo.

Dooms Cosmic And Personal

The Spectre fights to keep Earth-Two and Earth-X from colliding in hyperspace—while The Red Bee dies giving the other All-Stars a few precious seconds to break free. Art by Hoberg & Collins, script by RT. P. 15 (right) repro'd from photocopies of the original art (autographed by Hoberg), courtesy of Fred DeBoom. [© DC Comics.]

ALL-STAR SQUADRON ANNUAL #3 (1984)

COVER: Rick Hoberg (p) & Jerry Ordway (i)

STORY: (No Title) – 41 pp.

CO-PLOTTER: Dann Thomas

ARTISTS: Jerry Ordway, Rick Hoberg; Richard Howell; Keith Giffen (p&i); Rich Buckler, Wayne Boring, Carmine Infantino, Don Newton, Mart Nodell, George Pérez (p); Mike Machlan, Frank Giacoia, Bill Collins, Joe Giella, Jerry Ordway (i)

STARRING: TA, WW, SA, JT (w/TB), GL, DF, SP, HM, AT, HO, FL, SU, BM, RO, SM, HG.

SYNOPSIS: By focusing the Magic Sphere on mysterious documents, Wonder Woman and Tarantula see previously-unrelated events of June 28, 1941: The active and honorary JSAers—aided by Starman, Hawkgirl, Robin, Lois Lane, Joan Williams, and Inza Cramer—battle Ian Karkull and his pawns: Alexander the Great (Hawkman's foe), Catwoman (Batman's), Dr. Doog (Starman's), Lightning Master (Superman's), Sieur Satan (Flash's), Tarantula (Sandman's), Wotan (Dr. Fate's), and Zor (Spectre's). Karkull plans to assassinate FDR *and* the next nine men destined to follow him as President. The JSA save all but the unidentified last of these. The heroes are bathed in "chronal energy" which will keep them physically younger than their chronological ages in decades to come. Dr. Fate puts aside

the Helmet of Nabu, which is trying to take possession of him… GL steps down as JSA chairman… and Hourman resigns because of his Miraclo addiction. In 1942, Wonder Woman and Tarantula agree to keep the case a secret, yet never realize *why* Karkull wanted those other nine men murdered.

NOTES:

- This story was co-plotted by Roy's wife Dann Thomas, who researched what each of eight post-FDR Presidents was doing on or about June 28, 1941. (Dann had also assisted Roy, uncredited, on the plots of various other *All-Star Squadron* stories.)

- The single *Annual* page penciled by Rich Buckler, showing four JSAers in action as per *All-Star Comics #8*, was originally done for another project—possibly *America vs. the Justice Society.*

- This story, occurring right after *All-Star Comics #7*, was devised to explain things that happened *in between* it & #8: why GL stepped down as JSA chairman after only one session… why Hourman abruptly took a "leave of absence" and was unceremoniously replaced by Starman… why Dr. Fate's helmet became truncated between #7 & #8 and his powers became less magical.

- When Sandman fought a criminal called The Tarantula in *Adventure Comics #40* (July 1939), there was no masked *hero* of the same name.

- Yes, Virginia, The Catwoman really *did* originally wear a cat-mask like the one shown on p. 172!

- Due to an engraving error, characters have light green flesh on several pages; Wotan, of course, looked like that all the time!

- Inker Ordway altered the "S" penciled by Boring on Superman's chest insignia into the "Earth-Two" version, adapted from early-1940s Fred Ray covers.

- Since there wasn't room for solo chapters of every JSAer, Richard Howell drew a two-page spread showing what Hawkman (with Hawkgirl), Spectre, Sandman, and Atom were up to.

- The fully-hooded Atom is amused by Starman's referring to his own headgear as a "mask." By the Mighty Mite's standards, it definitely *wasn't* one.

- Wonder Woman became a member of the Justice Society months *after* what Sandman calls "the JSA mission the world's not ready to learn about, just yet."

Mirror, Mirror, On The Wall…

In late February 1942, Wonder Woman and Tarantula (as drawn by Jerry Ordway) use the Magic Sphere to eavesdrop on a Justice Society meeting of June 28, 1941 (drawn by Rick Hoberg)—the one detailed in All-Star Comics #8. Script by RT. [© DC Comics.]

And In This Corner...

The villains assembled by Ian Karkull were an all-star cast, as well. See issue synopsis to match evil-doer to JSAer. Art by Hoberg, script by RT. [© DC Comics.]

"One Day You May Grow Up To Be President"

Ian Karkull's great secret, of which only he of anyone in the Annual is aware, is that the persons attacked at his command were all destined to follow Franklin Roosevelt as US President: Harry S Truman (1945-1953)... Dwight D. Eisenhower (1953-61)... John F. Kennedy (1961-63)... Lyndon B. Johnson (1963-69)... Richard M. Nixon (1969-74)... Gerald Ford (1974-77)... Jimmy Carter (1977-81)... Ronald Reagan (1981-89).

The information on what those eight future Presidents were doing on or about June 28, 1941, was researched by Dann Thomas: the then still little-known Senator Truman was undergoing a check-up at Army and Navy Hospital in Hot Springs, Arkansas... Colonel "Ike" and wife Mamie were leaving Ft. Lewis, Washington, for a new post in Texas... JFK (a recent college grad) had returned to his family's home in Maine after a trip to South America... Congressman LBJ was in the process of losing a tight Senate race in Texas... young lawyer Dick Nixon and wife Pat were on a low-budget Caribbean cruise via fruit-boat (he was seasick most of the time)... Ford was setting up law practice in Michigan... Carter had just graduated from high school in Plains, Georgia... and minor movie star Reagan was working at Warner Bros. on Kings Row, which film historians consider his finest role—at least prior to 1981. (Though he still got third billing, after Ann Sheridan and Robert Cummings.)

But—who was the youngster Green Lantern was unable to save in his segment? We'll never know; but he was someone even younger than George Bush (then 16), who'd become President in 1989. [© DC Comics.]

Bush Pilot

(Left:) George Bush would be a decorated Navy pilot before World War II ended in the Pacific. On Earth-Two, he wouldn't have become the 41st President if not for Ian Karkull's causing the death of another, unidentified person.

The A-Team (As In "All-Star")

Even the artists of Annual #3 were an all-star cast (clockwise from top left): Superman by Wayne Boring & Jerry Ordway... The Flash by Carmine Infantino & Frank Giacoia... Batman by Don Newton & Mike Machlan...Green Lantern by (co-creator) Mart Nodell & Joe Giella...Hourman & Starman by George Pérez & Jerry Ordway...Dr. Fate by Keith Giffen. Script by RT. [© DC Comics.]

Nodell Unplugged

Actually, Mart Nodell both penciled and inked his three-page segment in Annual #3, as per the single panel at right... but the powers-that-were (not writer/editor Roy Thomas) had the sequence re-inked. Fortunately, RT saved photocopies of all three pages of the all-Nodell version, which were printed in Alter Ego V3#5. [© DC Comics.]

A Good Cast Deserves A Curtain Call

That line used to be tagged onto the end of some movies, and it's just as true re All-Star Squadron Annual #3. These artists of that epochal issue are the only ones not pictured earlier in this volume (clockwise from top left):

*Early Superman artist **Wayne Boring**, as per a 1954 issue of Coronet magazine [© the respective copyright holders]...*

***Carmine Infantino & Joe Giella**, a 1960s team supreme on The Flash, met circa 2000 for the first time in 25 years (photo courtesy of David Siegel.)...*

*Master inker **Frank Giacoia**, from the 1975 Mighty Marvel Comic Convention program book...*

*As per this photo from the Houston Chronicle for Aug. 12, 1973, **Don Newton** had fun as Captain Marvel at a Texas comicon [photo © the respective copyright holders]...*

***Mart Nodell**, artistic co-creator of Green Lantern, in a photo taken a few years back...*

*Modern super-star artist **George Pérez** as pictured in the 1985 book Focus On George Pérez (Fantagraphics Books, 1985), edited by Tom Heintjes...*

***Keith Giffen**, another contemporary star, in a photo taken by Glen Cadigan; thanks to Glen and to Michael Eury.*

☆☆☆☆☆☆☆☆☆☆☆☆☆☆☆☆☆☆☆☆☆☆☆☆☆☆☆☆

ALL-STAR SQUADRON #36
(Aug. 1984)

COVER: Rich Buckler (p) & Jerry Ordway (i)

STORY: "Thunder over London!" – 24 pp.

ARTISTS: Rich Buckler (p) & Richard Howell (i)

STARRING: SU, FL, WW, HM, BM, GL, SK, PL. (CM as "villain."—MM & CJ at end.)

SYNOPSIS: Superman, Batman, Wonder Woman, Flash, Green Lantern, and Hawkman watch a newsreel of Captain Marvel—who on Earth-Two is only a comic book character—battling RAF fighters and The Shining Knight over London. Superman investigates, while the others head for the White House, ignoring the frantic calls of two teenagers. FDR sends the five and Plastic Man to England. Marvel temporarily fells Superman at Hitler's orders, then flees to Berlin, where magic-vulnerable Superman, Wonder Woman, and Green Lantern dare not follow. The teens turn up in London and transform before their eyes into Mary Marvel and Captain Marvel Jr.

NOTES:

- Hitler calls the mesmerized Captain Marvel the first of his *Vergeltungswaffe—* his "retaliation weapons." This phrase (with initial) was used on our world in 1944-45 for the Germans' V-1 and V-2 rockets that rained down on London.

- One movie-goer refers to Edward R. Murrow, the American who gained fame making radio broadcasts during the Blitz of 1940, when Nazi bombers dropped deadly tonnage on London.

- The Shining Knight's lance has at least

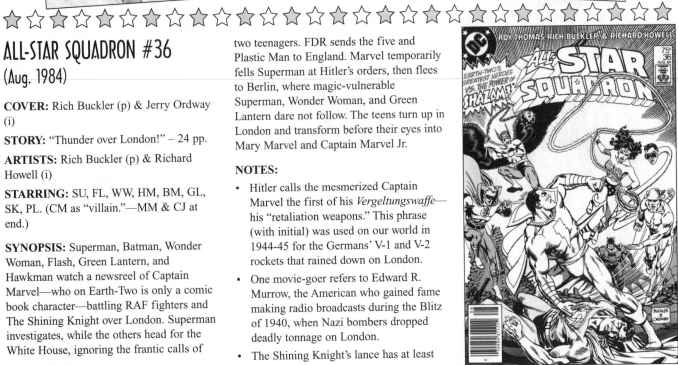

One For All—And All On One!

(Above:) The final Buckler/Ordway teaming—on the cover of #36—spotlighted DC's six most popular characters, plus the most popular super-heroes of Fawcett and Quality (if you don't count the non-super-powered Blackhawk). This is Buckler's penciled version of the cover. Note (on the previous page) the changes made by Ordway as he inked: more action in the Batman figure, the re-positioning of Hawkman's free-swinging mace, and GL's ring blasting away. Thanks to Jerry Ordway for the photocopy. [© DC Comics.]

"Mein Führer, I Can Fly!"

(Left:) Captain Marvel under Hitler's control in #36, due to the Spear of Destiny (see it hanging on the wall?). Adolf refers to President Roosevelt as a "Jewish warmonger" because of the spurious rumor that FDR's Dutch ancestors were Jews; his name was often rendered "Rosenfelt" by Nazis and other bigots. [© DC Comics.]

(Below:) In The Invaders #32 (Sept. 1978), an uneasy Führer has summoned Thor from Asgard—but soon convinces the thunder god (temporarily) that he should fight for Germanic peoples against Captain America & Co. Art by Alan Kupperberg & Frank Springer; script by RT. That issue's cover appears on p. 141. [© Marvel Characters, Inc.]

Three Of A Kind

(Above:) Seen with Hitler in the first of these two panels from #36 is Hermann Göring (center of panel 1), Reichsmarschall of the Luftwaffe (German Air Force); in the next is Propaganda Minister Josef Goebbels. [Art © DC Comics.]

(Right:) A few years earlier, Hitler, Goebbels, and Göring take a keen interest in the exploits of the German team at the 1936 Berlin Olympics. Their smiles suggest that they are not watching Jesse Owens (or Will Everett) win gold medals.

Shazam, Meet Shazoom!

(Below:) Maybe Captain Marvel resented Superman calling him an "impostor" because he knew that, on our Earth, National/DC sued Fawcett Publications for "copyright infringement" over similarities between the Man of Steel and the World's Mightiest Mortal, with the eventual result that Fawcett lost and left the comics field. Still, Roy and Rich had a blast doing this sequence. [© DC Comics.]

(Right:) Even so, they both defer to the best Supes/Cap battle ever staged: "Superduperman" in the four-color comic book Mad #4 (April-May 1953), with script and layouts by Harvey Kurtzman and art by Wally Wood—perhaps one of the best comic book parodies, or even comic book stories, of all time. [© EC Publications, Inc.]

some effect on Captain Marvel, since it was treated, centuries ago, by Merlin the Magician.

- The comic book cover of *Captain Marvel Adventures* #4 (Oct. 1941) and panels of Billy Batson changing into CM are skimmed by the All-Stars at a newsstand.

- Engineer Gootsden, who calls on Hitler, is the man who'll send eight JSAers to distant planets in *All-Star Comics* #13 (as well as in *All-Star Squadron* #50 ff.).

- Hitler uses the term "*Übermensch*"—which can be basically translated as "Superman." The word was coined by philosopher Friedrich Nietzche in the 19th century for a superior type of human being.

- FDR introduces the All-Stars to William Stephenson, the real-life Canadian who'd been a secret liaison for the British government with the President since 1940. Stephenson, whose story is told in the 1970s bestseller *The Man Called "Intrepid,"* was first mentioned in "The Untold Origin of the Justice Society" in *DC Special* (Vol. 7) #29 (Aug.-Sept. 1977).

- RT explains on the LP that the Quality-published heroine Lady Luck, whom one reader wants to see as an All-Star, is the property of Will Eisner.

- RT uses the LP to blast "one unperceptive fan-critic" who'd recently referred to the "retroactive continuity" of *All-Star Squadron* as a "pointless chronology." Roy made no bones about feeling that "the only thing 'pointless' was his review."

☆☆☆☆☆☆☆☆☆☆☆☆☆☆☆☆☆☆☆☆☆☆☆☆☆☆☆☆

ALL-STAR SQUADRON #37
(Sept. 1984)

COVER: Rick Hoberg (p) & Jerry Ordway (i)

STORY: "Lightning in Berlin!" – 23 pp.

ARTISTS: Arvell Jones (p) & Richard Howell (i)

STARRING: SU, BM, PM, HM, WW, FL, GL, CJ, MM, CM.

SYNOPSIS: Mary Marvel and Capt. Marvel Jr. explain that Captain Marvel, snatched from Earth-S, is under the spell of Hitler's Spear of Destiny. Batman, Hawkman, Flash, and Plastic Man—with Mary Batson and Freddy Freeman—enter Germany to destroy the Spear. Finding Billy Batson held prisoner, they're captured by a separated Captain Marvel (materialized by Nazi science and loyal to Hitler). An evil Junior and Mary are materialized, and the three Nazi Marvels fly off to demolish London. After the All-Stars escape, Superman, GL, and Wonder Woman

duke it out with the Marvels until Billy and the others enter Allied territory, freeing their super-selves of the Nazi spell. The Marvels return to Earth-S.

NOTES:

- This issue represents the first *All-Star Squadron* work of Arvell Jones, who would later become the mag's regular penciler.

- This story is set soon after Mary Batson first became Mary Marvel, in *Captain Marvel Adventures* #18 (Dec. 1942), which reflected events that had occurred months earlier. It makes sense, considering a December-dated comic went on sale in the fall, was printed in the summer, and would've been prepared in the spring, if not earlier.

- Superman, like many readers, finds it hard to understand why he's susceptible to magic: "Ma and Pa Kent found me as a baby in a rocket—not on a magic carpet!" That weakness (like the various shades of Kryptonite) had grown out of a need to keep the ever-more-powerful Man of

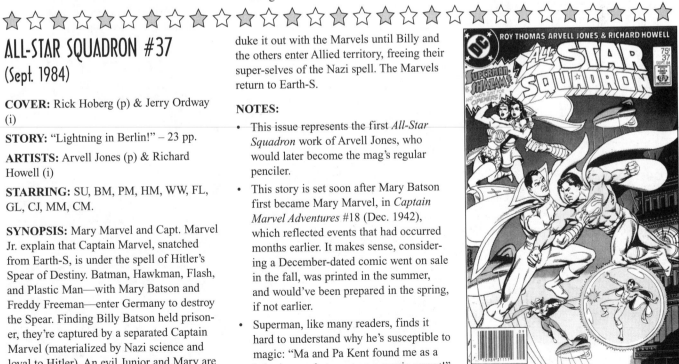

INTRODUCES MARY MARVEL

SHAZAM

SELENA GODDESS OF THE MOON — GRACE
HIPPOLYTA QUEEN OF THE AMAZONS — STRENGTH
ARIADNE SPIRIT OF SKILL — SKILL
ZEPHYRUS SPIRIT OF THE WEST WIND — FLEETNESS
AURORA GODDESS OF THE DAWN — BEAUTY
MINERVA GODDESS OF WISDOM — WISDOM

"We're Mad As Hell And We're Not Going To Take It Any More!"

(Left:) Mary Marvel joined Cap Jr. as a spinoff of the original Big Red Cheese in Captain Marvel Adventures #18 (Dec. 1942), courtesy of an unidentified scripter & Marc Swayze (artist)—as seen in the 1977 hardcover Shazam! From the 1930's to the 1970's.

(Right:) After all the preceding scenes on the past few pages of the All-Stars battling The Marvel Family, it's time we showed one of the DC and Fawcett heroes fighting side by side against the Nazis. Art by Arvell Jones & Richard Howell; script by RT. [© DC Comics.]

Steel from resolving every problem on page 1 of each story.

- A German officer tells an anti-Italian joke… something Nazis were given to, since Mussolini's forces had proved so ineffectual compared to the Nazis.

- Green Lantern calls the attacking Marvels "the Little Rascals"—a bit of an anachronism, since the comedy shorts later shown under that name on TV were originally titled *Our Gang.*

- Roy Thomas refers in the LP to the fact

that he now has the additional post at DC Comics of "Earth-Two Editor," courtesy of managing editor Dick Giordano. Other writers and editors now had to clear Earth-Two-related events through him; it was, incidentally, an unpaid position.

☆☆☆☆☆☆☆☆☆☆☆☆☆☆☆☆☆☆☆☆☆☆☆☆☆☆☆☆☆☆☆

ALL-STAR SQUADRON #38
(Oct. 1984)

COVER: Rick Hoberg (p) & Jerry Ordway (i)

STORY: "Detroit Is Dynamite!" – 20 pp.

ARTISTS: Rick Hoberg (p) & Bill Collins & Mike DeCarlo (i)

STARRING: RM, CS, LB, JQ, TA, FB, HO, HM, GL, AM. (Cameos: SA, DM, JT, AT, DF, SM, SP, CM, MM, CJ.)

SYNOPSIS: Robotman's metal legs are destroyed in a violent training exercise, but Commander Steel repairs them. Learning his ex-girlfriend's soldier husband is MIA, Steel reveals his true identity to her and vows to rescue him. At the Perisphere, several All-Stars watch newsreels of racial violence in Detroit, and of Will "Amazing-Man" Everett escaping from the fiery cross to which he was bound by the Ku Klux Klan-like

Phantom Empire. The All-Stars head for Michigan in their new plane. Real American, the Empire's superhuman champion, prepares to foment more trouble.

NOTES:

- "Detroit Is Dynamite!" is cited as the "title of a 1942 photo essay in *Life* magazine" that dealt with the race riot that formed the milieu of issue #38.

- The tank prototype which damages Robotman had been retrieved by the JSA from Japanese spies in #30 (which, in turn, retold events in *All-Star Comics* #12).

- Liberty Belle and Johnny Quick are embarrassed when Steel and Robotman spy her coming out of JQ's bedroom.

- Robotman mentions the Three Stooges because, in the 1940s, the main feature at a movie theatre was usually preceded by short subjects, newsreels, and animated cartoons.

- Hourman is working on his new "Miraclo Ray"—first used in *Adventure Comics* #71 (Feb. 1942). Apparently ray dependency is better than drug dependency.
- Some of the narration accompanying the newsreels (having been Photostatted into black-on-white) proved difficult to read.
- When a letter-writer asks that no stories feature such minor heroes as The Whip, Mr. America, et al., RT replies that the major All-Stars will bear the brunt of the action, but that minor heroes will be used when they fit the storyline.
  - The same letter-writer suggests avoiding any confrontations with the Japanese, to avoid overheated dialogue. RT responds that he won't sacrifice historical accuracy to avoid offending oversensitive souls.

(RT always had his own vision of what *All-Star Squadron* should be.)

- Starting with #38, *All-Star Squadron* devoted 2 or 3 pages each issue to special art relating to WWII super-heroes—starting with Marshall Rogers' stunning multi-hero cover for the house-produced *Amazing World of DC Comics* #16 (Dec. 1977).

There's No Place Like This Home, That's For Certain!

A panel in #38 (far left) featured a diagram of the Perisphere used as All-Star Squadron HQ. And look what erupts from the Trylon (left)—on a half-page of original art signed by penciler Rick Hoberg. Inking by Bill Collins & Mike DeCarlo, script by RT; repro'd from a photocopy of the original art, courtesy of Michael Dunne. Below is a photo of the real-world aircraft: the XP-55 Ascender. [Art © DC Comics.]

The Long Hot February

As per that "Detroit Is Dynamite!" title, here are a few of the things that lit the fuse:

(Above:) In #38, a b&w newsreel brings the All-Stars up to date on racial unrest in Detroit—as delineated by Thomas, Hoberg, Collins, & DeCarlo. [© DC Comics.]

(Right:) Detroit police lead a bloodied African-American away from the Sojourner Truth Homes in February 1942. [© the respective copyright holders.]

(Far right:) The Sojourner Truth Homes, flashpoint of the race riots, were a "new Negro housing project" named after a former slave, poetess, and abolitionist in the pre-Civil War USA. She had once resided in Battle Creek, Michigan, and is shown here in a symbolic portrait with President Abraham Lincoln. [© the respective copyright holders.]

ALL-STAR SQUADRON #39
(Nov. 1984)

COVER: Rick Hoberg (p) & Jerry Ordway (i)

STORY: "Nobody Gets Out of Paradise Valley Alive!" – 20 pp.

ARTISTS: Rick Hoberg (p) & Bill Collins (i)

STARRING: RM, JQ, HO, LB, FB, AM, GL, HM.

SYNOPSIS: The All-Stars encounter hostility at a Detroit diner. While Johnny Quick and Liberty Belle track down Will Everett, the others crash a Phantom Empire rally, where Real American incites an attack on the Sojourner Truth housing development. Amazing-Man, defending his father, uses his powers against the racist mob. The All-Stars break up the riot, but Real American defeats Amazing-Man, who is arrested.

NOTES:

• In 1942 "Paradise Valley" was the name of Detroit's "Negro ghetto." This slum would figure in further race riots in June 1943, as thousands of people, both black and white, continued to pour into Michigan from the South and elsewhere as its auto industry retooled for war production.

• Though such phrases are rare in the series, one diner patron calls the All-Stars "nigger-lovers." Hourman's response: "You've still got 32 teeth, pal. Would you like to try for none?"

• Real American says "federal bureaucrats" are trying to "force 18 acres of Negroes down our throats"—a reference to the Sojourner Truth housing project.

• One man uses the expression "dictator nations" to refer to Nazi Germany, Fascist Italy, and Imperial Japan, a term used in *All-Star Comics* #4 in 1941.

• The name of Will Everett's ladyfriend Rachel Lindsay was adapted from that of African-American poet Vachel Lindsay (1879-1931).

• When Johnny Quick says he'll bring The Phantom Empire to the President's attention, Rachel snaps that FDR did *nothing* the previous summer, when 50,000+

African-Americans were about to march on Washington, DC, to protest against discrimination. Roosevelt got his wife Eleanor to talk planner A. Philip Randolph into calling it off. FDR, in Rachel's words, then "made one speech against racism—created a toothless commission—and that was it!" (And it's true that the new Fair Employment Practices Commission was hardly likely to agitate for racial equality while war was raging.)

• FDR is equally noncommittal when GL and Hawkman try to enlist his aid. He insists the racial strife is "a local matter,"

Nighthawks At The Diner (Revisited)

(Left:) A quintet of All-Stars at an all-night Detroit diner. The surly proprietor Smiley and the top sign in the window ("We Reserve the Right to Refuse Service to Anyone") have their roots in George Stevens' Giant (1956), one of RT's favorite films. Therein, Bick Benedict (Rock Hudson) overcomes his own prejudices and slugs it out with a counterman named Sarge, defending the right of his son's Mexican wife and child to eat in a Texas diner. (Benedict loses the fight—bloodily but gloriously.)

(Right:) The other notice duplicates one actually circulated in 1942 Detroit. Art by Hoberg & Collins. [© DC Comics.]

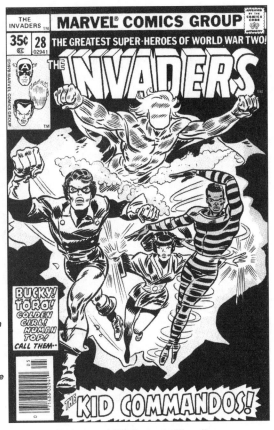

Race Against Time

(Above:) Firebrand makes a Ku Klux Klan-style burning cross really burn, in #38. Art by Hoberg & Collins. This echoes a scene RT'd written in Marvel's Fantastic Four #119 (Feb. 1972) in which The Thing, at the finale of a story set in the fictitious South African nation of Rudyarda, asks The Human Torch to wait a moment—while he demolishes a wall featuring separate, marked doors for "Europeans" and "Coloreds." [© DC Comics.]

(Right:) Most of the racism expressed by characters in RT's earlier Marvel series, The Invaders, was aimed against people of Japanese descent—but Bucky, Toro, and nisei Golden Girl fought alongside the young African-American Human Top. The latter pair, created for The Invaders #28 (May 1978), took the names of Caucasian 1940s Timely/Marvel super-heroes. Art by Frank Robbins & Frank Springer. Thanks to Dave Hennen & Michaël Dewally for the scan. [© Marvel Characters, Inc.]

and, as was his wont, deflects the conversation by asking Hawkman, "By the way, how's that gal of yours—Hawkgirl?"

- GL refers to a recent speech by FDR in which he stated that "Dr. New Deal" has been replaced by "Dr. Win-the-War"—meaning that social legislation such as was passed under his New Deal during the Depression 1930s would now have to take a back seat to whatever was necessary to carry on the war.

- The LP contains a letter from Mart Nodell about the creation of Green Lantern.

- One letter-writer suggests that, had FDR really known in advance about the attack on Pearl Harbor, he'd still have wanted super-heroes there to "greet" the Japanese, and US forces in Hawaii wouldn't have been as devastated as they were in our world.

- Special features in #39 include a 1947 house ad for the Junior Justice Society and *All-Star Comics* #37 (see p. 60 of this volume), RT's JJSA membership certificate, and a full-page '47 ad for *Flash Comics* #86.

☆☆☆☆☆☆☆☆☆☆☆☆☆☆☆☆☆☆☆☆☆☆☆☆☆☆☆☆☆☆☆

ALL-STAR SQUADRON #40
(Dec. 1984)

COVER: Arvell Jones (p) & Al Bradford (i)

STORY: "The Rise and Fall of the Phantom Empire!" – 21 pp.

ARTISTS: Richard Howell (p) & Bill Collins (i)

STARRING: HM, GL, FB, JQ, LB, HO, RM, AM.

SYNOPSIS: When Green Lantern and Hawkman intervene in another riot, Real American makes it seem the JSA is on The Phantom Empire's side. Accused of murder, Amazing-Man is targeted by a lynch mob. RA's hypnotic voice gains him control over all the All-Stars but Robotman, who frees Amazing-Man and makes him immune to RA's power. Real American is eventually exposed as an android and is destroyed;

heroes and citizenry are freed from its racist spell. The Phantom Emperor is unmasked as the diner owner (Smiley) from #39.

NOTES:

- RT recalls being told by DC in 1984-85 that the cover's "RACE RIOTS IN DETROIT" newspaper headline kept copies of #40 from being distributed in that city…but he never heard any details, or any precise verification.

- The "photo" image at top left of the cover is taken from that of the preceding issue.

- Page 2 of #40 quotes the 1979 book *State of War: Michigan in World War Two* by Alan Clive that, on 2-28-42, Detroit's mayor halted the scheduled move by African-Americans into the Sojourner Truth Homes, but "that news did not arrive at the battleground in time to prevent another clash at about 12:15 P.M." The move was put off till April.

- Reportedly, some middle-class African-Americans, who resided in nearby Conant Gardens, opposed the move, being worried about property values.

- A panel on p. 8 reveals that the android "Real American" was sold to the leader of The Phantom Empire by The Monitor, who would soon figure in the omnibus DC series *Crisis on Infinite Earths*.

- Amazing-Man stays in Detroit, to show that "we Negroes should be allowed to fight in this man's war—not just deliver toilet paper." A perhaps anachronistic reference to the fact that during WWII African-American soldiers were used only as support troops, not as frontline soldiers.

- The LP announces Rick Hoberg is departing, and Arvell Jones (fill-in artist on #37) will become regular penciler. Arvell, who got the news a few days before his June 27, 1984, wedding, said it was one of the best wedding presents he could've gotten.

- The issue's pin-up is a JSA drawing by Joe Staton (p) & Bob Layton (i) from *Amazing World of DC Comics #16*.

Voice Of America?

(Above:) These white picketers are acting on Feb. 27, 1942, to prevent blacks from moving into the Sojourner Truth projects. [© Archives of Labor and Urban Affairs, Wayne State University, Detroit, MI.]

The Direct Approach

(Above:) When Johnny Quick discovered that diner proprietor Smiley was the head of The Phantom Empire, he did what had to be done. [© DC Comics.]

Kill The Empire!

(Above:) The name The Phantom Empire originated in a 1935 Mascot movie serial in which singing cowboy Gene Autry, in his first "dramatic" role, battled hooded horsemen who rode forth from sci-fi hideouts in subterranean caverns. [© the respective copyright holders.]

(Right:) Some sources claim the "Black Legion" lauded by Real American to a gathered mob was a real-life murder cult, a Midwestern branch of the Ku Klux Klan (the so-called "Invisible Empire" whose name doubtless inspired that of The Phantom Empire)—but RT's sources were the Autry chapter-play and the melodramatic 1937 Warner Bros. film starring Humphrey Bogart. [© Time-Warner.]

(Far right:) In comics, The Secret Empire tangled with first the Hulk circa Tales to Astonish #81 (July 1966), then with Sub-Mariner. Script by Stan Lee, art by Jack Kirby & Bill Everett. [© Marvel Characters, Inc.]

[© DC Comics]

ALL-STAR SQUADRON #41
(Jan. 1985)

COVER: Arvell Jones (p) & Jerry Ordway (i)

STORY: "Catch a Falling Starman!" – 23 pp.

ARTISTS: Arvell Jones (p) & Bill Collins (i)

(Plot & partial script by Roy Thomas; partial dialoguer Paul Kupperberg)

STARRING: FB, SM, HM, GL, RM, TA, HO, JQ, AM, BM, RO, LB.

SYNOPSIS: An unconscious Starman falls from the sky over Squadron HQ. Tarantula recounts Starman's origins: Discontented playboy Ted Knight used the Gravity Rod, an invention of the missing Prof. Davis, to become the costumed Starman. His cousin Sandra, meanwhile, used Davis' black light ray to become The Phantom Lady. Starman rescued Davis from Dr. Doog and his Brotherhood of the Electron, and earned Davis' blessing to continue as Starman. In the present, Starman wakes— with a dire warning on his lips.

NOTES:

- Because of combined pressures of comics- and screenwriting, Roy Thomas had to turn over the dialoguing of all but four pages of the issue to newer scripter Paul Kupperberg—and also relinquish dialoguing chores on #43-44.

- In the framing sequence, a newspaper headline of March 4, 1943, notes Japanese claims of victory in the Battle of the Coral Sea (Feb. 27 - March 1). This encounter between the Allied and Japanese navies resulted in the sinking of several ships on both sides… but, for the first time, the Allied fleet had halted the enemy's advance in the Pacific.

- *All-Star Squadron* #41 features the first origin of Starman ever published. Since Ted Knight was inspired to become a costumed hero by seeing Batman in action, it was negated in the post-*Crisis on Infinite Earths* universe, where there hadn't been a Batman in 1941.

- Starman's origin is narrated by Tarantula, who'd learned it from Ted only a night or

Baby, Take A Bow

(Left:) Arvell Jones, who assumed the penciling reins with #41, entered comics as an assistant to fellow Detroiter (and original All-Star Squadron artist) Rich Buckler. Since the early 1970s, Arvell has drawn numerous comics for DC (New Gods, etc.), Marvel, et al. Vintage photo courtesy of the artist.

(Right:) Paul Kupperberg, who stepped in to dialogue pp. 4-22 of issue #41 at Roy Thomas' behest, has written comics since 1975. His 700+ story credits in the field include co-creating Arion – Lord of Atlantis, Checkmate, and Takion. He has also written on-line web animation, the syndicated Superman and Tom and Jerry newspaper strips, and young adult non-fiction books. Thanks to Paul K. for the photo.

two earlier, for his projected book on super-heroes.

- Sandra Knight's decision to become Phantom Lady is also related in flashback, as she defends her father, a US Senator, from kidnapers, in a scene adapted from *Freedom Fighters* #15 (July-Aug. 1978).

- When Starman first flies by means of the Gravity Rod, he wonders momentarily whether he should've "whipped up a mask to go with this get-up."

- FBI agent Woodley Allen originated in Starman's *Adventure Comics* tales; RT wouldn't have dared give a character a name so close to that of his favorite comedian!

- The portion of the story dealing with Dr. Doog is based on the first published Starman story, in *Adventure Comics* #61 (April 1941).

- The "special" page in #41 is the JSA drawing done by Joe Kubert for Jim Steranko's 1970 *History of Comics, Vol. 1*, used with both gents' permission.

I'm A Star, Man!

When, in issue #41, Ted Knight sees Batman and Robin in action, he is inspired to become a "mystery-man" himself. Here, he shares the secret of his and Prof. Davis' Gravity Rod discovery with his cousin Sandra, the future Phantom Lady—but his first "test flight" proves a bit unnerving. [© DC Comics.]

☆☆☆☆☆☆☆☆☆☆☆☆☆☆☆☆☆☆☆☆☆☆☆☆☆☆

ALL-STAR SQUADRON #42
(Feb. 1985)

COVER: Arvell Jones (p) & Rick Magyar (i)

STORY: "Oh, Say, Can't You See…?" – 22 pp.

ARTISTS: Arvell Jones (p) & Bill Collins (i)

STARRING: SM, LB, FB, HM, AM, HO, GL, TA, RM, JQ. (TS as villainess.) (Cameo: NP.)

SYNOPSIS: In a flashback to the previous day, Starman encounters two invisible Japanese bombers over Honolulu. They're commanded by spymaster Prince Daka to test his "inviso-inducer," which will enable the Axis power to make its bombers invisible. In thwarting their attack, Starman is injured, but his Gravity Rod carries him to safety. Daka enlists Kung, Tsunami, and Sumo in an attack on All-Star HQ to steal the Rod and other super-hero weapons. A handful of All-Stars, caught off guard and defeated, are ordered executed.

NOTES:

- The character Daka is called both "Dr. Daka" and "Prince Daka" in the 1943 *Batman* serial.

- One of Daka's Japanese henchmen in #42 states: "We have failed thus far to interest many American-born sons of Japan in serving our sacred cause"—a way of underscoring the basic loyalty of most *nisei* and the basic injustice of US "relocation centers."

- Tarantula is less than happy when Hourman asks Firebrand for a date before *he* gets around to it. "Maybe that's why they call him the Man of the *Hour*," quips Robotman.

- Liberty Belle unveils a new device in the Perisphere which enables them to hone in the whereabouts of any All-Stars currently in the New York-New Jersey area.

- The issue contains a sexy new pin-up of post-WWII JSAer Black Canary by Mike Hernandez (a.k.a. Michael Bair) and Terry Austin. (Roy T. planned to introduce a pre-Black Canary Dinah Drake as a mysterious teenage heroine called either Mockingbird or Blackbird, but never got around to it.)

- #42's LP contain small reproductions of the covers of three other JSA-related, RT-

scripted titles then on sale: *Infinity, Inc.*, the 2nd issue of the limited series *America vs. the Justice Society*, and *Jonni Thunder, a.k.a. Thunderbolt*, which introduces the Earth-One equivalent of Johnny Thunder.

Let's Play Daka

(Left:) Dr. (a.k.a. Prince) Daka and Tsunami plot their own sneak attack in #42—juxtaposed with a photo of J. Carrol Naish portraying Daka in the 1943 Batman movie serial from Columbia. For a photo of Naish as Daka with Batman, see Vol. 1 of this series. Of Irish descent, Naish apparently played characters (often villains) of virtually every nationality but Irish! [Art © DC Comics; still © the respective copyright holders.]

This Sumo Is No Wrestler!

Sumo, "a Samurai," meets Baron Blitzkrieg and Zwerg in his first comic book appearance, in the pages of All New Collectors' Edition, Vol. 7, No. C-54 (1978), with script by Gerry Conway and art by José García-López & Dan Adkins. This 72-page tabloid-size tale, billed on the cover as "Superman vs. Wonder Woman," took place in June 1942, three months after the events of All-Star Squadron #42. [© DC Comics.]

ALL-STAR SQUADRON #43
(March 1985)

COVER: Arvell Jones (p) & Tony DeZuniga (i)

STORY: "Ultimate Victory!" – 21 pp.

ARTISTS: Arvell Jones (p) & Bill Collins (i)

(Plot by Roy Thomas; dialogue by Mike Baron)

STARRING: LB, TA, SM, FB, GU, AM, RM. (TS as villainess.) (Cameos: JQ, HM, GL.)

SYNOPSIS: The timely intervention of The Guardian stops Daka's execution of six All-Stars. Daka, Kung, and Sumo escape with hostage Liberty Belle, but the heroes capture Tsunami. The heroes disagree whether to trade the Gravity Rod for Belle. Daka attempts a doublecross during the exchange,

but the All-Stars battle the villains to a draw. His dishonorable behavior leads Tsunami to question her allegiance to the Axis cause.

NOTES:

• The splash page features Admiral Isoruko Yamamoto's 1941 statement to his superiors about what may happen if Japan declares war on the United States. He promises he will "run wild" for the "first six months to a year," with "an uninterrupted succession of victories," but, "if the war is prolonged for two or three years, I have no confidence in our ultimate victory." He proved a good prophet—but he wouldn't live to see the war play itself out. When his itinerary for an inspection tour of the Pacific theatre of war was learned via the top secret American code-breaking operation known as "Magic," his aircraft was ambushed and shot down on April 18, 1943. To conceal that fact that Japan's codes had been broken, word was given out that a civilian coast-spotter had seen Yamamoto board the plane.

• The Guardian is the only one of three heroes called in the area who show up at the Perisphere; Sandman and Manhunter are apparently not minding their receptors.

• Tsunami, captured, expects to be tortured, but Firebrand says, "Americans don't go in for that stuff." Tsunami refers to US "concentration camps" for Japanese-Americans… though that's not the same thing as torture.

The Rising Sun Rampant

On the splash page, Daka and company stand victorious over several fallen All-Stars. It won't last. Art by Jones & Collins, script by RT & Mike Baron. [© DC Comics.]

• On the LP, *Alter Ego* founder and #1 JSA fan Jerry G. Bails lauds *Annual #3*, but jokingly chides RT that "there *is* still another story to tell between this adventure and *All-Star Comics #7 & 8*—one which explains how Hawkman was elected chairman." Roy never quite got around to that one. Maybe the other JSAers just *voted* for him.

• The two "extras" in #43 were a new Sandman pin-up by Canadian artist George Freeman, who'd drawn for both Marvel and *Captain Canuck*—and a different approach to the cover scene of *All-Star Comics #5* done by Howard Bender (who was then illustrating the 3rd and 4th issues of *America vs. the Justice Society*) and inker Dave Hunt.

(Left:) Guest dialoguer Mike Baron and Lucy. Mike has written for newspapers in Boston and for numerous magazines (Creem, et al.); he broke into comics with Nexus, his groundbreaking and award-winning science-fiction title co-created with artist Steve Rude. He admits to being "at least partly responsible" for The Badger and other comic book titles, and currently writes Detonator and Night Club for Image. He lives in Colorado with his wife and dogs. Lucy is one of the latter. Thanks to Mike for the photo.

(Right:) Tony DeZuniga was more closely associated in the 1970s and '80s with RT's sword-and-sorcery titles, first The Savage Sword of Conan at Marvel, then Arak – Son of Thunder at DC… but he has drawn innumerable comics over the year for both companies, including the well-remembered Jonah Hex. His photo is courtesy of Tony himself and Larry Crook.

ALL-STAR SQUADRON #44
(April 1985)

COVER: Arvell Jones (p) & Tony DeZuniga (i)

STORY: "Night and Fog" – 24 pp.

ARTISTS: Arvell Jones (p) & Pablo Marcos (i)

(Plot by Roy Thomas; dialogue by Paul Kupperberg)

STARRING: JQ, LB, HO, FB, PL, TA. (Cameos: GU w/ Newsboy Legion, SM, HG, HM, RM.)

SYNOPSIS: Johnny Quick and Liberty Belle catch a train to Philadelphia. Jim (Guardian) Harper and other All-Stars in mufti go to a Golden Gloves fight. Firebrand, Hourman, Tarantula, and Phantom Lady attend a masquerade party hosted by Brandy's father, steel magnate "Emerald Ed" Reilly. Superhuman assassins Night and Fog crash the party to strongarm Reilly, a former Nazi sympathizer, back into the fold. When he defies them, they murder him and nearly kill the other All-Stars before a vengeful Firebrand drives them off. She allows the police to believe the Nazis assassinated him only because "our war industries run on steel"… and the rain hides her tears.

NOTES:

- Usually, when super-heroes' civilian identities attend a costume party in comic books, they dress as themselves—so RT had two pairs of them switch costumes, even if it made the scripting (and perhaps the reading) a bit confusing at times.

- Ed Reilly, like some Americans of Irish descent, favors the Nazis over the English in the war—even though by early 1942 the US and Great Britain are allies against the Axis. He believes President Roosevelt "maneuvered" Japan into attacking America, to get the nation into the war via the "back door." In RT's opinion, that's at least a more plausible hypothesis than believing that FDR knew an attack was definitely coming at Pearl Harbor.

- Night and Fog (*Nacht* and *Nebel*) are personifications of the Night and Fog Decrees, a secret directive issued by Hitler on Dec. 7, 1941, under which political activists were to be "disappeared"

[© DC Comics]

throughout German-occupied territories. Figuratively speaking, potential enemies of the Third Reich would vanish into "night and fog."

Marcos Is Willing

Artist Pablo Marcos (right) entered the comics field at Skywald Publications in the 1970s, and has since drawn for DC, Marvel, et al. In late 2006 he and RT were reunited on the Dynamite one-shot Red Sonja: Monster Isle (above). Photo courtesy of Pablo. [Art © Red Sonja Properties, Inc.]

X "Marx" The Spot

Four All-Stars attend a costume party—disguised as each other—in #44's busy splash by Arvell Jones and Pablo Marcos. The "Groucho Marx" line is a reversal of the punch line of one of that comedian's best jokes, from the 1930 Marx Brothers movie Animal Crackers: "I once shot an elephant in my pajamas. How an elephant got in my pajamas, I'll never know!" Presumably this full, less savory version of the joke in #44 runs: "I once shot an elephant, cut open his stomach, and there were my pajamas—but how my pajamas got in an elephant, I'll never know!" But whether plotter RT or dialoguer Paul Kupperberg came up with the new punch line, or one of 'em heard it somewhere… or whether that's a guest dressed as Groucho, or Groucho himself… we dunno! [© DC Comics.]

- Phantom Lady finds that "you cannot blind Night with her own darkness!"
- A later LP notes a place or two where dialogue got confused between Tarantula and Hourman, who were wearing each other's costume.
- RT's friend Jim Harmon (author of several books on old-time radio) points out that the "five-day deodorant pads" mentioned by Tarantula in one panel didn't exist until some years after 1942.

Moonlight Sinatra

Frank Sinatra was still with Tommy Dorsey's big band when he sang for his supper at "Emerald Ed" Reilly's party in #44...but a bit later in 1942 he would launch his monumental solo career. Hourman didn't think he'd succeed: "Nobody's made it big on the solo route since [Bing] Crosby." The photo shows The Voice with Dorsey. [Art © DC Comics.]

ALL-STAR SQUADRON #45
(May 1985)

COVER: Arvell Jones (sketch) & Tim Burgard (finished art)

STORY: "Give Me Liberty—Give Me Death!" - 21 pp.

ARTISTS: Arvell Jones (p) & Pablo Marcos (i)

STARRING: LB, JQ, FL, GL, WW. (Cameo [on cover of *Time* magazine]: SM, RM, HM, DF, FB.) (Miss Liberty & Tomahawk seen in historical flashback.)

SYNOPSIS: Liberty Belle has recurrent nightmares of her 18th-century ancestor Miss Liberty being crushed to death beneath the true Liberty Bell. She and Johnny Quick visit Tom Revere at Independence Hall. The still-blinded Baron Blitzkrieg and the super-speedster Zyklon attack, killing Revere and outfighting the All-Star pair. Wonder Woman, Flash, and Green Lantern arrive too late to stop the theft of the Bell. Blaming herself for Tom's death, Libby abandons her costumed identity.

[© DC Comics]

NOTES:

- In 1779 or later, Miss Liberty battles "Hessians"— German mercenary troops fighting for the British crown against the American colonies—a foretaste of the 20th century, when America and England would be allied against Germany in two World Wars. She calls the British Redcoats "Lobsterbacks,"

Cover Story

Two covers were prepared for #45. The one used was drawn by the issue's inker, new pro artist Tim Burgard, based on a sketch by Arvell Jones (and on the story panel printed above)—while another take on that scene (left), penciled by Arvell and inked by Tim, became that month's Golden Age Gallery pin-up. And lucky you get to see all three versions! [© DC Comics.]

a real term of derision during the Revolutionary War.

- In a lame joke, Johnny Quick tells Belle, "I've got some riverfront property in Manila I'd like to sell you cheap"—a reference to the fact that most of the Philippines had already fallen to the invading Japanese since December 1941.

- Biting the bullet, RT decided to "kill off" Tom Revere in this issue—even though, in Liberty Belle's series in *Star Spangled Comics*, he was very much alive throughout the middle 1940s. In retrospect, the writer/editor feels he made a mistake in getting rid of Revere.

- The German word "Zyklon" ("Cyclone") became infamous at war's end, when it was learned the Nazis had exterminated millions of people in gas chambers using a poisonous gas called Zyklon-B.

- Flash, GL, and Wonder Woman arrive together because the latter two happened to be visiting Jay (Flash) Garrick in nearby Keystone City. If the earlier pattern of having the trio duplicate scenes from *Comic Cavalcade* covers had been followed here in order, the three would've been water-skiing!

- When Baron Blitzkrieg steals the Liberty Bell to see if its ring's vibrations can cure his blindness, events foreshadow 1948's

For Whom The (Liberty) Bell Tolls

Baron Blitzkrieg's powerful blow hurls Tom Revere against a wall with deadly force in issue #45. Johnny Quick would've caught him, but the equally fast Zyklon cut him off—and nearly defeated JQ himself in the battle of the super-speedsters. Art by Jones & Marcos. [© DC Comics.]

All-Star Comics #41, wherein the Second *In*justice Society steals the "Freedom Bell"—the same national treasure, under an inexplicable pseudonym.

- Besides the alternate cover for the issue, the "Golden Age Gallery" features a full-page 1942 ad for DC's eight monthly anthology comics with May cover dates.

For Whom The (Liberty) Bell Tolls

(Left:) In Liberty Belle's nightmare, which opens #45, her ancestor Miss Liberty is killed by the falling Liberty Bell itself. Art by Jones & Marcos, script by RT—detail from a photocopy of the original art, courtesy of Michael Dunne.

(Above right:) Miss Liberty (nee Bess Lynn) made her debut in Tomahawk #81 (July-Aug. 1962) and soon became a virtual co-star in that series set in America's Revolutionary War. The cover is probably by interior artist Fred Ray; the writer of "Miss Liberty—Frontier Heroine!" was reportedly France (Ed) Herron. Thanks to Bob Hughes & Bob Bailey for the scan. [Art © DC Comics.]

The Liberty Bell.

ALL-STAR SQUADRON #46
(June 1985)

COVER: Arvell Jones (p) & Pablo Marcos (i)

STORY: "Philadelphia—It Tolls for Thee!" – 22 pp.

ARTISTS: Arvell Jones (p) & Pablo Marcos (i)

STARRING: HM, JQ, HO, FB, TA, WW, FL, GL, AM, RM, HG, LB. (Cameos: CS, AT.)

SYNOPSIS: Johnny Quick and Libby Lawrence question Baron Blitzkrieg's aide Zwerg, captured last issue. JQ is injured putting out a fire. Libby, back in costume and backed by Hawkgirl, tracks down Blitzkrieg, who intends to use lightning, the Bell's mystic vibrations, and his own powers to cure his hysterical blindness *and* to level Philadelphia. The Baron's sight returns and he and Zyklon escape, but the heroines' interference saves the city—and a conflu-ence of circumstances gives Belle the new power to project pulses of sonic energy. At story's end, Belle and Johnny declare their love for each other.

NOTES:

- The fictitious *New York Eagle*, read by Hawkman, takes its name from a once-famous actual newspaper, the *Brooklyn Eagle*.

- When Liberty Belle yells to Zykon, "Don't touch that dial!," she's quoting a popular catch-phrase of the day, which meant not to touch the dial of one's radio—i.e., don't change the station, because you're about to hear something great!

- After this adventure, Belle tells Hawkgirl she'll never again think of her as just "a debutante with wings."

- The issue's LP contains letters on the recent limited series *America vs. the Justice Society*.

- Newcomer Dan Jurgens drew a full-page Dr. Fate pin-up for this issue.

ALL-STAR SQUADRON #47
(July 1985)

COVER: Todd McFarlane (p) & Tony DeZuniga (i)

STORY: "The Secret Origin of Dr. Fate" – 24 pp.

ARTISTS: Todd McFarlane & Mike Clark (p) & Vince Colletta (i)

STARRING: DF, SM, FB, TA, HO, RM, AM. (Cameo: HM half-image.)

SYNOPSIS: Dr. Fate tells Tarantula of his origins: In 1920, archaeologist Sven Nelson, excavating the Mesopotamian city of Ur, dies opening the tomb of Nabu the Wise. For twenty years, the revived Nabu trains Nelson's orphaned son Kent to replace him as mankind's mystic champion. Christening his protégé "Dr. Fate," Nabu reveals his true nature as a Lord of Order and vanishes. Fate is soon battling Nabu's ancient nemesis Wotan for the life of Inza Cramer. As he finishes his narrative, the Squadron receives an urgent message from Churchill requesting Fate or Spectre to come to England immediately.

Todd's In His Heaven

Todd McFarlane, still a fledgling pro when he penciled All-Star Squadron #47, had just begun his year-long gig with RT on Infinity, Inc., which would lead to Marvel, The Incredible Hulk, Spider-Man—and eventually to his own creation Spawn, as per illustration above. In the photo, he's seen (at left) next to Jim Salicrup, editor of his mega-successful Spider-Man run. Art courtesy of Todd M. & Carmen Q. Bryant; photo by Keith Simon & Jim Murtagh. [Spawn art © Todd McFarlane.]

They Stayed Too Long At The Pharaohs

(Left:) Archaeologist Howard Carter, discoverer of the tomb of King Tutankhamen, opens the door of the second gilded shrine, wherein he hoped to find the young pharaoh's coffin—though at this stage (early 1926) he encountered only a third gilded shrine. In the years that followed, people spoke of the "Curse of the Pharaohs," as nearly two dozen persons connected at some time with the unsealing of that tomb died under "mysterious circumstances."

(Above:) In More Fun Comics *#67 (May 1941)'s Dr. Fate origin, writer Gardner Fox and artist Howard Sherman transposed "King Tut's Curse" from Egypt to Mesopotamia, and had Kent Nelson's archaeologist father die instantly upon opening a secret chamber (in 1920). Even so, in the first of these three panels, young Kent suspects Nabu of helping to build the Pyramids—and the alien entity does not contradict him. Special thanks to Scott Nybakken, editor of the upcoming omnibus Golden Age Doctor Fate Archives. [© DC Comics.]*

NOTES:

- As noted in the LP, this story was prepared by RT for the upcoming series *Secret Origins*, which would debut with an April 1986 cover date; however, "due to the early scheduling of a new, monthly *Dr. Fate* series by DC, it was decided to use this story at once rather than later, so as not to confuse things."

- Newcomer Mike Clark, who had been suggested as a penciler of the title by DC's powers-that-be back East, drew the 2-page All-Star Squadron framing sequence in which Dr. Fate narrates his origin to Tarantula.

- In the LP, RT refutes a reader's complaint that a "group of slavering Japanese soldiers crawl[ed] out of the woodwork every few issues." RT felt that "the [Japanese] pilots, etc., shown in #42 were not depicted any differently than their American counter-parts," and that the letter-writer had been affected by looking at too many Golden Age comics with their "fang-toothed Japanese."

- RT will point out in the LP of #52 that there is a slight discrepancy in its account of how and when Inza Cramer first beheld the face of Kent Nelson behind Dr. Fate's mask. Don't ask!

A Helping Hand

(Right:) At the climax of #47, Todd displays the unique breakdowns that first attracted both readers' and pros' attention to him, as Dr. Fate gets to his feet—by grasping hold of a pair of comic book panels! People have been paying attention to McFarlane art ever since! Inks by Vince Colletta. [© DC Comics.]

☆☆☆☆☆☆☆☆☆☆☆☆☆☆☆☆☆☆☆☆☆☆☆☆

ALL-STAR SQUADRON #48
(Aug. 1985)

COVER: Mike Harris (p) & Tony DeZuniga (i)

STORY: "Camelot 1942" – 21 pp.

ARTISTS: Mike Harris (p) & Vince Colletta (i)

STARRING: SK, HO, RM, FB, BH (w/other 6 Blackhawks). (Cameo: HM image.)

SYNOPSIS: In the 1942 ruins of Camelot, The Shining Knight is felled by a dead ringer for King Arthur. 24 hours later, Dr. Fate and three other All-Stars turn the tide in an air battle over London between the

Luftwaffe (German Air Force) and the Blackhawks. Learning the Knight vanished while tracking down rumors of a mysterious force field, Blackhawk and the All-Stars find Camelot restored to its former glory and repopulated by the Arthurian court. "Merlin" defeats the heroes with "magic" before Fate exposes him and the others as Wotan-created robots. The evil scientist/wizard commands a spellbound Shining Knight to kill his fellow All-Stars.

NOTES:

- RT tossed a pair of Marvel references into the issue. In one panel, Firebrand says she "can play *Human Blowtorch* for you"—in another, Robotman, flying by means of a new rocket-pack, cries out:

  "'Okay, Axis—here I come!' Hmmm… must've *read* that somewhere." Yeah—like in a Timely/Marvel comic!

Good Knights, Sweetheart

(Above:) Mike Harris' graceful splash for #48, as inked by Vince Colletta. The Shining Knight of All-Star Squadron, clad in red and gold, followed the early-1940s rendition of the paladin by Creig Flessel, et al.

(Right center:) The Frank Frazetta-drawn Sir Justin of the early '50s wore armor of orange and white, with bare legs—an older Prince Valiant astride Pegasus—but who could resist that art? Nearly all of Frazetta's Shining Knight tales were reprinted by DC in two slick-paper comics for Phil Seuling's Sea Gate Distributors. This story from The Masterworks Series of Great Comic Book Artists #2 (July 1983) had originally appeared in Adventure Comics #161 (Feb. 1951).

(Bottom right:) In 1969, John Buscema drew this exquisite pencil illustration of Marvel's Black Knight for an issue of that era's Alter Ego, since RT had co-created the modern-day version for The Avengers.

Up In The Sky, Junior Birdmen!

The Blackhawks seldom appeared in All-Star Squadron, but when they did, they had the super-heroes outnumbered—and Mike Harris' aerial battle scenes were great! Actually, in the '40s and '50s, Blackhawk had been the Quality Comics Group's best-seller, ahead even of Plastic Man. Mike had said one of his foremost desires would be to draw DC war comics for the rest of his life, so this became his chance to audition. By our lights, he passed with, er, flying colors. Art by Harris & Colletta, script by RT. [© DC Comics.]

• When Hermann Göring's *Luftwaffe* bombs the English capital, Dr. Fate quotes the Brits' motto: "London can take it!"

• Hourman calls the German bombers "egg-men"—probably not an authentic WWII expression. RT picked it up from that odd late-'70s movie *All This and World War II*, which juxtaposed authentic war-era footage with a soundtrack of Beatles songs, including *I Am the Walrus* with its line "They are the egg-men." The "egg-men" shown dropping explosive "eggs" while that Lennon/McCartney classic played, however, were the Japanese at Pearl Harbor.

• Hourman refers to Robotman's new rocket-pack as "his little Buck Rogers gadget," alluding to the science-fiction comic strip whose title hero had entered the language since its debut in 1929.

• Hourman's mention of Canasta may be an anachronism—or it may not. The game came to the US in about 1949, but it was developed in Uruguay circa 1940, so it's possible Rex Tyler was an early devotee. Maybe the JSA learned it during their mission to Latin American countries in *All-Star Comics #9*—though none of the heroes went to Uruguay in that tale.

• #49 features dramatic pin-ups of Dr. Mid-Nite, Wonder Woman, and Green Lantern by newcomers Mike Clark (pencils) and Jerry Acerno (inks).

Camelot Without Kennedys

(Right:) #48's title, "Camelot 1942," was a tip of the hat to writer Mike W. Barr and artist Brian Bolland, whose 1982-84 Camelot 3000 had been the first direct-sales-only blockbuster. That 12-issue "maxi-series" had seen King Arthur and his Knights of the Round Table resurrected to fight marauding aliens 1000 years from now... with some real surprises along the way. Thanks to Mike Barr & Dave Billman for the scan of the cover of #1 (Dec. 1982).

ALL-STAR SQUADRON #49
(Sept. 1985)

COVER: Mike Harris (p) & Tony DeZuniga (i)

STORY: "Death-Sword at Sunrise!" – 23 pp.

ARTISTS: Mike Harris (p) & Vince Colletta (i)

STARRING: DF, FB, RM, SK, DO, HO, BH.

(**Note:** Cameos of HM, et al., left out of final panel—printed in #54.)

SYNOPSIS: Without the Helmet of Nabu, Dr. Fate is no match for Wotan and the ensorcelled Shining Knight. Fate, Robotman, and Firebrand are imprisoned in a machine that drains their powers; another captive is the psychic detective Dr. Occult. Wotan and Hitler want to demoralize the British by having their national hero King Arthur slaughter troops Churchill has dispatched to Camelot. Hourman and Blackhawk battle Wotan's robots. The Knight, waking from his trance, defeats Wotan. The robots are destroyed, but Hourman has a Miraclo-induced heart attack.

NOTES:

- The splash page quotation by Churchill is his response to the desires of many peoples and persons—including FDR—that Great Britain pledge to free its colonies, including India, after the war: "I did not become the King's First Minister to preside over the liquidation of the British Empire."

- Dr. Fate refers to Winged Victory as "a Mobilgas reject"; the symbol of that oil company was a (red) winged stallion (see p. 214).

- Wotan, like the All-Stars, doesn't recall that they all met in the events of *All-Star Squadron* #1-3.

- Wotan says there are certain "Places of Power" on Earth. This is a variant on a theory RT fleshed out in *Arak – Son of Thunder*: that there are Places of Power, Words of Power, and Objects of Power that a skillful sorcerer can tap into. One of the Places is the ancient site of Camelot.

- Hitler, speaking to Wotan via televisor, professes confidence his armies can mop up the "Bolshevik scum" of the USSR, even though they'd failed thus far to capture Moscow. He feels the half million additional men soon to come from "Axis partners" Italy, Hungary, Rumania, and Slovakia will crush "Stalin's ignorant peasants." It didn't work out that way.

- Wotan exclaims: "Thank Nyarlathotep!" That otherworldly entity was created by horror author H.P. Lovecraft in his 1930s stories for *Weird Tales* magazine.

- When a British soldier spots Wotan's green face through binoculars, he says skeptically: "It could just be the light."

- A tear streams down Churchill's face as

he realizes that, if Wotan's forces aren't defeated, his "island nation" may be lost. But then, the emotional Winnie's eyes were known to mist up at the drop of a hat. (Not to denigrate him, however; RT unblushingly admits that Churchill and Roosevelt are two of his heroes.)

- Despite misgivings because of his previous addiction, since his new portable Miraclo machine has been immobilized, Hourman swallows a Miraclo pill so he can help his fellow All-Stars.

- #49 revives the practice (originated in the 1940s *Adventure Comics*) of adding a small box at the bottom of each panel of Hourman in action, showing how many seconds of his "hour of power" remain to him.

- An editorial assistant in NYC left an overlay off the story's final panel—with the result that #49 became the only issue of All-Star Squadron in which no image of Hawkman appears.

Occult Following

Jerry Siegel & Joe Shuster's co-creation Dr. Occult made it into comic books before their Superman. Doc was a "ghost detective" (meaning a detective who chased ghosts, not a detective who was a ghost, like Siegel's later Spectre)—but in an issue or two of More Fun Comics (far left), while in another dimension fighting the demonic Koth, he wore a costume complete with cape and a triangular symbol "burned" onto his chest. He didn't otherwise appear in "costume" in any issue of All-Star Squadron, however. This Harris/Colletta page (near left) from All-Star Squadron #49 was a montage of his adventures—including a throw-away line by RT about "Pickman's inhuman models," a nod to one of the greatest horror stories by H.P. Lovecraft. [© DC Comics.]

☆☆☆☆☆☆☆☆☆☆☆☆☆☆☆☆☆☆☆☆☆☆☆☆☆☆☆

ALL-STAR SQUADRON #50
(Oct. 1985)

COVER: Jerry Ordway

STORY: "Crisis Point!" – 38 pp.

ARTISTS: Mike Clark & Arvell Jones (p) & Vince Colletta & Tony DeZuniga (i)

STARRING: HM, WW, JT, DM, SM, SP, AT, SA, CS, RM, SK, HO, TA, AM, DF, GU, FB, PL, DO, US, PM, RA, BL, DL, SD, MH/Q, HB, MN, JE, Blackhawk planes, GL, JQ, LB. (Cameo: FB/M.)

SYNOPSIS: The JSA (minus Dr. Fate) are captured by Nazi engineer Hans Gootsden, who launches them into space aboard eight rockets supplied by The Monitor… then captures Commander Steel. The entity Harbinger, time-traveling from 1985 to 1942, causes the ships to enter hyper-space instead. As several other All-Stars headline a war bond rally, Harbinger spirits Firebrand away. Blocked from returning to 1985 by interference from Gootsden's power generator, Harbinger forces her way through; the generator and Steel vanish in a flash of light. A number of émigré All-Stars join Uncle Sam on a one-way journey to Earth-X. Johnny Quick and Liberty Belle wed; they and Green Lantern promptly follow Harbinger through the dimensional rift. Steel awakens on Earth-One. On Earth-Two, Dr. Occult warns of an impending menace.

NOTES:

- Portions of *All-Star Squadron* #50-60 adapt the JSA story "Shanghaied into Space" from *All-Star Comics* #13 (1942).

- This story "crosses over" with *Crisis on Infinite Earths* #1. This celebrated 1985-86 limited series came into being because the DC powers-that-be became convinced that the various parallel worlds (Earth-One, Earth-Two, Earth-Shazam, Earth-X,

I've Got You Covered!

Happily, Jerry Ordway returned to All-Star Squadron to both pencil and ink a couple of latter-day covers—including that of #50. Below, repro'd from a photocopy sent by Rick Shurgin, is the original untrammeled art. This was the first issue of seven (#50-56) counted as a "Special Crisis Crossover." The crackling energy effects—what RT and others at Marvel used to call "Kirby bubbles"—were color-held on the printed cover—in gold (which doesn't just mean yellow, in this case). [© DC Comics.]

etc.) had become confusing to the average comics reader, and that all these spheres needed to be united into One Big Earth.

- While Marv Wolfman has called Roy Thomas one of the most "supportive" of DC's writers or editors with regards to the *Crisis*, RT cooperated with this storyline that would destroy Earth-Two, et al., for three reasons: (a) He liked and respected Marv and George Pérez (still does). (b) He figured DC was going to go ahead with the *Crisis* anyway, so he might as well ride the whirlwind in the direction it

was going. (c) It meant royalty money (though he'd have gladly foregone that if he could've preserved Earth-Two from destruction).

- Naturally, no actual German rockets developed during WWII could shanghai humans into space. Here, *Crisis* proved serendipitous, as RT could have the rockets supplied to Gootsden by its superhuman antagonist, The Monitor—so they could be capable of carrying the captive JSAers to *other-dimensional* versions of Mars, Venus, et al., which had livable climates, etc. The storyline of *All-Star Comics* #13 actually made a lot more sense this way!

- The Nazis transport the unconscious JSAers in a truck marked "Mayer Moving"—a nod to Sheldon Mayer, original editor of *All-Star Comics*.

- Rod Reilly, though still on crutches, tells Danette he's thinking of resuming his Firebrand alter ego.

- #50 features re-drawings of the covers of the *Preview* from *JLA* #193 and *All-Star Squadron* #1 by Rich Buckler (penciler) & Jerry Ordway (inker)—both incorporating Starman, who was left off the original covers.

That "Unghostly Breath" Again

(Top left:) The Spectre fights back, supposedly (if improbably, being a ghost) against the lack of oxygen—expanding on the opening chapter of All-Star Comics #13. Art by Mike Clark & Vince Colletta. See p. 24 of this volume for Jerry Bails' thoughts on why he thinks Spec evinces a weakness usually ascribed to the absent Dr. Fate.

(Top right:) At last, 40+ years late, we learn what Doc's up to while his fellow JSAers are being "Shanghaied into Space!": he and other All-Stars are doing their bit at a War Bond rally held in New York's Madison Square Garden. Fate plans to at least show up late at the JSA meeting, but misses the whole abduction. Which is a good thing, since the Nazis have only eight rockets available for their extraterrestrial exiles! Repro'd from a photocopy of the original Jones/Colletta art, courtesy of Mike Burkey. [Spectre & Dr. Fate art © DC Comics.]

(Left:) Popular comedian & singer Eddie Cantor is "makin' whoopee" (the title of his most famous song) to help sell War Bonds. His trademark "banjo eyes" didn't show up over the radio.

Uncle Monitor Wants You

(Above left:) Marv Wolfman wrote, George Pérez penciled (and co-plotted), and Dick Giordano inked issues of the 12-part maxi-series Crisis on Infinite Earths in advance of the "Crossover" issues done by those books' regular teams. On this half-page from Crisis #1 (April 1985), Harbinger recruits Firebrand as the representative of the All-Star Squadron to be taken to The Monitor's inter-world HQ. Danette Reilly was suggested by RT partly because she had no doppleganger on Earth-One.

(Above right:) The same sequence of events as adapted for All-Star Squadron #50. Art by Arvell Jones & Vince Colletta. Oh, and much as RT'd like to claim credit, Firebrand's quote from the MGM movie The Wizard of Oz (then less than three years old!) was lifted from Crisis #1. [© DC Comics.]

Down To Earth-X

(Above:) As the Crisis begins, Uncle Sam (in #50) propels his fellow Quality heroes to Earth-X, where they hope to stem the rampaging Axis tide. They didn't, as would be seen in Justice League of America #107-108. Art by Arvell Jones & Tony DeZuniga. [© DC Comics.]

So Did DC Have An "Earth-M"?

Before All-Star Squadron, but not before DC's Freedom Fighters title, Roy Thomas co-created and wrote two more WWII super-hero groups related to his 1970s Marvel series, The Invaders:

(Below left:) Captain America's boy ally Bucky led The Liberty Legion, composed of seven minor wartime Timely super-heroes, in search of the captive Cap, Human Torch, Toro, and Sub-Mariner. Its adult members are (l. to r.): Jack Frost, The Patriot, Miss America, Blue Diamond, Red Raven, Thin Man, and The Whizzer. From Marvel Premiere #29 (April 1976)—pencils by Don Heck, inks by Vince Colletta. [© Marvel Characters, Inc.]

(Below:) Invaders #14 (March 1977) introduced The Crusaders, six stalwarts of the British Empire who paralleled the Quality-spawned heroes who starred in DC's Freedom Fighters series of 1976-78. (L. to r.:) The diminutive Dyna-Mite (= Doll Man), Thunderfist (= Human Bomb), Captain Wings (= Black Condor), Tommy Lightning (= The Ray), Ghost Girl (=Phantom Lady), & The Spirit of '76 (= Uncle Sam). Pencils by Frank Robbins, inks by Frank Springer. [© Marvel Characters, Inc.]

ALL-STAR SQUADRON #51
(Nov. 1985)

COVER: Arvell Jones (p) & Tony DeZuniga (i)

STORY: "Monster Society of Evil!" – 22 pp.

(Dann Thomas, co-plotter)

ARTISTS: Mike Clark & Arvell Jones (p) & Vince Colletta (i)

Low Society

(Right:) The bad-guys in #51 are on view nowadays in old reprint comics or DC's hardcover series. (L. to r. on cover:) The Nightshade's 1942 run-in with Sandman and Sandy was recycled in Wanted! #9 (Aug.-Sept. 1973)... The Spectre's enemy, Oom the Mighty (from All-Star #3), can be seen in All Star Comics Archives, Vol. 1... Mr. Who (who debuted in More Fun Comics #73, Nov. 1941) will be back in the upcoming Golden Age Doctor Fate Archives... Hawkman's sultry foe Nyola, from All-Star #1, can be seen in Vol. 0 of that mag's Archives series.

(Above:) In #51, though, The Nightshade calls himself Ramulus (derived from another botanical term, relating to having numerous roots). Why? Because DC's heroine Nightshade, carried over from Charlton's Captain Atom, was appearing in Crisis on Infinite Earths. The panel is from World's Finest Comics #9 (Summer 1942) by Joe Simon & Jack Kirby. [© DC Comics.]

STARRING: DF, HO, HG, SN, JQ, LB, GL, CM. (Cameo: SP, FB—and, on cover, AT, SA, FL, HM.)

SYNOPSIS: Dr. Fate and Hourman walk into an ambush at JSA HQ, where the Monster Society of Evil—Mr. Who, Nyola, Oom the Mighty, Ramulus (formerly Nightshade), and their leader, Earth-Shazam's Mr. Mind—hold Hawkgirl prisoner. The timely arrival of Sandy saves the All-Stars' lives, but Oom teleports away with Fate. Green Lantern and newlyweds Johnny Quick and Liberty Belle emerge from Harbinger's dimensional portal on Earth-S—and instantly face a fighting-mad Captain Marvel.

NOTES:

- The four All-Stars utilized in #51 all have JSA connections: Sandy is Sandman's young partner—Dr. Fate missed the fateful meeting at which his colleagues were "Shanghaied into Space"— Hourman was a charter member—and Hawkgirl is engaged to Hawkman.

- Dr. Fate and Hourman do a conscious "Alphonse and Gaston" bit, aping the early-20th-century comic strip in which two self-effacing souls always implored the other to go first.

- When he realizes Charlie McCarthy is merely a ventriloquist's dummy, Mr. Mind seeks out his *second* choice of someone to pal around with on Earth: the Justice Society.

- Mr. Mind names his "Monster Society of Evil" after the JSA. Otto Binder, writer of the 25-chapter serial in *Captain Marvel Adventures*, claimed not to have heard of the Justice Society at the time—but RT

Never You Mind

(Above:) The true identity (and even species) of the mysterious Mr. Mind was unknown to both reader and even his creators for the first few chapters of "The Monster Society of Evil," a serial that ran in Captain Marvel Adventures #22-46 (March 1943-March 1945). In these panels by writer Otto Binder and artist C.C. Beck from the first episode, Mind addresses Marvel and minions alike through a long-distance radio.

(Top right:) By CMA #29 (Nov. '43), his wormic essence had been revealed; cover art by Beck. Since All-Star Squadron was set in 1942, RT preferred not to have his secret known even on Earth-Two—hence the flying "Mindtripper" (depicted on the cover), which travels from world to world via "Worm-Warp Drive." The heroes assume it's only a flying radio set, not realizing the miniature Mr. Mind is actually inside it.

(Right:) The World's Wickedest Worm, however, was seen by 1985 readers—in flashback panels, as where he delights in early-'40s radio shows such as Fibber McGee and Molly, Our Gal Sunday, and Suspense. Art by Clark & Colletta. [All art in this grouping © DC Comics.]

feels it unlikely the similarity is pure coincidence, and suspects at least a subconscious influence.

- An extra feature of #51 is Al Dellinges' painstaking tracing of Jack Burnley's cover for *All-Star Comics #13*, which wasn't so easily viewable in 1985 as it is today—but the Hawkman chapter of the adaptation of "Shanghaied into Space" is delayed till next issue..

- A letter-writer notes that *Squadron* continuity is incompatible with a tale in the 1976 *Flash Spectacular* in which the Earth-Two Flash and Johnny Quick meet for what is said to be the first time. The reader theorizes it may have been Johnny Quick *II* meeting Jay Garrick; RT says he just prefers to ignore that story. Even a "continuity freak" has his limits!

- RT quotes a letter printed in an issue of *Comics Buyer's Guide* which says a "close anticipation" of the JSA can be found in the circa-1597 book *The Seven Champions of Christendom* by Richard Johnson. We'll tell you all about it in *Vol. 3* of this series!

Who's On Earth-Two

(Left:) RT couldn't resist! When Hourman asks Dr. Fate about the evil scientist named Mr. Who, the two quickly get into an exchange based on the classic Abbott and Costello "Who's on First?" routine (for which Mr. Who berates them in the next panel). It's amazing how infinitely adaptable that bit of A&C verbiage is a variety of situations. Good thing neither hero knew about the Who's Who in the DC Universe series then on sale—they'd still be there arguing! Art by Clark & Colletta. [© DC Comics.]

I'm No Dummy

(Far left:) Mr. Mind's startled to learn his favorite radio star, Charlie McCarthy, is just a wooden dummy—a prop for a ventriloquist. Much of the dialogue in these panels is from actual radio scripts. Bergen is talking on the phone to NBC head David Sarnoff. (Incidentally, Edgar Bergen's equally famous daughter Candice will be born in 1946.) [© DC Comics.]

(Center:) Charlie (on left) and Bergen were radio and movie stars in the late 1930s and 1940s. Apparently, on the night of Oct. 30, 1938, Orson Welles' War of the Worlds radio broadcast on CBS panicked many people who'd been listening to the far more popular Bergen/McCarthy program on NBC when a commercial came on—they turned the dial and heard just the right segment of Welles' show to make them believe an "Invasion from Mars" was really going on!

☆☆☆☆☆☆☆☆☆☆☆☆☆☆☆☆☆☆☆☆☆☆☆☆☆☆

ALL-STAR SQUADRON #52
(Dec. 1985)

COVER: Arvell Jones (p) & Dick Giordano (i)

MAIN STORY: "From Fear to Eternity!" – 16 pp.

ARTISTS: Arvell Jones (p) & Alfredo Alcala (i)

STARRING: GL, LB, JQ, CM.

SYNOPSIS: On Earth-S, three dimensionally-displaced All-Stars join Captain Marvel's

Magic Word, Magic Lantern

Green Lantern's Power Ring needs recharging—but apparently nobody on Earth-S ever carved a piece of a certain green meteor into a train lantern. So Captain Marvel takes him directly to the source: the meteor itself, which had fallen in China. The pair never do find out if this part of China is in the hands of Chiang Kai-Shek's Nationalists or Mao Tse-Tung's Communists in March 1942. [© DC Comics.]

battle with strange shadow-beings—aspects of The Anti-Monitor from *Crisis on Infinite Earths*—which prove vulnerable to Green Lantern's ring. After putting them up for the night at Billy Batson's apartment, Marvel takes his guests to see Shazam. The spectral wizard sends the trio to the Rock of Eternity, whence they can return to Earth-Two.

SECOND STORY: "Shanghaied into Hyperspace!" – "Interlude One" – w/HM - 7 pp.

ARTIST: Al Dellinges (utilizing art of Joe Kubert & Alex Raymond)

STARRING: HM

SYNOPSIS: Hawkman's rocket lands on the Saturn of an alternate universe, where he becomes involved in a struggle between a peace-loving nation and its warlike rival. Made superhumanly strong by the planet's gravity, Hawkman outmuscles the dictator Hora, who yields the throne to his democratically-minded daughter.

NOTES:

• Captain Marvel remarks to Green Lantern, Liberty Belle, and Johnny Quick on the oddness of their names, but says Bulletman, Spy Smasher, and Mr. Scarlet and Pinky can "hold their own in that department."

• Also mentioned as existing on Earth-Shazam are Minute-Man and Ibis the Invincible. But at this time DC still didn't have the rights to *depict* any Fawcett heroes except The Marvel Family.

• Billy Batson lives in Fawcett City—a name that actually originated in the 1970s *Shazam!* series. From 1941-53, the city was unnamed.

• Johnny Quick learns Earth-S shares some radio programs with Earth-Two… including *Captain Midnight* (who was also a

licensed Fawcett hero from 1942-48). He considers seeing if Bing Crosby's on…but after all, he and Belle have only been married for an *hour*.

• Libby Lawrence wakes up remembering a "nightmare" about Firebrand running around with "a bunch of cowboys and Indians"—and a "Negro" Green Lantern. She's actually recalling events from *Crisis on Infinite Earths* #3.

• Kurt Mitchell reports that (aside from Firebrand) Amazing-Man, Johnny Quick, Liberty Belle, and Tarantula are the only 1942 All-Stars who figure in *Crisis*. Those four "pop up in some *Crisis* crowd scenes, but they don't play active roles."

• When his bride admonishes Johnny to "hurry up and get dressed," he replies: "One thing you should know about me,

Libby… when one of us is late getting dressed for a party…it's very rarely gonna be me." He's got on his Johnny Quick garb by the time he finishes the sentence.

- The Seven Deadly Sins in Shazam's tunnel remind JQ of "a leftover set from D.W. Griffith's old *Intolerance* epic." That 1916 film utilized gargantuan Babylonian sets built on a Hollywood sound stage and influenced many a comic book story in the 1940s.

- The Rock of Eternity was first seen in *Marvel Family Comics* #1 (1945)—but hey, if it's a Rock of *Eternity*, it was always *there*, right?

- Beginning this issue, because of the combination of *Crisis*-related segments and sub-chapters of "Shanghaied into Hyperspace," the Golden Age Gallery section is discontinued.

This Is For The Birds

(Right:) With #52, after a one-issue hiatus, All-Star Squadron featured back-up chapters relating what happened to each of the eight JSAers "Shanghaied into Hyperspace" in #50. As an admirer of young Joe Kubert's 1940s Hawkman art, RT invited another fan of that artist and era—Al Dellinges (photo)—to illustrate the first JSA-solo exploit, utilizing Hawkman figures from stories drawn by Kubert circa 1946. This splash panel is repro'd from a photocopy of the original art. [© DC Comics.]

(Right:) Al D., like 1942 Hawkman illustrator Sheldon Moldoff, drew Saturnians riding on giant land-birds, in panels based on the work of Flash Gordon artist Alex Raymond. Here's their source: a Raymond panel from the Sunday strip for April 9, 1939. [© King Features Syndicate.]

FLASH HAS SAVED THE LIFE OF QUEEN FRIA OF THE ICE WORLD. SHE HONORS HIM BY ASKING HIM TO DRIVE HER SNOWBIRD-DRAWN CHARIOT ON THE LONG DASH TO THE PALACE OF FRIGIA.

Al Dellinges in the 1980s.

Kane Was Able

(Above:) Though originator Mart Nodell, Irwin Hasen, Alex Toth, Carmine Infantino, Paul Reinman, and others all did well by the 1940s Green Lantern, the original Emerald Gladiator never look looked better than when Gil Kane, artistic co-creator of the Silver Age GL, drew him—as per this commission piece, courtesy of Michael Dunne. [Green Lantern TM & © DC Comics.]

☆☆☆☆☆☆☆☆☆☆☆☆☆☆☆☆☆☆☆☆☆☆☆☆☆☆☆☆☆☆☆

ALL-STAR SQUADRON #53
(Jan. 1986)

COVER: Mike Clark (p) & Steve Montano (i)

STORY: "Worlds in Turmoil" – 23 pp.

ARTISTS: Mike Clark & Arvell Jones (p) & Vince Colletta & Tony DeZuniga (i)

STARRING: SU, SK, RM, DO, AM, HG, HO, SN, TA, CA, GL, JQ, LB. (Cameos: FL, WC, DF, HM, WW, DM, SP, AT, SA, JT (w/ Thunderbolt), SM, FB, BM, MH, SG, MT, TNT, DD, AQ, ZA, AW, plus image of CM.) (plus various Earth-One heroes)

SYNOPSIS: Despite Superman's interference, the Monster Society of Evil free new member The Dummy from prison. Oom, claiming he's killed Dr. Fate, takes over leadership of the MSE; Mr. Mind flees to Earth-S. Returning from Earth-S, Johnny

Quick and Liberty Belle are snatched from Green Lantern's side to join dozens of super-heroes aboard The Monitor's satellite. JQ, the 1980s GL, the Silver Age Star Sapphire, and Deathbolt are dispatched on a special mission.

NOTES:

- This story crosses over into *Crisis on Infinite Earths* #5.

- Nyola wields power over the storm by calling on Tlaloc, the Aztec rain god.

- When Superman rips up his "Tendrils of Terror," Ramulus calls them his "babies," rages against the Man of Steel for "killing" them.

- Ironically, by this continuity, Superman fights Mr. Mind's Monster Society before Captain Marvel does!

- When The Dummy asks Mr. Who his name, he nearly gets into his own Abbott & Costello routine with him, echoing the

exchange between Dr. Fate and Hourman in #51 (see p. 195).

- Gazing at the Perisphere, Superman thinks back to when he helped set up the Infantile Paralysis exhibit at the 1939 New York World's Fair, as related in *New York World's Fair Comics 1939,* currently on view in *The DC Comics Rarities, Vol. 1.*

- Superman fails to recognize Dr. Occult—though (on our world) the two were created by the same Siegel & Shuster team.

- Hawkgirl points out the obvious—that her and Hawkman's wings "weren't exactly meant for sit-down dinners."

- The escaping Mr. Mind spies Green Lantern, Johnny Quick, and Liberty Belle coming back from another dimension… and he passes them going the other way. So *this* is how the World's Wickedest Worm first came to Earth-Shazam!

- Amazing-Man touches "a couple of old rubber bands in that trashcan" and becomes rubberized enough for a

Dummies For Dummies

(Above:) The Monster Society break into prison in #53, to free The Dummy—whose precise human status was always a bit uncertain in Golden Age tales, though he was definitely alive. Art by Clark & Colletta. A sentient ventriloquist's dummy would figure in the 1945 Universal horror film Dead of Night, but DC's Dummy came first, premiering in Leading Comics #1 (Winter 1941-42) as a foe of The Vigilante.

(Right:) From there, he went on to become Vigilante's recurring nemesis. This splash from Action Comics #59 (Feb. 1944) was reprinted in Wanted! #3 (Nov. 1972), with pencils by Mort Meskin and inks by Joe Kubert. [© DC Comics.]

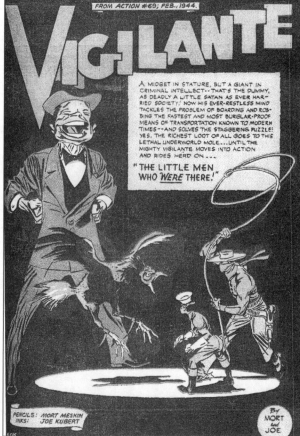

freefalling Johnny Quick to bounce off him.

- Three Earth-Two villains are pointed out by the '80s GL in The Monitor's stronghold: Per Degaton, Star Sapphire, and Deathbolt.

- This issue does not contain a JSA chapter

related to the "Shanghaied into Space" storyline—or, as RT retitled this version, "Shanghaied into Hyperspace."

- RT states on the LP that no Quality Comics heroes will henceforth appear in *All-Star Squadron,* as they've all departed for Earth-X.

Green Grow The Lanterns

The gathering at The Monitor's HQ—from the All-Stars' POV. Two young 1980s Earth-Two heroes can also be seen: Nuklon and Power Girl of Infinity, Inc. The twin Earths' Green Lanterns are shown shaking hands—but that's the Alan Scott of 1985! The 1942 GL was hurled back in the previous panel when he tried to follow Quick and Belle into a hole in the sky—because he can't exist in The Monitor's stronghold at the same time as his '80s self. Is your head hurting yet? Art by Jones & DeZuniga; script by RT. [© DC Comics.]

☆☆☆☆☆☆☆☆☆☆☆☆☆☆☆☆☆☆☆☆☆☆☆☆

ALL-STAR SQUADRON #54
(Feb. 1986)

COVER: Mike Clark (p) & Tony DeZuniga (?) (i)

STORY: "The Crisis Comes to 1942!" – 22 pp.

ARTISTS: Mike Clark & Arvell Jones & Jerry Acerno (p) & Alfredo Alcala & Vince Colletta (i)

STARRING: AM, SU, SK, HG, SY, RM, DO, GU, HO, BM, RO, GL, FL. (Cameos: SP, SM, HM, AT, WW, SA, JT, DM, DF, PM, BL, RA, PL, DL, FB, SS.)

SYNOPSIS: The All-Stars search for their missing teammates. The rechristened Society of Oom attacks the Perisphere, as Amazing-Man and Tarantula are spirited off to The Monitor's satellite. The Monster Society turn against the crazed Oom, who explodes when GL's ring destroys the mystic gem that gives him life. In 1985, Firebrand leads eleven historical heroes and heroines on a mission to Cape Canaveral, which is under assault by time-lost Indians led by Saganawahna (a.k.a. Super-Chief)—who's flying!

NOTES:

- This story crosses over into *Crisis on Infinite Earths* #5.
- Hourman gets frustrated when he can't beat Gernsback the robot at gin rummy.
- Firebrand refers to the time-tossed champions she leads as "History's Heroes" and "Classics Illustrated."
- Miss Liberty tells Brandy she was plucked from Tomahawk's side sometime in 1779—which means the Liberty Bell can't have crushed her (as seen in *All-Star Squadron* # 45) until after that date.
- Firebrand amuses Atom and Nuklon when she says she's got "only one question": "What the heck do they *do* down in this 'Cape Canaveral' place, anyway?"
- This issue's LP contains nearly a page's worth of corrections and additions to the Golden Age entries in the first eight issues of the 1985 *Who's Who: The Definitive Directory of the DC Universe*.

The Way Of All-Flash

This full-pager of The Flash rescuing Joan Williams was submitted by young artist Jerry Acerno as a pin-up. RT had discontinued the Golden Age Gallery because of the combination of Crisis-related sequences and sub-chapters of "Shanghaied into Hyper-Space," so he worked it in as a story page... after a fashion. It's signed by Acerno, but his name didn't make it into the splash page credits. [© DC Comics.]

Three... Two... One... Geronimo!

The Atlas missile launching at Cape Canaveral seen at left center might not have come off as well if the place had been attacked by "Indians," as in the page from #54 above. Why didn't the Russians ever think of that? [Art © DC Comics.]

The group of time-tossed adventurers led by Firebrand in All-Star Squadron #54-55 had all starred or co-starred in DC features at one time or another (clockwise, from top left—all © DC Comics:)

The Black Pirate had first set sail in Sensation Comics #1 (Jan. 1942), written & drawn by Sheldon Moldoff; he only donned a mask some time later, joined by his son **Justin**. This splash by Everett Raymond Kintsler (who didn't sign his last name) is from All-American Comics #89 (Sept. 1947).

The next four features all debuted in (sob!) All-Star Western #58 (April-May 1951)—and thanks to Robert Klein both for some of the creator info below, and for the scan of the house ad for it from Tomahawk #5 (May-June 1951), complete with the cover, which is credited to Gil Kane (pencils) & Frank Giacoia (inks):

The Trigger Twins were Walt and Wayne, a sheriff and a schoolteacher—only the latter was secretly the better gunfighter of the two, so when the lawman sibling got into trouble—well, you get the idea. Pencils by Carmine Infantino, with scripts by Robert Kanigher.

Strong Bow was a Native American brave in the days before Caucasians showed up and started calling them "Indians." Art by Frank Giacoia; script by Dave Wood.

The Roving Ranger (Jeff Graham on his horse Fury) was just another Texas Ranger (a lone one, but minus a mask)—but he had the advantage of Alex Toth pencils, inked by Bernard Sachs. Even so, he didn't last long. (Writers of this and the following feature unknown.)

Don Caballero was one of the "laughing cavalier" type of heroes Gil Kane loved to draw—a sort of Douglas Fairbanks/Zorro without the mask, in stories set in old Spanish California (one almost expected Donald Duck and his nephews to show up sometime). Too bad Gil never got a Golden Age shot at the JSA!

Miss Liberty (Bess Lynn) was a sort-of nurse during the US Revolutionary War, who donned a wig and mask to fight Redcoats alongside Tomahawk in the latter's mag. Apparently her friend Betsy Ross must've sewed her costume! This cover drawn by Bob Brown is for Tomahawk #110 (May-June 1967); thanks to Bob Bailey for the scan.

Super-Chief (apparently the English translation of "Saganowahna") was a "Wonder Warrior" in pre-Columbian America, created by writer Gardner Fox and artist Carmine Infantino for All-Star Western #117 (Feb.-March 1961). But the title died a few issues later.

Arak, Son of Thunder (a Roy & Dann Thomas concept) was an Amerindian who "discovered Europe" in the late 8th century AD when his canoe was intercepted in mid-Atlantic by wayward Vikings—while **Valda the Iron Maiden** was a knight of Charlemagne's court who debuted in his 3rd issue (Nov. 1981). She was considerably confused by happenings at "Castle Canaveral"—especially when she encountered Arak fighting for the other side! Cover by Arak/Valda co-creator Ernie Colón. Scan courtesy of Jonathan Jensen.

And finally, all three stars of The Brave and the Bold #1 (Aug.-Sept. 1955) were shown on the cover, in panels from the stories inside:

The Golden Gladiator, with art by Russ Heath, won his freedom in the Roman arena in the first issue. His prize was a helmet of pure gold—not the best protection in the world from a swordblow aimed at the head. Perhaps that's why Marcus only stuck around for the first few issues? Script by Ed Herron.

The comic's breakout star was **The Viking Prince**, scripted by Robert Kanigher and illustrated by Joe Kubert. Jon had amnesia from the moment he made his entrance—so we're not certain if he ever learned for sure if he really was of royal blood.

The medieval **Silent Knight** was actually a teenager named Brian, in a story written by Robert Kanigher and drawn by Irv Novick. When he donned special armor hidden in the Forest Perilous, he dared not speak lest he give away his identity as an evil lord's ward; but that caveat didn't apply in this crosstime adventure, so he talked up a storm in 1986. Thanks to Bob Hughes for the scan.

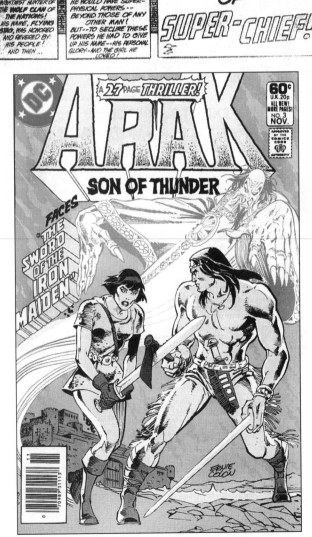

ALL-STAR SQUADRON #55
(March 1986)

COVER: Arvell Jones (p) & Tony DeZuniga (i)

MAIN STORY: "Crisis at Canaveral!" – 16 pp.

WRITERS: Roy & Dann Thomas

ARTISTS: Arvell Jones (p) & Vince Colletta (i)

STARRING: FB. (Cameos: HM, LB, GL, JQ, plus photo of AT.)

SYNOPSIS: The battle between Firebrand's team of "history's heroes" and Saganawahna's Indians turns into an alliance when Kennedy Space Center guards are exposed as fakes working for Ultra-Humanite. Ultra plans to steal the space shuttle and place a death ray in orbit around Earth-Two. Cyclotron, hurled forward through time at the moment of his death, sacrifices his life a second time to rescue Canaveral scientist Terri Rothstein, his now-adult daughter, from Ultra. Ultra "escapes" in the shuttle, unaware that Terri has programmed it to fly into the sun.

SECOND STORY: "Shanghaied into Hyperspace!" – "Interlude Two" - w/SA – 6 pp.

ARTIST: Tim Burgard

SYNOPSIS: Sandman lands on an alternate Uranus inhabited by crystalline humanoids plagued by Kafta the Evil One. Discovering his sand is the antidote for the deadly gas that is Kafta's major weapon, Sandman ends his threat.

NOTES:

- Miss Liberty, as she ropes several braves, speaks of quieting "drums along the Mohawk"—though she could hardly have read the 1936 book by Walter D. Edmonds, let alone seen the 1939 John Ford movie!

- The 1985-86 Ultra-Humanite taunts Cyclotron's daughter Dr. Terry Rothstein with references to Auschwitz, one of the Nazi death camps.

- *Arak, Son of Thunder* had recently been discontinued, with #50 (Nov. 1985), with Arak and his satyr companion Satyricus sailing off East, hoping to reach the North American continent, while Valda and the magician Malagigi watch from Asian shores. In *Squadron #55*, the lovers Arak and Valda know that, when this *Crisis* episode ends, they'll once again be many leagues apart… and indeed, they've never gotten back together since!

- RT mentions on the LP that his wife Dann, who has been co-plotting recent issues did the "preliminary dialoguing" on part of #55, in preparation for the couple's upcoming trip to Great Britain. (Dann had helped plot numerous earlier issues, as well.)

Smashing Atoms, Apes, And Crystal
Cyclotron turns on The Ultra-Humanite—again—at the climax of #55… while Sandman battles crystalline criminals on Uranus. Script by RT; art by Jones & Colletta and Tim Burgard, respectively. Tim soon moved on from comics to storyboarding for TV animation and major movies such as Stargate and Mars Attacks! He also does pretty good doodles of cute girls. [Comic art © DC Comics; good girl art © Tim Burgard.]

ALL-STAR SQUADRON #56
(April 1986)

COVER: Mike Clark (p)(?) & Tony DeZuniga (i)

ARTISTS (MAIN STORY): Mike Clark (p) & Vince Colletta (i)

MAIN STORY: "The Sinister Secret of the Sixth Sense!" – 19 pp.

STARRING: SK, CA, WI, SS, ST, GA, SY, VG

SYNOPSIS: The Seven Soldiers of Victory clash with The Five Senses—crooks given super-sensory powers by The Sense-Master, a paralyzed mastermind who hires them to steal five jewels for him. Despite the Soldiers, the thefts succeed. When the heroes invade his HQ, The "Sense-Master" is exposed as a wax dummy, a front for the real villain—a surgeon named Dr. Brett. He restores the jewels to the idol from which they came, giving him access to the mystic Lifestone which brings inanimate matter to life. During the subsequent battle with the Soldiers, Brett is exposed to its energy and is turned to stone.

SECOND STORY: "Shanghaied Into Hyperspace! - Interlude Three" - w/DM – 5 pp. (Cameos: WW, HM, SA)

ARTISTS: Mike Harris (p) & Tony DeZuniga (i)

SYNOPSIS: On an alternate Neptune, Dr. Mid-Nite saves a race of plant men from slavery and discovers a cure for the dreaded Crimson Plague.

NOTES:

• The Seven Soldiers say they'll stop The Sense-Master's hoodlums, "Red Skies or not!" During the *Crisis on Infinite Earths*, some DC issues were considered crucial to its main storyline. Others, more tangentially related to the *Crisis*, simply displayed the crimson-colored skies that accompanied the multi-world catastrophe—even stretching back into 1942. *All-Star Squadron* #56 was one of the so-called "Red Sky issues."

[© DC Comics]

• In his early exploits in *More Fun Comics* and *Leading Comics* (including #4 and this retelling thereof), Green Arrow had brown hair rather than blond.

• Dr. Mid-Nite's "Shanghaied into Hyperspace" chapter is the shortest of the JSA solo segments. Mike Harris penciled 6 pages, but a page's worth of panels had to be dropped when the Seven Soldiers adaptation ran a page long.

A House Call—On Neptune

(Left:) Dr. Mid-Nite tries out his bedside manner on a plant-man in his solo chapter in #56. He quickly diagnoses the "crimson plague" as—measles. Art by Harris & DeZuniga. [© DC Comics.]

Atlas Shrugs Again

At the story's climax, The Seven Soldiers of Victory battle the statue of Atlas in Rockefeller Center, brought to life by Dr. Brett in Leading Comics #4 (Fall 1942)—with art by Ed Dobrotka (scripter uncertain, though Bill Finger apparently wrote at least part of the issue)—and in All-Star Squadron #56 (center), with art by Clark & Colletta, script by RT. The panels above are repro'd from a vintage copy of Leading, but the whole tale's on view in DC's Seven Soldiers of Victory Archives, Vol. 1. The real McAtlas is seen in the photo at far right.
[Comic art © DC Comics.]

☆ ☆

ALL-STAR SQUADRON #57
(May 1986)

COVER: Mike Clark (p) & Jerry Acerno (i)

FRAMING SEQUENCE: Mike Clark (p) & Vince Colletta (i) – 4 pp.

STARRING: LB, JQ, FB, AM, TA, DF, SU, DO, GL, HG, SY, RM, HO. (Cameos: images of SA, HM.)

SECOND STORY: "Shanghaied into Hyperspace! – Interludes Four, Five & Six" - w/AT, SM, WW – 6 pp. each

ARTISTS: Rick Hoberg (AT); Arvell Jones (p) & Alfredo Alcala (i) (SM); Richard Howell (WW)

SYNOPSIS: Five All-Stars, their memories of the Crisis on Infinite Earths erased, return from the future. Drs. Fate and Occult conjure up images of the three still-missing JSAers in hyperspace. The Atom, on an alternate Mars, dethrones the dictator Butor, who uses control of the water supply to extort tribute. On an alternate Jupiter, Starman rescues armor-wearing subterraneans from the menace of the Big Red Spot, a living organism feeding on the planet. Wonder Woman helps the butterfly-winged women of an alternate Venus turn back invaders from the meteor Comas Sola.

NOTES:

• Three JSA-solo chapters are grouped in this issue to make up for segments being crowded out of a couple of recent issues by *Crisis*-related sequences.

• In *All-Star Comics #13*, Atom says he "won't be able to jump over trees any more"; RT changed that to: "I'm sure gonna miss not having real super-powers anymore." In 1948, the Tiny Titan's atomic strength would kick in (though writer

Gardner Fox had no inkling of that in '42), but he still wouldn't be leaping over tall Redwoods at a single bound.

• Rick Hoberg revealed, via the LP in #62, that much of his Atom chapter was inked by "newcomer Tim Gula."

• RT liked the look of the metal-helmeted, leopard-skin-clad villain Solaris, and would've brought him back if the mag had continued much longer.

• To readers unhappy with what *Crisis on Infinite Earths* had done to *All-Star Squadron* continuity, RT explained in the LP that *Crisis* had originally been intended "simply… to do away with the multiple-earths situation." When it was decided that its scope would be widened and the history of (a single) Earth would be "changed retroactively for all time," an agreement had been made between RT, *Crisis* conceptualizer Marv Wolfman, and DC that events in *All-Star Squadron* would be treated as happening *before* the *Crisis*, and that Superman, Batman, Robin, Wonder Woman, and Aquaman could still appear therein. It had been from Marv, at a comics convention both were attending in London in 1985, that Roy learned DC had changed its mind, and that after *Crisis* ended, none of the WWII incarnations of those heroes were to be used or even mentioned. This undercut not only what could occur in future issues of *Squadron*, but even what could be counted as having happened in *past* ones.

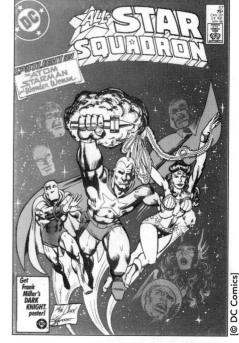

• A new arrangement was soon worked out between RT and DC managing editor Dick Giordano: after a few origin and fill-in stories following the conclusion of its *Crisis*-related story arc to buy time, *Squadron* would be canceled—and a new *All-Star Squadron #1* would be launched.

• RT voices his theory on the LP that the "energy" represented by the five negated super-heroes "can't just evaporate retroactively into nothingness. Something— *someone*—must take its place." In the end, this approach shaped the successor comic and led to its being titled *The Young All-Stars*.

Red Sky At Morning—All-Stars Take Warning!

One scene from each of the three solo-JSAer "Shanghaied into Hyperspace" chapters that comprised most of #57, all scripted by RT & © DC Comics:

The Atom, who can jump great distances in hyper-Mars' lesser gravity, compares himself to Superman rather than Hawkman, probably because All-Star Comics #13 scribe Gardner Fox (whose dialogue was adapted in these segments) still thought of the Man of Steel as "leaping tall buildings in a single bound"—even though by this time he was basically flying in the comic books. This panel foreshadows Al Pratt's gaining "atomic powers" in 1948. Art by Rick Hoberg.

Starman battles the famous Red Spot of (hyper-)Jupiter, which turns out to be a living menace. Art by Jones & Alcala.

Wonder Woman is feted after freeing the hyper-Venusians. RT planned to reveal later that a young butterfly-winged woman had stowed away on Diana's rocket back to Earth. "Krysalis" would've hung around with the All-Stars for a while—maybe even given Hawkgirl a bit of competition for Hawkman. But All-Star Squadron was nearing the end of its run, by the Red-Sky light of the Crisis. Art by Richard Howell, in homage to H.G. Peter.

ALL-STAR SQUADRON #58
(June 1986)

COVER: Arvell Jones (p) & Tony DeZuniga (i)

MAIN STORY: "I Sing the Body Robotic!" – 16 pp.

ARTISTS: Arvell Jones (p) & Vince Colletta (i)

STARRING: HG, SU, FB, DF, GL, FL, JQ, LB, HO, AM, TA, SN. (Cameos: HM, DM, JT, SA, AT, WW, SP, SM.)

SYNOPSIS: A damaged robot in female form falls from the sky. Not far away, the All-Star Squadron repair the damaged Perisphere. The sentient robot attacks them without explanation and is dealt with in kind, sustaining further damage. Robotman, offended by his fellow All-Stars' aggression toward what they dismiss as a mere machine, takes the intruder back to his lab for study.

SECOND STORY: "Shanghaied into Hyperspace! – Interlude Seven" - w/JT (& TB) – 5 pp.

ARTISTS: Mike Clark (p) & Jerry Acerno (i)

SYNOPSIS: His rocket landing on the alternate Mercury, Johnny is captured by one of the indigenous natives—an enormous insect—as a pet. When a giant anteater attacks the bugs' settlement. Johnny commands the Thunderbolt to relocate the insects to a place of safety before he has his electrical servant return him to Earth.

NOTES:

• Over the course of #58-60, cut into three parts, the splash page quotations comprise one of Prime Minister Winston Churchill's most famous utterances, from a speech made on Nov. 10, 1942, after the Allied forces' invasion of Axis-held territory in North Africa: "Now this is not the end. It is not even the *beginning* of the end. But it is, perhaps, the end of the beginning!" Was Winnie a phrase-maker, or what?

• In a flashback, Paul Dennis tells Joan Carter he can't see her again because he can't compete with the memory of her dead fiancé, Bob Crane. Of course, in actuality, Paul *is* Bob—or at least, Bob's brain resides in the metal body of Paul's

A Big Hand For The Little Lady

(Below:) We're printing #58's cover from a photocopy of the original Jones/DeZuniga art, sent to us by collector George Hagenauer. We don't mind that the issue number, price, date, and Comics Code seal are missing—but we wish we knew what happened to the small squarish area where Mechanique's hand has been whited out! [© DC Comics.]

[© DC Comics]

Zoot Story

(Right:) When Hourman, who's had to swear off taking Miraclo (with resultant loss of super-powers), says maybe he should "ditch this zoot suit," he's referring to a flamboyant clothing style popular in the late 1930s/early '40s with poor American youth of African, Mexican, and Filipino descent. It consisted of a long coat with wide lapels, wide (padded) shoulders, wide pantlegs (with "pegged" cuffs), and often a feathered felt hat. The War Production Board banned the manufacture of zoot suits in March 1942 as wasteful of valuable materials, but the fashion persisted at least through the infamous Los Angeles "Zoot Suit Riots" of 1943. At right, popular bandleader Cab Calloway wears a stage version in the latter year. So how is it more outrageous than the average super-hero costume? Like, does anybody really need a cape?

alter ego, Robotman. This sequence was based on a scene from *Star Spangled Comics*.

• Danette (Firebrand) says she'd "like to find out if Johnny Quick's finished re-plumbing the bathroom yet." Actual WWII super-heroes never had such problems, or at least never mentioned them.

• The injured female robot manages to whisper just one word to Robotman: "Rotwang." This is the name of the villain in the 1927 film *Metropolis*, from which she has been adapted into *All-Star Squadron*. She (if not the readers) probably pronounced it the German way: "*Roht*-vang."

Like A Bolt From The Pink

(Above:) Johnny Thunder's personal Thunderbolt explains the situation to "Master Johnny" in #58's chapter of "Shanghaied into Hyperspace." Art by Mike Clark & Jerry Acerno. [© DC Comics.]

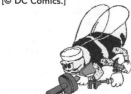

Seabees And Super-Heroes

(Above:) Green Lantern tells Superman and Flash, who're helping repair the Perisphere, they've done "more work than a hive full of Sea-Bees." The Seabees [correct spelling] were the militarized Naval Construction Battalions (CBs = Seabees) formed during World War II to build advance bases in war zones. Their insignia was an animated-style bee with an automatic weapon, pliers, and a hammer.

Popular Mechaniques

(Top center:) The golden robot who'll be called Mechanique makes a rough landing in our dimension in #58—near a leftover World's Fair poster which will remind her that she came from an alternate future in search of the All-Star Squadron. The classic film The Maltese Falcon had debuted in 1941. Art by Jones & Colletta. [© DC Comics.]

(Top right:) Mechanique was unabashedly modeled after the "Robot Maria" in the 1927 German film classic Metropolis, directed by Fritz Lang. In fact, it was soon revealed that Mechanique was that selfsame robot, as RT and the artists incorporated aspects of the movie into the milieu of All-Star Squadron. Thanks to John Day for the scan.

(Above center:) In 1996 RJM Lofficier & Roy Thomas would reverse the situation, and plunge a super-hero—Kal-El, no less—into the world inhabited by that golden robot, rather than the other way around, in Superman's Metropolis, an entry in DC's Elseworlds series. Art by Ted McKeever. [© DC Comics.]

Quick—Somebody Call A RoboCop!

(Left:) A confrontation between Mechanique and Gernsback—with the latter coming out the loser. Art by Jones & Colletta. [© DC Comics.]

★☆☆☆☆☆☆☆☆☆☆☆☆☆☆☆☆☆☆☆☆☆☆☆☆☆

ALL-STAR SQUADRON #59
(July 1986)

COVER: Arvell Jones (p) & Tony DeZuniga (i)

MAIN STORY: "Out of the Ashes… Mekanique!" – 16 pp.

CO-PLOTTER: Dann Thomas

ARTISTS: Arvell Jones (p) & Vince Colletta & Tony DeZuniga (i)

STARRING: AQ, SU, HG, GL, AM, DO, HO, VG, MT, GA, SY, DF, JQ, WH, TA, FB, TNT, DD, MA, ZA, SS, ST, SK, CA, WI, AW, WC, MH, GU, LB, BM, RO, SG, FL, RM. (Cameos: HM, SM, JT, SP, WW, SA, AT, DM, plus image of LBB.)

SYNOPSIS: Aquaman attends his first Squadron meeting. The heroes learn Robotman has repaired the robot he calls "Mechanique." When he refuses to return her to Squadron custody, Green Lantern, Shining Knight, Firebrand, and Air Wave confront him in his lab. When Robotman's overloaded generators explode, he thinks Mechanique has been destroyed and goes berserk. Mechanique steps between him and the All-Stars, vowing to kill anyone who threatens him.

SECOND STORY: "Shanghaied into Hyperspace! – Interlude Eight" - w/SP – 7 pp.

ARTISTS: Ron Harris (p) & Mike Gustovich (i)

SYNOPSIS: The rocket carrying The Spectre crashlands on an alternate Pluto, an icy world where war brews between The Pale Ones, living in huge subterranean cities, and The Furry Ones, barbaric surface-dwellers. After mending a breach in their protective dome, Spectre persuades the two sides' leaders to give peace a chance.

NOTES:

- RT directed that Aquaman's gloves be colored yellow, as a minor differentiation with the green-gloved Earth-One version… but the sea king's hand still wound up the same color as his face on page 1.

- Aquaman remarks: "I'm not exactly going to get a gold star for attendance, am I?" Well, no.

- Aquaman doesn't recognize Hourman, so the latter says he's "Forgotten, but not gone"… a line the humor mag *National Lampoon* used to refer to Mamie (Mrs. Dwight) Eisenhower while she was still living.

The More The Merrier

(Below:) This piece of original art from Roy Thomas' personal collection, given to him by penciler Arvell Jones years ago, depicts more members of the All-Stars than any other cover—plus Mechanique. Inking by Tony DeZuniga. [© DC Comics.]

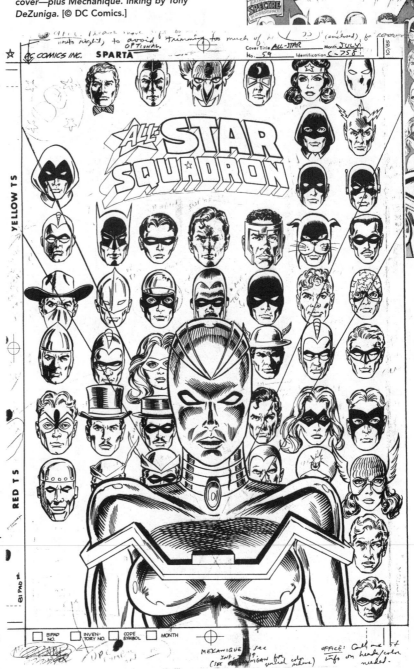

- When Batman says he and Robin were "awfully busy over in Gotham City," Firebrand snaps, "We're *all* busy, Batman." An offhand reference to the fact that Superman and Batman *always* seemed to be too busy to attend regular meetings of the JSA back in early *All-Star Comics*.

- Air Wave hopes his "radio powers" can determine if the robot is a menace.

- Faced with the All-Stars' vote against Mechanique, Robotman reminds GL "just how valid majority rule is when it comes to matters of science… or have you forgotten Galileo—Darwin?"

- The Spectre is the one JSAer who can

"Surprise!"

Issue #59 featured the Earth-Two Aquaman's first appearance "on-stage" in the series. This double-page splash depicts the largest gathering of All-Stars since #31, even with eight JSAers still off in hyperspace. Repro'd from a photocopy of the original art, courtesy of Michael Dunne. Art by Jones & Colletta. [© DC Comics.]

easily return to Earth under his own power (Johnny Thunder, of course, needed Thunderbolt).

• The LP includes a quote from the Nov. 11, 1985, issue of *Newsweek* by Mark A. Perigard: "Ironically… one comic book currently published that comes closest to capturing the noble, truer-than-blue heroes is DC's *All-Star Squadron*, a series set, appropriately enough, during World War II, perhaps the very last time in history that the United States had a clear sense of mortal righteousness."

One All-Star, One Vote

(Right:) Artist Arvell Jones sure didn't slough off in #59! Even so, Zatara had to settle for a word balloon from off-panel. Though it doesn't show here, a margin note changed Mr. America's vote from "Aye" and The Shining Knight's from "Nay." RT gave the matter of each hero's vote careful thought… but no way could he tell you today his rationale for most of them! Inks by Colletta. Repro'd from a photocopy of the original art, courtesy of Rick Shurgin. [© DC Comics.]

"A Robot May Not Harm a Human Being, Or, Through Inaction, Allow A Human Being To Come To Harm"

(Below:) Mechanique clearly has her own freewheeling interpretation of the First Law of Robotics (see above), which originated in I, Robot, Isaac Asimov's novel made up of related 1940s-50s short stories. Comic art by Jones & DeZuniga; I, Robot cover from a 1960s paperback. [Panel © DC Comics.]

[I, Robot © Asimov Estate.]

Last Chance To See...

(Above:) Little Boy Blue and his Blue Boys finally made it into an issue—at least visually. RT kept looking for the right spot to bring them in… but never found it. But then, he only had 100 issues or so, counting The Young All-Stars. [© DC Comics.]

A Spectre Is Haunting Pluto

(Below & left:) Ron Harris (no relation to Mike H.) penciled the Spectre segment, including the Metropolis-style Plutonian city in the background (inks by Mike Gustovich). He'd soon draw a number of issues of The Young All-Stars. Photo of Ron and wife Jan by their son Joey Harris. [© DC Comics.]

☆☆☆☆☆☆☆☆☆☆☆☆☆☆☆☆☆☆☆

ALL-STAR SQUADRON #60
(Aug. 1986)

COVER: Jerry Ordway

STORY: "The End of the Beginning!" – 22 pp.

ARTISTS: Mike Clark & Arvell Jones (p) & Vince Colletta & Tony DeZuniga (i)

STARRING: SP, JT (w/TB), HM, WW, SA, AT, SM, DM, RM, AW, FB, SK, GL, TA, BM, AQ, SS, ST, CA, WI, HO, VG, WH, ZA, AM, MH, WC, GU, SY, TNT, DD, MT, SG, MA, DO, LB, RO, FL, HG, SN, SU, GA, US, RA, PM, BL, PL, JE.

And There's a "Metropolis" In Illinois, Besides!

(Right:) On this page from #60 (narrated by Robotman), the All-Stars learn of Mechanique's origins. Wonder if Fritz Lang's 1927 film Metropolis existed on Earth-Two? Probably not—or else surely somebody would've recognized it as the source of her backstory—maybe even wondered about its connection to the name of the city where Superman hung out! Art by Jones & DeZuniga, script by RT. [© DC Comics.]

SYNOPSIS: Spectre and the Thunderbolt bring the scattered JSAers back to Earth, where they round up Gootsden and his spies. At Robotman's lab, Mechanique reveals she is from the far future, and claims she's come to halt a death that will result in Armageddon in her era. Green Lantern and Firebrand prevent that man's death. At All-Star HQ, Robotman learns Mechanique was actually sent to hold off the after-effects of the Crisis on Infinite Earths long enough to ensure the victory of the totalitarians who created her. She releases her hold and the Earth-Two universe is no more, reconfiguring into a universe where The Freedom Fighters never went to Earth-X and the careers of Superman, Batman and Robin, Wonder Woman, and Aquaman begin decades after the end of World War II.

NOTES:

- Pp. 1-7 of this issue adapt the final chapter of the Gardner Fox-scripted *All-Star Comics* #13, in which eight JSAers return to Earth from space.

- To validate her claim that she comes from the future, Mechanique reports that within minutes radio stations will announce that Iran has broken off diplomatic relations with Japan—a claim verified moments later. (That makes the date April 14, 1942.)

- Mechanique reveals that the event that will set in motion a *chain* of events destined to lead to a future Metropolis ruled by Rotwang will occur within minutes: A little girl will pursue her runaway cat into the street—a car swerving to avoid hitting her will strike a telephone pole—"and history is altered, forevermore, in a single instant of searing flame!" GL and Firebrand prevent that accident—in a scene adapted from the story "The War That Never Happened!" in *Wonder Woman* #60 (July-Aug. 1953), as detailed in *Alter Ego* #23 (2003). In the '53 tale, it was a rubber ball the little girl was chasing instead of a cat. (That cat, incidentally, was named Ignatz, after Roy & Dann Thomas' pet feline—who of course was named after the brick-throwing mouse in the classic comic strip *Krazy Kat*.)

- The reason that averting that car crash is so important turns out to be saving the life of a passenger, "Admiral Higby—one of the Navy's top strategists." This fictitious character was named in honor of a *real* Admiral Higby (ret.) whom Roy & Dann Thomas knew in LA in the 1980s. During WWII he'd been in charge of the

San Pedro port area. That colorful gent finally suffered a fatal heart attack—well into his 90s—while swimming laps at the local YMCA.

- Roy Thomas revealed in a later LP that, as a mid-1950s teenager, he'd written the averted car crash and other elements of the *WW* #60 tale into a JSA story he did for his own personal "*All-Star Comics* #58." Thus, the very *first* comics story he'd ever typed (as opposed to simply drawn) became the basis of the final Earth-Two issue of *All-Star Squadron*.

- The Red Skies of *Crisis* hung around for an issue or three longer in *All-Star*

Squadron than in other DC mags; only #60's last few pages take place on the post-*Crisis* Earth.

- Batman's line "Yes, Starman—there really *is* an Aquaman!" is, of course, a paraphrase of the famous quotation, "Yes, Virginia, there really *is* a Santa Claus!"

- Liberty Belle talks Hawkman into serving as co-chairman of the All-Stars "for the duration"—a popular expression of the day, meaning as long as the war lasted.

- By story's end, Mechanique and Robotman are an item—though whether she still represents a potential menace to Earth's future is unclear.

But Who's In Those Rockets?

Roy Thomas was delighted that Jerry Ordway agreed to pencil and ink the cover of issue #60, in which eight JSAers return to Earth from hyperspace. Repro'd from a photocopy of the original art, courtesy of JO. [© DC Comics.]

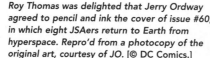

- A note on the LP reveals that, as reported in a recent issue of *Comics Buyer's Guide*, even British Prime Minister Churchill read comics on at least one occasion, in 1955, when he and his Cabinet colleagues were considering claims that comics had a "bad influence" on children. Left in a file of his personal papers from that period were copies of *Captain Marvel*, *Frankenstein*, and *Black Magic*—the first two of which had been *discontinued* by the time Churchill was perusing them!

Say "Big Red Cheese!"

The photo at top was snapped by the superfast Johnny Quick, who could click the camera and still make it back in time to be in the picture. To underscore what changes had been wrought in the DC Universe even retroactively to 1942, the version at bottom, when seen by FDR, has five of DC's major stars replaced by a quintet of Freedom Fighters—who, in the new continuity, never left Earth because there was no Earth-X to go to. FDR's dialogue assumes that "any costumed hero who isn't in this photo must be someone so obscure that nobody ever heard of them!" (Yeah... guys like Superman, Batman and Robin, Wonder Woman, and Aquaman!) The idea of "photos" as a way of visually underscoring the effects of Crisis was suggested by Dann Thomas.

Ironically, by the time #60 went on sale, even the second photo was "no longer operative," as DC had decided that Green Arrow and Speedy, as well, were now to be considered as having no World War II namesakes. Nice art job by Jones & DeZuniga, though! Script, of course, by RT. Another irony: not counting the guys in the photo, the last character to appear on-panel in the final issue of All-Star Squadron is President Franklin D. Roosevelt, who also popped up in the Preview in Justice League of America #193. [© DC Comics.]

SEE OUR LETTERS PAGE FOR A SPECIAL ANNOUNCEMENT ABOUT THE FUTURE OF ALL-STAR SQUADRON!

ALL-STAR SQUADRON #61
(Sept. 1986)

COVER: Mike Harris (p) & Tony DeZuniga (i)

STORY: "The Origin of Liberty Belle" – 22 pp.

ARTISTS: Mike Harris (p) & Tony DeZuniga (i)

STARRING: LB, JQ, TA. (Cameos: FB, HM, GL, FL.)

SYNOPSIS: Liberty Belle reveals her origin to Tarantula: Libby Lawrence is the daughter of Major James Lawrence, attached to the US embassy in Warsaw. After first fleeing a Blitzkrieged Poland in 1939, the swimming medalist Libby Lawrence escapes from the Nazi war machine by swimming the English Channel during the 1940 evacuation of Dunkirk, France. This feat earns Libby her own newspaper column and radio news show. Discovering a strange connection to the Liberty Bell, she adopts a costumed identity to tackle a Nazi spy ring. Concluding her narrative, she and Johnny Quick leave on their belated honeymoon.

NOTES:

- Libby's lovely hide is saved, first in Warsaw (Poland), then in France, by Capt. Rick Cannon, who seems to be a Nazi officer but is actually an agent of G-2, US Army Intelligence.

- In Poland, Rick gives Libby a "letter of transit" which, since America is still neutral in 1939, will enable her to safely reach Amsterdam. The specious genus called "letters of transit" was lifted from the 1942 film classic *Casablanca*, of course—and they make no more sense in this story than they did in the movie. They're really just a species of McGuffin, the term Alfred Hitchcock coined for an object that is of great importance to the characters in a story but of little interest to the audience. The other most famous McGuffin is probably *The Maltese Falcon*.

- The LP contains RT's listing of a half dozen additional All-Star Squadron-related errors in issues of *Who's Who: The Definitive Directory of the DC Universe*.

The Blonde And The Blitzkrieg

Libby Lawrence/Liberty Belle was modeled after Veronica Lake (top center), who by 1942 was famous for her sultry acting and peekaboo blonde hairstyle in such films as I Wanted Wings, This Gun for Hire, The Glass Key (based on the novel by Dashiell Hammett), and I Married a Witch (precursor to the 1960s TV series Bewitched).

All-Star Squadron #61 set the tone for most of the seven remaining issues of the series: a hero relating an origin story to Tarantula (writer Jonathan Law) for his projected postwar book on super-heroes. Law had promised not to divulge any secret identities without permission. The splash page at far right illustrates major elements of Belle's origin—Hitler's Blitzkrieg against Europe, abetted by Stuka dive-bombers and Panzer tanks. The story was adapted from Boy Commandos #1 (Winter 1942-43), as written by Don Cameron and drawn by Chuck Winter. 1986 script by RT; art by Mike Harris & Tony DeZuniga. [© DC Comics.]

Give Me Libby... Liberty... Whoever

(Above:) Libby Lawrence tries to talk her way out of a tight spot as the Nazis blitz Poland in 1939. (Above center:) Belle winds up her first night's work in costume. Art by Harris & DeZuniga; script by RT. (Right:) RT counted only her adventures in Boy Commandos #1-2 as occurring before the events in All-Star Squadron #1. This is the Chuck Winter-drawn splash from BC #2. [© DC Comics.]

★ ★

ALL-STAR SQUADRON #62
(Oct. 1986)

COVER: Tony DeZuniga

STORY: "The Origin of The Shining Knight" – 22 pp.

ARTIST: Tony DeZuniga

STARRING: SK. (Cameos: images of HM, SS, GA, FB.)

SYNOPSIS: When Camelot is threatened by the ogre Blunderbore, Sir Justin volunteers to rid the kingdom of this menace. Merlin enchants his sword and armor and gives his horse wings. The Shining Knight slays the monster but winds up frozen alive in a glacier. He is found and revived in 1941 by museum curator Dr. Moresby. The modern world meets the Knight and Winged Victory when they prevent thieves from looting the museum.

NOTES:

• RT blushes today to admit that, on #62's splash, he joined the legion of people who misspelled as "Craig" the first name of artist Creig Flessel, early DC and Sandman artist and the original illustrator/co-creator of The Shining Knight.

• In *Adventure Comics*, Justin's secret identity never had a last name, so RT called him Justin Arthur—a monicker he himself used on rare occasions as a pseudonym, standing for "just an author."

• The LP was brimful of reader suggestions as to how to carry on *All-Star Squadron* in a world now retroactively bereft of its most famed heroes: let Captain Marvel take Superman's place, let the Quality Miss America replace Wonder Woman, etc. Whether because of such letters, or because he already had it in mind, Miss A. did indeed fill that role in *Young All-Stars*.

• Some readers suggested RT ask DC to let him "create replacements for these characters [Superman, et al.]." In truth, he was already working that angle.

The Once And Future Super-Hero

The same events, as seen in Adventure Comics #66 (Sept. 1941) (left), and in All-Star Squadron #62 (right). The original writer (Henry Lynne Perkins, according to the Grand Comic Book Database) probably took inspiration from Mark Twain's classic work A Connecticut Yankee in King Arthur's Court—and/or from segments published between 1938-40 of T.H. White's The Once and Future King, a retelling of Arthurian legend that utilized anachronisms and in which Merlyn the Magician "lived backwards." In any event, DC's Merlin tells Sir Justin his armor is "bulletproof," though the knight has no idea what a "bullet" is. 1941 art by Creig Flessel; 1986 art by Tony DeZuniga, with script by RT. Thanks to Bob Hughes for the Adventure scan. [© DC Comics.]

You will battle the foes of the realm as THE BLACK KNIGHT!

SO BE IT!

BECAUSE I ONCE TOLD YOU THAT IF I HAD A SUPER POWER TO MATCH YOURS, THINGS WOULD HAVE TURNED OUT DIFFERENTLY-- REMEMBER??

OF COURSE! NOW I KNOW-- YOU'RE PROFESSOR GARRETT, THE TRAITOR! BUT-- HOW--??

A Mage Less Than Sage

(Above:) Merlin had his own problems, though. In this 1917 illustration by Arthur Rackam, the nymph Ninue tricks him into going under a stone—this trapping him and robbing King Arthur of his most trusted advisor. In other versions, didn't she turn into Merlin into a tree, the condition from which Sir Justin rescued him in the 1941 comic?

It Was A Black And Stormy Knight

(Above:) Timely/Marvel gained its own Arthurian warrior in Black Knight #1 (May 1955), which ran for five issues, originally written by Stan Lee and drawn by Joe Maneely. This secret-identity hero combined aspects of Prince Valiant and Countess Orczy's 1905 novel Scarlet Pimpernel (and 1930s film adaptations starring Leslie Howard)—and was given his enchanted armor and sword by none other than Merlin. [© Marvel Characters, Inc.]

(Right:) In the Giant-Man story in Tales to Astonish #52 (Feb. 1964), writer/editor Stan Lee and artist Dick Ayers introduced a criminal modern-day Black Knight—and this one had a flying stallion, à la Sir Justin's Winged Victory. (Marvel's third Black Knight, descendant of the first and nephew of the second, debuted in The Avengers #49, Jan. 1968, and can be seen on pp. 96 & 189.) [© Marvel Characters, Inc.]

Victory By Air Power

(Right:) The ultimate inspiration for Winged Victory was less anything Arthurian than the Pegasus of myth, ridden by the warrior Bellerophon when he killed the Chimaera. This illustration by the wonderfully-named Steele Savage appears in Edith Hamilton's popular 1940 book Mythology. [© Doris Fielding Reid or successors in interest.]

(Above:) The "flying red horse" that was the symbol of the Mobilgas Oil Company was easily the most famous winged stallion of the 20th century. The Shining Knight would've approved of this 1943 magazine ad. [© the respective copyright holders.]

★ ★

ALL-STAR SQUADRON #63
(Nov. 1986)

COVER: Mike Bair

STORY: "The Origin of the Golden Age Robotman" – 23 pp.

ARTISTS: Mike Bair (p) & Mike Machlan (i)

STARRING: RM. (Cameos: images of AT, LB, HM, CS, JQ, FB, SK, GL.)

SYNOPSIS: Gangsters shoot Dr. Robert Crane for refusing to hand over his latest experiment, a mechanical human body made of metal. Lab assistant Chuck Grayson transplants the dying Crane's brain into the robot. Crane awakens hours later to find Grayson accused of his murder. Creating a human disguise ("Paul Dennis"), Crane tracks down the real killers and, as Robotman, brings them to justice.

NOTES:

- Because Otto/Eando Binder's 1939 story "I, Robot" had been narrated in first person—by robot Adam Link—RT used the same approach in retelling the origin of Robotman.

- Penciler Mike Bair has also drawn comics under the name Mike Hernandez.

- Bair went to great lengths to find authentic circa-1941 fashions for Joan Carter, and the right vintage car for her to drive.

- The night Dr. Crane is shot, he and Joan plan to attend a performance of the hit Broadway play *Arsenic and Old Lace*, which was soon made into a film starring Cary Grant.

- Robotman is glad to know, via his power to monitor radio broadcasts, that Dr. Crane's murder is being driven off the front pages by news of a U-boat torpedoing a Navy destroyer on convoy duty near Iceland, even though the US and Germany are not officially at war. Since the *Reuben James* was sunk on Oct. 30, 1941, that "dates" the *All-Star Squadron* story—officially set on Oct. 31. Halloween seemed like a good day for Robotman to begin his masquerade as a human being.

- RT revealed he didn't intend to discount a previously published *DC Comics Presents* backstory, "Whatever Happened to Robotman?" in which Crane's brain eventually came to rest in the body of Chuck Grayson—some years in the future.

- RT announced his intention to (at some future date) transform Sparko, the robot dog from the 1939-40 New York World's Fair, into Robbie, the robot mutt who

later became less Robotman's pet than his sidekick.

- RT blushingly admitted in the LP that he'd totally forgotten that, in *All-Star Squadron* #17, Robotman had revealed his secret identity as Paul Dennis to Joan Carter; he vowed to hew to that version of events in the future.

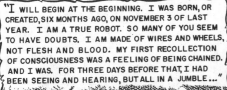
"I WILL BEGIN AT THE BEGINNING. I WAS BORN, OR CREATED, SIX MONTHS AGO, ON NOVEMBER 3 OF LAST YEAR. I AM A TRUE ROBOT. SO MANY OF YOU SEEM TO HAVE DOUBTS. I AM MADE OF WIRES AND WHEELS, NOT FLESH AND BLOOD. MY FIRST RECOLLECTION OF CONSCIOUSNESS WAS A FEELING OF BEING CHAINED. AND I WAS. FOR THREE DAYS BEFORE THAT, I HAD BEEN SEEING AND HEARING, BUT ALL IN A JUMBLE..."

Man And Superman—Robot And Robotman

(Left:) As related on p. 139 of this volume, Eando Binder's "I, Robot" short story from the 1939 *Amazing Stories* was in some ways was a precursor of Robotman—and was adapted by Binder and artist Joe Orlando in EC's *Weird Science-Fantasy #27* (Jan.-Feb. 1955). In it, Dr. Link gives his robot an artificial iridium brain. Repro'd from the Russ Cochran b&w hardcover volume *The Complete Weird Science-Fantasy*. [© William M. Gaines, Agent.]

(Below:) In *Star Spangled Comics #7* (April 1942), assistant Chuck Grayson transplants his dying scientist employer's brain into a robot body. Script by Jerry Siegel; art by Ed Dobrotka & (perhaps) others of the Joe Shuster studio that mainly turned out Superman art. With thanks to Tom Morehouse. [© DC Comics.]

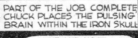

PART OF THE JOB COMPLETE, CHUCK PLACES THE PULSING BRAIN WITHIN THE IRON SKULL.
NEXT AND MOST IMPORTANT! THE ELECTRIC SHOCK TREATMENT!

AS CHUCK OPERATES THE CONTROLS, A GREAT ELECTRICAL DISPLAY BURSTS INTO BEING! SHAFTS OF FIRE CRASH MADLY ABOUT THE METAL FIGURE!

SHUTTING OFF THE POWER, GRAYSON EXAMINES THE FIGURE WITH TREMBLING HANDS----
IT'S *TRUE*! LIFE FLOWING THRU ITS VEINS! I'VE SAVED BOB! HE'S ALIVE! ALIVE!

Even A Robotman Can Cry

Robotman's torment—a living brain within a metal body—gave RT a chance to play with some of the same elements inherent in the Silver Age Vision he'd co-created for Marvel's Avengers #57. Above is a sequence from All-Star Squadron #63 by Mike Bair (pencils) & Mike Machlan (inks)—at right, the final page of The Avengers #58 (Nov. 1968), penciled by John Buscema and inked by George Klein. [Robotman art © DC Comics; Vision art © Marvel Characters, Inc.]

☆☆☆☆☆☆☆☆☆☆☆☆☆☆☆☆☆☆☆☆☆☆☆☆☆☆☆☆☆

ALL-STAR SQUADRON #64
(Dec. 1986)

COVER: Arvell Jones (p) & Tony DeZuniga (i)

STORY: "See You in the Funny Papers!" – 22 pp.

ARTISTS: Wayne Boring (p) & Tony DeZuniga (i)

STARRING: JQ, FB, SA, SN, TA, SM, LB, CA, WI, RM, AT, HM.

SYNOPSIS: The All-Stars investigate when famous comic strip villains begin committing robberies, a crime wave masterminded by the mysterious Funnyface. Captured, Firebrand learns of the strange "bio-ray" that brings the cartoons to life. The other All-Stars descend on Funnyface's hideout. Unmasked as a failed cartoonist, Funnyface destroys the bio-ray, sending the villains back to their imaginary worlds.

We Don't Much Care Who We Fight

The Sikela-drawn splash at left, from Superman #19 (Nov.-Dec. 1942), depicts the hero facing villains from five newspaper comic strips, come to life. Jones & DeZuniga made that splash the basis of their cover for All-Star Squadron #64—with five stand-ins for the Man of Steel. [© DC Comics.]

"See You In The Funny Papers!"

The Sikela-drawn, Siegel-scripted rendition of the Daily Planet's comics page in the story of that title. 1942's Superman #17 was in black-&-white, like a page from a daily newspaper. This made it easy to reprint in All-Star Squadron #64 (left), with Liberty Belle's (gloved) hand substituted for Lois Lane's, a bit of dialogue from Johnny Quick, and the Planet altered to The Daily Press (a New York newspaper on Earth-Two which apparently carries exactly the same strips as Metropolis' Planet). Could the name of cartoonist "C.C. Cook" on the Streak Dugan daily be a play on Captain Marvel artist C.C. Beck? The likely inspirations for the comic strips are fairly obvious (and are reproduced below):

Prince Peril is based on Harold R. Foster's epic and influential Prince Valiant—which actually appeared only on Sunday. This Nov. 27, 1937, panel is from the humongously gorgeous Prince Valiant: An American Epic – Volume One: 1937, from Rick Norwood's Manuscript Press. [© King Features Syndicate.]

Detective Craig is a cops-and-robbers strip, of which the epitome was Chester Gould's Dick Tracy. In 1944, Tracy would have a climactic showdown with The Brow, one of his most notable antagonists. [© Tribune Media Services, Inc.]

And could The Solitary Rider be anybody but The Lone Ranger, as per these panels from the Oct. 18, 1942, Sunday by longtime artist Charles Flanders? With appreciation for Dave Holland's excellent 1988 book From Out of the Past: A Pictorial History of The Lone Ranger. [© Lone Ranger Television, Inc.]

Streak Dugan could be either the first true science-fiction strip, Buck Rogers, which began in 1929 and was being drawn in the early 1940s by Rick Yager (as per the ad below left, prepared by the syndicate for newspapers)—or its later and even more influential rival Flash Gordon, created and drawn by Alex Raymond. (For a Raymond Flash Gordon panel, see p. 197.) [© Robert C. Dille or successors in interest.]

The probable inspiration of Happy Daze was C.W. Kahles' Hairbreadth Harry, as seen at bottom of page in 1931 panels wherein heroine rescues hero from a speeding train, for a change—even if she does it long-distance! Repro'd from Jerry Robinson's 1974 book The Comics: An Illustrated History of Comic Strip Art. [© the respective copyright holders.]

NOTES:

- RT chose Wayne Boring to pencil #64 because that artist had begun ghosting the *Superman* newspaper strip in 1939!

- This "Untold Tale of the All-Star Squadron" was, in writer/editor Roy Thomas' view, the bare beginnings of an answer to the question: "On the post-*Crisis* Earth, who fought the 1940s menaces that had been faced on Earth-Two by Superman, Batman and Robin, et al.?" #65 adapted the "Case of the Funny Paper Crimes!" from *Superman* #19 (Nov.-Dec. 1942), written by Jerry Siegel and drawn by John Sikela—with a coterie of All-Stars standing in for the now-nonexistent Superman. Other Earth-Two tales would be modified for the One Big Earth audience in *The Young All-Stars*.

- This story is stated to have occurred between events in *All-Star Squadron* #46-47, and thus is *retroactive* retroactive continuity!

- The splash page of *All-Star Squadron* #64 spotlights a list of the most popular comic strips of the war years, as reported by Richard R. Lingeman in his excellent 1970 book on the WWII home front, *Don't You Know There's a War On?* The top ten on whatever survey he was quoting were, in descending order: *Joe Palooka*, *Blondie*, *Li'l Abner*, *Little Orphan Annie*, *Terry and the Pirates*, *Dick Tracy*, *Moon Mullins*, *Gasoline Alley*, *Bringing Up Father*, and *The Gumps*. How many of these do *you* remember?

- Johnny jokes that Torgo's gone to "meet up with The Dragon Lady for lunch"—a reference to Milton Caniff's adventure strip *Terry and the Pirates*.

- Boring's 1986 Martian resembles Mr. Mxyztplk (see below).

- Sandy makes a reference to another fictitious science-fiction comic strip—*Buzz Roberts in the 30th Century*—since *Streak Dugan* is closer to *Flash Gordon*.

- Hinting at his opinion that there'd been no ample reason to get rid of the multiple Earths, RT says on the LP that he found "the parallel-earth stuff" confusing "only when the writers and editors themselves were confused, or didn't use any kind of logic," as when Vigilante, Wildcat, Spectre, et al., suddenly popped up without explanation on Earth-One. Clearly, he felt he and fellow DC editor Julius Schwartz (who in 1961 had originated the multiple-Earths concept with writer Gardner Fox) had no problems keeping it straight for most readers. Two decades have not altered his opinion.

The More Things Change...

(Above & right:) Superman never did quite manage to lay a hit on Prince Peril's foe Torgo; in #64 Johnny and Belle did, but it didn't do them any good, as the ogre vanished. Ditto with the Man of Tomorrow and the team of Starman, Sandman, and Sandy when each tangled with Streak Dugan's nemesis. Superman material by Siegel & Sikela; All-Stars by RT, Boring, & DeZuniga. [© DC Comics.]

Pay No Attention To That Man Behind The Mask

It's generally agreed that Shuster/Superman shop artist John Sikela drew the unmasked villain Funnyface to resemble scripter Jerry Siegel (vintage photo above), as an in-joke. Boring, penciler of the All-Star Squadron version (right), was aware of the joke, as he'd been one of the earliest artists of the Superman newspaper strip; inks by DeZuniga. In the 1986 adaptation, the villain's speech about wanting to be a celebrity is placed a few panels earlier. [Art © DC Comics; photo © the respective copyright holders.]

ALL-STAR SQUADRON #65
(Jan. 1987)

COVER: Arvell Jones (p) & Tony DeZuniga (i)

STORY: "The Origin of Johnny Quick" – 21 pp.

ARTISTS: Don Heck (p) & Tony DeZuniga (i)

STARRING: JQ, FL, SA, CA. (Cameos: TA, GL, HM, FB, RM, LB).

SYNOPSIS: Orphaned Johnny Chambers is raised by Professor Ezra Gill, discoverer of a "speed formula" he passes on to Johnny upon his death. As an adult, Johnny becomes a newsreel photographer with Sees All/Tells All News. On-the-job encounters with Sandman, Crimson Avenger, and especially The Flash inspire him to create his JQ identity, assuming it first to break up a circus-based crime ring.

NOTES:

• The official name of the Johnny Quick feature was sometimes "Johnny Quick and His Magic Formula." Of course, the latter term is a misnomer, since it was discovered by a mathematician. Perhaps the editors felt "Johnny Quick and His Mathematical Formula" would scare off readers? (The word "magic" isn't used in the 1986 adaptation.)

• There were actually *two* formulas—one to initiate super-speed, and one to stop it. The latter was soon dropped, however, even in the 1940s tales.

• For some reason, reciting the formula only works for Prof. Gill, then for Johnny Chambers.

• Chambers reveals he was filming at the New York World's Fair in 1939 the day the Fantom of the Fair attacked, but was knocked out before he could become Johnny Quick. This sequence is based in part on the Sandman story in *Secret Origins* #7 (Oct. 1986).

• FDR is shown giving three of his most famous speeches, as filmed by Chambers and Watts, to indicate passage of time from 1939-41.

• In a new sequence, Johnny C. observes The Flash in action at a 1941 Broadway performance of the play *DuBarry Was a Lady*, starring Bert Lahr and Ethel Merman. Tubby says he preferred Lahr as the Cowardly Lion (in the 1939 movie *The Wizard of Oz*), while Johnny wonders if he or Flash is faster—and whether the self-styled "Fastest Man Alive" might've been swift enough to save Prof. Gill's life the night he had his heart attack.

• In the 1986 story, Johnny modifies his costume the second time out, so people won't blame Sees All/Tells All News if he gets spotted "snooping around."

• As in the 1941 comic, the circus elephant is named Tantor, after the pachyderm in

Edgar Rice Burroughs' tales of Tarzan.

• In the 1986 version, the always-hungry Tubby Watts discovers a new delicacy called "pizza."

• JQ learns that, when he loses consciousness, his speed formula is deactivated and must be uttered anew to re-start it.

• Resentment against Britain in some circles in the US, for "trying to drag us into war with Germany," is exploited by Nazi spies.

Johnny Be Nimble, Johnny Be Quick

(Above:) When introduced in More Fun Comics #71 (Sept. 1941), Johnny Quick has a somewhat different costume, minus the winged insignia on his chest. Script by Mort Weisinger, art by Chad Grothkopf. (Sorry the repro from old photocopies isn't all it could be.) [© DC Comics.]

(Above:) According to More Fun #71, Johnny kept that outfit for "the following years," as seen in a montage of four otherwise-untold adventures. To get to the hero's more recognizable garb more, er, quickly, RT had those exploits occur after the circus tale. Art by Heck & DuZuniga. [© DC Comics.]

The Reel McCoy

(Above:) Maybe Johnny Chambers got into the newsreel business in 1939 because it was glamorized in such movies as MGM's Too Hot to Handle (1938), starring Clark Gable and Myrna Loy. [© MGM or successors in interest.]

ALL-STAR SQUADRON #66
(Feb. 1987)

COVER: Arvell Jones (p) & Tony DeZuniga (i)

STORY: "The Origin of Tarantula!" – 21 pp.

ARTISTS: Alan Kupperberg (p) & Tony DeZuniga (i)

STARRING: TA, SA. (Cameos: JQ, RM, LB, FB, CA.) (HM pin-up)

SYNOPSIS: While researching a book on so-called "mystery men" and after seeing Sandman in action in his gasmask, best-selling mystery novelist Jonathan Law decides to launch his own crime-fighting career. Armed with suction-soled shoes and a web-gun, Law creates the persona of Tarantula. His first solo case (following the tragic encounter with Sandman and Dian Belmont seen in issue #18) pits him against gangster Ace-Deuce.

NOTES:

• The flashback portion of #66 is divided between retelling Tarantula's origin from Star Spangled Comics #1 (Oct. 1941) and his encounter with Sandman in All-Star Squadron #18.

• The names of Jonathan Law's early best-selling mystery novels—The Dozen

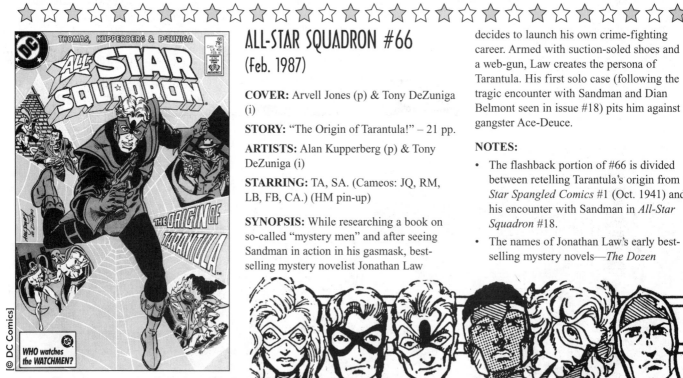

The Fandom Menace

The above pun is just in fun, honest! All-Star Squadron had long since inspired a reader-published fanzine devoted to it and to DC Golden Age heroes, titled All-Star Fandom. The LP in #66 reprinted this illo from it by "talented young artist Brian York." [Heroes TM & © DC Comics.]

Master Minds and *Crime and Crime Again*—are taken from the 1941 tale.

• A 1941 Broadway theatre marquee heralds a production of *Show Me a Rose*—a probably fictitious play (with two equally fictitious stars) penciled in by artist Alan Kupperberg.

• One Kupperberg panel shows a number of (unidentified) movie stars at a 1941 war relief party in Rockefeller Center. Among those depicted are Bob Hope, Clark Gable, Edward G. Robinson, Humphrey Bogart, Abbott and Costello, Ronald Reagan, Lucille Ball, and Desi Arnaz. The latter pair had been married in 1940, but their ultra-popular TV series was still a decade away.

• Olga begs Jonathan Law, at story's end, not to go out "spiderin'" again.

• A Hawkman illustration sent by then-*New Teen Titans* artist Eduardo Barreto made a nice addition to the penultimate #66.

Tarantulas Don't Actually Spin Webs, But...

(Left:) Tarantula and his landlady Olga, in All-Star Squadron #66; she'd also been seen in #24. Script by RT; art by Alan Kupperberg (pencils) & Tony DeZuniga (inks). [© DC Comics.]

(Above right:) Artists Alan Kupperberg (on right) and Jack Kirby, in a 1986 photo sent by AK.

(Right:) Olga nearly gets crowded out of a panel by a radio broadcast in Star Spangled Comics #7 (May 1942). Art by Hal Sharp. Mort Weisinger wrote the hero's origin in SSC #1, but it's not known if he scripted this story. [© DC Comics.]

Your Friendly Neighborhood Tarantula

Marvel had a couple of Tarantulas of its own, in between Star Spangled Comics #1 and All-Star Squadron #18.

(Left:) When Marvel picked up Magazine Enterprises' cowboy hero The Ghost Rider as an "abandoned trademark," Tarantula was the name of the whip-wielding outlaw in issue #2, complete with (fake?) Spanish accent. Art by Dick Ayers & Vince Colletta; script by Gary Friedrich. Thanks to Thomas Lammers for the scan.

(Above:) The South American super-villain called Tarantula first appeared in The Amazing Spider-Man #134 (July 1974), but was apparently killed off later. However, this alternate version—who turns out to be a Latin American patriot—is alive and well in the Spider-Man newspaper strip written by Stan Lee, as per this Sunday by Alex Saviuk (pencils) & Joe Sinnott (inks). [© Marvel Characters, Inc.]

ALL-STAR SQUADRON #67
(March 1987)

COVER: Tom Grindberg (p) & Tony DeZuniga (i)

STORY: "The First Case of the Justice Society of America" – 22 pp.

ARTISTS: Arvell Jones (p) & Tony DeZuniga (i)

STARRING: HM, GL, AT, SA, FL, SP, HO, DF, JT (w/TB).

SYNOPSIS: Around the turn of 1940-41, FBI Chief J. Edgar Hoover asks the newly-formed Justice Society of America to investigate the activities of fifth columnists. The heroes, on solo assignments, find that all roads lead to industrialist Fritz Klaver, leader of the Bund-style Grey-Shirts. Converging on his headquarters, the JSAers arrive in time to save Atom and non-member Johnny Thunder from death. With the aid of Johnny's Thunderbolt, they drop Klaver and his spies in Hoover's lap.

NOTES:

• This story is a truncated adaptation of *All-Star Comics* #4 (Spring 1941), the first actual published adventure of the Justice Society of America, since in #3 they had just sat around swapping stories. Most things of interest concerning #4 are covered in *The All-Star Companion, Vol. 1*—still available from TwoMorrows Publishing.

• Though *All-Star Squadron* was being discontinued (as much because of *Crisis* as for sales), RT was "gratified" to announce in its final text section that it had done well in the 1986 fan-voted awards given out by the weekly *Comics Buyer's Guide* tabloid. The title finished 9th in a field of "many, many dozens" of titles, while RT himself placed 6th in the "Favorite Writer" category and 4th among "Favorite Editors" in his 20th year as a comics pro.

• The final item on the text page was an extended thank-you from Roy Thomas to the artists, writers, editors, letterers, colorists, and publishers (most of them by name) who'd had a hand in making the half dozen years of *All-Star Squadron* among his most satisfying in the comic book field.

Washington, DC, Is A Jungle, Too

Tom Grindberg, cover artist of All-Star Squadron #67—and one of his recent paintings of Tarzan. [Tarzan TM & © Edgar Rice Burroughs, Inc..]

Comin' Right Atom

Most of the solo chapters in #67's retelling of events of All-Star Comics #4 were telescoped into one or two pages—but The Atom's, being the climactic episode, ran five. It was easy for Al Pratt to pretend to be a college student—because he really was one. Art by Jones & DeZuniga, script by RT—adapted from Gardner Fox's, natch. [© DC Comics.]

You Can't Take It With You

As detailed in Vol. 1 of this series, Nazi spymaster Fritz Klaver was probably modeled in part after Fritz Kuhn, 1936-39 leader of the American-German Bund. The high point of the latter's career was when he (seen at center in photo) and four others of the Bund's Uniformed Service (Ordnugs-Dienst) had an audience with Der Führer in Berlin in August 1936. Already, however, the Third Reich had severed most connections with the Bund.

When "Fritz Klaver" tried to blow up himself, his spy records, and the JSA (above center), Dr. Fate simply immobilized him via magic. In All-Star Squadron #67, it was clear that if Fate hadn't done so, The Spectre would have—or else The Flash or Green Lantern could've easily stopped him. That's the trouble with super-hero groups from a villain's perspective: they gang up on you! [© DC Comics.]

First Bow—And Last

(Above:) Issue #67—and All-Star Squadron itself—ended with FBI director J. Edgar Hoover (seen in photo at right) thanking the JSA for smashing the "dictator nations'" spy operations in the USA. Hoover's face had gone unseen in All-Star Comics #4. Script by RT; art by Jones & DeZuniga. [Art © DC Comics.]

Youth Wants To Know—Who Are These New Guys?

(Above:) The text pages in #67 announced that the new comic starring the DC super-heroes of World War II would be titled The Young All-Stars—and featured a drawing of its six principals, apparently by Brian Murray. Though two of the names below were held back for surprise value, the membership was to be (l. to r.): Neptune Perkins, who'd appeared in All-Star Squadron #33-35, as well as in two Golden Age Hawkman stories... Fury, introduced in the recent Secret Origins #12 and now "seem[ing] to be the mother of Lyta Trevor [of] Infinity, Inc." rather than Wonder Woman... "Iron" Munro, son of Hugo Danner, protagonist of Philip Wylie's 1930 "superman" novel Gladiator... Dyna-Mite, who'd appeared with his equally explosive mentor TNT in 1940s issues of Star Spangled Comics... Tsunami, who'd fought for the Imperial Japanese in Squadron #33-35... and Flying Fox, a Native American who could ride the winds. Other, previously-established All-Stars would appear, as well, readers were assured—and did, beginning in The Young All-Stars #1 (June 1987). More about these teenage titans in The All-Star Companion, Vol. 3, out in October 2007! [© DC Comics.]

And so ended *All-Star Squadron*. After a three-month hiatus, however, the 1942 super-group was back, at least after a fashion, for nearly three dozen issues of *The Young All-Stars*. Space precluded our covering that series in this book as originally intended... but watch for issue-by-issue coverage of that sequel series in *The All-Star Companion, Vol. 3*.

THE JUSTICE SOCIETY OF AMERICA IN THE 1980s

by Roy Thomas & Kurt Mitchell

During the 1981-87 run of *All-Star Squadron*, Roy Thomas was able to launch several other additional titles related in one way or another to the Justice Society and Earth-Two:

In 1984: *Infinity, Inc.*—starring the sons, daughters, and spiritual heirs of the 1940s JSA heroes…

In 1986: *Secret Origins*—revisiting, for modern readers, the roots of many of the greatest Golden Age stalwarts…

In 1987: *The Young All-Stars*—the adventures of a group of adolescent and young-adult super-heroes who're "trying out" to become full-fledged Squadron members—as a successor series to *Squadron*.

Along the way, in 1985, there was also a four-issue limited series in which, for the first time ever, the phrase "Justice Society" was used in the official title of a comic book.

And, as a 1986 footnote to the *Crisis on Infinite Earths*, there was the somewhat awkwardly titled *Last Days of the Justice Society Special*, which likewise contained the name of comics' first super-hero group—and which was (for a very brief while) intended to write "*finis*" for all time to the career of the JSA at DC.

No lie. It really was.

Because these five extra-size issues were all published during the period between the beginning and end of *All-Star Squadron*, we felt it appropriate to deal with them in this volume. Once again Kurt Mitchell wrote the basic story synopses and contributed other information and observations—and once again the meaning of the abbreviations of heroes' names on the ensuing pages can be found in the Key on p. 102.

Forty Years of Treason

(Above:) Original All-Star Squadron penciler Rich Buckler may have been slated at some stage to pencil America vs. the Justice Society, and the art he produced became pp. 1 (above), 4, 6, & 7 of #1. This splash, drawn as a "composite photo," was also produced by DC as a poster, as a promotion for the limited series. Inks by Alfredo Alcala; script by Roy Thomas. [© DC Comics.]

From Manila To Manhattan

(Right:) Alfredo Alcala inked nearly all of AVJS' four issues, as well as a few of All-Star Squadron. He was one of the foremost among the Filipino comic book artists who illustrated first for DC, later also for Marvel, beginning in the 1970s. He became especially noted for his embellishing of John Buscema's pencils in The Savage Sword of Conan. Alcala passed away in 2002. Photo courtesy of his son Christian Voltan Alcala & the Alcala family.

Stripped Away

(Above:) Alcala also drew the comic strip Conan the Barbarian for several months in 1980—but someone saw to it that his and RT's credit box was removed within it was printed in newspapers. [© Conan Properties International, LLC.]

AMERICA VS. THE JUSTICE SOCIETY

This quartet of issues was conceived by Roy Thomas as a vehicle for relating the entire previous history of the JSA chronologically, from its origin and first meeting in 1940 through the adventures of the 1976-79 revival, within the context of a storyline which took place in 1984-85. Giving it ample coverage thus presents a special problem, because all eight of its inside covers, front *and* back, were filled to the brim with typeset notes—a so-called "Skeleton Key" to each issue—which detailed the original 1940-plus source of the events retold. The idea behind this was to give the full provenance of each episode, each action, that had its roots in comics that had been published mere months or several decades before—while avoiding distracting readers with footnotes on virtually every page!

Twenty years later, that system seems to have worked fairly well. Thus, what follows is a severely truncated version of those page-by-page notes, plus such other commentary as seems worth adding in the early 21st century. If you want to know even more—go haunt the back issue bins.

But first, a few words about the series *America vs. the Justice*

Society (which will often be referred to by the abbreviation *AVJS* in what follows):

As stated in an inside-front-cover "Prologomena" by "Roy Thomas, writer/editor" in issue #1, this mini-series (the TV-derived term was still in common use in comics at that time) was originally intended to last six issues. A last-minute decision changed that to just four issues—but with the same page count, since #1 had 48 pages of story (plus covers), and the other three had 32 story pages between its covers, for a total of 144 pages. There were no ads in any of the issues.

RT indulged himself at the end of this prologue by saying:

"Hopefully, by the time we get to our grand finale three months from now, you will know, as the ads say, Everything You Always Wanted to Know about the Justice Society—and a Few Things You Never Dared Ask.

"And if you've never really cared about the JSA, you lack an historical perspective and I'm not interested in you in the first place. Sorry."

With that, the page-by-pages notes began there… and here.

AMERICA VS. THE JUSTICE SOCIETY #1
(Jan. 1985)

COVER: Jerry Ordway

STORY: "I Accuse!" – 48 pp.

WRITER: Roy Thomas (co-plotter—Dann Thomas)

ARTISTS: Rafael Kayanan, Rich Buckler, & Jerry Ordway (p)—Alfredo Alcala & Bill Collins & Jerry Ordway (i)

STARRING: WW, HM, GL, DM, SM, JT, HO, SU, SA, DF, AT, RO, WC, BM, SP, MT, HU. (Cameos: BC, BL, US, PL, PM.)

SYNOPSIS: The dozen surviving heroes of the original WWII-era JSA meet to discuss *The Batman Diary*, which was given to Prof. Carter Nichols by Batman years before, with instructions that it should be published should the Caped Crusader be deceased by a certain date. The diary relates a twisted account of the JSA's history, in which all the wartime members except Superman secretly served Adolf Hitler and the Third Reich. As the 1985 JSAers finish perusing the volume, federal troops take them—even Superman—into custody for treason. Publisher A.K. O'Fallon, son of the Senator who in 1951 had pressured the JSA into disbanding, leads a media crusade for a Congressional hearing. The JSAers tell defense attorney Helena (Huntress) Wayne their true history, as they recall it. Attorney Dick (Robin) Grayson is named special legal counsel to Congress' joint investigating committee. He is introduced by O'Fallon to the committee's star witness: none other than the heroes' old enemy, The Wizard!

Dann And Superman

Dann Thomas, Roy's wife, collaborated with him in plotting the AVJS series, as well as Infinity, Inc., Jonni Thunder a.k.a. Thunderbolt, most issues of Arak, Son of Thunder, and quite a few of All-Star Squadron. She often wrote first drafts of the dialogue on some of these series, though rarely on the latter. Though far from a comics fan, she'd begun co-plotting stories with Roy not long after they met in 1977. The Batman Diary aspects of the plot may well have been her concept. This 1980s photo was taken by a professional photographer as a gift from her friend Jennie-Lynn Falk, after whom the alter ego of Jade in Infinity, Inc. was named. Our apologies for this paragraph's heading to George Bernard Shaw.

[© DC Comics]

Comics Covers The Ord-Way

Jerry Ordway, who illustrated all four mini-series covers, had originally hoped also to pencil the interior art of all issues, as well as inking Mike Machlan's pencils on the new Infinity, Inc. title— but eventually it worked out that Jerry penciled and Mike inked Infinity, Inc. #1-10, so Jerry had to bow out of penciling the JSA series.

The "Justice Society" logo used on cover and splashes in this series had been designed, likewise minus the words "of America," for DC Special #29 in 1977. [© DC Comics.]

Raf And The World Rafs With You

(Below & right:) Rafael Kayanan has drawn comics professionally since the 1980s, and currently does designs and storyboards for films; he is also skilled in martial arts weaponry. America vs. the Justice Society #1 was one of his earliest assignments; he and Roy Thomas worked together again in the mid-1990s on Marvel's Conan the Adventurer. The Wonder Woman sketch at right was done as a commission drawing. Photo & art courtesy of Raf. [Wonder Woman TM & © DC Comics.]

Time And Time Again

(Above:) Beginning in Batman #24 (Aug.-Sept. 1944), Prof. Carter Nichols sent Bruce Wayne and Dick Grayson back in time via hypnosis on more than 30 occasions, to solve historical mysteries—which the pair invariably did as Batman and Robin, without the scientist/historian ever suspecting their secret. The vintage panel at left is from Detective Comics #116 (Oct. 1946), "The Rescue of Robin Hood!" Script by Don Cameron; art by Winslow Mortimer.

(Below:) In a flashback in AVJS #1, Batman shows his startling diary to Prof. Nichols not long before his death in Adventure Comics #462 (March-April 1979). Art by Rafael Kayanan (pencils) & Alfredo Alcala (inks); script by RT. [© DC Comics.]

Was Adolf Hitler Really Just A Spear-Carrier?

(Far left:) In AVJS #1, the eight charter JSAers "Heil Hitler" under the influence of the Spear of Destiny—as related in Batman's diary—a revamping of a scene from DC Special #29's origin of the Justice Society in 1977. Art by Kayanan & Alcala; script by RT.

(Left:) In addition to Trevor Ravenscroft's The Spear of Destiny (1972), another work which deals with Hitler's interest in the occult is Louis Pauwels and Jacques Bergier's The Morning of the Magicians (a.k.a. The Dawn of Magic), first published in English in 1963. Such books led writer Steve Englehart to utilize the legend of the Spear in Weird War Tales #50 (Jan.-Feb. 1977), whence it soon became integral to the first-ever origin tale of the JSA. [Comic art © DC Comics; book cover © the respective copyright holders.]

NOTES:

- Comics collector and researcher Rich Morrissey is listed as "consultant" in the credits of #1.

- The JSA return to Civic City, where they had met from *All-Star Comics* #45-57.

- Black Canary is not a part of these proceedings because she'd long since migrated to Earth-One and joined the Justice *League* of America—or rather, as was revealed around this time, her *daughter* had.

- The Sandman is absent because of a recent stroke, reported in *Infinity, Inc.* #1 (March 1984).

- On Earth-Two in the 1980s, Clark Kent is managing editor of the Metropolis *Daily Star*; a balding Jimmy Olsen is also an editor there.

- Batman is shown using a gun as per an adventure or two in 1939-40 issues of *Detective Comics*.

- It's highly improbable Hitler would've considered launching Operation Sea Lion—his planned invasion of England in 1940—as late in the year as November, as per the 1977 origin. That story would more logically have been set in September; but writer Paul Levitz probably felt the JSA should be formed not long before its first official get-together.

The Real McCarthy

(Above left:) Senator Joseph R. McCarthy (R.-Wisconsin), elected in 1946, became a driving force in what's been called a "witch hunt" for Communists in high places in the first years of the 1950s, before he was thoroughly discredited by his own excesses. He died in 1957.

(Above right:) In the 1951 of Earth-Two, super-heroes were suspected of being enemy secret agents (why else hide their identities?). Here, Senator O'Fallon prods the JSA to unmask, but they go into early retirement instead—in a reinterpretation of the scene from Adventure Comics #466 (Nov.-Dec. 1979), in which writer Paul Levitz and artist Joe Staton gave a rationale for there being no Golden Age JSA tales after All-Star #57. In AVJS #1, scripter RT and artists Kayanan & Alcala gave the Congressional committee's head a name and a face—that of O'Fallon, who on Earth-Two took over hearings after McCarthy's fatal car crash at the turn of '51. [© DC Comics.]

Dear Diary

The Batman Diary that sets in motion the plot of America vs. the Justice Society was inspired by the spurious Hitler Diaries unveiled in 1983. Though declared to be authentic by several historians of World War II, they were soon exposed as fraudulent, the work of a German named Konrad Kujau, who went to prison for his trouble. This is the cover of a Newsweek special edition on The Hitler Diaries soon after they were "discovered." [© the respective copyright holders.]

Nostalgia Isn't What It Used To Be

The mini-series saw inventive reinterpretations of scenes from the original 1940-1951 run of All-Star Comics.

(Above center:) Jerry Ordway's take on the cover of All-Star #4, drawn to be a pin-up, became a story page in AVJS #1. It's repro'd here from a photocopy of the original art, minus copy, courtesy of Jerry O.

(Above right:) Retroactive continuity was mixed with authentic tales in AVJS, as per this page from #1 which depicts the 1978 ending of All New Collectors' Edition, Vol. 7, #C-54, in which Superman and Wonder Woman had a 1942 encounter with Baron Blitzkrieg, plus new versions of scenes from All-Star #15, 18, 20, and 23. Art by Kayanan & Alcala; script by RT. [© DC Comics.]

- That first official JSA meeting, recorded in *All-Star* #3, is retroactively dated as having occurred on Nov. 22, 1940—by an amazing coincidence, the day Roy Thomas was born. In our world, that issue did go on sale in that month and year, and at least one copy has been found actually stamped "11-22" by a retailer or wholesaler.

- Various scenes from published JSA adventures, both in *All-Star* (from #4-14) and elsewhere, are recounted in #1. One or two episodes are recounted *twice*, with details differing greatly between the "revelations" of the *Batman Diary* and the heroes' own accounts. Part of this repetition occurred because two issues' worth of material was combined into one volume in the 11th hour.

- FDR made wire recordings of doings in the Oval Office—a fact only revealed in the early 1980s. This technology was a forerunner of audio tape recordings.

- Scenes from *All-Star Squadron* are also briefly recounted in #1, such as the events of Dec. 6 & 7, 1941, Uncle Sam's founding of The Freedom Fighters in that same month, and the menace of Prof. Napier's Flying Eye—as are incidents from several of the Justice League-Justice Society team-ups that began in 1963, and from the late-1970s revival of the JSA.

- There is mention of a "JSA reunion" at the funeral of President Franklin Roosevelt in 1945—a story which would be told in *Last Days of the Justice Society Special*.

- One of RT's retroactive concepts for *All-Star Squadron*, also utilized in *AVJS*, is the so-called "Time Trust," consisting of the scientists who in 1941 were researching time travel in *All-Star Comics* #10. None of these was given a name in the original comic, though Dr. Everson was

Heroes In The Hoosegow

Deciding not to resist the authorities, the Justice Society's older members are carted off to jail in issue #1. At the time, The Spectre was off in otherworldly realms. Art by Kayanan & Alcala, script by RT. [© DC Comics.]

identified in #21. Retroactively, RT added Prof. Zee (from *All-Star* #35) and Dr. Swanley (from #53) and even Dr. Doome from 1942's *Leading Comics* #2—and Per Degaton (of *All-Star* #35 & 37), already Zee's assistant in '41. It seemed logical that all these savants might have worked on the same World War II time-travel project.

- Infinity, Inc., are shown watching the Congressional hearings on TV, uncertain what to do about them.

- TV newscaster Andrew Vinson pops up from 1978 issues of *Showcase* starring Power Girl, the Earth-Two Superman's cousin.

- The death of Bruce Wayne, the Earth-Two

Batman, was depicted in *Adventure Comics* #462 (March-April 1979).

- Helena Wayne, Bruce's daughter, was introduced in *All-Star Comics* #69 (Nov.-Dec. 1977); her background was revealed at virtually the same time in a special 17th issue of *DC Super-Stars*.

- Dick Grayson wears a more adult variant of his Robin costume, introduced in *Justice League of America* #92 (Sept. 1971), worn by the older Earth-One Robin. The Earth-Two Robin donned a revamped version of it in *All-Star Comics* #58 (Jan.-Feb. 1976).

- The back cover of the issue is a re-creation by Al Dellinges of E.E. Hibbard's cover for *All-Star Comics* #4.

☆☆☆☆☆☆☆☆☆☆☆☆☆☆☆☆☆☆☆☆☆☆☆☆☆☆☆☆☆☆☆☆

AMERICA VS. THE JUSTICE SOCIETY #2
(Feb. 1985)

COVER: Jerry Ordway

STORY: "Trial by Congress!" – 32 pp.

CO-PLOTTER: Dann Thomas

ARTISTS: Mike Hernandez (p) & Alfredo Alcala (i)

STARRING: HM, FL, GL, SU, DF, DM, SM, WW, SA, WC, HO, AT, JT, SK, SP—plus HU (as Helena Wayne) & RO (as Dick Grayson). (Cameos: RM, LB, PM, JQ, CA, GA, SY, SS, ST, VG, FB.)

SYNOPSIS: The Congressional hearings begin. JSAers recounts the group's origin, early cases, and wartime history, revealing details never before made public. A mysterious figure watching the hearings on TV vows that, if Congress doesn't destroy the JSA, he will. The Spectre, now "all ghost [and] no part man," appears, threatening divine retribution until the JSA talk him out of it. Senator O'Fallon, who's convinced the JSA murdered his father, plots his next move with The Wizard.

NOTES:

- Sandman has recovered sufficiently from his stroke to appear at the Congressional hearing.

- The Earth-Two Clark Kent and Lois Lane were married in the early 1950s, as had been revealed several years earlier in the "Mr. and Mrs. Superman" series in *The Superman Family*.

- Al (Atom) Pratt's marriage to a woman named Mary (presumably the Mary James of 1940s stories) was revealed in *DC Comics Presents* #30 (Feb. 1981).

- Cryptic comments made by Flash and

Green Lantern as to the whereabouts of The Spectre refer to the latter's appearances with the Earth-One Batman in *The Brave and the Bold* in recent years, as well as to a Superman/Spectre confrontation in *DC Comics Presents* #29 (Jan. 1978).

- The JSAers relate their own versions of various of their 1940s adventures, both their origin (first told in 1977) and events from *All-Star Comics* #3-14, the first few issues of *All-Star Squadron*, and the "JSA case the world's not ready to learn about yet," as revealed in *All-Star Squadron Annual* #3 (1984).

- Aspects of Hourman's Miraclo addiction were revealed in *All-Star Squadron* #33-35 and in *Annual* #3, the issues in which he returned to crimebusting on Earth-Two.

- Shiera Sanders first flew as Hawkgirl in *Flash Comics* #24 (Dec. 1941); her first *All-Star* appearance was in #8.

- Diana Prince's husband Steve Trevor was badly injured during her battle with Infinity, Inc. in the latter's early days, at a time when the JSAers were under the influence of the Stream of Ruthlessness

first introduced in *All-Star* #36.

- The Shining Knight and Dr. Chuck Grayson—the latter now sporting the brain of Dr. Robert Crane that had once resided in the body of Robotman—appeared at the hearings as witnesses in defense of the JSA.

- The tale of the Seven Soldiers of Victory's sojourn in limbo was told in 1972's *Justice League of America* #100-102.

- Danette Reilly first donned (and altered) her brother's Firebrand costume in *All-Star Squadron* #5.

- The first disbanding of the JSA, and its reconstituting "for the duration" as the Justice Battalion, was related in *All-Star Comics* #11; it was expanded upon in *All-Star Squadron* #19-20.

- The brief recounting by Wonder Woman of events initially told in 1942's *All-Star* #13 reflects the "Shanghaied into Hyperspace" storyline that ran from *All-Star Squadron* #50-60.

- The back cover is a re-creation by Al Dellinges of the cover of *All-Star Comics* #3.

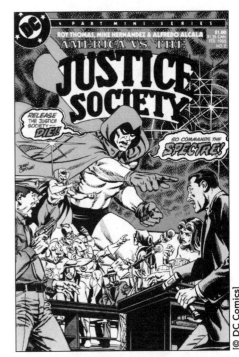

[© DC Comics]

"Release The Justice Society—Or DIE!"

Jerry Ordway's masterful cover showed The Spectre coming back from limbo and threatening to tear up half the world, if he must, to free the JSA. They talked him into cooling it. Somehow, the word "or" before "DIE!" in Spec's first balloon, though it appeared in a house ad for the issue, dropped off the cover as printed. [© DC Comics.]

Minority Report

(Above:) Congresswoman Valdez questions Green Lantern about why there were no minorities in the wartime JSA—and is defended by Wonder Woman. Hey, all the lady lawmaker had to do was pick up a copy of All-Star Squadron! [© DC Comics.]

(Right:) On our super-hero-deprived Earth, heavyweight boxing champion Joe Louis— "The Brown Bomber"—was good enough to be drafted, make personal appearances, and pose for posters; but neither he nor any other African-American was allowed to fight like a real soldier. Likewise on the Home Front, blacks staged a "silent parade" through New York's Union Square on July 25, 1942, in protest against ongoing racial discrimination; the action was sponsored by the March on Washington Movement, which FDR had talked out of actually marching on the nation's capital the previous year.

Pvt. Joe Louis says_

"We're going to do our part ...and we'll win because we're on God's side"

AMERICA VS. THE JUSTICE SOCIETY #3

(March 1985)

COVER: Jerry Ordway

STORY: "Hostile Witness!" – 32 pp.

ARTISTS: Howard Bender (p) & Alfredo Alcala (i)

(probably co-plotted by Dann Thomas)

STARRING: DF, DM, HM, SA, WW, SP, JT, AT, SM, GL, FL, HO, WC, SU, plus HU (as Helena Wayne) & RO (as Dick Grayson). (Cameos: SN, plus images of BM, MT, BC.)

SYNOPSIS: The second day of testimony continues the story of the JSA's wartime and post-WWII exploits. Dick and Helena argue about her intent to expose Batman's true identity, if necessary, to exonerate the JSA. The Wizard, called to testify, corroborates the *Batman Diary* but discredits himself by trying to escape. The mysterious watching figure is revealed to be Per Degaton.

NOTES:

• Again, many of the events related by the JSAers and other witnesses are culled from the 1940-1951 *All-Star Comics* (from #15 through #41), as well as from the 1970s JSA revival, *All-Star Squadron*, etc.

• Mention is made that occasionally, both in the 1940s and since, Wes (Sandman) Dodds' surname has been written as "Dodd."

If Ever, Oh, Ever, A Wizard There Was...

Jerry Ordway's cover for AVJS #3 featured The Wizard. It can be seen in its two separate halves— black-&-white line art and color overlay showing Hitler and the giant swastika—in Alter Ego #44 (2005), repro'd from photocopies of the original art, courtesy of JO. [© DC Comics.]

• Scenes from the solo exploits of several JSAers are depicted, reflecting in particular what happened to Starman, Sandman, Spectre, and Dr. Fate when their individual series were dropped in the mid-1940s from *Adventure Comics* and *More Fun Comics*. Some of the later changes in their solo stories were not reflected in their appearances in *All-Star*.

• In various issues of the late-1970s resurrected *All-Star Comics*, Police Commissioner Bruce Wayne had—under the influence of The Psycho-Pirate— become an adamant anti-JSA force in Gotham City. Though it perhaps wasn't made clear enough, Bruce was subconsciously resisting that villain's spell when he concocted the convoluted notion of *The Batman Diary* to energize the JSA.

• As per Chapter VI of this volume, there seem to have been from one to four never-published JSA stories. However, none of these, including "The Will of William Wilson," was covered in *AVJS*. Had RT purchased much of the art from it (from the late Mark Hanerfeld) a bit earlier, it no doubt would've been reflected in this story arc.

• The Wizard's finding the Spear of Destiny for Hitler is a new element of

retroactive history, added in this series, as is the revelation that his true name was William Asmodeus Zard. He used the name "W.I. Zard" in *All-Star* #34, but it was never certain whether that was his true name or just a pseudonym.

• The back cover of the issue is a re-creation by Al Dellinges of the cover of *All-Star Comics* #5, which RT and others suspect was originally prepared to be that of issue #3, before the Justice Society concept was devised.

Of Monsters And Men

(Above:) Much of AVJS #3 consisted of nuanced retellings of Golden Age JSA exploits—such as this montage of its first encounter with swamp-thing Solomon Grundy in All-Star Comics #33. Art by Bender & Alcala. [© DC Comics.]

Middle Relief—And Closer

(Right:) Howard Bender penciled the 3rd and 4th issues of America vs. the Justice Society. Photo courtesy of HB.

The Canary Sings—But Silently

(Left:) RT impishly gave Black Canary a thought balloon in recounting her finally being voted into official JSA member-ship at the end of All-Star Comics #41, after guest-starring in four issues in a row. Art by Bender & Alcala. [© DC Comics.]

★★★★★★★★★★★★★★★★★★★★★★★★★★★★★★★★★★★★

[© DC Comics]

AMERICA VS. THE JUSTICE SOCIETY #4
(April 1985)

COVER: Jerry Ordway

STORY: "D-Day for Degaton!" – 32 pp.

ARTISTS: Howard Bender (p) & Alfredo Alcala (i)

(Dann Thomas, co-plotter)

STARRING: AT, WW, DF, DM, HM, FL, GL, SU, WC, SA, JT, HO, SM, PG, SS, HU & RO (as Dick Grayson). (Cameos: images of BC, SK, ST, VG, CA GA, SY.)

SYNOPSIS: The JSAers narrate their postwar history up to the present. During an adjournment, Prof. Nichols tells Dick Grayson about the "Hundred Years Club," in which he and his fellow "Time Trust" scientists agreed to test their time travel methods by visiting the centenaries of their own births. Learning from Prof. Nichols that today would have been the long-missing Prof. Zee's 100th birthday, Dick rushes to the site of Zee's old lab. Degaton, lurking there, holds Dick at gunpoint until Zee's time machine materializes. Zee staggers from it; he had set it to transport him to this date before Degaton had shot him in 1947.

And The Wheel Goes 'Round And 'Round

Prof. Zodiak's alleged Wheel of Perpetual Motion (from All-Star Comics #42) was depicted in AVJS #4, as were events from the remaining issues #43-57 of the Golden Age series. #42's was the first JSA tale in which Hawkman sported a simpler cowl, and The Atom an entirely new costume. Black Canary and Wonder Woman were around, too—they just hadn't been strapped on the wheel. Art by Bender & Alcala. [© DC Comics.]

Through A Glass—Slowly

(Above:) As RT has often stated, one of his favorite comics covers is that of All-Star Comics #35. Here, Jerry Ordway does his own splendid reinterpretation of that classic scene of Degaton causing modern technology to revert to older, even ancient forms. [© DC Comics.]

He dies, but not before naming Degaton as his killer—with Dick and the arriving JSA and Congressional committee as witnesses. Degaton chooses suicide over surrender. The *Batman Diary* is exposed as a convoluted hoax designed by the terminally ill Bruce Wayne to focus attention on Degaton. (Feeling so negative toward the JSA, because of Psycho-Pirate's subconscious influence, Wayne hadn't been able to go to them directly… even though Helena Wayne reveals that her father had learned, shortly before his violent death, that he was dying of cancer.) The JSA is cleared of all charges.

NOTES:

• The JSAers relate their adventures from *All-Star Comics* #42-57, and their disbanding in 1951.

• Edmund Blake, who as a sick boy in 1948 was given the will to live by the JSA (in *All-Star* #48) vouches for the JSAers' character. Wonder if Edmund was any relation to Adam Blake (Captain Comet)—or to Dr. Don Blake (Marvel's Thor).

• When Green Lantern mentions the alien invasions by Fire People and Diamond Men (in *All-Star* #49 & 51), one aging audience member blurts out that he was in the National Guard troops sent up against "some of those outer-spacers," and if not for the JSA, "we'd have wound up like the people on that *V* show on TV!" *V* was a series about the conquest of Earth by aliens; it lasted from 1983-85.

• GL mentions how four ancient kings had put the JSA to sleep for an entire year—but the question of what happened to their personal lives and secret identities during that period is glossed over.

• Power Girl recounts a brief history of the All-Star Super-Squad version of the JSA to which she'd belonged during the 1970s revival. She says The Huntress wishes she could be here (and of course she is, actually—in her alter ego as Helena Wayne).

• Before he shoots himself to avoid capture, Degaton was about to launch his "ultimate plan"—which, like his earlier ones, was "to conquer the world, by plunging it back into the Dark Ages." But, this time, he's "had nearly four more decades to salt away the latest weapons—so that even the Justice Society won't be able to stand against me!" Yeah, right!

• The back cover of *AVJS* #4 is repro'd from the original Peddy/Sachs art for the cover of *All-Star Comics* #54, which Roy Thomas owned at the time. The story title "The Circus of a Thousand Thrills!" had fallen off, and had been replaced by lettering in a simpler style.

Fabulous '50s Felon-Fighters

Courtesy of Thomas, Bender, & Alcala, The Atom speaks in AVJS #4 of Superman, Batman & Robin, and Wonder Woman as if they were the only super-heroes who stuck around for the 1950s. But, of course, not only did DC's Aquaman, Green Arrow & Speedy, Captain Comet, Robotman, Vigilante, Johnny Quick, and The Shining Knight last into (and in a couple of cases far beyond) the decade of Ike and Elvis —but clearly the Mighty Mite had no inkling of divergent universes, where other colorful heroes had at least brief careers. (Clockwise from top center:)

Captain America, Sub-Mariner, and The Human Torch, plus a pair of kid sidekicks, returned for a year or two starting in 1953, as seen in Young Men #26 (March 1954), drawn by John Romita. [© Marvel Characters, Inc.]

Captain 3-D leaped off the pages of the mysterious Book of D just long enough to star in one issue of his own Harvey comic (dated Dec. 1953), which youngsters in our world needed red-and-green glasses to read. Art by Joe Simon & Jack Kirby. [© Home Comics, Inc., or successors in interest.]

Captains were big in the '50s! The atomic-powered **Captain Flash** *fought aliens as well as criminals in his own Sterling Comics series, as per this scene from the final issue (#4, July 1955). Pencils by future JLA artist Mike Sekowsky. [© the respective copyright holders.]*

Fighting American and Speedboy clobbered increasingly comical Commies for the Prize Group. Art by Joe Simon & Jack Kirby, from the cover of FA #3 (Aug.-Sept. 1954). [© Joe Simon & Estate of Jack Kirby.]

Another 1940s hero, **The Blue Beetle**, *made a brief comeback beginning in Space Adventures #13 (Oct.-Nov. 1954). Art by Al Fago for Charlton Comics Group, years before BB mutated into a DC franchise. [Blue Beetle TM & © DC Comics.]*

Plastic Man and **Doll Man** were likewise around for the early '50s, as per these Quality covers dated June 1953. Both became DC characters only after the late 1960s. (And what about aviator Blackhawk, who made the jump from Quality to DC in the mid-'50s?) [Plastic Man & Doll Man TM & © DC Comics.]

And that doesn't even count Harvey's **Stuntman**, *ME's* **Avenger & Strong Man**, *Ajax/Farrell's* **Black Cobra**, *et. al., Charlton's* **Nature Boy**, *and probably a few heroes we forgot!*

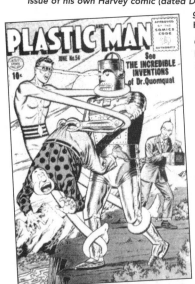

H-Hour For Degaton

(Above:) The late Prof. Zee had returned from his time trip and lived just long enough to point a bloody finger at Per Degaton as his killer—then the cavalry arrived to save Dick Grayson (and incidentally its own reputation). Thanks to Mark Trost for the scan. (Right:) Degaton took the coward's way out—and this time he didn't revert to being Zee's lab assistant in 1947. Art by Bender & Alcala; script by RT. [© DC Comics.]

SECTION B

LAST DAYS OF THE JUSTICE SOCIETY

As revealed in an "Epilegomena to *The Last Days of the Justice Society*" (sic) on the inside front and back covers of this 68-page one-shot, it was originally commissioned as a graphic novel, to be written by Roy Thomas, penciled by David Ross, and inked by Mike Gustovich.

It had arisen because Roy Thomas had sensed that the powers-that-be at DC would prefer to write the Justice Society entirely out of the post-*Crisis on Infinite Earths* universe. And so, at a 1986 DC editorial meeting in New York, he suggested the concept of a graphic novel that would write *finis* to the history of the JSA. The idea was enthusiastically accepted. In fact, marketing director Bruce Bristow said at the time, "This is such a sensible idea that I'm surprised anybody in this room thought of it!" Managing editor Dick Giordano, a friend of Roy's, proclaimed that, once this was done, it was his intention that, excluding their very limited 1940s use in *The Young All-Stars*, the JSA would never again appear in a DC comic while he was in charge.

Roy did not, of course, actually like the notion of getting rid of the JSA; but he could read the handwriting on the wall as well as anyone, and figured it would be better to give comics' first (and in his opinion greatest) super-hero group a strong send-off rather than simply let it peter out.

After the graphic novel had been well begun, DC decided that, instead of being a graphic novel (and thus more prestigious), it would be merely a "Special"—though its 64 pages would fill an entire comic, with no ads. Though not a party to this decision, Roy accepted it.

He used as his starting point the Spear of Destiny, which had figured in both the 1977 JSA origin and in *All-Star Squadron* #4, as well as in other 1980s issues. As the weapon which had supposedly pierced the side of the crucified Christ 2000 years ago, it was said to rank up there with the Ark of the Covenant (as per the 1981 Spielberg film *Raiders of the Lost Ark*) as a talisman in which the occult-obsessed Adolf Hitler had been interested.

LAST DAYS OF THE JUSTICE SOCIETY SPECIAL #1 (1986)

COVER: David Ross (p) & Mike Gustovich (i)

STORY: (No Interior Title)

CO-PLOTTER: Dann Thomas

ARTISTS: David Ross (p) & Mike Gustovich (i)

STARRING: DM, GL, FL, HM, PG, DF, HO, SM, SS, HG, SA, AT, SN, SP, MT, WC, WW, BM, SU, JT (w/ TB). (Cameos: images of RO, CM, & various heroes of defunct parallel Earths.)

SYNOPSIS: The JSA, Hawkgirl, and Sandy hold a memorial service for Robin and The Huntress, after which they intend to disband and retire. A dying Spectre passes a warning to Dr. Fate before discorporating. Fate fills the others' minds with images of a history that never was but is about to be: On the night of President Roosevelt's burial in April 1945, a crack opens in the fabric of reality. The nine JSAers not subject to magic of the Spear of Destiny invade Berlin to find the rift's source, most perishing in the attempt. As fireballs pour from the sky all over the world, Hitler uses the Spear to trigger the Gotterdammerung of Teutonic legend—and the Earth dies. To forestall this future/past, the present-day JSA time-travel to the moment Hitler launched his spell and enter the dimension of Asgard. By merging their essences with the Norse Gods, they prevent Ragnarok from destroying the world. But time in this netherworld is on an infinite loop, so the JSA must fight this same battle over and over again—till the end of time—to forestall the end of the universe. Fate propels Power Girl and Star-Spangled Kid back to Earth. A surviving avatar of Spectre appears and forces Fate to follow them before he himself is "called home." In the present, Infinity, Inc., learns of the JSA's sacrifice.

NOTES:

- Although the words "of America" appear in the cover logo, they are not part of the official title in the indicia.

"R.I.P. JSA"

The original art of the cover of the Last Days of the Justice Society Special, by David Ross & Mike Gustovich, is today the proud possession of collector Fred DeBoom, who sent us a full-size photocopy. Note that it's been autographed at the bottom by both artists and the writer. When Mike Gustovich signed it, he added the "R.I.P." phrase. [© DC Comics.]

- The material for the 4-page opening sequence in Hitler's bunker in besieged Berlin on April 12, 1945, was researched for accuracy, including the visit of munitions minister Albert Speer… even his failure to return the guards' Nazi salute. Of course, the main account we have is Speer's own controversial book *Inside the Third Reich* (1969; 1970, in English).

- Hitler was elated as he greeted Speer, because of the news that President Roosevelt had died earlier that day. He had long predicted a second "Miracle of the House of Brandenberg"—echoing the death of the Russian Czarina Elizabeth in the 18th century that saved his own "illustrious predecessor" Frederick the Great of Prussia by bringing an end to the

[*Continued on p. 237*]

Speer Of Destiny

Albert Speer had been Hitler's favorite architect before the war—and his minister of munitions during it. In the Bunker in April 1945 (above center), he had finally ceased to believe in Hitler—and refers to the horoscope actually drawn up for Der Führer on orders of S.S. chief Heinrich Himmler in 1933. According to the 1978 book The Bunker by James P. O'Donnell, much of what happened in between was predicted by that horoscope: the outbreak of war in 1939—astounding triumphs till 1941—then a series of setbacks—to be followed by overwhelming victory in the second half of that very month. Hitler thought of it as a miracle: the death of President Franklin Roosevelt, only hours before, would spell the doom of the "unholy alliance" between America, England, and Russia and save the Third Reich from destruction. [© DC Comics.]

(Above right:) Speer and Hitler in happier days, when they were planning together the remaking of the German capital Berlin into one of the world's greatest and most impressive cities. What amazes Roy Thomas is that, until he was working on this very volume, the pun of the "Spear of Destiny" and "Albert Speer," both of which are prominent in his story, had never occurred to him!

A Bunker In Berlin

(Above:) The facts concerning the situation in the besieged Berlin of April 12, 1945, as related in the first panel, are based upon several historical texts. The Third Reich was dying—and it looked as if all of Germany might die with it, pounded by Allied bombers and Soviet troops. Adolf Hitler's bunker beneath the Reichschancellery Building, and entered at a nearby point, probably looked very much as Ross & Gustovich drew it. [© DC Comics.]

"The Man From Missouri"

(Far left:) Dr. Fate confers, at FDR's funeral, with the new President, Harry S Truman. [© DC Comics.]

(Left:) Truman became President upon Roosevelt's death on April 12, 1945.

Death In Four Colors

(Left:) The surviving JSAers are gathered around the graves of Richard (Robin) Grayson and Helena (Huntress) Wayne, both dispatched in the Crisis on Infinite Earths.

(Above:) The ravaged Spectre crashes the wake. Gathering more and more power unto himself over the years, he has "become" the universe—and he is dying! [© DC Comics.]

And A Little Child Shall Lead Them—To Death

(Above:) In the reality in which the JSA find themselves, The Flash is fatally shot from behind as he carries the dying Starman, in search of a hospital—in bombed-out Berlin, April 1945. The soldier who has killed him is one of the many German children drafted into service in the last desperate days of the war. [© DC Comics.]

Maybe You Can Take It With You

(Top right:) Hitler's incantation with the Spear of Destiny sends out waves of destruction that destroy the world—and the universe embodied in the now-all-powerful Spectre—in 1945. [© DC Comics.]

Super-Heroes At Twilight

(Left:) Only by forever taking the part of the doomed Norse/Teutonic gods in Ragnarok—Gotterdammerung—the Twilight of the Gods—can the Justice Society prevent the end of all that is. So they make the ultimate sacrifice, battling Surtur, the fire god who burns everything that remains of the devastated Earth and Asgard. Art by Ross & Gustovich; script by RT. [© DC Comics.]

(Above:) The Norse Ragnarok had been portrayed more than once in Marvel comics, beginning with this scene from Thor #128 (May 1966) depicting Surtur—yes, that Surtur. RT felt that, because of Hitler's affinity for the operatic music of the German composer Richard Wagner, especially of his Ring Cycle whose last opera was Gotterdammerung, the Teutonic version of the Twilight of the Gods was a suitably dramatic ending for his beloved Justice Society. Art by Jack Kirby (pencils) & Vince Colletta (inks); script by Stan Lee. [© Marvel Characters, Inc.]

[Continued from p. 234]

alliance that opposed him. Hitler felt that FDR's death would spell the end of the "unholy alliance" between America, England, and Russia, and that soon the US and Red armies would be "exchanging artillery bursts over the roof of the Reichschancellery."

- Speer had indeed attended a concert that afternoon. He tells Hitler that he asked them to play the finale from Wagner's opera *Gotterdammerung*, which *Der Führer* loved. Odd that Hitler considered that a song of triumph; in the opera, it represents the Twilight (= death) of the Teutonic Gods.

- RT feels in retrospect he should have had Black Canary attend the memorial service for the four members of the Wayne family, since she (or her mother—take your pick) had been a JSAer long before she had joined the Justice League.

- In *Crisis on Infinite Earths* #10 (Jan. 1986), The Spectre had defeated The Anti-Monitor at the Dawn of Time, but at the cost of immense pain as "the universe explodes around him…. It is the death of all that is." After this "big bang," Deadman and The Phantom Stranger and Dr. Mist (of The Global Guardians) had conjured like crazy "to summon the essence of the still-comatose Spectre… to bring forth his infinite energies… and to wield them to save a universe."

- In this *Last Days Special*, it is revealed that The Spectre, over the decades, had become more and more powerful—so that, while he lay in his supernatural coma between the worlds at the close of *Crisis*, his unfettered mystic energy reached out unconsciously back into time, perhaps attracted by the magic of the Spear of Destiny. When his force was added to that inherent in the Spear—and when that force was wielded by a desperate but unsuspecting Hitler, who wanted to take the world with him when he died (in our world as well as in the comics)— that lethal combination was enough to destroy all time and space, starting from April 12, 1945, outward. And, granted the existence of both Spectre and Spear, it might very well have happened that way!

- Thus, The Spectre became the one thing which could cause the *destruction* of the brave new post-*Crisis* universe—and its salvation. For, though all but torn apart by the holocaust he and the Spear had unleashed, The Spectre survived long enough to reach the JSA—and to implant

"The Game Of The Gods"

In some retellings of the Twilight of the Gods, there are chess pieces shaped like manlike deities lying upon an empty field in the aftermath of the world's devastation. Last Days of the Justice Society ends the same way, as Infinity, Inc., walk away, leaving Dr. Fate alone to discover them. These "chessmen" in the shape of the heroes of the JSA—are they mere symbols? Or are they the JSAers themselves? Perhaps only Dr. Fate knows for certain… and he isn't saying. Incidentally, a short Dr. Fate dialogue balloon ("And when you do…") was accidentally left off the top right of the 2nd panel above by DC's production staff. [© DC Comics.]

his knowledge within the mind of Dr. Fate.

- The words the rector speaks graveside at FDR's funeral are as reported in Jim Bishop's 1980 book *FDR's Last Year*.

- With Hitler in the Bunker is his aide Martin Bormann.

- Much of the phrasing of the Ragnarok/ Gotterdammerung sequence of the *Special* was adapted from an 1847 book titled *Northern Antiquities* by M. Mallet, a copy of which RT's wife Dann had given him several years earlier.

- In both the *Special* and in our world, Adolf Hitler and his mistress Eva Braun were married in the Bunker on April 28, 1945—with the bride wearing black, because she and her new husband would commit suicide on April 30. The only witness was propaganda minister Joseph Goebbels—who would soon kill himself, his wife, and children to avoid their falling into the hands of the Russians.

- One of the two interior pages at the end of the *Special* is a JSA pin-up by Michael Hernandez/Bair.

- The final interior page is the first printing anywhere of a page from the JSA finale of the "lost" mid-1940s *All-Star Comics* story "The Will of William Wilson." No other art from that tale has ever been printed in an actual comic book to date.

- The back cover of the *Special* is a tracing by Al Dellinges of Jack Burnley's "V" cover for *All-Star Comics* #12. Since the cover's multi-printing of "V…-" (indicating both "V" for "Victory" and the Morse code symbol for "V" that was often utilized during World War II) was color-held, that part of the background had to be redone over a weekend by a DC staffer. Roy Thomas paid that gent $75 freelance for his time, so that the cover would look just as it had in 1942; little did RT dream that one day the original cover would be reprinted in a $50 hardcover edition of *The All Star Comics Archives*!

KURT MITCHELL is a database designer and freelance writer. A graduate of the University of Washington (class of '79), he resides in Tacoma, WA. His knowledge of JSA trivia, he maintains, is the sorry legacy of a misspent youth. He promises to turn up a photo of himself in time for *Vol. 3.*

AFTERWORD—& FOREWORD

And there you have it—more than 200 pages on *All-Star Comics'* Justice Society and its various successor series, from 1940 through 1989. At that point, except for a single 10-page story I was invited to write for the Sept. 1999 *All Star Comics 80-Page Giant*, my personal interest in ongoing JSA material pretty much drops off the radar... but I'm content to see that others continue to carry the flame, which only proves the ultimate vitality of what the *Overstreet Price Guide* has called "a breakthrough concept, second in importance only to the creation of the super-hero."

Two volumes' worth is far from all that can be said about the JSA or related titles, of course, as will be amply demonstrated in *The All-Star Companion, Vol. 3*, in the autumn of 2007. That book will deal in lavish detail with the original Justice League-Justice Society team-ups of 1963-85, the 1970s JSA revival, *The Young All-Stars* and other 1980s series—and even hitherto-unexplored aspects of the original 1940-51 *All-Star Comics* which have occurred to me while working on this tome (plus a few that will be doubtless be proposed by others when they *read* it).

But there could hardly be a better note to go out on than to print artist Carlos Pacheco's original layout for *Vol. 2*'s gorgeous wraparound cover, inspired by the 1947 cover of *All-Star Comics* #36. At John Morrow's and my suggestion, Carlos altered it slightly so that seven of the heroes would be fully featured on the front. Others are drawn larger or smaller on the sketch than on the finished art... Green Lantern, Captain Marvel, and Dr. Mid-Nite were replaced by different stalwarts. Carlos even worked in all six Blackhawk planes—no more, no less! If you want to see the entire complete illustration in black-&-white, not losing even a tiny bit of art to the book's "spine," you can peruse one of our *ads* for this tome, printed in various TwoMorrows publications.

It all just underscores our point:

There's always *one more way* to look at—and delight in—the Justice Society of America!

Bestest,

Roy

ROY THOMAS has been a writer and often editor in the comic book field since 1965, and was Marvel's editor-in-chief from 1972-74. He's noted at Marvel for his 1960s-70s work on *The Avengers, The X-Men, Dr. Strange, The Invaders*, the *Conan* titles, etc., and at DC for his 1980s series *All-Star Squadron, Infinity Inc., Captain Carrot and His Amazing Zoo Crew!, Secret Origins, The Young All-Stars*, et al. He is currently scripting several upcoming series for Marvel, as well as his World War II super-hero comic *Anthem* for Heroic Publishing. Roy co-wrote the films *Fire and Ice* and *Conan the Destroyer* and is the author of the hardcover books *Stan Lee's Amazing Marvel Universe* and *Conan: The Ultimate Guide to the World's Most Savage Barbarian*. He hopes Carlos Pacheco won't mind his usurping a little blank space in his banner for this bio.

Fin

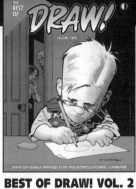

HERO GETS GIRL!
THE LIFE & ART OF KURT SCHAFFENBERGER

MARK VOGER's biography of the artist of **LOIS LANE & CAPTAIN MARVEL!**

• Covers **KURT'S LIFE AND CAREER** from the 1940s to his passing in 2002!
• Features **NEVER-SEEN PHOTOS & ILLUSTRATIONS** from his files!
• Includes recollections by **ANDERSON, EISNER, INFANTINO, KUBERT, ALEX ROSS, MORT WALKER** and others!

(128-page Trade Paperback) **$19 US**

SECRETS IN THE SHADOWS: GENE COLAN

The ultimate retrospective on **COLAN**, with rare drawings, photos, and art from his nearly 60-year career, plus a comprehensive overview of Gene's glory days at Marvel Comics! **MARV WOLFMAN, DON MCGREGOR** and other writers share script samples and anecdotes of their Colan collaborations, while **TOM PALMER, STEVE LEIALOHA** and others show how they approached the daunting task of inking Colan's famously nuanced penciled pages! Plus there's a **NEW PORTFOLIO** of never-before-seen collaborations between Gene and such masters as **JOHN BYRNE, MICHAEL KALUTA** and **GEORGE PÉREZ**, and all-new artwork created specifically for this book by Gene! Available in Softcover and Deluxe Hardcover (limited to 1000 copies, with 16 extra black-and-white pages and 8 extra color pages)!

(168-page softcover) **$26 US**
(192-page trade hardcover) **$49 US**

COMICS ABOVE GROUND
SEE HOW YOUR FAVORITE ARTISTS MAKE A LIVING OUTSIDE COMICS

COMICS ABOVE GROUND features top comics pros discussing their inspirations and training, and how they apply it in "Mainstream Media," including Conceptual Illustration, Video Game Development, Children's Books, Novels, Design, Illustration, Fine Art, Storyboards, Animation, Movies & more! Written by **DURWIN TALON** (author of the top-selling **PANEL DISCUSSIONS**), this book features creators sharing their perspectives and their work in comics and their "other professions," with career overviews, never-before-seen art, and interviews! Featuring:

• BRUCE TIMM
• BERNIE WRIGHTSON
• ADAM HUGHES
• LOUISE SIMONSON
• DAVE DORMAN
• GREG RUCKA & MORE!

(168-page Trade Paperback) **$24 US**

COMIC BOOKS AND OTHER NECESSITIES OF LIFE

WERTHAM WAS RIGHT!
SUPERHEROES IN MY PANTS!

Each collects **MARK EVANIER'S** best essays and commentaries, plus new essays and illustrations by **SERGIO ARAGONÉS!**

(200-page Trade Paperbacks) **$17 US EACH**
ALL THREE BOOKS: $34 US

THE DARK AGE
Grim, Great & Gimmicky Post-Modern Comics

By MARK VOGER
with photos by Kathy Voglesong.

Documents the '80s and '90s era of comics, from **THE DARK KNIGHT RETURNS** and **WATCHMEN** to the "polybagged premium" craze, the **DEATH OF SUPERMAN**, renegade superheroes **SPAWN, PITT, BLOODSHOT, CYBERFORCE,** & more! Interviews with **TODD McFARLANE, DAVE GIBBONS, JIM LEE, KEVIN SMITH, ALEX ROSS, MIKE MIGNOLA, ERIK LARSEN, J. O'BARR, DAVID LAPHAM, JOE QUESADA, MIKE ALLRED** and others, plus a color section! Written by **MARK VOGER**, with photos by **KATHY VOGLESONG.**

(168-page trade paperback) **$24 US**

DICK GIORDANO
CHANGING COMICS, ONE DAY AT A TIME

MICHAEL EURY's biography of comics' most prominent and affable personality!

• Covers his career as illustrator, inker, and editor, peppered with **DICK'S PERSONAL REFLECTIONS** on his career milestones!
• Lavishly illustrated with **RARE AND NEVER SEEN** comics, merchandising, and advertising art (includes a color section)!
• Extensive index of his published work!
• Comments & tributes by **NEAL ADAMS, DENNIS O'NEIL, TERRY AUSTIN, PAUL LEVITZ, MARV WOLFMAN, JULIUS SCHWARTZ, JIM APARO** & others!
• With a Foreword by **NEAL ADAMS** and Afterword by **PAUL LEVITZ!**

(176-pg. Paperback) **$24 US**

ALTER EGO COLLECTION, VOL. 1

Collects the first two issues of **ALTER EGO**, plus 30 pages of **NEW MATERIAL!** JLA Jam Cover by KUBERT, PÉREZ, GIORDANO, TUSKA, CARDY, FRADON, & GIELLA, new sections featuring scarce art by GIL KANE, WILL EISNER, CARMINE INFANTINO, MIKE SEKOWSKY, MURPHY ANDERSON, DICK DILLIN, & more!

(192-page trade paperback) **$26 US**

AGAINST THE GRAIN: MAD ARTIST WALLACE WOOD

The definitive biographical memoir on Wood, 20 years in the making! Former associate **BHOB STEWART** traces Wood's life and career, with contributions from many artists and writers who knew Wood personally, making this remarkable compendium of rare and critical commentary! From childhood drawings & early samples to nearly endless comics pages (many unpublished), this is the most stunning display of Wood art ever assembled! **BILL PEARSON**, executor of the Wood Estate, contributed rare drawings from Wood's own files, while art collector **ROGER HILL** provides a wealth of obscure, previously unpublished Wood art.

(336-Page Trade Paperback) **$44 US**

ART OF GEORGE TUSKA

A comprehensive look at Tuska's personal and professional life, including early work with Eisner-Iger, crime comics of the 1950s, and his tenure with Marvel and DC Comics, as well as independent publishers. The book includes extensive coverage of his work on **IRON MAN, X-MEN, HULK, JUSTICE LEAGUE, TEEN TITANS, BATMAN, T.H.U.N.D.E.R. AGENTS,** and many more! A gallery of commission artwork and a thorough index of his work are included, plus original artwork, photos, sketches, previously unpublished art, interviews and anecdotes from his peers and fans, plus George's own words!

(128-page trade paperback) **$19 US**

TRUE BRIT
CELEBRATING GREAT COMIC BOOK ARTISTS OF THE UK

A celebration of the rich history of British Comics Artists and their influence on the US with in-depth interviews and art by:

• BRIAN BOLLAND
• ALAN DAVIS
• DAVE GIBBONS
• BRYAN HITCH
• DAVID LLOYD
• DAVE McKEAN
• KEVIN O'NEILL
• BARRY WINDSOR-SMITH
and other gents!

(204-page Trade Paperback with COLOR SECTION) **$26 US**

COLLECTED JACK KIRBY COLLECTOR, VOL. 1-5

See what thousands of comics fans, professionals, and historians have discovered: The King lives on in the pages of **THE JACK KIRBY COLLECTOR!** These colossal **TRADE PAPERBACKS** reprint the first 22 sold-out issues of the magazine for Kirby fans!

• **VOLUME 1:** Reprints TJKC #1-9 (including the Fourth World and Fantastic Four theme issues), plus over 30 pieces of Kirby art never before published in TJKC! • (240 pages) **$29 US**

• **VOLUME 2:** Reprints TJKC #10-12 (the Humor, Hollywood, and International theme issues), and includes a new special section detailing a fan's private tour of the Kirbys' remarkable home, showcasing more than 30 pieces of Kirby art never before published in TJKC! • (160 pages) **$22 US**

• **VOLUME 3:** Reprints TJKC #13-15 (the Horror, Thor, and Sci-Fi theme issues), plus 30 new pieces of Kirby art! • (176 pages) **$24 US**

• **VOLUME 4:** Reprints TJKC #16-19 (the Tough Guys, DC, Marvel, and Art theme issues), plus more than 30 pieces of Kirby art never before published in TJKC! • (240 pages) **$29 US**

• **VOLUME 5:** Reprints TJKC #20-22 (the Women, Wacky, and Villains theme issues), plus more than 30 pieces of Kirby art never before published in TJKC! • (224 pages) **$29 US**

HOW TO CREATE COMICS
FROM SCRIPT TO PRINT

REDESIGNED and **EXPANDED** version of the groundbreaking **WRITE NOW! #8 / DRAW! #9** crossover! **DANNY FINGEROTH** & **MIKE MANLEY** show step-by-step how to develop a new comic, from script and roughs to pencils, inks, colors, lettering—it even guides you through printing and distribution, & the finished 8-page color comic is included, so you can see their end result! **PLUS:** over 30 pages of **ALL-NEW** material, including "full" and "Marvel-style" scripts, a critique of their new character and comic from an editor's point of view, new tips on coloring, new expanded writing lessons, and more!

(108-page trade paperback) **$18 US**

(120-minute companion DVD) **$35 US**

SILVER STAR: GRAPHITE

JACK KIRBY'S six-issue "Visual Novel" for Pacific Comics, reproduced from his powerful, uninked pencil art! Includes Kirby's illustrated movie screenplay, never-seen sketches, pin-ups, & more from his final series!

(160 pages) **$24 US**